POLITICAL MANHOOD

Political Manhood

Red Bloods, Mollycoddles, & the Politics of Progressive Era Reform

Kevin P. Murphy

COLUMBIA UNIVERSITY PRESS *New York*

Columbia University Press
Publishers Since 1893
New York Chichester, West Sussex

Library of Congress Cataloging-in-Publication Data
Murphy, Kevin P., 1963–
Political Manhood : Red Bloods, Mollycoddles, and
the politics of Progressive Era Reform /
Kevin P. Murphy.
p. cm.
Includes bibliographical references and index.
ISBN 978-0-231-12996-1 (cloth : alk. paper) —
ISBN 978-0-231-50350-1 (electronic)
1. Masculinity—United States—History. 2. Male homosexuality—
United States—History. 3. Sex—United States—History. 4. Social reformers—
United States—Sexual behavior. 5. United States—Politics and government—
1865–1933. 6. United States—History—1865–1921. I. Title.
HQ1090.3.M867 2008
306.76'62097309034—dc22 2007038665

Columbia University Press books are printed on
permanent and durable acid-free paper.
This book was printed on paper with recycled content.
Printed in the United States of America
c 10 9 8 7 6 5 4 3 2 1

Contents

Acknowledgments

I have accumulated many debts over the course of researching and writing this book, which began its life as a dissertation at New York University. Foremost, I thank my dissertation advisor, Thomas Bender, who offered intellectual guidance and support above and beyond the call of duty and who stood as an exemplar of intellectual generosity. I also thank Lisa Duggan, who taught me so much about the history of sexuality and about the politics of academic production. She remains a friend and an inspiration. I also owe much to the members of my dissertation committee—Daniel Czitrom, Martha Hodes, and Molly Nolan—for sharing their wisdom. I am indebted as well to other members of the history faculty at NYU for generously sharing their wisdom during my time there. These include Barbara Abrash, Rachel Bernstein, Walter Johnson, Robin D.G. Kelley, Paul Mattingly, Carl Prince, Jeffrey Sammons, Daniel Walkowitz, and Susan Ware.

For their incisive critiques of various dissertation chapter drafts, I thank the members of Thomas Bender's dissertation seminar, including Stephen Mihm, Jasmine Mir, Greg Robinson, and Andrew Schroeder. I'm especially thankful to Molly McGarry and Mark Elliot, whose close readings of dissertation chapters, friendship, and support have been invaluable. Thanks also to fellow NYU graduate students whose intelligent and good-humored companionship sustained me through the arduous dissertation process. These include Joy Anderson, Katie Barry, Dan Bender, Steve Corey, Duane Corpis, Betsy Esch, Lori Finkelstein, Kim Gilmore, Dayo Gore, Dave Kinkela, Karen Krahulik, Rachel Mattson, Micky McElya, Jane McNamara, Ellen Noonan, and Dawn VanderVloed. Special thanks to Rebeccah Welch for her creative and insightful responses to my work, as well as for her warm friendship.

New York City friends and *Radical History Review* comrades Adina Back and Jeffrey Escoffier also contributed to this project in significant ways. I was especially fortunate to work with Terence Kissack and Molly McGarry; I learned much from them about the history of sexual politics, and our conversations influenced the conceptualization of this project in significant ways.

Colleagues at the University of Minnesota have been enormously supportive as I transformed dissertation into book. I'm especially grateful to David Chang, Tracey Deutsch, Karen Ho, Malinda Alaine Lindquist, Keith Mayes, Hiromi Mizuno, and Karen Sue Taussig, members of my junior faculty "boot camp," who offered challenging and constructive advice on several chapters. I also thank members of the history department writing group, Chris Isett, Michael Lower, Patrick McNamara, J. B. Shank, and Tom Wolfe, for comments on several chapters. I have benefited from the wisdom and generosity of other colleagues in the departments of History and American Studies, including Kirsten Fischer, Lary May, Elaine Tyler May, M. J. Maynes, Lisa Norling, Ann Waltner, and Barbara Welke. I'm indebted to my colleague Anna Clark, whose kind mentorship and broad knowledge of political history and the history of sexuality have enriched this project and my professional life. Rod Ferguson, Jennifer Pierce, and Jeani O'Brien have also shared their insights and friendship with me; they've made life in the Midwest a real pleasure.

At Minnesota I've had the great pleasure of working with smart and talented graduate students who've helped to expand my intellectual horizons. I'm thankful especially to Aaron Carico, Lisa Blee, Michael David Franklin, Brian Tochterman, and Andy Urban, who have provided excellent research assistance. Thanks also to graduate student collaborators

Ryan Murphy, Polly Myers, N'Jai-An Patters, Andrea Robertson, Jason Ruiz, Mark Soderstrom, Amy Tyson, and Alex Urquhart.

For astute comments on chapter drafts, articles, and conference papers, I thank Henry Abelove, Gail Bederman, Mary Blanchard, Howard Brick, Mark Carnes, Patricia A. Cooper, John D'Emilio, Edward Ross Dickinson, Stefan Dudink, Nancy F. Gabin, Andrea Friedman, Jim Greene, David Johnson, Felicia Kornbluh, Seth Koven, Ian Lekus, Laura McCall, Leisa Meyer, Joanne Meyerowitz, Doug Mitchell, Pablo Mitchell, Richard Morrison, Claire Potter, Siobhan Somerville, Donald Yacovone, and Bonnie Yochelson.

This project has received generous institutional support. At the dissertation phase, I benefited from a Sexuality Research Dissertation Fellowship from the Social Science Research Council with Funds from the Ford Foundation, a Prize Teaching Fellowship from the New York University Department of History, and the Gregory Sprague Prize from the Committee on Lesbian and Gay History of the American Historical Association. Support for the book came from a Mellon Postdoctoral Fellowship at the Wesleyan University Center for the Humanities. I thank Center Director Henry Abelove, as well as staff and wonderful fellow peers, especially J. Kehaulani Kauanui and Shelley Rosenberg, for an extraordinary postdoctoral year. The History Department, Graduate School, and College of Liberal Arts at the University of Minnesota have generously supported this project with research grants and teaching leaves. It's been my privilege to work with supportive and talented department chairs David Good, M.J. Maynes, and Eric Weitz. I also owe much to remarkably efficient and supportive staff members in the Department of History and the Institute of Advanced Study at the University of Minnesota.

I am extraordinarily fortunate to have received insightful and challenging comments on several chapters from very smart friends Margot Canaday, Tracey Deutsch, and Dara Z. Strolovitch. Special thanks go to my newest colleague, Regina Kunzel, who has been friend, mentor, and incisive critic for many years now. I owe a great deal to Gail Bederman, Timothy Gilfoyle, and Michael Moon for extraordinarily astute and generative readings of an earlier version of this manuscript.

Lisa Blee and Mandy Keifetz have lent their editorial skills to this project. I am also indebted to Peter Dimock, Leslie Kriesel, and Anne Routon at Columbia University Press for their editorial expertise and patience. I am grateful and honored to have received recognition as well as financial support from the Society of American Historians.

Finally, thanks to my closest friends and companions, who have offered unwavering support over the years and have helped me through writing blocks and other crises. Steven Cutri supported my commitment to graduate school and to this project in countless ways; it would be hard to overestimate how much his continued friendship means to me. I am eternally grateful to Bob Burns for his wit, humor, and optimism, and for rescuing me from technological disasters on a regular basis. Finally, I thank all the members of my huge family, especially my siblings, whose insouciant humor and loving support made rough times less so.

POLITICAL MANHOOD

Introduction

In a 1907 lecture to Harvard undergraduates—one of many such addresses he gave at American colleges and universities—President Theodore Roosevelt asserted that to "neglect . . . political duties . . . shows either a weakness or worse than a weakness in a man's character." He warned the young men not to become "too fastidious, too sensitive to take part in the rough hurly-burly of the actual work of the world." Roosevelt contended that one's physical, moral, and mental strength—indeed, the quality of one's manhood—depended on such participation. Asserting that colleges should never "turn out mollycoddles instead of vigorous men," he cautioned that "the weakling and the coward are out of place in a strong and free community," and further warned of the dire consequences of such weakness: "if you are too timid or too fastidious or too careless to do your part in this work, then you forfeit the right to be considered one of the governing and you become one of the governed."[1] This widely reported and discussed speech, while typical of Roosevelt's promotion of the virtues of strenuous manhood, proved exceptional to the extent that it fixed the "mollycoddle" as an ineffective and weak male figure—the debased other to the idealized "strenuous man"—within popular American discourse.[2]

The British philosopher and classicist Goldsworthy Lowes Dickinson, who was touring the United States at the time, responded to Roosevelt in a brief essay entitled, "Red-Bloods and 'Mollycoddles.'"[3] Dickinson commented on the American enthusiasm for the "gospel of strenuousness" and attempted to delineate the characteristics of the "red blood" and the "mollycoddle." "Red bloods," he asserted, were "men of action" who "carry on the business of the world," including soldiers, businessmen, and politicians. The "mollycoddle," in contrast, was "all inner life. He may indeed act . . . but he acts, so to speak, by accident. . . . The Mollycoddle in action is the Crank: it is he who accomplishes reforms; who abolished slavery, for example, and revolutionised prisons and lunatic asylums."[4]

Nations too, according to Dickinson, could be divided into these two male categories. Mollycoddle nations included "the ancient Greeks, the Italians, the French," whereas red blood nations included "the Romans, the Germans, and the English," with the United States as "the Red-Blood nation *par excellence*." Indeed, Dickinson concluded, in relation to America, "Europe as a whole might almost be called Mollycoddle." The reason, he argued, was that European cultures had accepted that both red bloods and mollycoddles, although often hostile to one another, were necessary for the proper functioning of "civilized" society. The United States, on the other hand, appeared not to value the civilizing influences of the mollycoddle: "To be born a Mollycoddle in America is to be born to a hard fate. You must either emigrate or succumb."[5]

Dickinson's essay was clearly intended to be polemical and provocative, as is evinced by his acknowledgment that "strictly neither the Mollycoddle nor the Red blood exist, and that real men contain elements of both mixed in different proportions."[6] Yet Dickinson's abstracted male types, and the political qualities he assigned to them, remain useful for understanding historical connections between categories of gender and sexuality and American political culture. I accept Dickinson's central contention that, by the turn of the twentieth century, a "red-blooded" Rooseveltian model of masculinity proved ascendant and functioned as a prescriptive ideal for American men, especially for those of the white middle and elite classes. A growing and convincing body of scholarship has demonstrated that popular ideals of American masculinity coalesced around the figure of Roosevelt and his ideology of the "strenuous life."[7] This study builds on and expands upon this body of scholarship in two important ways. First, it offers a historicized analysis of the political and class contexts and contests in which the ideal of strenuous manhood was produced; second, by centering on the rhetorical figure of the mollycoddle (as opposed to the red blood), it illuminates competing ideologies of manhood and demonstrates how the strenuous model was deployed in order to marginalize the careers and projects of political actors successfully stigmatized as weak and effeminate. This process of stigmatization became possible, in part, through a powerful correlation of weakness and effeminacy with homosexuality at the turn of the century.[8] As I argue, and as Dickinson suggests only obliquely in his essay, the mollycoddle functioned as an intelligible and powerful rhetorical figure largely because of its similarity to the emergent "homosexual" type.

This study historicizes the emergence of a strenuous model of manhood within political culture by examining the careers and writings of a generation of male reformers who became active in political and social reform causes in New York City in the late nineteenth century. In the 1880s and early 1890s, this group, which included Roosevelt, joined an older generation of elite liberal reformers referred to, often derisively, as "mugwumps" and "goo goos" (for "good government"). I argue that this younger generation departed from the mugwump tradition by aligning themselves more closely with white working-class men.[9] Building on the concept of "homosocial desire" developed by literary scholars, I show that many male reformers of this generation eschewed their elite forebearers' distaste for working-class political culture. Indeed, they came to believe that Tammany men and the laboring classes possessed the virile and "manly virtues" that men of privilege had lost due to the effeminizing influences of cultured civilization.[10] As a result of this perception, male urban reformers borrowed from the style and practices associated with working-class men, constructing more aggressive forms of political manhood that legitimized reform as an appropriately masculine endeavor. Although this new style of masculinity did not yet cohere around the notion of strenuousness, it had many of the characteristics that would come to mark the Rooseveltian model.

By focusing on this dynamic of cross-class appropriation, this book reassesses the oppositional model so often used to characterize the relationship between political "machines" and social and municipal reformers at the turn of the twentieth century.[11] While reformers viewed excessive loyalty to Tammany Hall, the democratic New York City machine, and the "spoils system" of political patronage as corrupting influences in American political life, they began to argue that machine politics performed a necessary social function, bonding men of diverse backgrounds together and introducing immigrant men to American political and economic structures and institutions. Therefore, male urban reformers attempted to replace what they believed was a corrupt system with new sets of institutions and associations that organized men across class, ethnic, and generational lines. Paying attention to the historical workings of ideals of manhood reveals a much more complex and dialectical relationship between Progressive reformers and urban party politicians than has been captured in the historiography.[12]

Political Manhood also analyzes the shifting gendered and sexual meanings attached to political and ideological positions during this period. I argue that one reason this generation of reformers recast themselves in the working-class masculine mold was to insulate themselves from charges of effeminacy leveled by party politicians, who had long ridiculed men who took up reform causes such as abolitionism and temperance.[13] By the late 1880s, the language used in these attacks—such as "third sex" and "political hermaphrodite"—converged with terminology applied to non-normative gender and sexual types identified by sexologists. Just as medical "experts" invoked the notion of a "third sex" to impose order on the seemingly chaotic and disruptive pattern of sexual relations they believed characterized modern life, so did American party politicians and journalists utilize an analogous concept to make sense of threats to the two-party system and the workings of patronage that structured American political life. By the early twentieth century, prominent Progressive-era reformers, including Theodore Roosevelt, appropriated this sexual invective to cast aspersions on reform opponents, many of whom held anti-imperialist and socialist views. Such invective most often stigmatized more radical reformers as "sentimental," "impracticable," and sexually suspicious—as mollycoddles—in contrast to the practical and centrist red blood embodied by Roosevelt.[14]

The importance of sexuality to reform politics of this period extends beyond the realm of rhetoric, however. Many Progressive-era reformers shared

Jane Addams's belief that "the sexual impulse" not only motivated heterosexual reproduction but also served as a primary force in the forging of all social relations.[15] The social reformer and anti-imperialist Ernest Howard Crosby, for example, declared: "Sexual love is the origin not only of the human race, but of all our altruism, all our idealism, all our art, all our religion. Falling in love, in its larger implication, is the one thing in life worth doing."[16] Reformers influenced by this broad vision of the social role of sexuality incorporated it into a political ideology that I call "social brotherhood." This stressed the importance of universal love in motivating reform and called for the establishment of direct and personal relationships across class lines. Several prominent reformers discussed in this study, including settlement leaders Charles B. Stover and John Lovejoy Elliott, imbued this ideology with homoerotic significance. Drawing inspiration from writers and thinkers who celebrated male comradeship and eroticism across class and generational lines—among them Socrates, Walt Whitman, and Edward Carpenter—these men forged their primary attachments to young working-class men. In so doing, they developed a politics of same-sex eroticism that stood in contrast to emerging medical models of homosexual pathology and heterosexual normativity; indeed, this model affixed many performative attributes associated with the red blood to a politics that celebrated homoerotic expression. Yet, I argue, while such masculine self-presentation often worked to shield reformers from the mollycoddle label, they too became subjects of sexual and political suspicion as object-based understandings of sexual identity took hold, especially in the nineteen-teens.[17]

Political Manhood engages important questions that have emerged in the field of gender history; in particular, it draws from and builds on more than two decades' worth of feminist scholarship on women's political activism, ideologies of "separate spheres," and the gendering of political rhetoric. First, it expands on recent work on the role female reformers played in shaping American social policy by analyzing cross-gender collaborative reform efforts as well as gendered conflicts that arose over claims to expertise and authority. In particular, it shows that, along with the well-documented legacy of maternal reform, a tradition of masculinist militarist reforms aimed at working-class men and youths was carried into New Deal social policy.[18]

Second, by amplifying the cross-class dimensions of male identity construction, this study enriches recent scholarship on the history of American manhood at the turn of the twentieth century. Historians have identified two prominent sets of concerns relating to the nature of male power in American political and cultural discourse. The first set involved the fear that middle-class American men, estranged from physical labor and emasculated within the feminine confines of the middle-class home, had lost the manly vigor that stood at the center of the American national character. According to a number of scholars, these fears were so profound as to constitute a "crisis of masculinity," which led to a widespread obsession among middle-class men with physical fitness and chivalric ritual.[19] The second set involved the massive influx of Southern and Eastern European immigrant men, primarily to cities, during the last two decades of the century. Journalists and reform writers of the era expressed a great deal of anxiety about the presence of these men. This anxiety encompassed fears of violent political and labor unrest and of individual acts of crime, as well as concerns about the power these immigrant men would have as American citizens and voters.[20]

With some notable exceptions, these sets of concerns about male power have been treated separately by scholars. The "crisis of masculinity" is usually embedded in discussion of middle-class formation and has been analyzed as a response to the growing power and independence of middle-class women and as a nostalgic identification with medieval warriors and American frontiersmen. In contrast, historians have typically addressed concerns about the power of immigrant men within discussions of labor conflict and anti-immigration rhetoric. Moreover, scholarship has emphasized expressed fears of working-class male power within a social control model, arguing that elites acted on such fears by supporting arguments for suffrage restriction and repressive police measures.

Although all of these interpretations contain significant explanatory power, I argue that the two sets of concerns were crucially and inextricably linked and that poor and working-class urban neighborhoods functioned as physical sites for this connection, places of cultural encounter and creative reinvention. Interactions on the streets of tenement districts shaped the ideologies and strategies of male New York City reformers and facilitated the construction of male relationships and identities across class and ethnic lines. By treating urban neighborhoods and urban politics as dynamic spaces of exchange, this study eschews limiting models of social control and cultural hegemony in favor of a paradigm that accounts for ambivalent social interactions and an uneven flow of power. At the same time, however, this project pays heed to the material factors that constrained and formed the contours of this process. Although it focuses most directly on New York City reformers and political culture, it has significance beyond this local context; the reformers, reform projects, and politicians at the center of this book achieved national stature and proved influential throughout the United States. Moreover, they participated in reform networks and discourses that extended across the country and even abroad; this broader geographic frame shapes my analysis.

The first chapter of this book, entitled "Of Mugwumps and Mollycoddles: Patronage and the Political Discourse of the 'Third Sex,'" sets out the concept of political manhood and explores the gendered and sexual stigmatization of independent mugwump and civil service reformers who challenged the party and patronage system. I locate the roots of this rhetoric in the contest over the meaning of political manhood in the years after the Civil War. Whereas party adherents subscribed to a communal model linked to participation in the homosocial rituals of partisanship, mugwumps remained attached to the model of individualist and independent manhood that characterized the abolitionist movement. This chapter argues that party stalwarts understood the civil service reform advocacy of the mugwumps in social Darwinist terms. The mugwump's rejection of patronage—the dispensation of which brought young men into the political system—rendered him unable to reproduce politically. The label "third sex," associated with sexual sterility, therefore seems an apt description. I conclude by showing that a younger generation of reformers enjoined this critique of their mugwump forbearers and called for a more "masculine" reform image.

The next two chapters concentrate on reform efforts to replace political patronage in municipal politics, chiefly through competition with machine politicians to win the votes and allegiance of newer populations of immigrant men. Chapter 2, "The Tammany Within: Good Government Reform and Political Manhood," examines attempts by municipal "good government" reformers to emulate the methods and style of the Tammany Hall organization and, at the same time, transcend what they believed to be the corrupt operation of party politics on the local level. This chapter rethinks the relationship between the reformer and the machine politician, which has been described as one of antagonism. I show that not only did municipal reformers pattern crucial reform institutions—including the Citizens' Union and the Good Government Clubs—on the Tammany ward model, but they also transformed their own political personae to approximate the rough and practical style of "the boss."

Chapter 3, "White Armies and the White City: Civic Militarism, Urban Space, and the Urban Populace," argues that Progressive municipal leaders, inspired in part by the belief that the strict military discipline of Tammany Hall accounted for its success, employed militaristic rhetoric and modes of organization within New York City. Through an analysis of two reform projects carried out during the 1890s, this chapter analyzes an emerging ideology I call "civic militarism," which called for the application of the qualities of manly camaraderie and communal purpose identified with warfare to domestic reform. While this ideology worked to legitimize the projects of militarist reformers as appropriately masculine, it also evinced a model of urban social organization that subjugated egalitarian principles to hierarchical ones, contributed to a model of urban citizenship based on whiteness, and deauthorized female reformers.

Chapter 4, "Socrates in the Slums: 'Social Brotherhood' and Settlement House Reform," examines the construction of an ideal eroticized cross-class social brotherhood in the careers of two New York City settlement leaders: John Lovejoy Elliott and Charles B. Stover. This chapter shows that notions about the social role of sexuality stood at the center of the settlement movement and examines the intersection of reform and two traditions of male homoeroticism (the "social mobility" model associated with Horatio Alger and the "democratic comradeship" model heralded by Walt Whitman) as well as the influence of Socratic pedagogy in shaping the praxis and personae of the settlement leaders. I argue that the ideal of social brotherhood encouraged more reciprocal and egalitarian relationships with reform constituents than did the ideology of civic militarism.

Chapter 5, "Daddy George and Tom Brown: Sexual Scandal, Political Manhood, and Self-Government Reform," deals with reformers' attempts to bring the kind of education in "self-government" associated with the settlement movement to populations defined as both criminal and dependent: namely, prison inmates and juvenile delinquents. These reformers wanted to create alternatives to what they believed was a critical association between street gangs and Tammany Hall. The chapter focuses on two, William R. George and Thomas Mott Osborne, who, like the settlement reformers, developed intimate relationships with the objects of their reform projects. Yet, in large part because these men posed a significant challenge to traditional distinctions between the criminal and the citizen (as well as between dependency and independence), the nature of their personal interest in reform became subject to significant public scrutiny; indeed, both became embroiled in sensational sexual scandals.

The final chapter, "The Problem of the Impracticables: Sentimentality, Idealism, and Homosexuality," examines the persistence of gendered and sexual political invective in the Progressive era. Whereas previously, this rhetoric had been leveled against reformers by party politicians, turn-of-the-century reformers revived the figure of the "intermediate sex" and employed it within fiercely waged battles over the future of American reform. The chapter focuses on the most influential use of such invective, Theodore Roosevelt's attack on former reform colleagues as effeminate "impracticable idealists," arguing that Roosevelt and allied figures effectively marginalized those who proposed more radical responses to social and political problems. This chapter also discusses attempts by two prominent reformers—John Jay Chapman and Ernest Howard Crosby—to resist the label of the "impracticable idealist" as well as the broader doctrine of the strenuous life. Their responses revealed the narrowness of political ideals based on masculinist assumptions. Moreover, their attempts to extricate a politics of homoeroticism from the tradition of idealism pointed to a deepening entrenchment of homophobic political discourse.

The epilogue, "Red Bloods and Mollycoddles in the Twentieth Century and Beyond," traces how political conceptions of effeminate weakness and masculine strength—the mollycoddle and the red blood—have retained their discursive power in our own time.

1

Of Mugwumps and Mollycoddles

Patronage and the Political Discourse of the "Third Sex"

On April 14, 1907 the following passage appeared in the *Minneapolis Journal* editorial under the headline ALAS THE MOLLYCODDLE!:

> The mollycoddle controversy continues to rage.
>
> The latest definition is "a man over 30 who goes to a skating rink." The best, probably, is, "A combination of a woman and a man with the weaknesses of each and the strong points of neither." The male mollycoddle is the womanish man. His complement is the mannish woman.
>
> . . . We do not know what a mollycoddle is, but we all know him when we see him. Indeed, we are uncomfortably conscious of his presence before he comes in sight. He carries his atmosphere with him . . . He is elusive. . . . We do not know why we should rather kick him than shake hands with him, but we would.

The editorial went on to define the elusive and undesirable figure of the mollycoddle in the context of American political life:

> The President [Theodore Roosevelt] made it plain . . . that his mollycoddle is a man who won't take hard knocks, who flinches from the crowd. . . . Curiously enough, it was only a few years ago that such opprobrious epithets were invented to describe men like George William Curtis and others like them, who put on their neckties before they went to vote. This raises the question, when is a mollycoddle a mollycoddle?
>
> . . . In the last New York campaign the *New York Journal* thought it had found a perfect specimen. It was Richard Watson Gilder, editor of *Century* magazine. Mr. Gilder didn't drink; didn't swear. He enjoyed feeble health, and he wrote pale, ineffectual verses. If he was not a mollycoddle, what was he? . . . Then a veteran came forward with testimony that Richard Watson Gilder was a perfectly dashing soldier. . . . Another paid tribute to Mr. Gilder's work in cleaning up the slums in New York. . . . On both the military and the civil side Mr. Gilder belied his looks. He was not a mollycoddle, even if he did wear polkadot hose.

The editorial concluded by advising caution in the use of the "mollycoddle" epithet: "It appears to be unsafe to classify any man as a mollycoddle unless he has proved it, and then he classifies himself."[1]

The "mollycoddle controversy" invoked in the pages of the *Journal* referred specifically to a well-publicized and vituperative exchange between the publisher and politician William Randolph Hearst and Richard Watson Gilder, editor of the *Century* magazine and a prominent New York City reformer. On October 18, 1906 Gilder published a letter in the *New York Times* scathingly critical of Hearst's decision to enter the race for the New York governorship as the Democratic candidate after flirting with running as an independent candidate. Like other elite reformers of his generation, Gilder characterized Hearst's candidacy as a travesty: an "absolutely grotesque" attempt at self-glorification, financed by his own personal fortune and waged in the pages of the disreputable newspapers he published. He painted Hearst as a dangerous demagogue who merely posed as a friend to the working man.[2]

While Gilder and his reform colleagues certainly feared that Hearst's appeals to the working class would threaten their own class interests, they represented their concerns as issues of character. Even as their own manhood was challenged, the reformers remained committed to a distinctive ideal of manhood that espoused hard work and self-sacrifice. They found Hearst utterly lacking in either. "Are we prepared to cast to the winds all our hitherto admiration for unselfish public devotion, for . . . modesty in our public men?" Gilder asked. He continued: "Are we to give our suffrage and our praise and the tribute of imitation to the sheer force of money, to blatant self-seeking, to brutal and unscrupulous success?"[3]

Shortly thereafter, the *New York Times* published a similar critique in an editorial called "A Question of Manliness," which contrasted Gilder's "modesty and reserve" with Hearst's "attitude of unbridled hatred and abuse."[4] Gilder and the *Times* referred only obliquely to another element of Hearst's character that they deemed offensive to ideals of respectable manhood—namely, his scandalous penchant for consorting with show girls and participating in the *demimonde* of commercialized vice. As David Nasaw has shown, Hearst had been criticized earlier that year on the floor of the U.S. House of Representativesas a "moral degenerate who insolently casts his eyes upon the noblest of women whose virtue places them beyond the contamination of lust."[5] For some reformers, Hearst's sexual proclivities only deepened their feeling that he was a dangerous political figure. Thomas Mott Osborne, for example, called him "a new and sinister figure in our political history," and likened him to "those degenerate Roman millionaires who bought their offices with bread and circuses."[6]

Hearst retaliated in an editorial published in his newspaper, the *New York Journal*, which purported to respond to a reader's suggestion that Hearst physically attack Gilder. It read: "Reader, surely you have NEVER SEEN MR. GILDER. Who should as think of 'ripping up' the fluffy, feebly-scratching incubator chick as to attack Mr. Gilder . . . in face, in form, in voice, and in movement he is a pathetic imitation of a young girl." The editorial continued this denigration of his physical appearance, referring to the spectacle of "Mr. Richard Watson Gilder, with his gray hair falling around his little mouse eyes, and his thin body shivering in his black cape, gliding into a room among men."[7] Although exceptionally harsh, this kind of gendered and sexual invective was not unique to Hearst.[8]

Although Hearst clearly branded Gilder as insufficiently manly, the 1907 *Minneapolis Journal* editorial interpreted such characteristics as representing a third gender category: a "mollycoddle" was "a combination of a woman and a man with the weaknesses of each and the strong points of neither." As invoked in the editorial, the mollycoddle resembled the figure of the "invert"—or member of a "third sex"—introduced into medical discourse in the latter part of the nineteenth century. The mollycoddle also resembled the "fairy" or "pansy," a familiar urban figure commonly understood to belong to a "third sex."[9] In both the medical and the urban social contexts, this figure connoted not only the inversion of gender roles but also same-sex desire. In so doing, it functioned as a precursor to the modern figure of the "homosexual."[10]

However, the terms in which this editorialist sought to define the mollycoddle pertained directly to American *political* life. The two men subject to the label, Richard Watson Gilder and George William Curtis, were leaders of a group of prominent, elite political reformers in the latter half of the nineteenth century—commonly referred to as the "mugwumps"—who criticized American party politics as thoroughly corrupted by the spoils system of patronage distribution and advocated a disavowal of strict party loyalty.[11] Beginning in the late 1870s, politicians and journalists opposed to this political stance asserted that mugwumps posed a threat not only to the binary structure of the two-party system but also to essentialist distinctions between men and women. They utilized the concept of a third sex to make sense of threats to the political system, while medical "experts" invoked the notion to explain the seemingly chaotic and disruptive pattern of sexual relations that they believed characterized modern life.[12]

The "mollycoddle controversy" sheds significant light on the gendered meanings of politics in the Gilded Age and Progressive Era. The struggle to shape the American political system during a period of intense social upheaval was intricately connected to contests over the meaning of American manhood. Party politicians employed gendered language and sexual invective to denigrate the elite reformer as incapable of participating in the rough and manly world of politics. Indeed, such participation stood as a crucial marker of manhood; reformers who criticized the system appeared to be attacking the very foundations of that communally sanctioned ideal. By linking their critique of reformers to the stigmatization of the sexual invert, party stalwarts discovered a powerful rhetorical weapon with which to oppose reform. Recognizing the potency of this invective, a younger generation of reformers at the turn of the twentieth century constructed their political identities in opposition to the image of the much-maligned mugwump.

The *Minneapolis Journal*'s assertion that such epithets as "mollycoddle" were "invented to describe" mugwump reformers suggests that state politics served as a crucial site for the creation of modern sexual typologies. Much attention has been paid to the emergence of the concept of a third sex in medical discourse, in working-class street life, and in literature, but not in the arena of electoral politics.[13] Writing in 1962, Richard Hofstadter offered some intriguing insights into the interplay of political reform and sexual invective in *Anti-Intellectualism in American Life*. Referring to the occasional denunciation of mugwump reformers as "political hermaphrodites," Hofstadter suggested that such a characterization marked "an easy transition from their [mugwumps'] uncertain location as to political party to an uncertain location as to sex." Hofstadter also linked such rhetoric to the political culture of the Cold War, claiming that "more recent attacks by Senator McCarthy and others upon the Eastern and English-oriented prep-school personnel of the State Department, associated with charges of homosexuality, are not an altogether novel element in the history of American invective."[14]

Historians have expanded on Hofstadter's insights, demonstrating that anxieties about the growing political presence of women and concerns about a broader "feminization" of American culture motivated antimugwump sentiment. In a 1980 essay, "The Mugwump Reputation, 1870 to Present," Geoffrey Blodgett compared historians' negative assessments of the mugwumps to the "brutal invective they sustained from their contemporaries." Like Hofstadter, Blodgett argued that the anti-intellectualism that predominated in American life assigned to "the preservation of culture a somewhat ladylike function." He also asserted that "the exaggerated differentiation and rigid role definitions" inherent in the Victorian attachment to a doctrine of separate spheres "seem to have left males with strong, ambivalent attitudes toward the cultural meaning of sex difference, causing them to equate manliness with both potency and animal aggression while the female symbolized not only virtue but fragile passivity." Mugwumps, who attempted to mix "virtue and virility in public life," found themselves on hazardous gendered terrain, especially in relation to party politics, which "remained of course a wholly male enterprise":

> Regularity was a credential of manliness and rootedness, and party deviates paid a predictable price, especially if the public environment enforced their isolation and rootlessness in other ways. The man who proposed to tame, cleanse, or elevate public life by means of his own special code of purity violated role stereotypes as brashly as the suffragist who asked for woman's place in politics. Both ran the risk of acquiring a queer, desexed public reputation.[15]

Following Hofstadter again, Blodgett argues that the mugwumps' refusal to commit to a party, notably their famous "bolt" from the Republican Party to support the presidential bid of Democrat Grover Cleveland in 1884, precipitated their abuse at the hands of party stalwarts.[16]

More recently, scholar Harlen Makemson, who studied the visual representation of mugwumps in the satirical press, has shown that gendered constructions of the mugwumps referenced a much-discussed male type of the period, "the 'dude,' who was most often upper-class, English in manner, obsessed with eccentric sartorial style, and somewhat ambiguous in his sexuality." The "dude" carried meaning in a discourse of American nationalism that figured American men as unadorned and plain-spoken in opposition to European men, often depicted as decadent, frivolous, and unduly interested in aesthetics. Discussions of the dude often invoked a negative image of Oscar Wilde as an effeminate English aesthete. That some American men looked like Wilde generated worries about what the *New York Daily Tribune* referred to as the "enfeebled and effeminate state of the youth of America." Makemson has shown that, although the popular depiction of the mugwump overlapped with that of the dude, the latter term never took hold with regard to the reformers.[17] While certain dude qualities applied—especially elitism, effeminacy, and a European orientation—mugwumps, who embedded their calls for reform in a rhetoric of moral righteousness, belied the association of the dude with the decadent and disreputable qualities of the "dandy" or "swell."[18]

The connections that Hofstadter and others have made between anti-mugwump rhetoric, cultural elitism, and party "irregularity" are persuasive. The most ridiculed mugwumps were patrician, highly educated white men with literary associations. Refined and cultured editors such as Gilder and George William Curtis of *Harper's Weekly*, who was also singled out in the mollycoddle editorial, became favorite targets, in large part because the sentimental literature they published in their magazines was perceived to wield a feminizing influence on American culture.[19] The mugwumps also attacked the ideal of strict party loyalty. Curtis, for example, asserted that "the constant, watchful, deadly enemy of republican government is the party spirit."[20]

The question remains whether independence from party implied gender indeterminacy, as Hofstadtder suggested. This contention becomes more convincing when one considers that members of the Populist Party and the Prohibition Party were sometimes labeled "she-men" in response to their challenges to the two-party system in the 1890s.[21] Moreover, party politicians and the party press tended to heap gendered abuse on independent reformers during or after important elections, including the election of 1880, when "Young Scratchers" in New York, led by R. R. Bowker, crossed off the names on the ballot of Republican politicians they deemed corrupt, and the "bolt" to Cleveland in 1884.[22] During that same year, editorialists and politicians used the pejorative term "political hermaphrodites" to describe the bolting mugwumps. This became common in press coverage of independent politics thereafter. In 1896, for example, the *New York Sun* published a letter criticizing the Citizen's Union, a newly established nonpartisan political organization, as "a crowd of paltry politicians, Miss Nancys and insufferable bourgeois creatures." The headline given it was IT WILL BE A STRUGGLE IN WHICH THERE WILL BE NO USE FOR POLITICAL HERMAPHRODITES.[23]

Yet the mugwumps' stance of independence from party politics, in and of itself, hardly appears to have justified the passionate abuse heaped upon them. First of all, mugwumps made only a limited critique: while they condemned *excessive* party allegiance, most remained convinced of the value of the political parties to the American democratic system. Charles Francis Adams, for example, declared in 1880 that both the greatness and the weaknesses of the American system lay in the machinelike organization of political parties:

> The American has a natural aptitude for machinery and organization. He believes in system and in order and in combination. In doing so, also, he is entirely right;—that he believed in and practiced these things is the secret of his success in the past, and is its best guarantee

> for the future. Even system, order, and combination, may however, be carried to excess; and there is such a thing, in politics especially, as too much of the machine:—and this too, I say, while fully acknowledging that the machine in itself, in politics as well as elsewhere, is a most indispensable and beneficent institution.[24]

Likewise, Curtis spoke with ambivalence about the "romance of party loyalty upon which politicians trade." He maintained that such loyalty represented "a sentiment indeed, but so is love, so is patriotism, so is religion" and argued that party spirit, "not as a mere agency, but as a living and inspiring organism," had encouraged American men to achieve "splendid results for . . . country, for liberty, and for mankind."[25] Like Adams, Curtis concluded that the problem lay not in the "romance" of party spirit per se but in its unchecked reign over political principle.[26]

Second, with the memory of the disastrous consequences of the Liberal Republican campaign of 1872 fresh in their minds, few mugwumps even advocated the establishment of a third party. Instead they preferred to think of themselves as an informal "party of the centre"—to use Henry Adams's words—that offered its votes to the party most willing to accept its demands.[27] New York mugwump R. R. Bowker, for example, claimed that "it is by the free flux of independent votes on the edge of party lines, the fluidity of parties, so to speak, that politicians can most practically be controlled and politics be most effectively reformed."[28] Curtis, who always considered himself an heir to the rightful tradition of the Republican Party, maintained that "it is only independence *within* the party which secures political progress by means of party."[29]

For their part, party politicians never believed that mugwump reformers represented a large enough constituency to seriously affect the outcome of elections, especially at the state and national levels. Historians of the period have tended to agree, pointing to the fact that mugwumps were frequently unsuccessful in convincing liberal Republicans who shared their overall political perspective to support Democratic or independent candidates.[30] In the 1884 presidential election, for example, the majority of such men refused to bolt the party to vote for the detested Democrats and even joined in the public criticism of those who did.[31] Indeed, party politicians delighted in pointing out the mugwumps' limited numerical base. Referring to mugwump reformers as the "*unco guid*," Blaine asserted that "They are noisy but not numerous, pharisaical but not practical, ambitious but not wise, pretentious but not powerful! They can be easily dealt with . . . I could handle them myself without trouble." Likewise, New York Republican Roscoe Conkling numbered mugwumps at "about three hundred persons."[32] Still, there was in their reform agenda something that provoked intense reaction and a sustained challenge to their masculinity. The stakes were large: the set of masculine values and practices that would sustain political participation and power.

Patronage, Civil Service Reform, and Political Manhood

If Gilded Age party politicians expressed skepticism about the threat of mugwumps to party membership, they did fear their influence on elected officials and on the voting public—despite protests to the contrary. This fear focused primarily on the most potent cause advocated by the independents: reform of the civil service. At the end of the Civil War, liberal reformers began to turn their attention away from the South and toward Northern cities and identified the spoils system as the most egregious social evil. Growing more resolute at each revelation of patronage abuses, reformers—led by the triumvirate of George William Curtis, Carl Schurz, and Dorman B. Eaton—studied the English civil service code with the intention of applying it to the American system.[33]

Liberal reformers, who had organized voluntarily on behalf of civil service reform since the 1850s, achieved greater influence on federal and state legislatures after the "Southern Question" faded from political prominence in the late 1870s. During the presidential election of 1876, Curtis implored Rutherford B. Hayes to make civil service reform the premiere Republican issue in light of "the universal prostration of industry and stagnation of business . . . and the absence of any overpowering vital issue like slavery, the war, or reconstruction."[34] Although Curtis and his colleagues grew disappointed by the low priority given their cause in Hayes's stump speeches, the president ultimately proved an ally. Indeed, after ordering the last of the federal troops from the South, Hayes wrote in his diary, "Now for Civil Service reform."[35] Soon after taking office, he appointed a Civil Service Commission with Curtis at its head.

Through constant advocacy of civil service issues in journals sympathetic to mugwump causes (including the *North American Review*, Curtis's *Harper's Weekly*, and E. L. Godkin's *Nation*), vigorous campaigns to influence elected officials, and clever exploitation of the public furor over the assassination of President Garfield by a deranged office seeker, Curtis and his allies achieved substantial successes in the 1870s and 1880s. Their signal achievement was the passage in 1883 of the Pendleton Act, which required that certain federal positions be staffed through "impartial" examinations administered by the newly established Civil Service Commission. Within the year, state legislatures in New York and Massachusetts passed legislation modeled on the Pendleton Act pertaining to state and city employment.[36]

It was in response to such successes, as well as to various efforts to "bolt and scratch," that party politicians unleashed their most vituperative criticism of mugwump reformers. The mugwumps themselves asserted that reform of the civil service constituted their central aim. They routinely justified their decision to cross party lines and to promote independent and fusion candidates as efforts to attack party patronage, which they maintained was the central evil of machine politics, and to replace patronage with civil service measures. Curtis, for example, declared:

> Useful as scratching is as a corrective, it does not strike at the heart of the machine, and it is therefore only a corrective, and not a radical remedy. That remedy can be found only by finding the source of the power of the machine, and that source is official patronage. It is the command of millions of the public money spent in public administration; the control of the vast labyrinth of place, with its enormous emoluments; the system which makes the whole civil service, to the least detail and most insignificant position, the spoils of party victory; which perverts necessary party organization into intolerable party despotism.[37]

Curtis's assertion that the spoils system "perverted" American democracy typified the mugwump view, which held that control of patronage gave party leaders a dangerous level of power and that the "grab" for positions subordinated political virtue to materialist greed and rampant corruption. Many (but not all) mugwumps imbued this critique of patronage with nativist sentiment and racist claims; they maintained that unworthy and inferior immigrant men (especially Irish men) threatened to control American politics through the exploitation of political spoils.[38]

For their part, party politicians often defended the spoils system and vehemently opposed civil service reform. Urban machine politicians, in particular, attacked the mugwump expressions of ethnic superiority and characterized civil service reform as a gambit to disempower the "urban masses" at the expense of native-born elites who, they charged, would fare much better on civil service examinations.[39] Likewise, party politicians both urban and rural contended that civil service measures would favor elite and educated men over "plain men"—namely, industrial and agricultural workers. Moreover, a number defended the patronage system on principle, maintaining that the dispensation of political positions represented the "practical" workings of American democracy and promoted party loyalty and patriotism among the masses of constituents. These men dismissed civil service reformers as "impractical" idealists who were too weak and snobbish to participate in the Machiavellian rough-and-tumble of party politics. Republican Senator John J. Ingalls, for example, called civil service reform an "iridescent dream" and charged that "Government is force. . . . Politics is a battle for supremacy. Parties are the armies. The decalogue and the golden rule have no place in a political campaign. The object is success."[40]

The bitter disagreement over the role of patronage in American democracy helps to explain the passion with which party politicians attacked mugwump reformers, but it does not, on the surface, account for the gendered and sexualized dimensions of such attacks. In order to better understand the imbrication of gender and sexuality within this political debate, one must pay attention to an underlying contest over the meanings of political manhood. This contest involved sharply divergent disagreement over the gendered meanings of the individual and the collective, the ideal and the practical.

Mugwump reformers had originally exemplified an individualist style of manhood that emphasized self-restraint and the power of the will. Influenced by Emersonian transcendental individualism and Garrisonian abolitionism, proponents of this ideal posited that manhood required a forceful and persistent resistance to social evil and corruption. Above all else, the true abolitionist man was not to allow his moral self to be subsumed in a corrupt system; he was not to sacrifice principle to achieve practical ends. Of course, such a moral stance did not necessarily require abstaining from party politics, although some abolitionists—most famously Garrison—took that position. Unlike the Garrisonians, George William Curtis, who began his political career in the abolitionist movement, forcefully argued that young educated men of principle should "take a practical and active interest in politics." In a series of lectures to college graduates delivered from the 1850s through the 1870s, Curtis asserted that engagement in political affairs represented a noble and manly duty:

> There is no intellectual or moral life without liberty. Therefore, as a man must breathe and see before he can study, the scholar must have liberty, first of all; and the American scholar is a *man* and has a voice in his own government, so his interest in political affairs must precede all others. He must build his house before he can live in it.[41]

In these addresses, Curtis insisted that such a manly political role would necessarily lead young men "to party association and cooperation." He asserted that the "spring of party" promoted "great public results" but at the same time warned young men that it could lead to "the deadliest peril": overzealous party loyalty.[42]

Curtis's lectures navigated between two sets of binary categories suffused with class and gender meanings: the independent versus the communal and the ideal versus the practical. Critics associated elite calls for "independence" with a genteel disdain for association with the masses. Recognizing this, Curtis urged that rather than "cultivating the feeling that politics are tiresome and dirty, and politicians vulgar bullies and bravoes," educated men should engage in "united action." He also attempted to refute the "popular idea" of the educated, "unpractical and impracticable man" for whom "heaven itself is not pure enough."[43] Beginning in the antebellum era, party politicians negatively compared the professed idealism and "purity" of the elite educated man to the "practical" nature of the "self-made man" whose strength of character was forged through manual labor and business success. They also portrayed expressions of idealism and political "purity" as moral qualities that properly belonged in the female sphere. Recognizing the strength of such charges of unmanliness and impracticability, Curtis and other mugwump leaders attempted to chart a new course for educated men that recalibrated the balance between independence and collective action as well as between idealism and practicality.[44]

Mugwumps also challenged such negative assessments by defining themselves through the gender-laden rhetoric and imagery of Christian warfare. After the Civil War, reformers made distinct connections between the "manly" fight to end slavery and the subsequent battle against the spoils system.[45] James Russell Lowell, for example, said of the mugwump cause: "A moral purpose multiplies us by ten, as it multiplied the early Abolitionists. . . . They emancipated the negro; and we mean to emancipate the respectable white man."[46] Richard Rogers Bowker, who compared civil service reform to the "anti-slavery crusade," also made connections between the mugwump movement and the American War of Independence: "The independent voter of today is the independent soldier of a hundred years ago," he wrote. "His ballot is the bullet of the bloodless revolution for which we must hope and work. He has had for some time a guerrilla fight, like the farmers who popped away at the British . . . but the force is now getting pretty strong."[47]

While party politicians criticized mugwumps as too rarefied to participate in "politics as warfare," male reformers countered that excessive party loyalty represented an affront to the manhood of the true soldier. Although mugwumps generally agreed that politics represented a form of warfare, they argued that the militarism of "practical politics" required excessive discipline, making "strict party men" obsequious sycophants rather than manly soldiers.[48] Charles Francis Adams, for example, maintained that "the habit of individual political action" proved impossible in a system requiring "complete suppression under the rigid discipline of party." Mark Twain declared that the emasculating effects of such discipline extended beyond the individual: "I am persuaded . . . that this idea of consistency—unchanging allegiance to the party—has lowered the manhood of the whole nation—pulled it down and dragged it in the mud."[49]

Mugwumps also believed that the system of patronage—the "engine" by which such discipline was achieved—represented a significant affront to the ideal of independent manhood. Curtis compared the loyalty of the patronage recipient to the party boss to "that of a dog to his master who throws him a bone" and maintained that "his tenure corrodes his manhood and self respect."[50] Mugwumps argued that the enormous power of patronage threatened to corrupt the entire American population. The National Civil Service Reform League warned voters in 1882 that "the young American is taught that the qualifications for public employment are not integrity, intelligence and industry, but sycophancy and servility, cheating and bribing to swell the party vote . . . When personal favor has thrown him a place he learns that he can retain it not by personal service . . . in a word, that he must be a parasite instead of a man."[51] For mugwump reformers, the primacy of patronage in American political life deprived every man, and by extension the nation, of autonomy, self-respect, and virtue—the hallmarks of independent manhood.

The system of patronage proved much less problematic to most party loyalists, who subscribed to a model of manliness that differed sharply from the individualist tradition of the abolitionists and mugwump reformers. Nineteenth-century partisan politics were rooted in a cross-class homosocial world in which, according to historian Elliot Gorn, "manliness had to do more with valor, strength, and prowess than with upright behavior. . . . Manliness on the urban streets was tied to honor, to one's status among peers; it inhered in an individual's reputation for toughness. Bravado, group loyalty, and a defiance of outsiders were marks of leadership in this world."[52] Party politics played a crucial role, tying men of various classes and backgrounds into a communal society of political manhood. According to historian Michael McGerr:

> An intense partisanship, epitomized by the press, simplified the task of choosing among candidates and politics; independence from party was virtually unthinkable. The rallies and parades of spectacular campaigns at once gave men a sense of their power and importance and put subtle communal pressure on them to participate. For men, politics was work, entertainment, camaraderie, and above all a form of self-revelation. A man demonstrated his identity and power by wearing a party button, turning out to listen and cheer at rallies, marching in parades, and casting a ballot on election day.[53]

For many nineteenth-century men, allegiance to party and participation in political rituals and spectacles functioned as badges of collective male identity.

The system of patronage played a crucial material role in cementing the collective male world. Party membership functioned as a central, if not essential, site for the economic and social mobility of poor, working-class, and immigrant men in nineteenth-century America. In fact, party politicians often explained that their control of patronage extended beyond the disbursement of political appointments; their status as political leaders gave them access to information and influence with regard to a variety of private positions as well. It was their ability to make such opportunities available, they argued, that opened up avenues to material success and imbued young men with the principles of patriotism and nationalism. Indeed, party politicians asserted that this network of public and private patronage prevented men from turning to lives of crime or to "dangerous" radical political ideologies.[54]

The importance of patronage to the homosocial culture of party politics accounts for much of the fierce resistance among party loyalists to mugwump reformers' advocacy of civil service measures. Whereas mugwumps maintained that the civil service examinations would free men from corrupting servility to party officials and produce a meritocracy based on individualist values, party politicians viewed such provisions as potentially disastrous to the intricately woven web of male social relations and maintained that such a system of civil service employment would favor already privileged elites at the expense of the working classes. To these politicians, the mugwump attack on patronage represented an assault on not only the party system but also the very foundation of shared principles of male identity and camaraderie.

Political and Medical Discourse on Sex and Gender

To understand why the attacks on the spoils system by Curtis and other advocates of civil service reform found expression through the language of sex and gender, it is helpful to examine a parallel, and often intersecting, medical discourse that sought to make sense of cases of deviance from binary notions of gender and sexual order. In recent years, scholars have shed new light on the emergence of a new science of "sexology" in the United States, showing that beginning in the early 1880s, American scientists, influenced by a burgeoning literature in Europe, identified a perverse or "contrary" sexual instinct. Although American medical professionals used different terms and disagreed about issues of causation, they most often referred to a person with this instinct as a "sexual invert," the precursor of the twentieth-century "homosexual." As historian Jennifer Terry has noted, early descriptions of the "invert" collapsed categories of gender and sexuality: not only were inverts "attracted to members of the 'same' sex," but they were also described as having "bodies, conduct, attitudes, tastes, and personalities characteristic of the 'opposite' sex."[55] Americans tended to perceive inversion as threatening. According to Terry, "inversion signaled the alarming effacement of gender distinctions upon which social order (i.e., male dominance) had been based."[56]

The first published American treatment of sexual inversion drew on the archives of American political history. In 1881, Edward Spitzka, a European-trained neurologist who gained fame as a medical witness testifying for the defense of Garfield assassin Charles Guiteau, published a short essay, "A Historical Case of Sexual Perversion," on Lord Cornbury, the colonial governor of New York and New Jersey (1702–1708). Spitzka described Cornbury as perverted based on evidence that he "dress[ed] himself as a woman" and, citing sexologist Richard von Krafft-Ebing, asserted that he manifested "'contrary sexual sensation.' Here a male feels himself drawn to males, the female to females, and either feels himself or herself as if a person of the opposite sex." Evincing the broader American tendency to judge inversion in harshly negative terms, Spitzka judged Cornbury "a degraded, hypocritical, and utterly immoral being." He associated his "disease" with his elite status and described him as inverting the manly character of political and military leadership, asserting that "New York frequently saw its Governor, the commander of the colonial troops, and a scion of the royal stock, promenading the walls of the little fort, in female attire, with all the coquetry of a woman."[57] Spitzka's assessment of Cornbury parallels in many ways the critique of the elite and effeminate mugwump, whose lack of manliness made a mockery of his political ambitions. It is noteworthy that Spitzka assumed that inversion of gender comprised sexual desire for males, although he offered no supporting evidence.[58]

Medical professionals did not invent the invert from whole cloth, of course. As historians writing on Europe and the United States have argued, in many ways sexologists responded to and elaborated events happening in society; in particular, they responded to urban subcultures comprising individuals who inverted gender roles and engaged in same-sex practices that gained public notice over the course of the eighteenth and nineteenth centuries.[59] To this complex genealogy of modern sexual and gender meanings, we might add those produced within political discourse. Indeed, the fact that Spitzka used Lord Cornbury as the vehicle for introducing American physicians to the theory of inversion suggests the importance of politics as terrain for making sense of sex and gender in the U.S. context. As historian Patricia U. Bonomi has shown, the earliest assertions that Cornbury cross-dressed emerged in the context of his factional struggles with colonists; in attempting to enforce the rule of the crown, the governor was understood to undermine values of independence and religious freedom. In order to discredit him and have him removed from office, opponents asserted that he wore women's clothing.[60]

This association of gender inversion with political values and goals believed to threaten national strength and independence became a hallmark of nineteenth-century American political discourse, which introduced such figures as the political hermaphrodite and the third sex reformer. Although the connections between these types and those identified within medical discourse were often tenuous, they emerged within the same broad historical context and represent important strands in the making of modern understandings of sexuality. One example of the interconnection of political and medical discourse is the use of the epithet "political hermaphrodite." This term held some resonance prior to the Gilded Age. For example, Samuel Galloway, a judge advocate appointed by Abraham Lincoln during the Civil War, in a letter to Lincoln described a Union Army official as "a sort of political hermaphrodite," on the grounds that he suspected the man of supporting Lincoln rival Samuel S. Cox.[61] Although sporadic references, similarly linked to ambivalent party identification, appeared in the 1870s, the term did not achieve real currency until the 1880s, when Abigail Dodge, a cousin of James G. Blaine who wrote under the pseudonym Gail Hamilton, used it to denounce Blaine's opponents. In 1880, Hamilton referred to Massachusetts Senator George Frisbie Hoar, a vocal critic of Republican Party policies, and his followers as "political hermaphrodites." Thereafter, the

New York Times frequently used the term to refer to Hoar and his supporters and especially in reference to the mugwump "bolt" of the Republican Party in 1884.[62]

The most widely recognized elaboration of the concept came in March 1886, in a speech that stalwart Republican Senator John J. Ingalls of Kansas delivered during a debate over the application of civil service rules in the U.S. Postal Service. After ridiculing President Cleveland for supporting civil service reform and proudly defending partisanship and the patronage system, Ingalls offered the following description of civil service reformers who, "standing on the corners of the streets . . . loudly advertise their perfections, thanking God that they are not as other men":

> Mr. President, the neuter gender is not popular either in nature or society. "Male and female He created them." But there is a third sex, if that can sex be called which sex has none, resulting sometimes from a cruel caprice of nature, at others from accident or malevolent design, possessing the vices of both and the virtues of neither; effeminate without being masculine or feminine; unable either to beget or to bear; possessing neither fecundity nor virility; endowed with the contempt of men and the derision of women, and doomed to sterility, isolation, and extinction. But they have two recognized functions. They sing falsetto, and they are usually selected as the guardians of the seraglios of Oriental despots. . . . These political epicenes, without pride of ancestry or hope of posterity, chant in shrill falsetto their songs of praise of non-partisanship and civil-service reform.[63]

Journalists sympathetic to the mugwump movement characterized Ingalls's speech as "one of the most vulgar and disgusting ever heard in the chamber" and noted that it prompted "ladies [to] fly from the gallery and Republican Senators [to] roar with laughter."[64]

However, Ingalls's contention that civil service reformers constituted another sex held rhetorical power in two crucial ways. First, as Hofstadter suggested, the concept of a third sex served as a pointed metaphor for describing those who refused to commit to either party. Second, by labeling reformers "third sex" and associating them with hermaphrodites and eunuchs, party politicians raised the issue of procreation. The emphasis on a lack of fecundity was important, for it implied that allied goals of nonpartisanship and an end to political patronage were impractical and unproductive: "doomed," in his words, "to sterility, isolation and extinction."[65] Other critics made similar connections between procreation and reform politics. Colonel Robert G. Ingersoll, for example, declared that "a Mugwump, like the mule, has no pride of ancestry, nor hope of posterity." Republican John Hay implied both sterility and frustrated sexual desire by comparing the attraction of a mugwump for a "rascal" with "the Eunuch's admiration for the ram."[66]

Such charges of reproductive sterility become especially interesting when considered in conjunction with the positive defenses of the patronage system put forth by a number of machine politicians at the end of the nineteenth century. Virtually every successful politician of the era paid special attention to young men; indeed, in many published interviews and memoirs, party politicians bragged of their skill in attracting them to the fold. New York Republican Thomas Collier Platt, for example, in a special section of his autobiography entitled "Advice to Young Men," maintained that "the young men are the reliance of the country. . . . About the strongest argument that can be advanced in a candidate's favor before a political convention is that he is popular with the young men."[67]

George Washington Plunkitt, a Tammany leader in New York City, also spoke of the importance of attracting young men and argued that, in this regard, civil service reformers could not compete because they had nothing to offer. "How are you goin' to interest our young men in their country," he asked, "if you have no offices to give them when they work for their party?"[68] Platt, Plunkitt, and other party politicians effectively argued that patronage functioned as the means by which the American political system—and the ideal of political manhood—reproduced themselves. Divorced from the two major parties and without patronage positions to offer, mugwump reformers stood outside the cycle of political reproduction.

This discourse was firmly embedded within ideologies of social Darwinism. The publication of Darwin's *Origin of the Species* (1859) and Herbert Spencer's subsequent application of Darwin's findings to human behavior revolutionized the ways individuals on both sides of the Atlantic interpreted human social, political, economic, and cultural life.[69] Party politicians used the Spencerian phrase "the survival of the fittest" to characterize political struggle and legitimize their methods. Just as social thinkers like William Graham Sumner invoked Darwinian theory to naturalize the workings of laissez faire capitalism and justify the inequities the system produced, Ingalls and other political leaders and allied journalists described patronage as resulting from the natural and unregulated functioning of the American political system. Reformers who criticized patronage, therefore, were dismissed not only as "sentimental" idealists unwilling to engage in such life-and-death struggle but also as impotent and stunted. Thus, the *New York Sun* described the mugwump movement as "an arrested development" (a term used by Darwin) that "will not grow, save to grow beautifully less."[70] Mugwumps, who lacked the means to reproduce themselves, were fated to become casualties of the process of political evolution.[71]

The Darwinian notion of "arrested development" also structured the understanding of a newly defined figure in the latter half of the nineteenth century—the sexual invert—and this is where the political hermaphrodite intersects with the discourse of sexology. As introduced into the scientific literature in the 1860s by Karl Heinrich Ulrichs, who sought a scientific framework to explain same-sex desire, "third sex" referred to men with male bodies and female psyches. Ulrichs also referred to such men as "psychical hermaphrodites." He viewed members of the third sex as benign, and hoped his research would achieve emancipatory consequences for them. Other sexologists followed, including Richard von Krafft-Ebing, whose work was highly influential in American medical circles. Krafft-Ebing adopted the notion of third sex or sexual invert, but imbued it with negative meanings. He argued that homosexuals were arrested at a primitive stage of development and therefore, according to historian Jennifer Terry, functioned "as living signs of modern nervous degeneracy."[72] Like Ulrichs, Krafft-Ebing linked inversion to hermaphroditism, but he concluded that inverts possessed the least desirable traits of man and woman.[73]

It is uncertain, perhaps even unlikely, that Ingalls and others who critiqued reformers as inverted would have been familiar with the work of European sexologists in 1886. Theories of sexual inversion were discussed in medical publications throughout the 1880s but would not be widely disseminated to the American public until the following decade.[74]

However, the category of the political hermaphrodite and the political invocation of the third sex bear more than a passing resemblance to the concept developed in that new "scientific" field.[75] In both contexts, the third sex figure was understood in terms of both gender ambiguity and estrangement from reproduction and was perceived as threatening to sexual and gender order. Moreover, both medical and political models at times suggested that inversion was congenital; for example, Krafft-Ebing's assertion in 1888 that the condition represented a "freak of nature" recalls the terminology Ingalls used in his 1886 speech.

This suggestion of the congenital roots of inversion is linked to the influence of degeneration theory, which held that negative traits, whether inherited or acquired through environmental conditions, could be passed from one generation to the next. Concerns about degeneration often manifested in expressed anxieties about the effects of industrial life on poor people and became explicitly racialized through the "science" of "eugenics." At the same time, the upper classes were understood as susceptible to degeneration due to the effeminizing and enervating effects of "overcivilization."[76] Krafft-Ebing and his American followers interpreted sexual inversion as one symptom of degeneration and noted its prevalence among the poorest and wealthiest classes. As degeneration theory became more influential in the mid-1880s and after, critics of the overcivilized and of mugwumps increasingly presented them as congenitally and constitutionally abnormal (see figure 1.1).[77]

Medical and political discourses of the third sex differed in terms of the explicit association of gender inversion with same-sex desire. While such desire was constitutive of the medical model of sexual inversion in the 1880s, it rarely found direct expression within political discourse. Often presented as effeminate—terms of opprobrium included "Miss Nancy," "man-milliner," and "long-haired man"—the mugwump was also often figured as lacking sexual desire entirely—as "unsexed" or "neutered." Yet the femininizing terms applied to mugwumps and other reformers may well have connoted same-sex desire. Effeminacy had long been linked to those who engaged in same-sex relations; male prostitutes, for example, were described as effeminate in the nineteenth century. Same-sex desire was also suggested by the use of feminine pronouns and names—like "Charlotte Anne" and "Miss Nancy"—in reference to males.[78]

Titled "The Persecuted Mugwump: A Refuge at Last," this cartoon likens the mugwump reformer to a dime museum curiosity. Not only outdated and useless, the mugwump also resembles the biological "freaks" exhibited in such venues. By embodying the mugwump's political position in this way, the cartoon reflects broader depictions of elite reformers as estranged from both political and biological (sexual) norms.

Frank Leslie's Illustrated Newspaper, November 14, 1885, cover

At the turn of the century, this connection between gender inversion and same-sex desire became more fixed in the public imagination as a result of a range of historical transformations, including the expansion and increased visibility of urban "fairy" cultures, bohemian enclaves, and the dissemination of medical theories of sexual inversion in the periodical press and in newspapers reporting on sensational trials, such as the 1892 "girl lover" trial of Alice Mitchell.[79] These developments also served to more firmly link the political discourse of the third sex to an increasingly pathologizing medical mode, as demonstrated by the appearance of the phrase "inverted mugwump," beginning in the early 1890s, as well as by the use of the terms "degenerate" and "pervert" in critical analyses of Lord Cornbury's tenure as colonial governor produced by American historians at the end of the century.[80]

American press coverage of the Oscar Wilde trial in 1895 also illustrates the extent to which sexological and political definitions of "third sex" became intertwined. The *New York Sun*, for example, published an editorial that held that Wilde suffered from an "intellectual and moral disease and abnormality" and defined this disease in medical terms, asserting that the symptoms had been documented by alienists. The editors also insisted, however, that this malady commonly afflicted social reformers who considered themselves "superior to their fellows in sensitive perception and refinement." They contended that the warped impulse to reform

> has its origin in a diseased discontent with conditions and passions and ambitions which are inseparable from social health and indicative of normal human nature. The natural instincts and the rugged virtues of the people; the invigorating spirit and the hearty sentiment necessary for the preservation and strength of the race, are treated as the evidences of an inferiority of development.

The *Sun* further identified Wilde as a source of medical, social, and political contagion. The editorial not only advocated that he be committed to an insane asylum and separated from society "like an incurable leper," but also stated that the ideas he espoused "must be resisted by all the uncontaminated moral and normal influences of society."[81]

A similar collapsing of the political and sexological languages of the third sex was certainly evident in the critique of the "New Women" who had become active participants on the American political scene at the turn of the century. As Carroll Smith-Rosenberg has shown, opponents of the political causes promoted by these women began to paint them as sexual deviants, "mannish lesbians" who threatened the nation's social, sexual, and political order.[82] Indeed, in 1890 Ingalls used the third sex model to condemn both male and female supporters of the woman suffrage movement:

> Its advocates, outside this chamber, so far as I know them, are the unsexed of both sexes. Men (long hair) without manhood: women (S. H.) [short hair] without womanhood: males without virility, and females without fecundity. . . . I am sure I voice the sentiments of a vast majority of the women of America in protesting agt [against] this movement to abolish the distinction between the sexes as a loathsome unnatural heresy—an obscure dogma at war alike with the ordinances of nature and the laws of God.[83]

However, the convergence of the political and sexological paradigms of the third sex had different implications for men and women. Whereas New Women who *violated* the traditional ideals of private womanliness by entering into the political arena were stigmatized as members of a third sex, men were similarly stigmatized for *adhering* to a traditional genteel style of manhood associated with the upper classes and to the traditional mugwump critique of party politics.

A new generation of male reformers at the dawn of the Progressive Era chafed at the taint of effeminacy and inversion associated with their forbearers. Many struggled to imbue the image of the reformer with a sense of virility and heroism while laying claim to the moral idealism and cultural authority of those who preceded them. They sought to maintain a critique of the party machines as corrupt and contrary to American democratic values and also to reposition themselves as "practical" reformers unafraid to deal with party bosses on their own terms.

This vexed relationship to the older genteel reformers was reflected in the mollycoddle editorial presented at the beginning of this chapter. The men who defended Gilder from Hearst's attacks were, in essence, attempting to recuperate the reform tradition from the stigma of effeminacy and inversion. Thomas Mott Osborne and Jacob Riis, among others, intervened in the vituperative debate by praising Gilder's military service in the Civil War and his work on the New York City Tenement House Commission of 1895.[84] The defense of Gilder on these grounds reflected the importance of an ethos of militarism to the ideals of political manhood at the turn of the century. This ethos was manifested not only in the

"Inexplicable. Miss Anthony Susan—To think that thing can vote and I can't." This cartoon reflects the gendered and sexualized connotations of citizenship in the late nineteenth century. "Miss Anthony Susan," the more imposing and masculine figure and the epitome of the New Woman, is contrasted with the effeminate dude on the right. In the early twentieth century, "mollycoddle" replaced "dude" as the most common epithet used against allegedly effeminate, upper-class men, including those involved in political reform efforts.

Judge Publishing Company, 1896

jingoist campaign to involve the United States in the war against Spain but also in the realm of domestic politics. Linking reform efforts to the grand and noble cause of the Union Army, a number of influential reformers and scholars called for a new principle of civic militarism, which identified city bosses and monopolists as the enemies to be vanquished. Promoters believed it had the capacity to redeem an American class in danger of losing the "manly virtues."

Many of the primary architects of this new brand of political manhood began their political careers aligned with mugwump reformers. Indeed, younger reformers often joined in the gendered critique of their older colleagues. Richard Rogers Bowker, a civil service reform leader who was somewhat younger than Curtis and Gilder, publicly criticized the genteel timidity of his elders. In an open letter to Curtis he charged that party politicians "rely on your elegant politeness, sir, not to say anything acrimonious, not to make any 'personal attacks,' not to disturb the 'harmony' of the convention. . . . Wanted, a man who dares! Who dares not only to write before the convention, but to talk in it, and to act after it!"[85]

Theodore Roosevelt, who began his political career in the early 1880s resembling the "effeminate" mugwump reformer, proved an even more strident critic. When Curtis, E. L. Godkin, and other mugwumps criticized Roosevelt for refusing to "bolt" the Republican Party to vote for Cleveland in 1884, Roosevelt responded by brashly attacking them as "liars, lunatics, and political hermaphrodites."[86] In his autobiography, he characterized his former colleagues with great contempt:

> Most of the newspapers which regarded themselves as the especial champions of Civil Service Reform and as the highest exponents of civic virtue, and which distrusted the average citizen and shuddered over the "coarseness" of the professional politicians, were, nevertheless, given to vices even more contemptible, although not so gross as, those they denounced and derided. Their editors were refined men of cultivated tastes, whose pet temptations were backbiting, mean, slander. . . . They were not robust or powerful men; they felt ill at ease in the company of rough, strong men; they often had in them a vein of physical timidity. They . . . were almost or quite as hostile to manliness as they were to unrefined vice—and were much more

> hostile to it than to the typical shortcomings of wealth and refinement.[87]

In the years after his break with the mugwumps, Roosevelt strove to create his own political persona and style in opposition to the maligned image of the genteel and effeminate reformer and frequently advised young men of privilege to eschew that example in favor of his own "strenuous" brand of political manhood.

Bowker and Roosevelt were not alone in their treatment of "mugwumpery" as a negative referent for participation in the political arena. Indeed, many of the educated and privileged young men interested in political and urban reform at the turn of the twentieth century looked not to their mugwump forbearers but to their purported nemeses—machine politicians—as paradigms of virile political manhood. By discovering "the Tammany within," this generation remade reform as an appropriately manly endeavor. Moreover, they worked to replace the spoils system of party patronage with new forms of cross-class male relations through political and educational initiatives. Ironically, the close connections some of them forged with working-class male constituents made them vulnerable to the same kinds of gender- and sexuality-laden criticism that had been directed toward their reform predecessors.

2

The Tammany Within

Good Government Reform and Political Manhood

In early autumn 1897, two seeming adversaries met on the deck of the ocean liner *New York*, which was en route from London to its namesake city. These two men—the influential British reformer and journalist W. T. Stead and the "boss" of New York City's Tammany Hall, Richard Croker—engaged in a lengthy conversation about the political scene in New York City. In so doing, they staged a debate between machine and reform political styles that would dominate turn-of-the-century urban politics.

Stead, determined to "portray a man as he seems to himself at his best moments rather than [as] he appears to his enemies at his worst," asked Croker how he accounted for his own success and for the endurance of Tammany Hall as the predominant force in city politics, despite the many reform campaigns to remove that organization from power. Croker ventured three major arguments. First, Tammany Hall had successfully rid itself of outright, or "illegal," graft and had thereby become an upright and "respectable" political organization. Second, Tammany pursued a "practical" brand of politics as opposed to reformers, whose "lofty" political theories could never be realized. Third, Tammany Hall served the large foreign-born and working-class populations primarily by seeking out young men and bringing them into the fold. Croker argued that "the encouragement of young men" was crucial because it promised a level of social mobility and immediate material rewards for those with few alternatives. In this way the machine made loyalists not only of the young men themselves but also of their "fathers and elder relations."[1]

When Stead published this conversation as a "character sketch" of Croker in October 1897, many anti-Tammany reformers reacted with great outrage. Prominent lawyer Matthew P. Breen, for example, insisted that the interview was "manufactured out of whole cloth" and that Croker was incapable of speaking in such an intelligent and philosophical fashion.[2] E. L. Godkin, editor of *The Nation*, railed against the interview as a vile apologia for Tammany corruption. For such mugwump reformers who had battled Tammany Hall during the infamous scandals of the Tweed ring in the 1870s, any account of Tammany or Croker that fell short of utter condemnation was tantamount to treason.[3] Often motivated by nativist prejudice and convinced of their own position as the city's "best men," municipal reformers of this generation found the hated machine unredeemable.[4]

A younger generation of reformers proved much more willing to, in Stead's words, "give the devil his due." The members of this group, who came of age in the 1880s and 1890s, were in many ways similar to their mugwump forbearers. They came from prominent, well-to-do, native-born families and were highly educated. They also took up many of the causes associated with mugwump municipal reform: securing the election of "honest and capable citizens," separating municipal affairs from state and national party issues, achieving "home rule" and "business management" for the city, and rooting out corruption and the spoils system from municipal administrations.

Yet significant differences marked the two generations. Whereas mugwumps believed that the mostly Irish Tammany leaders were inherently criminal and undeserving of respect, the "good government" reformers—or "Goo Goos" as they came to be called—developed a much more complex analysis of the sources of corruption in politics due, in part, to Tammany's own bid to present itself as a respectable organization. Whereas the mugwumps so feared the taint of party politics that they were reluctant to form any lasting organizations, earning a reputation as lofty "do-gooders" without a realistic sense of the political process, the Goo Goos cast themselves as committed "practical" politicians capable of making real and lasting changes in the city. Finally, most reformers abandoned mugwump calls for denying suffrage to the uneducated or foreign born and instead recognized that they would need to win the support of a large portion of the immigrant working classes in order to obtain power.

The good government reformers also rejected the genteel style of their mugwump predecessors. In order to successfully compete in the urban political arena and to attract young working-class men to the cause, many municipal reformers attempted to emulate the "rough" manly style of Tammany leaders. Moreover, because they recognized the success with which Tammany had organized men socially and politically, they looked to their old nemesis for models of political organization and institution building. Retaining a critique of the spoils system as a corrupting influence, the good government reformers attempted to establish a new system that would bring men of various classes together to work for the public good.

This willingness to challenge accepted orthodoxy vis-à-vis Tammany Hall represents a significant shift in the history of reform politics from the Gilded Age to the Progressive Era. Although some historians have characterized the municipal reform movement of the 1880s and 1890s as a continuation of the mugwump effort to impose the rule of the "best men" on urban populaces, an examination of evolving reform characterizations of and engagement with machine politics shows that good government reformers attempted to create a broader constituency for their campaigns against municipal corruption and challenged reductive notions of ethnic supremacy. Such an examination reveals the dialectical process through which, by borrowing from the style and practices associated with working-class men, reformers constructed a more aggressive form of political manhood that legitimized reform as an appropriately masculine endeavor.

The good government reformers first emerged on the political scene in 1882 through the City Reform Club, an organization devoted exclusively to municipal reform. Members included Theodore Roosevelt, at the time a young New York assemblyman; lawyer and essayist John Jay Chapman; and Richard W.G. Welling, a lawyer and Harvard classmate of Roosevelt who went on to become a leader in educational reform. In 1892, the City Reform Club was remade into the City Club, a larger and more powerful organization that launched efforts to bring good government municipal reform to New York City. Reformers affiliated with the City Club played a leading role in many of the major political developments in New York City at the turn of the century, including the election of the reform-oriented mayoral administrations of William L. Strong (1895–1897) and Seth Low (1901–1903), the routinization and professionalization of city services including police and sanitation, and the drafting and passage of "tenement house" legislation improving living conditions for working-class residents.[5]

This chapter traces the interventions of good government reformers in the last two decades of the nineteenth century and examines the shifts and political subjectivities of the men who initiated a new mode of reform politics that emphasized cross-class collaboration, even if efforts to reach out to working-class men were not always successful. The first section, "Discovering the Tammany Within," examines good government reformers' reassessment of Tammany Hall as the exclusive agent of political corruption and the development of a critique of corruption promulgated by members of their own class, including Republican Party leaders and New York business interests. The second section, "The Tiger Behind the Mask: Tammany After Tweed," argues that Tammany leaders, faced with reform pressure and electoral success, incorporated elements of middle-class respectability and, in an effort to shore up their own political power, represented themselves as the "true" reformers. Good government reformers developed new political strategies in response. The third section, "Alternatives to Patronage: Tammany Points the Way," argues that good government reformers, recognizing that Tammany achieved political success through forging personal relationships with male constituents and disbursing patronage, developed new strategies for attracting working-class men to reform causes. The fourth section, "Pursuing Manhood Through Urban Politics," shows that reformers saw these efforts to engage with working-class men in the arena of urban politics as an opportunity to remake and redeem their own compromised manhood. The final section, "The Pure, the Practical, and Political Manhood," examines a cleavage among good government reformers over the concept of political "purity," a concept associated with the feminine virtue of "chastity." While one faction, led by Theodore Roosevelt, argued that political compromise represented manly practicality, another group, represented most vociferously by John Jay Chapman, argued that successes in the 1890s had led erstwhile reformers to a cowardly abandonment of their political ideals and to complicity in a political system that retained much of its corruption.

Discovering the Tammany Within

"The world has wondered that New York could not get rid of its famous incubus," wrote prominent good government reformer John Jay Chapman in 1898. He referred, of course, to Tammany Hall, which had survived the spectacular corruption scandals and imprisonment of leader William M. Tweed in the 1870s only to achieve even greater power in city politics in the last decade of the century.[6] Chapman believed that the city's municipal reformers had failed to recognize that Tammany Hall was just one part of a larger and hopelessly entangled web of political and financial corruption that dominated life in the modern city. By making Tammany the sole object of attack, the reformers had only perpetuated this system of corruption and obfuscated its workings. Chapman compared these men to "a child with a toy" who "did not see that the same mechanism which caused Punch to strike caused Judy's face to disappear from the window." He argued that virtually all citizens were implicated in some way in the corruption of the city and that even those who worked to "expel Tammany Hall" would find, upon introspection, that "Tammany is within them."[7]

Chapman was not alone in discovering a "Tammany within." These men and their colleagues initially believed that municipal corruption stemmed from the perverted local workings of the political party system and that the remedy lay in separating city issues from the party apparatus. Yet, over time, they came to believe that the sources of corruption were much more diffuse, and accordingly, that vanquishing "the municipal evil" was much more complex than they had previously believed. This shift in perceptions stemmed from both the changing balance of power within the city itself and from broader developments on a national level, namely the development of a critique of the corrupting influence of large corporations on American society.

Perhaps the most significant factor leading to the good government reformers' reassessment of machine politics was the major realignment of the New York political landscape in 1886. Tammany Hall, which had experienced a steep decline in political influence after the Tweed scandal of the 1870s, reemerged as a powerful force in New York City when Richard Croker took over leadership. The mayoral contest of that year featured a spectacular third-party campaign by single-tax reformer Henry George, whose candidacy had galvanized the city's working classes, bringing an unprecedented level of organization to New York's trade unions and socialist and radical groups within the newly formed United Labor Party (ULP). In a shrewd political maneuver, Croker threw Tammany's support behind wealthy "swallowtail" Democrat Abram Hewitt, a candidate he believed would draw the votes of middle- and upper-class residents terrified at the prospect of labor rule.[8] The Republican Party nominated Theodore Roosevelt, recently graduated from Harvard and a political novice, realizing full well that he had little chance of winning and that many Republicans would throw their vote to Hewitt. Croker's maneuver paid off: Hewitt prevailed over George by a narrow margin. When the ULP fragmented after George's loss, Croker worked hard to win over the "labor vote" and to consolidate Tammany's operations in the city's working-class and immigrant neighborhoods, establishing clubhouses in every assembly district and bringing the entire organization under tighter control.[9]

During this same period, the state's Republican Party underwent a consolidation of its own. Thomas Collier Platt, who had lost his seat in the U.S. Senate, staged a political comeback by centralizing the party apparatus and bringing it firmly under his control. Called the "easy boss" because of his seemingly detached manner, Platt proved as capable as any Tammany politician in manipulating state and city patronage to his own ends.[10] This new level of organization in both the Democratic and Republican parties worked to the benefit of the city's business interests, which could now deal with one "boss" rather than numerous district leaders when seeking to "grease the wheels" of the municipal government. Indeed, Croker and Platt worked together to parcel out lucrative city contracts.[11]

This unprecedented coordination of political and financial power led New York's reformers to reevaluate their critique of Tammany as the city's singularly corrupt political institution. For many, the newly reorganized state Republican Party appeared practically indistinguishable from the

Tammany democracy. Older reformers, who had been fiercely loyal Republicans, felt particularly betrayed by strong-arm tactics practiced under Platt's leadership. George Gunton, president of the Institute of Social Economics, "refused to believe" that his beloved party would engage in spoils politics until he observed the fixing of nominations at a state convention:

> The people have no alternative but to choose between the candidates these dictators [Croker and Platt] present. Each machine trades with the other as to which shall have the nominal power in consideration for a certain amount of patronage afterwards. . . . It is not Democrats, it is not Tammany Hall alone, but it is the political managers of both parties that are thus corrupting the very sources of our political life. They are prostituting the force of free government and making our institutions misrepresent the people.[12]

Gunton's realization that Tammany now *dwelled within* the Republican Party was widely shared among reformers and liberal journalists at the end of the century. Indeed, editorialists and cartoonists who had long singled out Tammany leaders as objects of ridicule began to depict Croker and Platt as two heads of the same beast, which they labeled "bossism."[13]

Reformers also "discovered" that this system of corruption extended beyond the Democratic and Republican parties; it characterized the city's business community as well. Lincoln Steffens, a good government advocate who worked as a reporter for the *New York Evening Post* in the 1890s, had initially accepted "unthinkingly" the image of Tammany Hall as "absurd, illegal, disgraceful" held by his editor, mugwump E. L. Godkin. And he had accepted Godkin's proposed solution to the problem of political corruption: "Elect to office good business men who would give us a business government." But Steffens's experiences on the *Post*'s Wall Street beat eventually led him to draw different conclusions:

> I asked myself suddenly what was the difference between a political boss and a banker boss. None that I could see, except that one was a political, the other a financial, boss. Both political government and business government were run on the same lines, both had unofficial, unresponsible, invisible, actual governments back of the legal, constitutional "fronts."[14]

Steffens, aided by a series of candid off-the-record conversations with Tammany's Richard Croker, transformed this analysis into a full-blown critique of the "commercial spirit," arguing that close ties between business and political interests had disastrous consequences for American civic life and represented "the Shame of the Cities."[15]

In the 1890s, Steffens and other good government reformers found even more reason to challenge accepted truths about political corruption when a series of state investigations of municipal "abuses" in New York City, intended to discredit Tammany, revealed widespread corruption that extended beyond the political machine and even the corporate boardroom. John Brooks Leavitt, for example, responded to the findings of the Lexow Committee, convened to investigate corruption in the Tammany-controlled police force, by publishing an article entitled "The Criminal Degradation of New York Citizenship," in which he argued that "the inquiry has disclosed the terrible fact that the quality of our American citizenship is being destroyed in the race for wealth. The 'plain people,' as Lincoln called them, the bone and sinew of our country, the respectable, common-sense, every-day sort of persons, who are supposed to do a good deal of homely vigorous thinking, and who want to do the right thing without regard to practices or policies . . . have taken to buying police favors." The seemingly vast reach and deep roots of urban corruption caused Brooks to question his former conviction that overthrowing Tammany Hall would result in the establishment of responsible city government.[16] The problem appeared to be much more intractable.

The Tiger Behind the Mask: Tammany After Tweed

As reformers discovered corruption throughout the urban populace, Tammany politicians began a concerted effort to rehabilitate their public image and rid themselves of the taint of the Tweed years. This process began with the rise to power of "Honest John" Kelly, a former New York City sheriff and devout Roman Catholic, who swept Tammany clean of Tweed's "cronies" and brought a new level of centralization and discipline to the organization.[17] Moreover, unlike Tweed, Kelly eschewed overtly illegal means of accumulating wealth in favor of what George Washington Plunkitt famously referred to as "honest graft"—or the production of wealth through trading on political influence and acting on inside information.[18] Richard Croker, who succeeded Kelly as Tammany's leader, refused to apologize for amassing a large fortune through "honest graft." Indeed, when he appeared before the Mazet Commission in 1899, Croker famously acknowledged that he was working for his own pocket "all the time" before pointing his finger at his examiner: "the same as you."[19]

During the 1880s and 1890s, Kelly, Croker, and other Tammany politicians frequently turned the tables on reformers in this way, maintaining that municipal politics was a business like any other, and one in which politicians could make their fortunes. Such claims created problems for municipal reformers, who had long argued that city government should be run like a business organization to promote efficiency. Ironically, Tammany leaders, including Croker and Kelly, had become wealthy precisely by bringing business management to the local political process, primarily by streamlining organizational hierarchy and centralizing patronage distribution. Sounding in many ways like a good government reformer, Croker asserted in an 1892 article published in the *North American Review*: "The affairs of a vast community are to be administered. Skillful men must administer them. . . . The principle is precisely the same as that which governs the workings of a railway, or a bank, or a factory." He added that, like business leaders, municipal officials must be "well paid" for their work.[20]

Tammany assertions of respectability extended beyond the realm of business, however. As soon as Tweed was removed from power, Tammany leaders began to claim the mantle of municipal reform for themselves. Indeed, Kelly and Croker readily conceded that the Tweed administration had been corrupt and took great pains to separate themselves from its legacy. Croker, who referred to municipal reformers as "counterfeit" and to Tammany as "the genuine article" of reform, claimed that he and Kelly had come to power as part of "the anti-Tammany reform party" and had "made the old sink of corruption the headquarters of Reform."[21]

Although Tammany's attempts to remake itself might be dismissed as mere rhetorical posturing, municipal reformers expressed genuine worry that these assertions would be accepted by the voting public. In 1894, John D. Townsend, a Republican judge and the author of *New York in Bondage*, complained that Tammany "used the ghost of poor old Bill

Tweed" in order to "actually pose as reformers and virtuous men."[22] In the same year, good government reformer Richard Welling described Tammany as a "wolf in sheep's clothing" that wore "an air of tolerable respectability" and posed "as the poor man's friend and the friend of honest government." Welling argued that unless reformers and the clergy exposed this "shrewd Tammany programme," the organization would continue to win support and elections.[23]

Tammany men's attempts to repackage themselves as respectable agents of reform represented a predicament for municipal reformers accustomed to taking the moral high ground in their struggles with the machine. This predicament reached a pinnacle in 1901, when Tammany supported the mayoral candidacy of Edward M. Shepard, a well-heeled Brooklyn lawyer and independent Democrat, in opposition to Republican candidate Seth Low, a prominent municipal reform proponent backed by the Citizens' Union, a good government reform organization. This election proved difficult for municipal reformers because they had long considered Shepard one of their own. Indeed, only a few years before he received the Tammany nomination, Shepard had warned "high-minded" Americans of accepting Tammany claims that its method of administration was "both inevitable and beneficent" and had characterized the previous machine mayoral ticket as "the most insolent and audacious as well as the most sheerly reckless assault we have yet known upon the welfare of greater New York and of the masses."[24]

The good government reformers developed several strategies to oppose this candidate whose political philosophy and campaign platform differed little from their own. Foremost, they portrayed his backers as insidiously cunning and duplicitous; through dishonest trickery, they had enticed "an anti-Tammany man [Shepherd] to head and mask a thoroughly Tammany ticket."[25] Indeed, the Citizens' Union worked assiduously to convince voters that Tammany was not what it seemed "despite the mask at its head."[26] They relayed this to the voting public through several illustrated posters. One depicted a tiger—Tammany's mascot—wearing sheep's clothing; another presented an image of Shepard bound to Croker by a chain with the caption, "Unlike the proverbial leopard, this one can change his spots to stripes"; a third featured an enormous tiger hiding behind a small mask of Edward Shepard's face and bore the caption "Nobody'll know it's me!"[27]

The Citizens' Union addressed a number of campaign pamphlets and posters to working-class voters, claiming that while Tammany posed as "the poor man's friend," it was actually "robbing him of his very shirt." This attempt to sway voters centered on the wealthy lifestyle of Richard Croker, who sported expensive clothing and owned a country manor in England where he raised racehorses. While Croker, who was born in Ireland before emigrating to the United States with his poor family, presented himself as an American success who had risen from rags to respectability, the Citizens' Union maintained that he had betrayed his working-class constituents and had stolen their money to cavort in Europe "with the lecherous sons of a rotten aristocracy."[28]

These elite reformers, traditionally distrusted by immigrant and working-class voters due to their wealth and social position, attempted to change the class dynamics of local political elections. Croker was a country "squire" and "absentee landlord" whose wealth came at the expense of poor New Yorkers, while good government reformers were concerned with improving life in tenement neighborhoods through the provision of social programs. As an allied tactic, Citizens' Union propaganda attempted to turn Irish voters against Croker by implying that his associations with the British upper crust represented a betrayal of the fight for Irish independence.[29]

Alternatives to Patronage: Tammany Points the Way

The Citizens' Union's efforts to make Croker's wealth a target of working-class outrage were linked to another major difficulty faced by municipal reformers during the mayoral election of 1901. Tammany had long contended, and reformers had begun to concede, that participation in local machine politics represented the primary route for immigrant men to achieve economic advancement. Richard Croker, for example, boldly defended the spoils system of patronage in his interview with Stead:

> We need to bribe them [immigrant working-class men] with spoils. Call it so if you like. Spoils vary in different countries. Here they take the shape of offices. . . . I admit it is not the best way. But it is for practical purposes the only way. Think what New York is and what

> the people of New York are. One half, more than one half, are of foreign birth. We have thousands upon thousands of men who are alien born, who have no ties connecting them with the city or the State. . . . They are raw material with which we have to build up the state.[30]

Tammany leader George Washington Plunkitt echoed Croker's claims that political patronage, because it led to economic success, encouraged patriotic ideals of citizenship among working-class immigrants. "When parties can't get offices," he concluded, "they'll bust."[31]

Municipal reformers had routinely, and largely unsuccessfully, attempted to persuade immigrant voters that the institution of civil service policies in city employment would create such opportunities in a more equitable and efficient fashion. Yet with Tammany's support of Edward Shepard, who had established his public career as a crusader for civil service reform, this argument held even less power. Indeed, the Democratic nomination of Shepard reflected the machine's growing realization that civil service regulations, which had already been instituted on the state and national levels, would inevitably be adopted at the municipal level. Thus, Tammany's endorsement represented a shrewd attempt to exercise some influence over (or, according to some critics, to undermine) the shaping of a new civil service apparatus in New York City.[32]

Because Tammany had nominated a respectable reformer with an unassailable record on civil service issues, the Citizens' Union eschewed attacking the patronage system. Instead, the union alleged that Tammany patronage extended beyond the disbursement of political offices into the world of vice and crime through an illicit shadow system of prostitution procurement. This operation, termed the "cadet system" by the Committee of Fifteen, an organization formed by the Citizens' Union and led by municipal reformer and economist Edwin Seligman in 1900 for the purpose of investigating prostitution in the city.

The Committee of Fifteen, acting on the belief that women were forced into prostitution through the "white slave trade," publicized revelations that prostitution in New York was much more organized than had previously been thought, and that Tammany Hall and the police department were complicit in it. The committee alleged that men connected to Tammany used boys and young men to coerce girls and women into prostitution and to manage the business for them. Young boys, they argued, would first become employed as "lighthouses" or lookouts before moving on to the position of "cadet . . . a young man averaging from eighteen to twenty-five years of age" who essentially functioned as a pimp.[33]

During the 1901 campaign, the Citizens' Union made prostitution a prominent political issue, not by lamenting the plight of the "fallen woman" but by addressing the ill effects of the cadet system on boys in working-class neighborhoods. A campaign pamphlet addressed to "Citizens of the Lower East Side," for example, asserted that "Tammany has surrendered the tenements to Vice. . . . Under its shameless system, children have become 'lighthouses,' 'cadets' and vendors and advertisers of vice. From such protection Tammany receives an enormous income." Another pamphlet alleged that, due to the machine, "vice in tenement houses uses little children as its decoys and trains them to its infamous trade."[34] Lacking proof that Tammany directly controlled the cadet system, Citizens' Union reformers implied that this system was intricately bound up in the functions of the organization, so boys in tenement neighborhoods who joined risked becoming involved in criminal activity. One piece of campaign literature advised working-class women to encourage their male relatives to vote for the reform ticket so that they "need not fear that the lives of their sons will be ruined by doing the will of the bosses . . . they need not dread the orgies of world-wise politicians, through which their sons must go in order to 'stand in for promotion.'"[35]

The Citizens' Union's efforts bespoke a desperation on the part of municipal reformers who, because of their ideological aversion to patronage, had little to offer working-class men. For their part, Tammany leaders freely acknowledged that patronage was the fuel that kept the organization running. George Washington Plunkitt, for example, asserted "that you can't keep an organization together without patronage. Men ain't in politics for nothin'. They want to get somethin' out of it."[36] Yet Plunkitt also insisted that "there is more than one kind of patronage" and argued that, even if Tammany lost control of city jobs, it could draw on its immense network of influence to help obtain private employment for constituents. He explained that this system of private patronage worked because Tammany men, unlike reformers, had forged personal relationships between their organization and every individual it represented: "I know every man, woman, and child in the Fifteenth District. . . . I know what they like and what they don't like, what they are strong at and what they are weak in, and I reach them by approachin' at the right side."[37] Indeed, machine politicians of both parties named such personal relationships as the chief factor contributing to their success, especially with regard to young men. Croker, for example, asserted that "No small part of my hold on Tammany, and through Tammany on the city, came from the fact that I always made a point of pushing young men to the front." "If you get a reputation for picking out the young fellows," he added, "all the smartest lads will crowd around you. . . . You are giving them the chance they want today."[38]

In the decade that preceded the 1901 mayoral election, good government reformers had already acknowledged the importance of this personal network and had begun to assert that the reform element would need to produce similar networks to have a chance at long-term success.[39] Unlike their mugwump forbearers, they recognized that civil service policies, which required the establishment of impersonal and "objective" standards, by definition worked against the establishment of such bonds between reform organizations and their potential constituents. Indeed, party politicians boasted that they were able to draw reform-minded men away from organizations like the Citizens' Union because so many of them failed stringent civil service examinations. Reformers paid new attention to Tammany's success and explored other options for winning the support—and maintaining the loyalty—of immigrant and working-class men.

Henry Childs Merwyn, a journalist who supported the good government movement, for example, theorized that Tammany gained the allegiance of recent immigrants, to whom they were not tied by ethnicity, through "the power of personal leadership and the power of the totem." By "personal leadership" Merwyn meant the Tammany system of ward leaders and charismatic "bosses" who had close personal contact with their constituents. He defined the "totem" as "some bond . . . which binds men together, which leads them to common cause, which inspires them with a contagious enthusiasm." He offered political parties and baseball

This cartoon depicts the professional party politician as a dangerous seducer and corrupter of young working-class men. Caption reads: "Beware! Professional Politician: 'Take hold, and I'll show you how to use it.'"

Frank Leslie's Illustrated Newspaper, August 14, 1886

teams as examples and asserted that personal leadership and the "totem" represented "the coherent, dynamic forces which only can knit men together, and inspire them with the necessary heat and fury."[40]

Theodore Roosevelt also praised Tammany's ability to join men together in common cause. In his 1886 article "Machine Politics in New York City," he stressed that Tammany's influence in working-class neighborhoods was not limited to elections:

> On the contrary, they [Tammany political associations] exist throughout the year, and for the greater part of the time are to a great extent merely social clubs. . . . These men congregate in the association building in the evening to smoke, drink beer, and play cards . . . The different members of the same club become closely

> allied with one another, and able to act together on occasions with unison and *esprit de corps*; and they will stand by one of their own number. . . . Naturally all the men so brought together gradually blend their social and political ties.

Roosevelt believed that this kind of "*esprit de corps*" was sorely lacking among middle- and upper-class men "whose social instincts interfere, instead of coinciding with their political duties."[41]

While Roosevelt stressed that Tammany's social function was a distinct advantage in the city's political contests, some of his reform colleagues emphasized that it offered economic opportunities for young working-class and immigrant men that were not available elsewhere. Merwyn heralded the chance for upward mobility. "Tammany is very hospitable to rising talent," he argued; "young men find that Tammany is ready to advance them as fast as their capabilities will permit." Merwyn, who considered the machine "the best object lesson in city government this generation has seen," maintained that reform organizations must offer similar benefits in order to attract young working-class and immigrant men.[42] Likewise, City Club founder Edmond Kelly argued that Tammany's philanthropy went "hand in hand with their politics," whereas reform organizations "divorced" their philanthropy from politics, thereby failing to build enduring ties.[43]

Municipal reformers also expressed admiration for the strict and efficient organizational structure of Tammany Hall. If the hallmark of the Progressive Era was a "search for order," as Robert H. Wiebe contends, then New York City reformers had found a model.[44] Following the lead of Richard Croker, who proclaimed that "politics is war" and heralded the obedience of his "foot soldiers," reformers invariably described the Tammany machine as an "army" mobilized to conduct political warfare. In 1893, journalist Oswald Garrison Villard described it as "essentially military in its organization, for it has its commanding officer (at present Richard Croker), his staff, regimental and battalion commanders and captains and lieutenants, only they bear other titles."[45] While some critics agreed with civil service reformer Dorman B. Eaton's view that Tammany's "crushing military discipline" represented a "savage and venal" perversion of American democratic values, younger reformers such as Villard and Roosevelt waxed enthusiastic about that militarism, arguing that reform forces should band together in armies of their own.[46]

Pursuing Manhood Through Urban Politics

These expressions of admiration for Tammany's success in organizing working-class and immigrant men in New York City reveal reformers' deeply held belief that men of their class lacked the kind of vigorous masculinity necessary to compete in the political arena. This belief corresponded with a broader cultural anxiety that native-born elite and middle-class men were losing their claim to manliness due to a variety of factors, including their estrangement from physical labor and the rise of the assertive New Woman. Theodore Roosevelt, for example, argued that "the general tendency among people of culture and high education has been to neglect and even to look down upon the rougher and manlier virtues." He chastised educated men for "a certain effeminacy of character" and asserted that "our more intellectual men often shrink from the raw coarseness and the eager struggle of political life as if they were women." He concluded that this effeminacy effectively rendered "refined and virtuous" men "entirely out of place in the American body-politic."[47]

Roosevelt's critique of cultured men closely resembled the characterizations of mugwumps promulgated by machine politicians. Indeed, Roosevelt himself, like other good government reformers—especially in the early years of the movement—was subject to the same kind of gender and sexual ridicule that had been leveled against the older generation. One facetious 1882 account of the City Reform Club published in the *New York World*, for example, characterized those in attendance as frivolous and effeminate "dudes" slavishly devoted to their leader Roosevelt. Laden with phallic and homoerotic references, the account alleged, for example, that after Roosevelt finished speaking "the other dudes took the tops of their canes out of their mouths . . . and then they lighted cigarettes."[48] Roosevelt was singled out for such derision. When he entered the New York State Assembly in 1882, his colleagues assigned him such nicknames as "Jane-Dandy," and "Punkin-Lily."[49]

Although likely offended by this gendered and sexualized derision, municipal reformers shared the belief that men of their class had become feminized, and to a remarkable extent, this belief influenced the way they constructed their own identities and life stories. Participation in the municipal reform movement offered an opportunity to remake themselves as virile and useful. In this sense, they subscribed to what Jane Addams referred to as the "subjective" motive or "necessity" of reform work. Addams held that involvement in reform facilitated both the healing of the "social organism" through the establishment of reciprocal class relations and the social invigoration of middle-class youths who had "no recognized outlet for their active faculties."[50] For reform men, the latter process was imbued with classed notions of manhood. The rough homosocial arena of urban politics served as a crucible in which they could test and remake their own masculinity and, at the same time, free themselves from the effeminate stigma that had been attached to the mugwumps.

An examination of the experiences of three leading good government reformers offers some insight into the way gender and class anxieties shaped "subjective" motives for reform. Theodore Roosevelt's struggle to remake himself as a "strenuous" man is the most familiar of these stories. A scrawny and asthmatic youth, Roosevelt struggled in his college years (1876–1880) to build his body through boxing and other vigorous sports. Still, he was ridiculed by fellow students at Harvard for his high voice, fancy clothing, and "effeminate" self-presentation, which earned him the nickname "Oscar Wilde."[51] Although he did not desire to become a politician as a young man, he soon discovered in the tumultuous arena of New York Republican politics an opportunity to enter into the "hurly burly" of life. Indeed, one of his objects in forming the City Reform Club in 1882 was to introduce other young men of his class to the "robuster virtues" that would result from contact with rough politicians.[52] Yet the taint of effeminacy would remain with Roosevelt even after he won a seat in the New York State Assembly in 1882. As has been well documented, Roosevelt continued to remake his masculine persona in the American West and in the Spanish-American War.[53]

John Jay Chapman, four years behind Roosevelt at Harvard, also worried about the quality of his manhood as a young man. As a boy he was "an inward creature" unable to "answer a question in class or catch a ball." He suffered from physical ailments and debilitating emotional collapses, which he later described as neurasthenia "fifteen years before it would be diagnosed in American businessmen." So severe were these episodes of physical and mental sickness that Chapman was removed from school to be educated at his home on Washington Square by tutors, including mugwump civil service reformer Horace Deming.[54]

Chapman's struggles with mental illness continued into his adolescence and adulthood. The most devastating episode took place in 1887 when, after becoming infatuated with the young aristocrat Minna Timmins, Chapman attacked Percival Lowell, a man he apparently imagined to be courting her. Upon returning to his flat in Cambridge after the attack, Chapman placed his left hand in a coal stove, burning it so severely that it had to be amputated. The events that contributed to this act of self-mutilation remain unclear, but an examination of correspondence between Chapman and Timmins during his recuperation sheds some light on the incident. Chapman had confessed to Timmins that he had a "shameful"—and unnamed—"defect" that he believed would make it impossible for the two to have children (although he and Timmins later did marry and had three children).[55] When Timmins conveyed this information to Chapman's mother, and perhaps to others as well, Chapman became enraged. He felt that the revelation of his secret amounted to the ruin of his future. "I blame you—for spoiling my life," he wrote to Timmins. "I too had a life to live and I wanted to be proud of it."[56]

Chapman biographer Richard Hovey has speculated that the "defect" was impotence, and this is certainly a possibility.[57] It is also possible that Chapman confessed to Timmins a sexual attraction to men. This is supported by Chapman's allegation that Timmins, upon learning of his secret, "went on and said [he] was like Michelangelo," whose sexual history may well have been familiar to an educated woman.[58] Chapman's certainty that the revelation of his confession would have devastating consequences for his future also contributes to such a hypothesis.[59]

In any case, in the aftermath of these events, Chapman expressed ambivalent feelings about his gender and sexual identity. In one letter to Timmins he wrote, "Don't think of me as hero but as a *lusus naturea* ["trick of nature" in Latin]—neither a man nor a woman. There is an awful pathos about such a being."[60] During this same period, he wrote to his friend Mrs. Benoni Lockwood, "God has used me as a clinical demonstration. Like a woman. My soul was like a woman's in many ways."[61] In the months following the hand-burning incident, Chapman also repeatedly expressed the desire to seek refuge in the company of men. In one letter to

Timmins, he wrote, "the woman thing in me got pretty well mangled. . . . What I need is to be with men . . . but the soul of me loved women and will still while [*sic*] I live." In another letter he lamented, "I ought to have stayed in Cambridge and been with men all the time." Chapman reported emerging from his state of psychic distress when he began to take up the work of the City Reform Club in 1888. Dismissing literature, his previous passion, as a "woman's business," he exclaimed, "The time is for action and political organization. Better cast a vote than write a book."[62]

Richard W.G. Welling, a Harvard classmate of Roosevelt's and a close colleague of Chapman's in the good government club movement, also reported being taunted for his lack of vigor as a youth. Plagued by "monstrous self-consciousness and shyness," Welling turned to reading Roman history and found a compelling model for manhood in the ascetic lives of Roman soldiers. He took to testing his physical endurance through a grueling exercise regimen and by refusing to protect himself against the elements, refusing even to wear a winter coat. In a story with striking parallels to Chapman's experience, Welling recounted being so impressed with Muscius Scaevola, "the Roman . . . who held his hand in the fire to prove his scorn of pain," that he refused to withdraw his hand when his father beat it with a "trunk strap" as punishment for misbehavior.[63]

In his adolescent and college years, Welling found companions who shared his enthusiasm for the ascetic life, including Leonard Opdycke and James Pryor, two men who would become prominent figures in the good government movement. Throughout most of his life, Welling boldly pronounced his preference for the rugged company of men. He maintained that it infused him with a sense of "social spirit," a quality he had lacked in his early childhood. Although typically proud of his commitment to bachelorhood and male camaraderie, Welling admitted to insecurities about this way of life occasioned by two "harangues on the good citizen and his duty to marry" by his friend Theodore Roosevelt.[64] In an unpublished autobiography bearing the intriguing title "The Arrested Development of Johnny Doe," written near the end of his life, Welling recast his decision to "avoid the double harness" of marriage in Freudian terms, arguing that adverse experiences in early childhood kept him from forming romantic relationships with women.[65]

For all these men and for many of their reform colleagues, interaction with Tammany "heelers" and with men from the tenement neighborhoods represented an opportunity to pursue an ideal of social brotherhood. John Jay Chapman wrote in his book *Practical Agitation*, published in 1900: "Our intercourse with the laboring man is a great teacher to ourselves. It brings out, as nothing else can, the magnitude and perfection of the system, whose visible top and little flag we can see, but whose dimensions and ramifications nothing but experiment can reveal; philosophy could not guess it."[66] In this passage and in numerous other writings Chapman insisted that an individual wishing to effect social change must immerse himself in the political life of the community and work "with people unlike himself for a common object." Such activity provided the only means to "social enjoyment" because "the strands of prejudice and passion that bind people together pulsate with life." The chief mode of such activity, he argued, was "the great machinery of government," which "was designed to be at the service of anybody."[67]

Chapman and other reformers endeavored to create what Theodore Roosevelt called a "machine . . . for the good" by emulating Tammany methods.[68] They believed that "fellow feeling" could replace patronage as the glue that would bind men together. To this end, they attempted to emulate Tammany's military style while imbuing this form of organization with a noble sense of purpose. It resonated with male reformers for a variety of overlapping reasons: it appealed to the popular ideal of "muscular Christianity," which promoted the notion that Christian men should serve as active forces for good in a corrupt world; it promised adventure to young men who felt constrained by middle-class ideals of respectability; and it imbued reform work with a distinctly masculine quality—a crucial stamp of legitimacy for a generation so often characterized as foppish and effeminate. Most important, however, was the promise that a militarist organization could replace venal self-interest with a sense of camaraderie and common purpose.[69]

Indeed, reformers found in the struggle against municipal corruption a grand and worthy cause—something William James would later characterize as "the moral equivalent of war."[70] Writing more than a decade before James, the Reverend Josiah Strong, invoking the legacy of the Civil War, called for a "new patriotism" in the fight to redeem "our boss-ridden cities":

> This new peril demands a new patriotism—not new in spirit, but in manifestation; one which is civil rather than military; one which

> devotes itself to the principle actually endangered; not a patriotism which constructs fortifications and builds navies, but one which purifies politics and substitutes statesmen for demagogues; not one which "rallies round the flag," so much as rallies round the ballot-box; not one which charges into the deadly breach, but one which smashes the machine.[71]

Roosevelt, in particular, embraced and promoted the idea that political struggle in the nation's cities offered an opportunity for the redemption of middle-class men who were in danger of losing the "virile fighting qualities" essential to a nation's well-being.[72]

The Pure, the Practical, and Political Manhood

Ultimately, however, the fight against municipal corruption did not produce the "new patriotism" that Strong envisioned. Good government reformers largely failed to attract working-class men to their cause, mostly because they could not offer any material alternatives to patronage. The movement foundered due to internal dissension about the extent to which it should cooperate with political parties. This conflict played out in terms of "pure" versus "practical" politics. The gendered and sexualized rhetoric that infused the debate became increasingly divisive and acrimonious over time.

The conflicting meanings of "pure" and "practical" took center stage at the very beginning of the good government movement. Within weeks after founding the movement's first organization, the City Reform Club, Theodore Roosevelt resigned to enter party politics as a member of the New York State Assembly in October 1882, embarking on a path that would eventually take him to the White House. In his resignation letter, Roosevelt endorsed the view that an association like the City Reform Club must remain independent of party politics: it was "of vital importance that the club should not contain among its members any who are either at present office-holders or who may become so in future."[73]

Roosevelt's decision to "be one of the governing class," as he put it, institutionalized a policy of pure political independence within the club.[74] Directly after accepting his resignation, the club resolved "that no office holder or candidate for office be eligible for membership, and that the club hereby pledges itself not to support any of its members for office until a year after his public resignation from the club." This resolution, informally referred to as the "chastity clause," inspired a series of similar measures, including the denial of membership to "any man who can be called a 'political worker'" and the provision that the club would not nominate its own candidates.[75]

That Roosevelt initiated the "chastity clause" and its related provisions is in many ways ironic. Already aligned with the Republican Party in the early 1880s, he began to craft a masculine public image around his ability to succeed within the "rough and tumble" of party politics, leaving the remaining members of the City Reform Club to determine how they might be both "practical" and "pure" at the same time, given that they lacked a significant base of political power to put into action the kinds of changes they advocated. By using the term "chastity," with its gendered and sexual connotations, club members acknowledged their weak position. Within the ideology of separate spheres, chastity was a quality valued mainly in women, deemed responsible for protecting the home from sexual corruption, and hardly represented an admirable public virtue for men. The *Tammany Times*, the weekly of the Tammany Democrats, attested to this in an article entitled "The Professional Reformer" that accused reformers of threatening accepted notions of male and female virtue through misplaced ideals: "All men should be pure; but they are not; in fact the pure man is the exception and not the rule."[76] This conflation of political and sexual purity helps to explain the prevalent use of sexological terms—like "third sex"—to deride reformers. Those who ranted against "corruption" in the manly and public world of politics by adopting the private and feminine value of "chastity"—or political independence—subverted widely shared ideals of private and public, of masculine and feminine.[77]

A gendered understanding of purity and corruption also undergirded the City Reform Club's approach to class difference. Mugwump forbearers in the municipal reform movement had believed that the "best men" in American cities came from the upper classes and that it was their duty to educate the illiterate and immoral masses in the virtues and practices of self-government. This view was held by the more conservative members of the club who, at a sparsely attended meeting, pushed through a resolution that membership would "be restricted to that class in the community from which its members have hitherto been chosen."[78] Although Welling and others succeeded in overturning this resolution at the next meeting, they made no subsequent effort to attract working-class—or even middle-class—men to the cause until the inception of the good government clubs more than a decade later.

Even though the City Reform Club remained exclusive, its leaders—including Welling and Chapman—advocated more direct contact with working-class men, especially after they gained greater control of the organization in 1886. The form this contact took, however, was largely adversarial. The most significant endeavor of the club in the late 1880s consisted of an effort to enforce an excise law that required saloons within a quarter mile of the polls to be closed on election day. Upon learning that New York City police failed to enforce the law, the club sent letters to saloon owners and the police department demanding that the bars be closed. When this failed, Welling, Pryor, Opdycke, and several other club members visited saloons, dressed in working-class garb, in an undercover operation. They reported their experiences to the press, which enthusiastically published the exploits in sensational terms, presenting the reformers, according to Welling, as "a dangerous body of law enforcers."[79]

Excited by their clandestine activities and thrilled by the positive attention from the press, club members broadened their scope to include the undercover observation of pool halls, allegedly a site for the transaction of political graft. During this period, club members also served as poll watchers in working-class districts. In this capacity, they frequently engaged in direct confrontation with men they felt to be voting illegally. Chapman proved especially fond of such combat, "with his one arm arresting and taking to the police station a lawbreaker."[80] He was effusive about the newfound sense of power achieved through this activity:

> There is nothing one may not do. I almost throw some men out of the window—I get so violent, and I suddenly turn as heavy and icy as cold lemon-pie. Some men are to be taken by the throat, some jollied, some taken aside into an alcove—and, by Jove, all men are nothing but dough so far as I can see.[81]

By taking their reform activities out of the genteel clubhouse and to sites of working-class manliness—saloon, pool hall, and polling place—Chapman and his colleagues found a means by which to experience "corruption" firsthand and at the same time attest to the purity of their motives. Moreover, they could redeem their public personae and rid themselves of the taint of effeminacy. The public relations benefits of such operations were not lost on other reformers eager to present themselves as simultaneously manly and virtuous. In the 1890s, vice reformer Reverend Charles Parkhurst and Theodore Roosevelt, as New York City police commissioner, would adopt these undercover and confrontational tactics.

In spite of the publicity windfall resulting from these measures, the City Reform Club failed to effect any significant changes. The club's lack of power and influence—along with the general unpopularity of the cause—doomed the effort to enforce the excise law. After successfully transcending the image of the genteel and feminine reformer, the City Reform Club men grew increasingly frustrated by their inability to escape the limitations of their "chaste" political position.[82]

This coterie of reformers could, in fact, count few substantive accomplishments until 1892, when Welling, Chapman, and several other City Reform Club members joined Edmond Kelly, an international lawyer recently returned to New York from Paris, in forming the City Club. This organization effectively supplanted the City Reform Club, although the two coexisted for several years. The original plan was ambitious; it called for a central social club composed of upper- and middle-class men interested in the cause of municipal reform as well as a network of neighborhood civic clubs throughout the city that would function as branches. Membership in the districts would be open to men of all classes. The club would draw a diverse citizenry together as an organized political force promoting good government: Tammany-like, but without a fixed connection to political party.[83] To signify that this was to be a new kind of organization and to free it from the negative and effete image of the reformer, the group agreed, upon Welling's initiative, to delete the term "reform" from the club's name.

This grand plan for the City Club originated with Kelly, an intellectual who eventually published several books on the relationship between evolutionary theory and government. Toward the end of his life he joined the Socialist Party, although at the time he conceived of the City Club his politics were generally in line with those of Chapman and Welling. Yet the plan, which called for nothing more than creating a larger and more aggressive organization to secure traditional municipal reform objectives, met with intense resistance. In order to secure support and financial backing, the small group of City Club founders opened their ranks to leading independents, including older members of the mugwump movement. These men feared that an activist organization would be co-opted by corrupt party politicians, and they vehemently objected to the idea of district branches encompassing the working classes. Because this more conservative group comprised the majority of the expanded organizing committee, the resulting club was stripped of virtually every innovative feature. In the end, it became a social and civic association with the vague purpose of "tak[ing] action as may lead to the honest, efficient, and independent government in the City of New York."[84]

While City Club members opted not to institute a "chastity clause," the organization's overwhelming emphasis on nonpartisanship and the shared hostility to party politics on the state and local levels ensured that its membership would not include individuals actively engaged in political work. The executive committee also proved unwilling to commit to the development of district civic associations. In response, Kelly and Welling decided to organize local "good government clubs," one for every district in the city, and they persuaded City Club members to grant them affiliate status. The good government scheme achieved striking success among New York City's middle classes: by 1895, 24 clubs and over 6,000 members. It was aided by a series of scandals unleashed by the Society for the Prevention of Crime led by the Reverend Charles Parkhurst. In 1892, the fiery orator had charged Tammany politicians with "official and administrative criminality that is filthifying our entire municipal life, making New York a very hotbed of knavery, debauchery, and bestiality." When challenged to provide evidence for his accusations, Parkhurst obtained the research on vice and police corruption compiled by Welling, Chapman, and other City Reform Club members. He also adopted their tactics, conducting his own spectacular undercover excursions in the city's "underworld" and securing banner headlines. Parkhurst's campaign caused the State Senate to appoint the Lexow Committee to investigate police corruption. The committee made public its lurid allegations of vice and official misconduct, inspiring much alarm (and titillation) among New York's "respectable" population.

After capitalizing on middle-class furor over these scandals, good government club leaders immediately directed their energies toward the

1894 mayoral campaign of William R. Strong, a wealthy banker running on a fusion ticket backed by Republicans, anti-Tammany Democrats, and reform groups. Strong's candidacy benefited from the groundswell of anti-Tammany sentiment touched off by the Parkhurst and Lexow Committee allegations, as well as from an unprecedented unity of support among reform factions. This unity resulted, in large part, from Strong's status as a political novice—he had yet to be tested in the crucible of partisan politics. However, it quickly collapsed after Strong took office.

The reformers who had worked so hard to elect Strong became the new mayor's earliest and most vocal critics. Members of the various clubs chastised him for making appointments they deemed politically motivated and expressed outrage when he signed a bipartisan police bill that had been opposed by municipal reform groups. These conflicts deepened in 1895 when good government club leaders refused to endorse a fusion slate of judicial candidates on the grounds that it represented "a deal ticket, in which the Republican Party gets the big spoils." When the Council of Confederated Good Government Clubs nominated their own candidates, independent reformers and Republican leaders alike became enraged. Charles Dana, publisher of the *New York Sun*, dismissed their lofty calls for a "pure ticket" as "the infantile blubber of the goo-goos," thereby introducing a nickname that would be widely adopted.

In manifestos and editorial letters, the "Goo Goos" depicted their cause as a heroic one in which the very principles of American democracy were at stake:

> Some of us believe that the greatest need of the hour is not the possible partial defeat of Tammany Hall in a minor election, but rather the removal of the cancer of corrupt municipal administration, contracted through the control of municipal affairs by National partisanship, of which cancer Tammany Hall is but a single symptom. Why should we support an inferior ticket, nominated on a platform embodying every vicious principle of city government and already doomed to defeat? We believe it is wiser, more expedient, better morals to support a "model" ticket, on which "every man on the list is a public-spirited citizen and entirely qualified for office. . . . Down with Tammany and down with Platt, death for machine politicians in the City of New York."[85]

The Goo Goos embedded their calls to idealism in a rhetoric of manly heroism, comparing themselves to the patriots of the American Revolution. Chapman went so far as to liken the cause to that of the early Christian martyrs.

Of all the voices decrying this position of purity, former ally Theodore Roosevelt's sounded loudest. His most severe denunciation of Goo Goo methods came in the form of a published letter to Preble Tucker, president of Good Government Club C, who had accused Roosevelt of "defending expediency against plain duty." Roosevelt objected in particular to Tucker's claim that the good government clubs had carried on the legacy of the "founding fathers":

> Do you know how our Constitution was formed? Have you ever read the Federalist? If so, you know that the Constitution could not have been formed at all if questions of expediency had not been given full weight no less than questions of principle. You also know that Alexander Hamilton, the chief champion in securing the adoption of the Constitution, was entirely opposed to most of the provisions incorporated in it. Had he obeyed your principle, and because he could not get everything, refused to support the best of the only two practicable courses, he would have been a mere curse to the country.[86]

Roosevelt employed other historical arguments in denouncing the "purity" of his former comrades, offering the failed 1864 attempt of "the queer abolitionist group" to run a presidential candidate against Lincoln as an example.

This conflict over Mayor Strong's policies marked a major schism in New York City's municipal reform movement. Roosevelt and his allies maintained that the Goo Goos had not learned the lesson of the mugwumps—that their commitment to purity rendered them ridiculously impotent. For Chapman and his supporters, the compromises made by the Strong administration represented a capitulation on the idealistic principles of the movement—stunning evidence that the spoils system continued to work its corrosive effects on American politics. Indeed, many of those in the Chapman camp became so disillusioned that they abandoned the cause altogether.

Embedded in this vituperative debate among the municipal reformers were the now familiar tropes of political manhood. Roosevelt, in particular, began to wield the gendered rhetoric that had once been used against him. Emerging from the Spanish-American War with immense political power, he used it not merely to demean particular political enemies but rather to argue that the unrestrained moral idealism that had characterized nineteenth-century reform had no place in—and even endangered—the practical, competitive, and masculine culture of modern America.

Conclusion

At the dawn of the twentieth century, New York's good government reformers could count a number of important accomplishments. They had twice challenged Tammany's control of New York City politics by electing the reform-fusion mayoral administrations of William L. Strong (1895–1897) and Seth Low (1901–1903). To a significant extent, these administrations succeeded in dismantling the workings of party patronage in municipal employment. The reformers also established two important political organizations, the Citizens' Union and the City Club, which would continue to play a leading role for decades to come. Moreover, from the ranks of the good government movement emerged the country's leading Progressive figure, Theodore Roosevelt, who as New York State Governor and U.S. President instituted many of the reforms espoused by the movement.

However, the good government reformers also counted a number of notable failures. First, the movement failed to separate city government from the workings of state and national party politics; more important, it failed to uproot Tammany from power. Indeed, when the machine successfully defeated Low's bid for a second term in 1903 and elected George McClellan as mayor, it emerged stronger than ever, launching a three-decade period of domination of New York City politics described by historian David C. Hammack as Tammany's "one great age."[87] Yet Tammany achieved such hegemony in part by remaking itself as a reform-minded organization supporting many of the social policies and causes espoused by Progressives. This transformation, directed and personified by Charles Francis Murphy—Croker's successor as Boss of Tammany Hall—was at least to some extent a response to the challenges of the reformers.[88]

The failure that loomed largest for many good government leaders was their inability to attract working-class men to the cause. Indeed, this led many to embark on new reform projects, discussed at length in subsequent chapters. Edmond Kelly, founder of the City Club and good government clubs, worked to recruit "carpenters, masons, plumbers, electricians," but "not one could be induced to join the movement." Kelly found that most working-class men believed the clubs would undermine their party loyalty and distrusted the motives and goals of municipal reformers. After considerable effort, he resigned from both the good government clubs and the City Club, convinced that any attempt to build cross-class coalitions within the municipal reform movement were doomed to fail. He was disgusted, moreover, with the conservatism and obstinate devotion to "pure" politics of the other reformers. In 1895, Kelly and Ernest H. Crosby, another ex-City Club member and the author of books on Tolstoy and Edward Carpenter, established the Social Reform Club, devoted exclusively to labor reform. Richard W.G. Welling, on the other hand, interpreted the movement's failure to cross class boundaries in a more conservative manner, maintaining that working-class immigrants failed to oppose corruption because they lacked the appropriate education in American ideals of self-government. As a result of this belief, Welling emerged as a leader in the civic education and student government movement in the decades to come.

The good government movement also produced an ambivalent legacy with regard to ideals of political manhood. On the one hand, the leaders' embrace of the notion of "civic militarism" effectively challenged the legacy of the effete and ineffective reformer inherited from the mugwump generation. Theodore Roosevelt was only the most famous individual to have effectively recast the gendered meaning of reform through this ideal. Yet this new militarized political manhood also worked to marginalize male reformers who failed to espouse or fully embrace it. They sought alternative versions of political manhood and democratic solidarity.

3

White Army in the White City

Civic Militarism, Urban Space, and the Urban Populace

At the end of Edward Bellamy's 1887 utopian novel *Looking Backward*, Julian West emerges distraught and depressed from his dream of a perfectly organized Boston in the year 2000. Returning to 1887, he wanders the streets of the city and sees only disorganized squalor and commercialism—until he encounters a military parade:

> A regiment was passing. . . . Here at last were order and reason, an exhibition of what intelligent cooperation can accomplish. The people who stood looking on. . . . Could they fail to see that it was their perfect concert of action, their organization under one control, which made these men the tremendous engine they were, able to vanquish a mob ten times as numerous?[1]

A little more than a decade later, the influential reformer and journalist Jacob A. Riis, wandering the streets of New York City with a European companion, also saw signs of hope in a passing military parade. With great admiration, he described a scene of "white duck trousers glimmering in the twilight, as the hundred legs moved as one." Riis's companion, upon observing that a gang of immigrant boys quickly fell in with the march, queried whether Americans feared such expressions of the military spirit. Riis replied that they did not: "Let them march; and if with a gun, better still. Often enough it is the choice of the gun on the shoulder, or, by and by, the stripes on the back in the lockstep gang."[2]

The power invested in military parades in these accounts points to a central, if underexamined, current in urban reform in the early Progressive Era. During a period of escalating social conflict, when the fear (or promise) of class war occupied a prominent place in public discourse, militarism—as rhetoric, ideology, and mode of social organization—operated in powerful ways in negotiations over categories of class, gender, race, and nation in American society. For many male reformers and social thinkers, in particular, militarism provided a framework for interpreting the meanings of social conflict and for imagining a transformed urban society and environment. Moreover, reformers found in militarist modes of organization an alternative to a political system they believed had been perverted by excessive partisanship and the corrupt workings of patronage. Militarism also seemed to work against the prospect of a culture in which allegiance to class—through labor unions and workers' parties—threatened to supersede the interests of society as a whole.

Numerous scholars have noted the flourishing of militarist imagery and ideology at the turn of the twentieth century and have offered diverse explanations for it. Several studies have stressed the power of a military ideal to redeem and reinvigorate native-born men who, it was feared, had become overcivilized and feminized. T. J. Jackson Lears, for example, argues that "the martial ideal" offered elite American men "the chance to escape the demands of bourgeois domesticity and reintegrate a fragmented sense of self by embracing a satisfying social role."[3] Other accounts have emphasized the simultaneous emergence of a militarist ethos and the American quest for an overseas commercial empire. Historian Kristin Hoganson argues that an ideal of "militant manhood" brought diverse groups of American men together to support the Spanish-American and Philippine-American wars, reinforced a sense of the United States as a superior and "manly" power in world affairs, and stifled opposition to U.S. imperial endeavors by casting anti-imperialists as weak and effeminate.[4]

Although they are compelling, the many excellent studies of militarism and constructions of masculinity at the turn of the century have tended to deemphasize or ignore several important factors. First, most accounts fail to recognize that the turn to militarism among elite men emerged in a dialectical relationship with military forms of organization among working-class and immigrant men. Not only did working-class men understand and explain their participation in electoral politics in military terms, as discussed in chapter 2, but displaced workers also organized in military fashion to make demands on federal and state governments during the depression of the 1890s. The famous 1894 march of Coxey's Army, comprising hundreds of unemployed workers demanding greater economic democracy, is one of numerous examples of poor and working-class men organizing as self-proclaimed "industrial armies" during this period. Middle-class reformers and journalists described groups of immigrant and poor men who banded together and traveled the country looking for work using military terminology. Reform writer Washington Gladden, for example, declared that an "army of invasion . . . is assaulting in overwhelming force the citadel of every one of our municipalities."[5]

This tendency of American elites to view poor, immigrant, and working-class men in military terms is linked to a second development that has failed to receive adequate attention in scholarship on militarism and masculinity. American reformers began to devise militarist solutions to domestic problems in order to defuse the threat of class warfare and promote social unity. Indeed, prominent reform partisans advocated a new ethos—which I call "civic militarism"—in order to bring the discipline and collective values associated with waging war to the domestic arena. The ideology of civic militarism encompassed not only the fight against corrupt machine politics and partisanship but also the struggle against poverty and other social injustices.

Edward Bellamy's notion of the "industrial army," first espoused in *Looking Backward*, represents an early expression of the values of civic militarism. Bellamy's "industrial army," which required that each citizen contribute his "industrial or intellectual services" to the welfare of the nation, perfectly melded the labor and civic responsibilities of every individual.[6] The concept held enormous appeal for many Americans at the end of the nineteenth century, even for those who did not embrace Bellamy's entire socialist vision. Such an organization offered an antidote to the unbridled "self-interest" that many believed had produced corporate monopolies, wide-scale political corruption, and consequently, horrendous working and living conditions in industrial cities. The ideal of a frictionless, rational, and equitable social structure represented by the industrial army also provided, for many, a possible solution to the alarming incidents of violent confrontation between capital and labor that threatened to tear the nation apart.[7]

The philosopher William James echoed Bellamy's advocacy of collective militarism in his influential 1910 essay, "The Moral Equivalent of War." A committed pacifist, James nevertheless believed that "the higher aspects of militaristic sentiment" were essential to the success of American democracy:

> We must make new energies and hardihoods continue the manliness to which the military mind so faithfully clings. Martial virtues must be the enduring cement; intrepidity, contempt of softness, surrender of private interest, obedience to command, must still remain the rock upon which states are built—unless, indeed, we wish for dangerous reactions against commonwealths fit only for contempt, and liable to invite attack whenever a centre of crystallization for military-minded enterprise gets formed anywhere in their neighborhood.[8]

James and other proponents argued for civic militarism based on a belief that middle- and upper-class Americans had lost—or were in danger of losing—the kind of "manly hardihood" that made for national greatness. He expressed concern that a growing awareness of the futility and "bestial" aspects of warfare would lead Americans to abandon the more noble qualities associated with militarism, such as patriotism, honor, and sacrifice for the common good.[9] This idea that militarism might restore a lost sense of American "manliness," was shared by many turn-of-the-century men of privilege, who experienced a sense of enervation and feminization due not only to the dislocations of "modernity" but also to a growing fear that the immigrant working classes owned a more primal and fecund masculinity.[10]

Although scholars have identified the ideal of civic militarism as espoused by social thinkers like Bellamy and James as an important precursor to the large-scale public works projects of the New Deal, scant attention has been paid to the workings of this ethos in social reform projects of the Progressive Era. Yet principles of civic militarism worked in important ways during this period, especially with regard to urban reform. First, reformers wielded militarist ideals and rhetoric to argue for an ordered and rationalized reconfiguration of urban space and to reorient the allegiance and labor of working-class men and youths away from loyalty to party or class and toward the service of the city and nation. In particular, they sought to provide alternatives to the militarist parading, ceremony, and spectacle that had bound men together during the "party period."[11]

Second, civic militarist principles promised to link men of various classes together in new forms of social and political organization, replacing patronage with a more efficient and allegedly more equitable structure. Universalist on its face, this process rested on a racialized logic, however; advocates saw civic militarism as a means of producing a white male polity in which obedience to civic military order granted Southern and Eastern European men access to a provisional and inferior form of racial whiteness.

Third, an ethos of civic militarism allowed male urban reformers to cast their projects as both legitimate and appropriately masculine and to create for themselves a new subjectivity as "reform warriors." In so doing, they defied the effete and overcivilized stereotype by investing urban reform with a sense of "manly" vigor, honor, and adventure.

This chapter examines two examples of successful militarist reforms in New York City carried out between 1895 and 1897, under the administration of Mayor William Strong, elected through the efforts of good government reformers. The first involved collaboration between Jacob Riis and Theodore Roosevelt, who was at that time police commissioner in the Strong administration, to demolish a Lower East Side immigrant neighborhood, "the Mulberry Bend," and build a park in its stead. Riis and Roosevelt structured this endeavor as a military battle against both the dangerous environmental conditions and the unruly and potentially hostile male inhabitants of overcrowded and unhealthy tenement districts. The two reformers envisioned their project as a military drama in two acts, in which the men of Mulberry Bend first played the role of a hostile enemy, then were defeated and remade as a corps of disciplined and obedient allies.

The second project involved the refashioning of the city's street cleaning department into a militarized force—popularly referred to as the "white army"—under the leadership of Colonel George E. Waring. Waring brought Edward Bellamy's concept of the industrial army to the field of civic employment. His goal was to replace what reformers believed to be the inefficient and corrupt workings of the party spoils system with a smoothly functioning "nonpartisan" military hierarchy that would, theoretically, hire and promote employees based on merit rather than on political affiliation and connections. During Waring's tenure, clean streets and the associated spectacle of the white-uniformed street cleaning army functioned as a symbol of urban order that brought dangerous urban spaces and potentially unruly male immigrant men under control. Considered together, these reform efforts provide insight into the ideological underpinnings and gendered meanings of an ethos of militarism in the turn-of-the-century city.

Manhood in Mulberry Bend: Urban Reform as Warfare

"The Mulberry Bend Goes at Last!" wrote Jacob Riis in his scrapbook on May 25, 1895.[12] The famous reformer had spent much of his career writing and lecturing about this irregularly shaped block on New York's Lower East Side, which housed a growing community of Italian immigrants. Riis, who described himself as "the Mulberry Bend crank," considered "the Bend" a symbol of urban squalor and depravity: "a crooked three-acre lot built over with rotten structures that harbored the very dregs of humanity."[13] During the early 1890s, he had invested much energy in lobbying the city government to have the block demolished and a park built in its place. Although Mulberry Bend had been slated for demolition in 1887, it was not until the reform administration of Mayor William Strong came to power that Riis found a sympathetic ear at City Hall. Even then, Riis had to call on his good friend, Police Commissioner Theodore Roosevelt, before action was taken.[14]

When Mulberry Bend Park opened to the public in June 1897, the *New York Times* reported on the "colorful," multiethnic crowd that gathered for the festivities in a scene that "formed a striking antithesis to the picture of the old Mulberry Bend, reeking in filth, where men too often met for dark deeds instead of mirth. The wide space and the grass and the open air had banished crime, and let in sunlight and open, cheerful life."[15] The image of the "old Mulberry Bend" invoked here, a dark and reeking masculine menace, is one Riis had helped to popularize in his stories and illustrated lectures. Indeed, in advocating for reform, he had warned his primarily middle-class audience that immigrant men lurking in Mulberry Bend and other neighborhoods like it were threatening the very fabric of American society. To head off this danger, Riis argued, Americans needed to reconfigure the urban environment in ways that would produce better citizens. For him, urban parks represented the antithesis of dark and crooked urban alleyways; they provided an open, regulated space that would foster more "appropriate" masculine behavior.[16]

In both his writing and his photographs, conceptions of manhood were central to Riis's Mulberry Bend campaign. Although Riis never set out an explicit ideology of gender, he frequently invoked dominant ideas about appropriate male roles in his characterization of the immigrant poor. Implicit in his representation of manhood on Mulberry Bend was the notion that working-class immigrant men transgressed middle-class gender values and therefore represented a threat to American society. Until they conformed to more acceptable male and female models, immigrants would never become productive and virtuous members of that society.

The "battle" against urban evil became embedded in a militarist discourse on social order and reform that combined constructions of masculinity and social Darwinist theories of racial superiority. Middle-class reformers began to attribute what they believed to be the threatening power of the immigrant working class to racially conceived ideas of gender: Southern and Eastern European immigrants were more primal, fecund, and virile—and therefore potentially more powerful—in their masculinity. To combat and reform this masculine threat, middle-class men needed to recapture their own "primitive" masculinity while maintaining their superior reason and control. Reformers framed this contest as "war" and "battle," but the rules were not absolute: the masculine enemy could be reformed through a process of evolution, discipline, and Americanization. As we shall see, Jacob Riis and Theodore Roosevelt—the primary players in the campaign to transform Mulberry Bend—helped to define this process. They conceived of a war on poverty that was also a war on poor immigrant men; it would result in the immigrants' successful assimilation and bolster the reformers' confidence in their own manhood.

Jacob Riis, along with other reform writers at the turn of the century, described and disseminated to a large audience a portrait of insidious urban menace. In addition to his career as a reformer and photographer, Riis was a successful newspaper reporter for the *New York Sun* with a police department beat. He often reported on crime on the Lower East Side in a sensational, if sometimes sentimental, style. In this capacity, he churned out articles on murders, rapes, robberies, and gang conflict, typically making note of ethnic characteristics that he linked to specific crimes. Indeed, according to writer Lincoln Steffens, Riis even "created" crime waves by enhancing urban crime reportage at the request of a greedy editor.[17]

Riis continued to warn audiences about the dangers represented by urban immigrants in his reform-oriented writings. In his famous 1890 book, *How the Other Half Lives*, he appealed not only to his audience's Christian conscience but also to their fear of class violence, asserting that "[tenements] with their restless, pent-up multitudes . . . hold within their clutch the wealth and business of New York, hold them at their mercy in the day of mob-rule and wrath. The bullet-proof shutters, the stacks of hand-grenades, and the Gatling guns of the Sub-Treasury are tacit admissions of the fact and of the quality of the mercy expected."[18] Riis made this threat seem more direct and authentic through photographs of the streets and tenements of the Lower East Side, which were reproduced as halftones and as illustrations in his book. He took the photographs for a period of about three years, from 1887 to 1890, but he continued to include them in slide lectures, books, and articles well into the first decade of the twentieth century.[19] Over time, Riis would rearrange and recontextualize the same stock of images to suit the needs of his changing agendas.[20]

Riis had singled out Mulberry Bend early in his reform career. "The Bend," as he called it, became the subject of many of his photographs and the central focus of *How the Other Half Lives.* Riis presented the block as the symbol of urban degradation and menace for his era, just as the nearby Five Points neighborhood had been a similar symbol for a previous generation of reformers.[21] Mulberry Bend received more attention than any other immigrant neighborhood in his famous book, and Riis often described it as representing in microcosm the problems and dangers of New York's immigrant "slums." In a chapter entitled "The Bend," he wrote:

> Where Mulberry Street crooks like an elbow within hail of the old depravity of the Five Points, is "the Bend," foul core of New York's slums. . . . Around "the Bend" cluster the bulk of the tenements that are stamped as altogether bad, even by the optimists of the Health Department. Incessant raids cannot keep down the crowds that make them their home. In the scores of back alleys, of stable lanes and hidden byways . . . they share such shelter as the ramshackle structures afford with every kind of abomination rifled from the dumps and ash barrels of the city. Here, too, shunning the light, skulks the unclean beast of dishonest idleness. "The Bend" is the home of the tramp as well as the rag-picker.[22]

Riis also referred in this chapter to rampant crime in the neighborhood: "Abuse is the normal condition of 'the Bend,' murder its everyday crop."[23] Alongside these descriptions of crime and idleness, he presented images that illustrated his points in graphic terms.

In the years before 1897, Riis continued to draw attention to the area as an apotheosis of squalid immigrant life and to publicly advocate its demolition and reconstitution as a park. In 1891, for example, he led three British noblewomen on a tour of Mulberry Bend to show them the worst example of "poverty and vice" in America.[24] In an 1895 lantern slide lecture, he called Mulberry Bend "a block that is reputed . . . to be the worse spot in the country," an estimation with which he concurred.[25] After the tenements were torn down in 1896, Riis wrote several articles and newspaper stories, including "The Clearing of Mulberry Bend," "Letting in the

Light," and "Goodbye to the Bend," that celebrated "the going of the wickedest of American slums" as a high point in New York City reform and as a major victory in his career.[26] He echoed this theme in his autobiography, where, in a chapter entitled, "The Bend Is Laid by the Heels," he stressed the importance of the campaign and claimed that "until the Bend was gone, it seemed as if progress were flat down impossible."[27]

When Riis depicted Italian immigrant men on Mulberry Bend during the 1890s, he called upon two primary tropes of manhood: the violent and passionate criminal and the idle tramp.[28] Both were images of men who transgressed dominant middle-class ideals. Passionate criminals, although virile, were incapable of controlling their masculinity and given to sudden, antisocial violence. Tramps were lazy and inept providers, transgressing male values of hard work and industry. Riis described them in *How the Other Half Lives*:

> Tramps and toughs profess the same doctrine, that the world owes them a living, but from stand-points that tend in different directions. The tough does not become a tramp, save in rare instances, when old and broken down. Even then usually he is otherwise disposed of. The devil has various ways of taking care of his own. Nor is the tramps' army recruited from any certain class. All occupations and most grades of society yield to it their contingent of idleness. . . . Of the tough the tramp doctrine that the world owes him a living makes a thief; of the tramp a coward. Numbers only make him bold unless he has to do with defenseless women.[29]

To illuminate Riis's characterizations, I analyze two images that he presented over and over again in published works and slide lectures dealing with Mulberry Bend: "Bandit's Roost" and "The Tramp (in a Mulberry Street yard)."[30] Although the two "types" bear some relationship to actual men who lived in Mulberry Bend, Riis embedded them in narratives that speak more to the preconceptions of a primarily middle-class and native-born audience than to the experience of working-class men.

"Bandit's Roost," perhaps the most famous image of Mulberry Bend, can be said to reflect—at least superficially—some facets of Italian immigrant life in New York at the turn of the century. Its depiction of a public space dominated by men corresponded to the demographic composition of the community—the Italian immigrant population of Mulberry Bend was overwhelmingly male—as well as the gendered use of space. Historian Robert Orsi, for example, has shown that in Italian immigrant communities, "the streets were predominantly a male place . . . the public arena of male authority." Orsi and other historians have noted that men in Italian communities congregated there to talk, play sports, and gamble.[31]

Although Riis documented this male environment, he did not stress conviviality. Instead, he embedded the brooding image in a narrative of male violence. As Maren Stange has noted, Riis emphasized a sense of male menace by sometimes cropping out of Bandit's Roost the figures of two women who appeared on the left-hand side in the original print.[32] Over the course of the 1890s, the idea of a male menace associated with this image became more exaggerated. Whereas in *How the Other Half Lives*, published in 1890, Riis drew attention not only to the activities of the men depicted but also to the crowded physical conditions, by 1895 he communicated a more sinister message: in a slide show delivered to an audience of church workers, he contended that men playing card games in Bandit's Roost "generally in the end [take] to the knife; then murder comes in to finish the business."[33] In a newspaper article of the same year, Riis wrote of the "blood-letting" in the area, informing his audience that men in Mulberry Bend "have a way of settling their own scores" in violent fashion: "The stiletto is their favorite tool."[34]

Exaggerated as it was, Riis's attention to this extralegal use of force within the Italian community nonetheless suggests an alternative interpretation of the "Bandit's Roost" image that has less to do with an unbounded social menace than with resistance to and suspicion of outside authority among New York's Italian immigrants. They were extremely wary of city institutions, especially of the police. Often treated in uncaring and even brutal ways by police officers, Italian immigrants had little reason to make official complaints and often acted to "police" perceived infractions within their own community.[35] Their distrust extended to reformers, whom many immigrants eyed suspiciously as interlopers; one native-born reformer even complained that most Italians automatically

Jacob A. Riis, "Bandit's Roost, 391/2 Mulberry St.," 1887.

Courtesy Museum of the City of New York

assumed that charity workers took part in the system of graft that permeated municipal affairs.[36] Riis directly addressed this distrust in 1888, when he commented that Italians whom he photographed might "return a smile" but at the same time would keep their hands on their weapons in anticipation of a potential conflict.[37] This quality of wariness and resistance can be detected in the expressions and postures of the men depicted in "Bandit's Roost." What Riis constructed as social menace might also be interpreted as evidence of communal solidarity and resistance to outside authority.

In fact, resistance to outside authority was a central component of a southern Italian code of manhood, *omerta*, that differed in crucial ways from native-born conceptions of masculinity. Historian George Pozzetta asserts that the "manly character trait or *omerta* was much prized by southern Italians, particularly Sicilians. It called for firmness and seriousness in carrying out one's affairs; each man was to look to himself to settle any difficulties." Pozzetta adds that "no one was ever to place their trust or confidence in civil authorities for justice. Revenge was to be carried out quietly and personally, 'like a man,' or possibly with the aid of a trusted relative."[38]

The Italian American reformer Gino Speranza, an elite member of the *prominenti* who lived in Mulberry Bend during the 1890s, attempted to explain to native-born audiences the cultural basis for Italian immigrant noncooperation with the police. He too characterized Italian immigrants as "criminal," but he contended that although *omerta* was a "dangerous principle," it was born from a "communal spirit nourished into a spirit of intimate fellowship."[39] Angered by the press focus on acts of retributive justice by Italian immigrant men, Speranza asserted that "acts of love, and of courage and of manhood pass unchronicled."[40] In sum, he attempted to explain and counteract, at least partly, the stereotype of "the tough," disseminated by Riis and by countless newspaper reporters and magazine writers.

If "Bandit's Roost" represents Riis's image of the threatening tough, "The Tramp (in a Mulberry Street yard)" is his symbol of the idle, vagrant immigrant. This image too tells us something about the experiences of Italian immigrant men in Mulberry Bend; many in the late 1800s were "tramps," insofar as they traveled to work in rural areas and returned to New York City in the winter, and often were unable to find work or housing then.[41] Riis, however, presented "the tramp" to his audience as an individual with no desire to work. Following is an account of his narration that accompanied this picture in an 1895 slide lecture:

> On one of my visits to "the Bend" I came across this fellow . . . sitting there in the yard on the rung of a ladder, and he struck me as being such a typical tramp that I asked him to sit still for a minute and I would give him ten cents. That was probably the first and only ten cents the man had earned by honest labor in the course of his life, and that was sitting down at which he was an undoubted expert. [Laughter.] He was too lazy to say "Yes," but simply nodded. [Laughter.] I fixed my camera, and just as I got ready to take his picture he took the pipe out of his mouth and put it in his pocket. I said, "That belongs in the picture." But no; he would not have it. Less than fifty

> seconds at work and he was on a strike! [Laughter.] He knew what his labor was worth. That pipe was one of the two-for-a-cent kind, and I had to pay him a quarter to get the pipe in. [Laughter.] As he sits there, he is worth a quarter, and that is all he is worth.[42]

The inclusion of audience response in this account is valuable, as it provides insight into the way that Riis was able to play on class prejudices in his depictions of immigrant subjects.

This passage also provides further insight into Italian immigrants' resistance to outsiders. The man clearly realized that his photographic image was of some value to Riis, and perhaps understood why Riis felt it so important for him to be smoking a pipe in this constructed view. His response indicates that he assumed that posing and following Riis's directives represented the performance of a service, for which he expected to be compensated. Indeed, the qualities that Riis and his audience took to be evidence of laziness and greed on the part of an unmanly tramp might also be said to represent both resistance to exploitation and assertion of the right to earn a wage. As historians have argued, Italian immigrant men, motivated by a desire either to return to Italy with some wealth or to pay for the passage of family members to America, were driven to earn as much money as quickly as they could.[43] Far from lazy, most worked at physically demanding and often dangerous jobs, such as digging sewers and subways and construction work on buildings.[44] As he did in the case of the tough, Gino Speranza attempted to counter the prevalent image of the Italian immigrant man as a tramp; he often called on his middle-class audience's esteem for such "manly" values as hard work and bravery. He wrote, for example, of the "characteristically Italian quality . . . [of] daring or indifference to danger" and their "readiness . . . to undertake highly hazardous labor."[45] Speranza even hinted at the underlying insecurity about masculinity that may have contributed to male reformers' attacks on immigrant men. Writing of the Italian laborer, he asserted, "we utilize his brute strength in such heavy labor as our higher standards of feeding render us unfit to engage in."[46]

In presenting the image of the tramp, Riis eschewed descriptions of physical strength and bravery among Italian working men—qualities deemed "manly" by middle-class standards—in favor of an image of weakness and cowardice. In fact, he derided the courage of the tramp by

Jacob A. Riis, "The Tramp (in Mulberry Street yard)," 1887.
Courtesy Museum of the City of New York

comparing him unfavorably to the tough: "They are not thieves. They have not spunk enough for that. At most they might summon up courage to rob a clothes line, when no one is looking."[47] Yet although this tramp was an unmanly coward as an individual, he posed a real threat as a member of a larger population; Riis frequently warned his audience of the "hordes" and "armies" of Italian tramps who roamed the city streets. In an article published after the demolition of Mulberry Bend, he referred to "the grip of the tramp on our throat."[48] Such an image undoubtedly resonated with a middle-class audience, familiar with groups of laboring men on the road looking for work during the severe depression of the 1890s.[49]

Riis presented the men of Mulberry Bend as inferior to their middle-class counterparts in manliness, yet also as potent threats to American social order. By constructing Italian immigrants as both cowardly and passionately violent, he both sounded the alarm about potential class violence and reassured his audience that such violence could be thwarted. In so doing, Riis joined a vast number of reporters and writers in creating a stereotype that played on nativist fears. The voices of those—like Gino Speranza—who tried to complicate this image often became lost in the din.[50]

The meaning of these tropes of manhood in Mulberry Bend become clearer when one considers that Theodore Roosevelt played a key role in Riis's campaign and was Riis's greatest intellectual influence during this period. Roosevelt was also the primary spokesman for late nineteenth-century values of passionate and vigorous manhood, and he undoubtedly helped to shape Riis's thinking about gender. The two first met in 1890, when Roosevelt was serving in the New York State legislature. After reading *How the Other Half Lives*, he expressed his admiration and support for Riis's work. Riis characterized this initial meeting "like a man coming to enlist for a war because he believed in the cause, and truly he did."[51] Riis treated Roosevelt as a hero, so much so that contemporaries chided him for his unwavering admiration of the man. The bond between them grew even tighter when Roosevelt became New York City Police Commissioner in 1895. They were virtually inseparable during the two years that Roosevelt served on the commission. He commented that "[Riis] and I looked at life and its problems from substantially the same standpoint. Our ideals and principles and purposes, and our beliefs as to the methods necessary to realize them, were alike."[52] Roosevelt and Riis were crucial allies in supporting each other's causes.

This close relationship is important to an examination of manhood in Mulberry Bend. Roosevelt was in the process of developing his influential ideas about manhood, ethnicity, and American virtue, which would later form the foundation for his famous 1900 essay, "The Strenuous Life."[53] He allowed for both a process of immigrant assimilation and a conception of Anglo-Saxon culture as racially (ethnically) superior. During the mid-1890s, according to historian Thomas G. Dyer, Roosevelt came to believe that superior Protestant Northern European immigrants would more readily "intermix" with native-born American stock; Catholics, from Southern and Eastern Europe, would take longer.[54]

This process of Americanization as conceived by Roosevelt was complicated by his views on racial and ethnic conflict. During the same period, he began to espouse a theory of racial hierarchy based, in part, on Charles Pearson's *National Life and Character*, which explained national development in social Darwinist evolutionary terms.[55] Roosevelt came to believe that the nobler, English-speaking "races" were quickly reaching an "effete" stage of development and would soon be eclipsed by the lower races, who possessed a more primal and fecund virility but were inferior socially and intellectually. Significantly, Roosevelt singled out southern Italians—the majority population of Mulberry Bend—as "the most fecund and the least desirable" European population. To combat this race threat, Roosevelt warned, Americans of Northern European stock needed to become manlier, more "strenuous," and to procreate at greater rates. Roosevelt cloaked this theory in the rhetoric of "battle," "crusade," and "warfare" between races, and raised the specter of "race suicide" if white America did not heed his call to the strenuous life.[56]

Roosevelt's understandings of race, gender, and Americanization shed some light on the images and rhetoric Riis employed in his work on Mulberry Bend. The Italian men are depicted in seemingly contradictory ways: they are both dangerous enemies to be fought on the reform battlefield and potential allies and possessors of civic virtue; they are both excessively manly and excessively unmanly; and they are at once exploitative *padrones* and picturesque victims of capitalist greed. These constructions ultimately reveal more about middle-class anxieties concerning class conflict and changing gender relations than they do about the lives of the immigrant men. They illuminate the ways that working-class assertions of power caused middle- and upper-class men to reassess their own privilege and reformulate their conceptions of their own manhood.

Riis's depictions of the men of Mulberry Bend rely in important ways on the language and symbols of warfare. Like Roosevelt, Riis conceived of reform as contentious, as is encapsulated by his maxim "those who would fight for the poor must fight the poor to do it." He referred explicitly to "the battle with the Bend," and entitled a chapter of his autobiography, "The Bend Is Laid by the Heels." Such language appears elsewhere in his work, notably in the titles of two of his books that deal with reforming the Lower East Side, *The Battle with the Slum* and *A Ten Years' War*. The language of Christian warfare was certainly not new in reform efforts; it was used in the abolitionist movement and in social reform movements after the Civil War. But in the context of the Mulberry Bend campaign, this terminology took on a new meaning that had to do with contested class notions of masculinity. By waging a battle against the poor men of Mulberry Bend, male reformers like Riis and Roosevelt appropriated the passionate manhood of the immigrant enemy. They both vanquished that threat and presented a portrait of revitalized and aggressive middle-class manhood to their white middle-class audience.

This notion that combating urban vice and crime would augment one's own masculinity was explicitly addressed by key players in the campaign. Theodore Roosevelt, upon accepting his position on the Police Commission in 1895, wrote his sister Anna that he was glad to take it because "it is a man's work."[57] Likewise, Lincoln Steffens, a young reporter who joined Riis and Roosevelt in their forays on the Lower East Side, told his father that he was glad to do this work because "it would make a man of me."[58] In similar fashion, Riis often cast himself as a courageous "war correspondent" or a member of "a raiding party" in the slums.[59] On several occasions, he boasted of conflicts with armed immigrants when snapping pictures.[60]

Such assertions of aggressive militarist masculinity are telling, given that during the late nineteenth century male social reformers, like their counterparts in municipal and civil service reform, were often ridiculed by politicians as effeminate dilettantes. In 1890, for example, a reporter commented directly on the inefficacy of reformers—"the daintiest of bric-a-brac"—in combating violent "dagoes." The criticism was apparently directed at Riis; it referred to reformers "who have exhausted . . . the entire science of photography."[61] In response to such broadsides, recasting reform as an aggressive military campaign allowed men like Roosevelt and Riis to attest to the potency of their own manhood.[62]

Likewise, the act of "investigating" sites of working-class male entertainment, especially at night, allowed reformers the chance to associate with the immigrant sporting world and at the same time maintain a superior moral stance. Riis became well known for leading nighttime tours to sites of immigrant vice on the Lower East Side. The most famous example of this type of "reform slumming," however, was by the Reverend Charles Parkhurst, one of Riis's allies. In 1892, Parkhurst, disguised as a dandy, spent several nights visiting brothels and "bawdy" performances. Parkhurst recounted his nocturnal exploits in sermons, often portraying himself as the shocked object of unwanted sexual advances. His accounts received a great deal of press attention; they were even published in a popular 1894 book that sensationalized working-class sexuality.[63]

Following Parkhurst's lead, Theodore Roosevelt also roamed the city streets at night, disguised in a black cape and hat and often accompanied by Riis and Lincoln Steffens. Roosevelt's nocturnal forays, which earned him the nickname "Haroun-al-Roosevelt," were also heralded in press accounts, which positioned him as both a brave, daring adventurer and a protector of middle-class values. These encounters with working-class sexuality allowed Roosevelt to claim for himself some of the virile, sexual manliness that was thought to belong to working-class men, but also rendered vulnerable his claims to manly self-control and propriety. Recognizing the instability of the "Haroun-al-Roosevelt" image, the police commissioner's opponents waged a campaign to ruin his career by circulating the story that he was an enthusiastic participant in sexual revelries on the Lower East Side.[64]

Just as Riis depicted Mulberry Bend in terms of warfare between immigrant men and middle-class reformers, so did he use a military model in discussing reform of "the Bend." Riis argued that immigrant men and boys had to be brought into line, to be regimented, before they would become good citizens and true American men. Yet if Riis saw military regimentation as an effective means of re-forming the masculinity of immigrant men, he was even more hopeful about the use of this strategy with second-generation boys. Like many other reformers of his era, Riis believed that without intervention, "the sins of the father" would be passed down from one generation to the next.[65] He was especially concerned with second-generation male children: he argued that the "boy . . . is the one for whom we are waging the battle with the slum."[66] Immigrant boys, who joined street gangs and were potential "thieves in the making,"[67] also showed great promise. Brought under proper control, these potential thieves could be remade into American men.

Riis paid considerable attention to boys' gangs, which he differentiated from the bands of adult toughs and armies of tramps that he posed as such a threat to American values. By joining a gang, Riis argued, a boy was not necessarily acting out of wickedness, but was "demanding his . . . right to his childhood . . . that makes a self-respecting manhood." Gangs represented the "instinct[ual]" desire "to fall in and march in line that belongs to all boys." By capitalizing on this desire, exploiting "the boy's instinct for organization" and taking advantage of his "military spirit" in a more controlled fashion, reformers could defuse the immigrant menace in the second generation.[68] Riis depicted an example of such control in his photograph, "Drilling the Gang in Mulberry Street." For him, this approach meant shifting the dynamics of the reform battlefield: brought under a military style of discipline, Riis argued, the gang was transformed into "our ally, not our enemy."[69]

The eventual reconfiguration of Mulberry Bend as a park was central to this strategy of transforming second-generation immigrants. By the end of the 1890s, Riis had become a leader in the "small parks movement," which held that urban parks and playgrounds had enormous power to hasten the assimilative process for the children of immigrants. The movement found much of its inspiration in the popular and influential "recapitulation theory of play," developed in the late 1800s by psychologist G. Stanley Hall and YMCA founder Luther Halsey Gulick Jr. The recapitulation theory, which combined Darwinist evolutionary precepts and genetics-based psychological theory, held that the human life cycle approximated, or "recapitulated," the stages of human evolution: children began life as "primitive" individualists, entered into a stage of communal "savagery" as adolescents, and finally, if correctly socialized in an "advanced" society, became "civilized" adults.

Central to the recapitulation theory was the notion that engaging in vigorous physical play developed sound moral character and civic virtue. Not all forms of play resulted in this advancement, however: adolescent boys who participated in unruly and violent street gang activities remained mired in a lower stage of evolution, and "ethnic" immigrants merely recapitulated the "savage" stage of their own community.[70] Reformers who worked with boys, including Riis, saw in this theory the means of providing for the socialization of immigrant youth. By directing their group play in formalized institutions like parks and playgrounds,

Jacob A. Riis, "Drilling the Gang in Mulberry Street" or "A Cure for Truancy: Drilling in Mulberry Street," c. 1888.

Courtesy Museum of the City of New York

reformers might help toughs evolve into civilized American men. This connection is made explicit in a photograph of boys playing in Mulberry Bend Park by Jesse Tarbox Beals captioned, "Annexing Mulberry Bend to the U.S.A."[71]

In the years after Mulberry Park opened, Riis called on the recapitulation theory to interpret the success of that reform effort, most notably in the form of a new lantern slide lecture entitled, "Tony's Hardships," which he toured throughout the country. According to newspaper reports, Tony, Riis's fictional "representative of the street gamin," was said to have grown up in a tenement in Mulberry Bend where "there is no family, no manhood and no patriotism." Tony "grows up in the street" and is destined to "lead a life of vagrancy and vice" and "to vote for the man we do not want him to vote for" unless the law forces him to go to school. Even that does not really help until Tony is provided with a place to play, "for play is Tony's normal condition." Riis went on to depict organized play as working a kind of magic: once a playground or a boy's club is made available to the boy, he learns to respect the law, recognizes "the dignity of labor," shuns the saloon, and renounces support for Tammany. Riis presented the opening of Mulberry Bend Park as the shining symbol of this transformation: "Three years of sunlight in Mulberry Bend have banished crime. . . . Let each of us do our part, and we need have no fear for the future of Tony." The character who plays in the Mulberry Bend Park emerges as a solid American man, no longer the "savage" who previously lurked in the neighborhood's dark alleyways.[72]

Riis also applied the recapitulation theory to his own experience as an adult, middle-class reformer. He was strongly influenced by the writing of G. Stanley Hall, who contended that the "overcivilized" middle-class American man had much to learn from the theory. In America's modern, corporate society, Hall argued, the majority of middle-class men had passed through adolescence without properly recapitulating the "savage" stage. Overly controlled by the "civilizing" influences of women when they were children, most now led sedentary lives, which resulted in an effete moral condition. By engaging in recreation and team sport, he argued, middle-class men could reinvigorate their manliness and morality.[73] As historian E. Anthony Rotundo has shown, Hall's theories helped to encourage a widespread "manly embrace of boyhood" at the end of the nineteenth century. Men began to celebrate the boy within them and were concerned to a much greater degree with the play activities of boys and male adolescents.[74]

This concern is evident in the language and strategies that Riis and Roosevelt used in their reform efforts on the Lower East Side, as well as in the images that contemporary writers used to depict their efforts. Although Riis and Roosevelt frequently constructed "the battle against the slum" as warfare, they also tellingly treated reform work as a type of play. Riis acknowledged this duality in the dedication of his 1902 book, *The Battle with the Slum*:

> To Theodore Roosevelt
>
> Ever in the thick of the fight for a brighter to-morrow, whose whole life is a rousing bugle-call to arms for the right, for good citizenship, and an inspiration to us all,
>
> This record of some battles in which we fought back to back and *counted it the finest fun in the world* is inscribed with the loyal friendship of the author. [emphasis added]

This inclination to conceive of reform as "fun" is evident elsewhere. Indeed, Riis, Roosevelt, and Steffens thought of themselves as a sort of boys' gang knocking about the immigrant neighborhoods. Steffens, who characterized Roosevelt as an overgrown boy, reported that whenever Roosevelt wanted to summon Riis and himself, he would lean out of his second-story window at police headquarters and yell "his famous cowboy call, 'Hi yi yi.'"[75] This "playful" adventurousness was also evident in the three reformers' nocturnal incognito excursions on the Lower East Side. Contemporary writers picked up on this spirit, sometimes exploiting it to poke fun at the reformers. Reform on the Lower East Side, then, became a form of adolescent group play, encompassing both "savagery" and "civilization."[76]

In the context of Riis's campaign to transform Mulberry Bend, the recapitulation theory intersects in illuminating ways with Roosevelt's thinking on racial/ethnic hierarchy outlined above. Riis, who always wavered uncertainly between expressions of racial superiority and a belief in a democratic form of assimilationism, achieved a kind of synthesis by bringing these two theories together. Through controlled and organized play, immigrant boys could advance beyond the "degradation of the family, of manhood, and of patriotism" that characterized the older generations of their ethnic community.[77] Moreover, by collapsing notions of life-cycle evolution and racial evolution, Riis both asserted the superiority of Northern European values and allowed for the successful assimilation of second-generation immigrants. He and other male reformers simultaneously demonstrated their own adolescent—"savage"—virility without relinquishing their claim to moral and ethnic superiority. The urban playground, then, served as a stage upon which reformers brought together middle-class and immigrant working-class styles of masculinity in a drama of accommodation and Americanism that allowed for both the taming of the immigrant masculine menace and the vigor of middle-class manliness.

Waring's White Army: Militarism and Municipal Employment

In his book, *A Ten Years' War: An Account of the Battle with the Slum in New York*, Riis paid special homage to Colonel George E. Waring, a Civil War veteran and noted sanitary engineer who served as Street Cleaning Commissioner in the Strong administration.[78] Waring proved to be an ally in the Mulberry Bend campaign when he insisted that the "truckmen of the Sixth Ward" remove carts that they routinely stored on the vacant block after the tenements had been demolished. According to Riis, Waring's action, carried out over the protests of Tammany leaders, paved the way for the completion of the park. In response, Riis made the hyperbolic claim that Waring, who died in 1898, "made his last stand" in Mulberry Bend.[79] To Riis, he stood as a reform hero second only to Roosevelt. Both men, he maintained, possessed the "primary virtues of honesty and courage in the conduct of public business" and demonstrated "that simple, straightforward, honest dealing as between man and man is after all as effective in politics as in gun-making."[80]

Riis was not the only American to hold the colonel in such high esteem. Although largely ignored in the historiography of the early Progressive Era, Waring stood as one of the most famous and admired reformers of his day. Indeed, reform partisans hailed him as a singular hero whose "physical courage," manly vigor, and "forthright" style redeemed the much maligned reputation of the male reformer.[81] Prominent civil service advocate Everett P. Wheeler, for example, praised Waring as a "man amongst men" who "had the will and manliness to back his opinions, which placed him in the front rank of men to be emulated and entitled him to be ranked among the great men of the country, certainly the first of any officers who have ever served the city."[82] Likewise, *The Charities Review*, in a lengthy 1898 obituary, portrayed Waring as the embodiment of civic manliness and drew an implicit contrast to the figure of the effete and ineffective reformer:

> George E. Waring was the true and faithful citizen. In the first place, he had no nonsense about him. He did not live an artificial life upon

> a plane which needed to be supported upon stilts. He had the courage of his opinions. As a public officer it was not his habit to plead the baby act. . . . He did not ask to be let, or wait to be hindered. When he thought he saw clearly his duty, he went ahead and did it, and took the consequences. When shall we see more public men with knowledge and with principles, who are ready to bear themselves like men? Is it wise to let the devil have all the grit on his side?[83]

Because Waring invested reform with the related qualities of manliness and efficacy, reform partisans bemoaned his loss long after his death. In 1901, for example, a *New York Times* editorial, noting that the current crop seemed too passively "academic" to engage adequately in the "battle," lamented the absence of a "man who may now be . . . likened to Waring."[84]

Waring captured such rapturous admiration among reformers and journalists and masculinized the popular image of the reformer through his use of militarist rhetoric and spectacle in the reorganization of the Department of Street Cleaning. His brand of militarist reform differed from that of Riis and Roosevelt, however. While they stressed the vigorous glories of combat, he embraced a militarist vision of harmonious order. When Colonel Waring accepted the commissionership from Mayor Strong in late 1894, the appointment was greeted with much fanfare in the local press. Waring quickly announced his broad and far-reaching goals: to increase the mileage of streets to be cleaned by the department tenfold; to make the department more efficient by managing it like a "business"; to eliminate the corrupting influence of "political considerations," including the dispensation of patronage positions within the department; and to secure greater discipline and accountability among department employees.

Such efforts reflected the broader Progressive reform strategy of bringing "scientific management" to city services, which reformers believed had been mismanaged by wasteful and corrupt machine politicians. For Waring, scientific efficiency could only be achieved through a strict military style of organization. To this end, he reorganized the department along the lines of a military chain of command and, most conspicuously, required that the predominantly Italian street cleaners wear white cotton duck military uniforms. Moreover, the cleaners were required to conduct their work in military formation. The masses of white-uniformed street cleaners moving through the city in regimented fashion became a public spectacle, and the street cleaners earned the military monikers "white wings," the "white brigade," and the "white army."[85] The image of the white army soon proliferated as the subject of poems, photographs, dramatic works, paintings, and tourist literature. The annual street cleaner parades instituted by Waring during his first year in office receiving the most attention in the local and national press and drew huge crowds of spectators.

Waring's enthusiasm for military organization came from a number of sources, including his admiration for the German achievement of national unity and imperial glory through the creation of a modern, rationalized military force under the leadership of Bismarck. The most important influence, however, was his own service in the Union Army. Like many other men of his generation, Waring, who was commissioned as a colonel in the Fourth Missouri Cavalry in 1862, viewed the war as a crucible of manhood and struggled to recapture the sense of adventure, camaraderie, and discipline he had experienced as a soldier. Long afterward, Waring remembered his service in the Civil War as belonging to "a dreamland," so "different from all the dull routine of home." Like Roosevelt and Riis, he identified warfare as the antithesis of feminine civilization. He recalled with nostalgia "the circumstances of authority and responsibility" of active service "that fan[ned] the latent spark of barbarism, which, however dull, glows in all our breasts, and which generations of republican civilization have been powerless to quench."[86] Waring also remembered the Union Army as a democracy of merit, in which men could succeed regardless of their class background. He gave voice to this idealized vision of the military in an 1894 article on education at West Point:

> Here, as elsewhere in life, "equality" means only the equality of opportunity. Wealth, social standing, influence, and favoritism can secure no advantage. The poor youth from a remote agricultural region meets the son of the millionaire of the city on an absolutely equal footing, and they have the same privileges and opportunities. There is a fair field and no favor, and the best man wins by his own unaided effort.[87]

Waring concluded that such military principles had civic applications and would produce "success in the vocations of peace" as well as in "the operations of war."[88] This idea received powerful expression in the reform writings of Edward Bellamy, most prominently in his wildly popular novel *Looking Backward*. Indeed, Bellamy's vision of a harmonious and productive nation in which the members of a vast industrial army work together in the interests of the polity profoundly influenced Waring and many other veterans of the Civil War. Bellamy produced his utopian vision in response to what he saw as the rampant commercialism, economic inequality, and civic disorder in urban America in the late nineteenth century. The industrial army remedied these conditions by applying the principles of business efficiency to the state through a system of hierarchical military organization, in which all mobility was determined by merit. The perfect order of the national industrial army was achieved not through armed revolution or labor protest but through the bloodless evolution of the capitalist system. Spatially, the society of this army was the epitome of the city beautiful; its ordered streets, classical public buildings, and open green spaces symbolized its harmony.[89]

By attempting to produce an industrial army in microcosm in the Department of Street Cleaning in New York City, Waring acted on shifts in Bellamy's own thinking. Alarmed by the repressive and violent response of American military forces to labor struggles, Bellamy argued that rather than the military itself, "it is the post office . . . the civil service in which the prototype of nationalism is to be found."[90] His belief that the growing American civil service apparatus provided the perfect venue for the promotion of the camaraderie and order associated with the Union Army was, of course, shared by many of the leaders of the civil service reform movement, as discussed in chapter 1. Indeed, when Mayor William Strong (who himself had achieved the rank of colonel in the Union Army) took office in 1895 after a new wave of civil service legislation had been passed, prominent reformers immediately pressured him to hire "military men" to oversee the city's municipal departments. For example, Lincoln Steffens reported that he found himself "the agent of . . . the committee of Seventy, Doctor Parkhurst and the reformers on an expedition to find a military man for the Superintendent of Police." Indeed, with the exception of Roosevelt (who had not yet established his military career), all of Strong's appointments to the Police Commission had military backgrounds, including Fred D. Grant, the son of former President Ulysses S. Grant, and Avery D. Andrews, another graduate of West Point.[91]

The motivation behind appointing military men to lead municipal departments was, in the words of Police Commissioner Andrews, to instill in the civil service "that spirit of military discipline and military honor which in our Army . . . had been the true secret of success."[92] Reformers believed that this civic militarism would replace the spoils system of patronage appointments, which they charged had fully corrupted the entire municipal workforce and had undermined the proper functioning of city services. Waring described the effects of political patronage on the Tammany-controlled Department of Street Cleaning in an 1896 article, "The Necessity for Excluding Politics from Municipal Business":

> They were as nearly an utterly worthless crowd as you could find anywhere. They had three duties to perform; they had been appointed for those duties, and in the performance of two of those duties they had been diligent enough. The first duty was to make contributions regularly every week of a certain percentage of their pay to the agents of Tammany Hall; the second duty was to obey all the orders of the men who had given them their place; and the third duty was to sweep the streets.[93]

Characterizing the workings of the two-party system as a "menace to our safety, a danger to our liberty, a source of corruption to the people, and a disgrace to the nation," Waring immediately acted to remove "politics" from his department—to "put a man instead of a voter at the other end of the broom handle."[94] He did this not through the wholesale dismissal of Tammany appointees but by refusing to grant appointments requested by the mayor and other reform colleagues and by establishing an extensive and detailed list of dismissible employee offenses.

Bellamy's conception of the industrial army also bespoke antipathy toward party politics. Indeed, in *Looking Backward*, Bellamy argued that participation in representative politics would destroy worker discipline and "tempt candidates to intrigue for the support of the workers under them."[95] Thus, as Arthur Lipow argues, Bellamy effectively replaced government with the bureaucratic administration of the industrial army.[96]

His influence of is also apparent in Waring's stance toward labor unions. Both Bellamy and Waring believed that unions were divisive and counterproductive institutions that the militarization of civic employment would make both unnecessary and unattractive to workers. Waring put this belief into practice with the white army, declaring that "the strikes will not be tolerated for one moment" and encouraging street cleaners to inform him of any organizing activity within the ranks.[97] When the New York chapter of the Knights of Labor objected to this policy, Waring expressed his antipathy toward unions with considerable vitriol: "I regard your organization as an anti-labor organization, opposed to workingmen and opposed to work—an association carried on in the interests of idleness."[98]

Waring attempted to deal with labor conflicts and complaints internally through an elaborate arbitration scheme based on "the Belgian method of 'Arbitration and Conciliation.'" He established a "committee of forty-one," comprised of representatives elected from within the ranks, to address minor disciplinary matters, and a "board of conference," which included five members from that committee and an equal number of Waring's staff, to settle major disputes. According to Waring, after initial suspicion, fomented by labor agitators—"false teachings received from falser prophets"—the men "welcomed [the plan] in a manly spirit, and entered heartily into every detail of organization."[99] Indeed, Waring presented the "committee of forty-one" scheme as a remarkable success in the management of labor relations, through which conflict was replaced by mutual respect and poor and immigrant workers achieved self-respect and learned good citizenship. Urban reformers and allied journalists overwhelmingly accepted Waring's rosy depiction of labor relations in the department, urging other employers in both the public and the private sectors to emulate this novel experiment. The *New York Times*, for example, claimed that "The Commissioner of Street Cleaning has practically solved the 'labor question' in his department" and asserted that "the system adopted by Col Waring . . . may be studied with profit by all employers of large bodies of men."[100] Felix Adler, founder of the Society for Ethical Culture, called Waring "the advance guard of a new race of civic servants" who had "taken the discord out of the relations between employers and employees." Journalist Charles A. Meade declared that Waring's system of labor management represented a "master stroke . . . which has probably never been surpassed, if equaled, in this or any other country."[101]

In spite of such claims by reform advocates, available records indicate that the picture was not so free of trouble. For example, although the majority of street cleaners were of Italian descent, no Italian names appear in the records of elected representatives within the department, suggesting that the influence of Tammany Hall may have remained far greater than Waring let on. Moreover, the mayoral records of the Strong administration contain numerous letters and petitions of complaint about the unfair treatment, low pay, and unsubstantiated dismissal of department employees, in particular those who worked on a part-time basis, as well as several letters alleging that street cleaning employees continued to agitate for the Knights of Labor and other labor organizations.[102] In any case, Waring's attacks on municipal patronage and organized labor met with vociferous opposition by Tammany politicians and leaders of the Knights of Labor and New York's Central Labor Union throughout his tenure.

Yet, although labor leaders and party politicians had considerable experience launching public critiques against reformer incursions, they faced new obstacles with Waring and the white army. Waring's embrace of militarism as a mode of organization and, especially, as *public image* insulated him. As has been discussed previously, by the end of the century it had become commonplace to dismiss male reformers as effete and effeminate "do-gooders." By emphasizing his own military background—he insisted that he be addressed as "Colonel" and always dressed in full uniform—Waring constructed a uniquely masculine reform persona all but impervious to such criticism. At the same time, his transformation of the public image of his workforce—from potentially dangerous and volatile working-class men to obedient and respectful "soldiers of cleanliness"—helped protect the labor practices he instituted. Waring's brilliant public relations strategies proved highly influential to a generation of Progressive Era male reformers, who found in the "reform warrior" a role with remarkable public resonance and authority.[103]

Waring communicated his militarist social vision to various urban constituencies through the spectacular movement of street cleaning employees throughout the city. For Waring and his supporters, clean and ordered streets meant clean and orderly men. The conflation of space and bodies in this manner represented an emerging brand of reform ideology that Waring and Riis helped popularize. Referred to by historians as "pragmatic environmentalism," it held, essentially, that dangerous and unhealthy urban conditions were largely responsible for the moral and physical problems of poor people, and therefore, improved conditions would bring about improved behavior.[104] Moreover, the white army functioned as a bodily manifestation of the ideals of the "White City" displayed to stunning effect at the 1893 Columbian Exposition in Chicago. As M. Christine Boyer has argued, in the White City, Progressive reformers merged a desire to discipline the urban populace "with their desires to transform and improve its physical fabric."[105] This symbolic relationship was heralded in the *New York Times*: "If clean streets mean anything, they tell of an alert and honest municipality; they are . . . vast aids to inculcating the true principles of the comity of citizenship."[106]

Waring's symbolic drama took its most conspicuous form in street cleaner parades, initiated in 1896. The white-clad men marched in lockstep behind the colonel, who signified his leadership by riding horseback, dressed in black. These parades, viewed by tens of thousands of citizens, were described by journalists as a "magnificent . . . object lesson" and as a "revelation" and were often compared to the grand military processions familiar to New Yorkers.[107] But at the same time, the parades drew on a very different kind of tradition: the working-class militia parading connected to party politics and trade identification. Thus the street cleaner parades implicitly challenged both traditional communal expressions of class-based solidarity and power and Tammany Democrats' claims on the loyalty of immigrant voters.

Judging from the voluminous letters of praise and works of poetry submitted to the *New York Times*, many middle- and upper-class New Yorkers embraced the spectacle of the white army and the ideal of a compliant nonpartisan civic workforce that it promoted. One typical example, a poem entitled "The White Brigade," appeared in the *Times* in 1897:

> So you that wear the City's garb, whose art
> Is but to cleanse its pathways, have good heart!
> Your tasks well done, we count our street gains
> Yours not to reason, yours to deal with facts

Yours not to glory, nor even to boast;
Yours but to do an honest day's work for hire.[108]

A good number of people responded enthusiastically to calls for public surveillance of the white army by reporting a wide range of alleged infractions—including the presence of "white wings" in saloons, which Waring strictly forbade.[109]

Such reactions operated within late nineteenth-century discourses of race and ethnicity. The white army functioned as an idealized symbol of an assimilated and harmonious white polity of American men, in which potentially unruly southern Italian men—whose "whiteness" was open to question—were brought under military control and homogenized, their immigrant identities subsumed under the category of civic employee. Much of the press participated in producing this Lamarckian narrative of social and moral elevation. In the words of one reporter, "The men who had been the scoff and butt of the people became the 'white wings' of a renovated city, and proudly wore the much-ridiculed badge of their calling as an evidence of its dignity."[110] This process of elevation and assimilation was largely denied to non-Europeans, even though street cleaning had long been thought of as the lowest form of municipal employment.[111]

The racial aspects of this process were reflected in newspaper accounts that portrayed white skin as an integral characteristic of the white army. A reporter from the *New York Post*, for example, described the street cleaners as "rank after rank of men, dazzling white from helmet to ankles (except where the face of a colored brother appeared in high relief against this effective background)."[112] This literary depiction correlates with the composition of the Street Cleaning Department. In 1895, according to the *New York Times*, the vast force counted only twenty-seven "colored" workers, only one of whom was in a managerial position. This in spite of the fact that Waring, in keeping with his critique of the "corrupted" patronage system of Tammany administrations, claimed that he was concerned only with hiring "good men" and that it did "not make the slightest difference . . . whether a man is green, blue, black, or white."[113] Not until Waring's Tammany-appointed successor took over did the number of African Americans in the department increase. Unlike Waring, Tammany politicians were interested in seeing any color "voter at the end of a

Newspaper illustrations of the white army emphasized the whiteness of street cleaner bodies and uniforms.

"Waring's White Army," New York Tribune, *May 26, 1896, 13*

broom handle," and, beginning in 1897, routinely offered street cleaning positions to African Americans who supported Tammany candidates.[114]

The press dissemination of visual and literary images of white-clad and white-skinned street cleaners, when considered alongside Waring's disinterest in hiring non-European men, offers some understanding of the racialized underpinnings of the ostensibly color-blind politics espoused by the colonel and embraced by many white middle-class New Yorkers. It is significant that skin of street cleaners was colored white in this context, given that contemporaneous accounts depicted southern Italians often as dark-skinned "guineas" and sometimes as "black." Thomas A. Guglielmo has argued that, while Italians were often "dark" during this period and subject to racialized derision and prejudice, in "numerous critical ways," including in the context of immigration law, they were "white on arrival."[115] The spectacle of Waring's white army, then, might be understood as a testament to and performance of the white racial status of the force.

Critics of Waring's policies, namely Tammany leaders, resisted the attempt to mark the street cleaners as white. Indeed, they played on racial and ethnic hostilities and fears in their relentless attacks. An 1895 parody in the *Tammany Times*, for example, depicted Waring literally painting the bodies of hapless and sycophantic Italian street cleaners white.[116] Tammany politicians also invoked slavery in their racialized critiques, arguing that the reform administration unduly controlled the labor of the employees and that this represented a threat to free labor principles. Tammany judge Tom Grady, for example, referred to the white uniform as "a badge of slavery," a "mark of degradation," and a "stinging disgrace to a free American citizen."[117] Such characterizations played to a long-standing racist discourse that held that slavery threatened white labor and that formerly enslaved peoples were part of the problem. Tammany critics charged that reform efforts to refigure municipal employment enacted a new form of "wage slavery" while making a racialized critique of Italian men who submitted to the control of their labor and bodies.

Labor leaders, in contrast, complained that behind the symbolism of the white uniforms lurked very real problems for the workers themselves. Such criticism peaked in the very hot summer of 1895, when Waring insisted that all street cleaners wear full uniforms. including buttoned jackets and caps. One letter of protest was excerpted in several newspapers:

> It is extremely doubtful that your Honor would approve of allowing pet dogs to be blanketed and strapped in this hot weather, let alone requiring upward of 1,500 human sweepers to be dressed in heavy suits of duck cloth, through which neither sunshine, air, nor rain can penetrate, but only heat, and then apply strict, rigid military rules, to keep the coat full buttoned and the belt fastened or suffer the penalty of being laid off from work. Under these conditions the men are afraid to complain or say anything, and so work on and bear.[118]

Others protested the fact that street cleaners were required to purchase their own expensive uniforms and to keep them spotless, which imposed hardship on their wives and mothers. Waring vehemently and publicly objected to these complaints. For example, in a letter published in the *New York Times,* Waring informed a complainant that his "sympathy [was] entirely misplaced," and asserted that "the advantages of the exaction of conformity of the rules concerning uniforms are so great that . . . there is no prospect of my changing my regulations."[119]

Tammany and labor critics alike employed gendered rhetoric to subvert the militarist image that Waring promoted, alleging that his preoccupation with the white uniform—which he designed himself—represented not military manliness but feminine vanity and superficiality. For example, a satirical piece in the *Tammany Times* listed the following "Regulations Governing the Uniforms of the Waring Battalion": "Coat: White duck Mother Hubbard . . . lined with white swan's down . . . puffed sleeves and narrow cuffs, designed by Colonel Waring; Shoes—White duck, shovel-toed, low instep and high-heeled."[120] Moreover, Tammany leaders called into question Waring's own claims to military service, maintaining that he was not a "valorous soldier" but in fact "never was in battle but was always in retreat."[121] Representatives of the Central Labor Union, who frequently petitioned the mayor's office for Waring's removal, also challenged his self-depiction as a rugged war hero by presenting him as a Europeanized dandy from Newport society, a "lackey of the idle classes" who used his office to enrich himself rather than serve the public good.[122]

Conclusion

The militarist reform projects of Riis, Roosevelt, and Waring, of course, did not achieve the kind of hegemonic power their creators had envisioned. Indeed, Tammany Hall, rallying around the slogan "To Hell With Reform," took control of the municipal government in the very next election.[123] The new administration immediately dismissed Waring, and most of the signature policies he had instituted—including the labor arbitration scheme—were quickly abandoned. Likewise, Riis's vision of a vast network of small urban parks offering organized military drilling and play to immigrant youths did not come to be.

Despite their failure, these projects hold considerable historical and political significance. First, their promoters, especially Waring and Roosevelt, served as the first real heroes for a generation of male reformers who constructed themselves and their projects in militarized terms, thereby claiming reform as a practical and manly, rather than idealized and feminine, endeavor. The use of militaristic images and rhetoric became commonplace for Progressive Era men, who, like Roosevelt, embraced this new notion of civic militarism and cast themselves as manly soldiers in the battle for the social good. The emergence of the reform warrior depended upon a reconfigured racial hierarchy in which Southern and Eastern European men were granted access to a form of provisional whiteness.

These militarist projects also challenge a dominant understanding of the trajectory of American political culture in this period, which holds that elite liberal reformers attempted to replace the passionate male world of popular politics—characterized by mass militarist parading, ceremony, and spectacle—with a dispassionate, allegedly objective brand of electoral politics based on education and advertising. According to Michael McGerr, a prominent architect of this understanding, the reformers "dismissed all else—emotion, partisanship, display, public mobilization—as irrelevance." Historians have connected the elite liberal efforts to the concomitant rise in women's political activism, arguing that women pioneered voluntarist pressure-group politics by employing the educational style, thereby contributing to the "domestication"—or feminization—of political society.[124] The projects discussed in this chapter, however, suggest that a tradition of militarist, masculinist urban reform politics actually incorporated the passionate and spectacular qualities associated with the "party period." If politics were indeed domesticated and feminized during this time, reform was undergoing a process of militarization and masculinization.

4

Socrates in the Slums

"Social Brotherhood" and Settlement House Reform

The settlement house movement of the late nineteenth century occupies a central place in the history of American women. The two most prominent and influential American settlement houses, Chicago's Hull House, led by Jane Addams, and New York's Henry Street Settlement, led by Lillian Wald, functioned as sites where educated and committed middle-class women could live and work together for the "social good." Located in urban immigrant neighborhoods, settlement houses provided material assistance and educational and cultural programs primarily targeted at poor women and children. Recent scholarship has shown that through this movement, American women built political skills and networks that not only launched the careers of famous female reformers and politicians but also established the blueprint for twentieth-century American welfare policies.[1]

The settlement house movement also occupies a central place in the history of American women's sexuality. Scholars have long noted that the majority of American settlement women remained unmarried and formed their primary relationships with one another.[2] The prominence of these relationships, or "romantic friendships," has raised a number of interesting questions: Were they sexual? Are such "romantic friendships" appropriate subjects for lesbian history? What connections, if any, existed between these romantic attachments and the political ideologies and practices of the movement?[3] Although vigorously debated in the 1970s and 1980s, these issues have retreated to the background in more recent studies of the settlement movement.[4]

A new perspective on the connections between same-sex eroticism and settlement house politics emerges from an examination of men's involvement. Although women quickly came to dominate, many men lived and worked in urban settlement houses. Indeed, the early American movement began as a collaboration between middle-class men and women influenced by European reform efforts. Two of its most prominent builders were Charles B. Stover, leader of the University Settlement on New York's Lower East Side, founded in 1887 as the earliest American settlement, and John Lovejoy Elliott, of the Hudson Guild on Manhattan's West Side. Stover and Elliott, like their more famous counterparts, took their inspiration from the world's first settlement "experiment," London's Toynbee Hall; drew to a remarkable extent on the same intellectual traditions; and embraced the social democratic notion of cross-class "social brotherhood" rooted in humanist ethical theory. Moreover, all became active participants in national political matters.[5]

Elliot and Stover shared two other important similarities with settlement women. First, they embedded a critique of middle-class sexuality and gender roles within their ideal of social brotherhood. In this they echoed the concerns of women like Jane Addams, who wrote a great deal about the limitations of the "family claim"—the constraints imposed by marriage and family—on young members of the middle class. Like Addams, Elliott and Stover argued that the nuclear family was not sufficient; other forms of social family, linked to what Addams called "the universal claim," were necessary to achieve social democracy.[6] Second, Elliott and Stover lived their lives in a way that reflected and supported this view. Like many settlement women, they forged their primary emotional and erotic attachments to members of the same sex. Settlement houses represented experiments in creating this alternative family, in which sexuality was not linked to reproductive ends. Through these experiments, both men and women developed a politics of same-sex eroticism that stood in contrast to emerging medical models of homosexual pathology and heterosexual normativity.

The male settlement leaders' embrace of the ideal of social brotherhood also distinguished them from militarist reformers like Roosevelt and Waring in two crucial ways. First, whereas the militarist reformers borrowed from the "rough" style of working-class men to legitimate themselves as worthy opponents and eventual leaders of these men, Stover and Elliott adopted similar personae to pursue a form of cross-class solidarity that encompassed social, political, and erotic desires. Second, while Stover and Elliott joined the fight against the patronage system and actively participated in anti-Tammany campaigns, they shared neither the oppositional pugnacity nor the commitment to strict hierarchical organization of the militarist reformers. Rather, these settlement leaders and their colleagues, through the establishment of political clubs and organizations linked to the settlement houses, worked to form a new, more reciprocal set of male relations that would provide an alternative to the Tammany-controlled patronage system. The settlement leaders aimed to create political and social outlets for young men who might otherwise look to Tammany for a sense of community and the prospect of upward mobility. Of course, the ultimate shape of the new relations never aligned with this democratic vision. Settlement leaders operated from a position of class and cultural privilege vis-à-vis their often younger working-class constituents; the reforms and the relationships they pursued reflected and were structured by their relative power.

Like the more famous female leaders of the American settlement house movement, John Elliott and Charles Stover came from comfortable, middle-class families that stressed education and social involvement. Elliott, born in 1868, grew up in Princeton, Illinois. His father was a Civil War colonel and his mother was an abolitionist.[7] Stover, born in 1861, was raised in a prominent and religious Presbyterian family in eastern Pennsylvania. Both men attended college, Elliott at Cornell University, where he was president of his senior class and a member of the football team, and Stover at Lafayette College and the Union Theological Seminary. Both had rejected mainstream Protestantism. Elliott's family belonged to no religious organizations, but at a young age he adopted the religious convictions of the famous agnostic orator Robert Ingersoll, a close family friend. Stover, who underwent a painful "crisis of faith" as a young man, renounced his Christianity and abandoned plans to enter the ministry.[8]

Rejection of organized Christianity left both men adrift in search of organizing spiritual or moral principles. Elliott remembered feeling aimless at Cornell, even though he was a popular and active participant in the college's social life.[9] Stover, who traveled to the American West and Europe after leaving the seminary, suffered from such a "phalanx of terrible doubt" about the "genuineness of [his] divine calling" that he described the experience as being "like a thunder-clash in the clear heavens." This assault upon his faith, "after years of agony, led to its total eclipse."[10]

Both men soon found direction in the form of the secular Society for Ethical Culture. Elliott first encountered the organization when Felix Adler, its leader, came to speak at Cornell. Adler's declaration that "it is possible to live without a formal creed" and his call to social commitment through "right action" and ethical living inspired Elliott. Stover was first introduced to ethical culture by Stanton Coit, a prominent follower of Adler who had founded the Neighborhood Guild. Coit convinced Stover that, although he had lost faith in the Christian doctrine, he could carry out the kind of "Christ-like life" he believed in at the settlement.[11] Through Adler and Coit, Elliott and Stover had found powerful secular principles that could replace the Christianity each had abandoned.

The Society for Ethical Culture, a well-funded organization with branches in the United States and Europe, also provided a powerful institutional base from which Elliott and Stover could develop and disseminate their philosophical beliefs and enact social reform programs. After meeting Adler, Elliott immediately affiliated himself with the organization and, at Adler's insistence, attended the University of Halle in Germany to study for a doctorate in philosophy in preparation for a position as Adler's assistant. Stover became a resident at the Neighborhood Guild in 1887, and took charge of that organization when Stanton Coit left to lead the Society for Ethical Culture in Great Britain. In 1894, Stover took brief leave from the guild to make a second trip abroad, in part to learn about European reform movements.

Stover and Elliott took advantage of their travels by immersing themselves in secularized European discourses on ethical philosophy and reform. They studied the works of Thomas Carlyle, John Ruskin, and Matthew Arnold and visited Toynbee Hall, the famous London settlement house. Exposed to unfamiliar intellectual traditions and separated from the constraints of American moral conventions, the young men further questioned the foundations upon which they had constructed their identities. As a result of their European travels, they reimagined themselves and their gendered social roles. For both, this self-reconstitution involved the formation of primary bonds with other men.

For Stover, this process was filled with considerable anguish and persistent religious doubt. Throughout his life, he suffered from spells of severe depression. In the few instances when he communicated to friends about the cause of his psychic distress, he linked these problems to issues of procreation and marriage. Stover continued to employ a rhetoric of Christian sin and divine will, despite his renunciation of the Christian faith. When he suffered from one of these depressions during his second trip to Europe, for example, he wrote to friends about his suicidal thoughts and spoke bitterly of the "greatest crime of which a man can be guilty"—the perpetuation of the human species. He also referred to an unspecified problem "outside of himself" that had caused his loss of faith.[12]

Only in later years did Stover begin to resolve his anxieties. At the University Settlement, he separated himself from family life and eschewed potential romantic interactions with women. In 1899, a Miss Greene of the neighboring College Settlement accused Stover of a "sad short-coming," which she referred to as a "blind bias" and "indiscriminate hostility" that characterized his dealings with women. Stover responded that he felt "unqualified by disposition" to visit socially with the women at the College Settlement. He added that, although Miss Greene "may have good authority for some outward facts" regarding his interaction with women, "the fault lies in the interpretation. I confess to frequent sinning against conventionalities. No, not sinning, for I would have it otherwise." Stover went on to argue that the fault lay not with himself, but with some outside "power . . . with whom I have not yet arrived at a satisfactory understanding. This I hope yet to accomplish." Many years later, in 1916, he indicated that he had come closer to such an understanding. In apologizing for not attending dinner at the home of a woman friend, he wrote, "The Almighty . . . wills that I have no participation in home pleasures."[13]

Stover had, in the words of his settlement colleague James Kirke Paulding, a "following on the East Side [that] was a preponderantly masculine one."[14] Yet not all of Stover's female colleagues saw him as distant and antagonistic. He maintained friendly relationships with such leading settlement workers as Lillian Wald, Jane Addams, and Mary Kingsbury Simkhovitch. Some of these women had sympathetic insight into Stover's "peculiarities" and "occasional erratic movements," including his periods of depression and occasional sudden disappearances. Simkhovitch, for example, thought that for all his gregariousness, "there was something withdrawn about him, as if he cared only to disclose his activities, while holding shyly and inviolate some core of his personality which was simply his love for all his fellow men."[15] Wald spoke of "a probable deeper struggle within" Stover.[16]

All of these comments point toward a common element linking Stover's vexed relationships to women, his alienation from the traditional family, and his primary interest in relationships with males. Although tentative and coded, these expressions invoked a model of gender and sexuality first explained in the late nineteenth century by sexologists as homosexuality: an innate quality, a sexual inversion that constituted the personality. Such a model did not inherently stigmatize "the homosexual," although many reformers and politicians deployed it to that end. In fact, as developed by British intellectuals J. A. Symonds and Edward Carpenter—whose work was well known and highly regarded by many settlement reformers—this new model provided "homosexual" people with a unique social role, and even an inherent superiority.[17] Wald, in particular, utilized this positive model in her memorial to Stover. She fondly remembered her first visit to the book-lined quarters that Stover shared with fellow settlement resident Edward King, recalling the "frank and instructive" advice that this "unconventional pair" gave her. She credited this experience with inspiring her to take up residence in the nearby College Settlement with her companion, Mary Brewster. That Wald made the move from an account of Stover and King's domestic scene to a reference to her own relationship with Brewster—with whom she also formed an "unconventional pair"—suggests that she saw some basis for comparison between male and female same-sex relationships. Edward Carpenter drew similar comparisons in his theorizing on the politics of what he called "homogenic" love, and suggested that male same-sex relationships should be modeled after the relationships of "New Women."[18]

John Elliott appeared to be less troubled by his bachelorhood. Like Stover, at a young age he structured his life around primary relationships with other men, but he did not interpret these relationships as especially problematic or sinful. In 1892 and 1893, during his years of graduate study in Germany, Elliott enthusiastically wrote home about the men he met and his experiences with German fraternal organizations. In his letters, Elliott juxtaposed expressions of delight in this fellowship with those of disinterest in forging romantic relationships with women. "I've met some nice fellows here," he wrote in one letter, "some . . . professors whom I like very well, much better than the girls. I'll tell you when my heart is in danger, but so far it has never even been exposed."[19] Later, when he returned to the United States, he responded to his mother's complaints about his unmarried status by writing that he had nothing against marriage, "in principle."[20] Elliott expressed a disenchantment with the limitations of reproductive family life that echoed Stover's. He did not denounce the institution of the family but espoused other models of familial association linked to broader forms of social organization. As teacher of ethics at the Hudson Guild and at the school of the Society for Ethical Culture, Elliott spread his new gospel that such alternative associations would promote social "brotherhood."

Like the great settlement reformer Jane Addams, Elliott and Stover embedded their dissatisfaction with circumscribed sexuality and traditional family life within an idealistic vision of a cross-class "brotherhood." They called on Platonic models of a society dedicated to the common good and invoked the figure of Socrates to argue for their social vision. Stover and Elliott also had access to two nineteenth-century traditions that linked male homoeroticism to particular social ideologies and practices: "social mobility," best exemplified by writer and philanthropist Horatio Alger, and "democratic comradeship," heralded by poet Walt Whitman. Although seemingly at odds, these two traditions intersected in significant ways in the two reformers' careers.

The social mobility model of male homoerotic ideology and practice has been brilliantly explicated by literary scholar Michael Moon. Moon has shown that American reform narratives—whether produced as nonfiction, as in the life story of Children's Aid Society founder Charles Loring Brace, or as fiction, most famously in Horatio Alger's stories of social ascent—romanticized fraternal relationships among working-class boys and men. Alger, whose Harvard education concentrated on a study of Hellenic culture, eroticized relationships between the middle-class "saviors" and the poor youths, framing the act of "saving" as one of seduction. These narratives of "rescue" involve the crossing of "seemingly intractable class lines" and terminate, happily, with a romantic portrait of masculine domesticity.[21]

The narratives produced by Brace and Alger posited overlapping trajectories of middle-class reformers' and benefactors' "descent" into the working-class slums. Juxtaposed with the social and economic ascent of poor working-class young men, these trajectories created an eroticized portrait of masculine cross-class amicability during a time of considerable labor unrest and violent class conflict in urban America. In this sense, the narratives share certain characteristics with the literary work of Walt Whitman, especially *Leaves of Grass*, which included the highly homoerotic Calamus poems. In fact, one of Whitman's early efforts, the 1841 short story "The Child's Champion," forecasted the plot line of "the most popular literary forms of the post-Civil War era . . . the rags-to-respectability stories of Horatio Alger."[22]

Whitman's later writings presented a more leveling model of male homoerotic attachment. *Leaves of Grass*, published in 1855, created a politicized utopian narrative of masculine comradeship and "adhesiveness" that would bind American men together in democratic society. In the Calamus poems, Whitman explicitly sexualized these bonds, presenting himself as both "the poet of homosexual love and the bard of democracy."[23] Whitman himself commented on the political significance of these poems:

> Important as they are in my purpose as emotional expressions for humanity, the special meaning of the Calamus cluster of Leaves of Grass . . . mainly resides in its Political significance. In my opinion it is by a fervent, accepted development of Comradeship, the beautiful and sane affection of man for man, latent in all the young fellows, North and South, East and West—it is by this, I say . . . that the United States of the future, (I cannot too often repeat), are to be most effectually welded together, intercalated, anneal'd into a Living Union.[24]

For Whitman, as for Brace and Alger, personal desire and the public politics of class relationships were intricately linked.

This connection between homoerotic desire and homosocial class relations is illustrated not only in the literary productions of Alger and Whitman but also in their life stories. In a sense, both writers lived their narratives by forging eroticized personal relationships with young working-class men. While Alger was writing his famous stories, he also worked as a social reformer in the Newsboy's Lodging House founded by Charles Loring Brace's Children's Aid Society. He "adopted" several young working-class men, who lived with him and assisted him in his work.[25] Alger, who had previously been dismissed from a ministerial position for "the abominable and revolting crime of unnatural familiarity" with a young male parishioner, embedded his erotic interests within his social roles as philanthropist and author.[26]

Walt Whitman also formed primary relationships with young working-class men who lived with and worked for him. Yet Whitman constructed his social performance in a way that both reflected and influenced the theme of a leveling manly democracy that characterized his writing. Rather than assuming the role of philanthropist, he presented himself as a physically virile man who shared the habits, attire, and pastimes of the "rough" working-class men whose company he kept. Reflecting popular notions of the manly virtue of the American yeoman, Whitman situated this communion between men in an idyllic Arcadian setting, thereby naturalizing a "community of desire sharing a sexual, social, and psychological condition."[27] The idealized expression of manly comradeship and desire that Whitman expressed in his work and lived with his body provided a compelling discourse for late nineteenth-century men—including Stover and Elliott—who resisted the growing stigmatization and pathologizing models of male same-sex attachments. Whitman served as a major influence for intellectual leftists on both sides of the Atlantic who sought to incorporate a more positive model of such relations within their broader political visions.[28]

Among those inspired by Whitman were the famous British theoreticians of "homogenic" love, John Addington Symonds and Edward Carpenter.[29] Whitman's influence on them reflects a broad cross-Atlantic collaboration in the discourses of homoeroticism and class relations. Symonds and Carpenter drew on Whitman's model of manly comradeship and on the models of pederasty and pedagogy of ancient Greece to construct an explicitly political argument that presented homosexual relations as morally valid and socially useful and that challenged the repression of homosexuality by the state. Carpenter, in his 1894 essay, "Homogenic Love," expanded on arguments previously made by Symonds that, if freed from government repression, homosexuality could effect a major social transformation. Homosexual relations could draw "members of the different classes together" by forming "an advance guard of that great movement that will one day transform the common life by substituting the bond of personal affection and compassion for the monetary, legal and other external forces which now control and confine society."[30]

The political theories espoused by Symonds and Carpenter circulated in socialist intellectual circles in Great Britain, especially at Oxford and Cambridge universities, and found an institutional setting in London's settlement houses. At the end of the nineteenth century, young Carpenter enthusiasts, including C. R. Ashbee and Frank Llewellyn-Smith, took up residence in Toynbee Hall, to re-create "the relationships, comforts and rituals of the all-male world" and to form relationships with the "rough" working-class boys. These privileged reformers boxed and roughhoused with the young men, recording the sights and smells of these experiences in their journals, and took the "lads" on "idyllic weekend gambols" that resulted in an "eternal love" between the reformers and the East End boys. Historian Seth Koven argues that these young reformers, who used the same sexualized and class-based rhetoric of the "rough lad" developed in London's gay subcultures, sought to "create nation and community through vertical bonds of comradeship across class lines."[31]

A similar combination of same-sex desire and social reform characterized the careers of Stover and Elliott. Stover exulted in the companionship of young working-class men at the University Settlement, developing a following referred to by others as "Stover's boys."[32] He fashioned himself as a "rough" Whitmanesque figure and was especially close to a "belligerent and excitable" group of young men who belonged to the Chadwick Juniors club. Their ringleader was Jacob Epstein, who would later become a renowned sculptor. Stover and his associate James Kirke Paulding were extremely "permissive" with this crowd, and when other residents felt that the youths' mischievous antics had gotten out of hand, Stover "sided with their belligerence" and invited them to meet in his private quarters.[33]

Like his British counterparts, Stover integrated his desire for comradeship with young working-class men into a decidedly Arcadian vision.[34] He believed that natural settings provided the ideal location for forging social bonds and was influential in establishing a settlement camp in upstate New York. He maintained quarters at the camp and was happiest spending time there with youths from the settlement, to whom he taught natural history. Stover carried this belief in the transformative power of nature—especially for working-class boys—into his other reform activities, especially in his capacity as New York City Parks Commissioner between 1910 and 1914. In fact, his commitment to making parks accessible for the recreation of working-class men contributed to his losing that position. He advocated "popularizing" the parks, including Central Park, by providing playing fields. Wealthy New Yorkers, appalled at a policy that they thought would mar the landscapes and fearful that the parks would attract "gangs of hoodlums," lobbied for his removal.[35]

Like Stover, Elliott was drawn to the "rough" masculine culture of New York's working-class neighborhoods. According to Algernon Black, Elliott's colleague in the Society for Ethical Culture, when Elliott first heard about the "rough and tough" Manhattan neighborhood Hell's Kitchen, he responded with great enthusiasm. Black reported that Elliott began to frequent the area, where he "walked through the streets and along the docks" and "watched the men working on the docks unloading the ships, the truck drivers taking the cargo away to factories and markets."[36] Elliott rented an apartment in the neighborhood and soon attracted a gang of boys called the Hurly Burlies, with whom he boxed and shot craps. He reported that their visits to his apartment would sometimes end in a brawl, with the lights turned off and objects broken. One neighborhood minister, according to Elliott, reported that the boys who visited were "a menace to neighborhood morality . . . and . . . a disturber of the peace."[37]

In reminiscing about his experiences with the Hurly Burlies, which led to his establishment of the Hudson Guild, Elliott recalled being immediately taken with one "blond haired boy" who was "the first to box." This "handsome and strong boy with a wonderful Irish brogue" was Mark McCloskey, with whom Elliott formed the closest relationship of his life.[38] He took a special interest in McCloskey, to whom he referred in his letters as "Marksie" and "Beloved."[39] He financed McCloskey's education at Princeton University, and thereafter named him as his successor as director of the Hudson Guild. McCloskey went on to play a leading role in several federal programs during the New Deal era and World War II. In later years, Elliott established similar relationships with other youths from the neighborhood.[40]

Elliott also constructed his persona in the Whitmanesque mold. He eschewed coat and tie in favor of shabby casual clothing and often walked through the streets of the West Side followed by a gang of "Elliott's boys."[41] Those who met him inevitably commented on his large stature, handsome face, booming voice, and "manly" personality. His associates often queried why a man so "handsome and affectionate and loving" never expressed any interest in marrying. This question proved to be a source of troubled speculation, especially in the years after his death. Those who addressed the topic frequently invoked a gendered model of the homosexual male as "effeminate" in contrasting Elliott's virile, charismatic personality with his unmarried status. One explanation, which circulated among his acquaintances, was that he lived his life "like a priest"—that his overwhelming social commitment would have been diluted if he gave his attention to a wife and family. Algernon Black, in a chapter of an unpublished biography of Elliott suggestively titled, "The Gay Life," discussed this and other possible explanations before concluding that "No matter how much people asked and guessed, no one was ever able to find out the real truth about why John never married. All they could do was guess and wonder."[42]

Elliott did not interpret his homosocial and homoerotic desires only as matters of personal preference. Lesson plans from the ethics classes he taught in the early years of the twentieth century indicate that his conceptions of male homoeroticism and comradeship bore a striking resemblance to the political models espoused by Carpenter and Symonds. For example, Elliott shared those two writers' penchant for making political arguments about class relationships through eroticized retellings of stories about two sets of famous comrades: Damon and Pythias of Greek mythology and David and Jonathan from the Bible.[43] In one lesson, Elliott set up the stories through a voyeuristic account of the body of the young shepherd, David:

> You will see a shepherd boy, about fifteen or sixteen years old, playing and singing. . . . If you look at the boys [*sic*] arms you would

> see the great large muscles and large bones, and his wrists are strong. He is a strong young fellow. His back was straight, and his chest is large and his legs are long and muscular, and he was swift of foot. He was a splendid young chap if there ever was one. . . . He is a mighty nice kind of a youth. So big and brave and skillful. He touched the harp with skillful fingers and such beautiful deep music like religious music, and then just love music, and then nature music, or of the eagle flying in the sky.[44]

Elliott continued with a description of David's battle with Goliath and subsequent "beautiful friendship" with Jonathan, relating the story as a class-infused morality tale by claiming that David was "a poor boy" to whom Jonathan "gave his best things."[45]

In similar fashion, Elliott framed the story of Damon and Pythias as one of "the love of brothers . . . too rare to be destroyed." He contrasted the "beauty" of their relationship to the tyranny of the king who was ready to execute Damon: "The meaning of the story is that the tyrant king cannot learn or know friendship." In one telling, he defined modern types who "cannot join in this friendship" as the wealthy industrialists, "Rockefeller, Whitney, and Ryan. . . . Money cannot cure Rockefeller's indigestion." Elliott also linked these tales to an argument that validated the decision to remain unmarried. After giving examples of "unmarried brothers who lived their whole life together," he stated that "This was a very lovely life. . . . When they marry they separate. That is a very beautiful relation and there are other beautiful examples."[46]

More stories of loving brotherhood appear in the context of the University Settlement. Although there are no extant records of the pedagogical strategies employed there, the artistic production of members of boys' clubs led by Stover and Paulding suggest that they were taught lessons similar to those of Elliott. One example in visual form are the homoerotic *Calamus* drawings by the famous modern sculptor Jacob Epstein. In the 1890s, Epstein, who hailed from a family of Russian-Jewish immigrants on the Lower East Side, was active in the Chadwick Juniors, modeled after a social reform club founded by Stover and other settlement leaders, and the Social, Educational, and Improvement (SEI) Club, dedicated to the study of literature and political philosophy. Epstein credited his participation in these settlement clubs with forging his commitment to leftist politics and with educating him about Whitman's writings.[47] When Epstein went to study art in Paris and London in 1902, Paulding and another reformer associated with the University Settlement, Edward W. Ordway, corresponded with him; Ordway even provided financial support for his studies. Epstein likely produced the drawings in 1902, and, with an introduction by Ordway, showed them to an impressed George Bernard Shaw in 1905. The *Calamus* drawings launched Epstein's career and led to the commission of his famous design for the *Oscar Wilde Memorial* in Paris.[48]

Other examples of cultural production from the University Settlement are found in literary magazines, published by the young members of the clubs, that include numerous poems and stories on the beauty of comradely love. One such story, "A Tale of Two Souls," tells of the love between "the flower-like Elmer" and his friend Enoch, who had eyes as "blue as the calmest summer-sky" and hair "like gold—beautiful gold." One typical passage reads:

> They were very great friends. Sometimes, out of the busy striving and struggling world, two souls reach out, recognize in each other the inmost desires of their hearts and cling to each other forever. The friendship of Enoch and Elmer was such a fellowship of souls. There was not a joy for the one, but that it was born from the other's gladness and not a tear, but shed because of the other's grief.[49]

Similar themes were sounded throughout the pages of these journals, often in explicitly classed political contexts. For example, David Colin, a member of the Emerson Club, celebrated the ability of the poet to "Proclaim on high, True Friendship and Fraternity" and thereby "awake the weary slave of toil" and "destroy the chains that bind him tight."[50]

This ideal of loving bonds between male friends was not restricted to artistic expressions. Members of turn-of-the-century University Settlement clubs—with names like the Comrade Club, the Spartan Athletic Club, Athenians, and the Young Citizens—considered it the basis of their very existence and of their social mission. The constitution of the Promethean Club, for example, stated that because "conditions exist which are contrary to the ideals of truth, justice and brotherhood . . . we youths do hereby band together to preserve and foster by education of word and

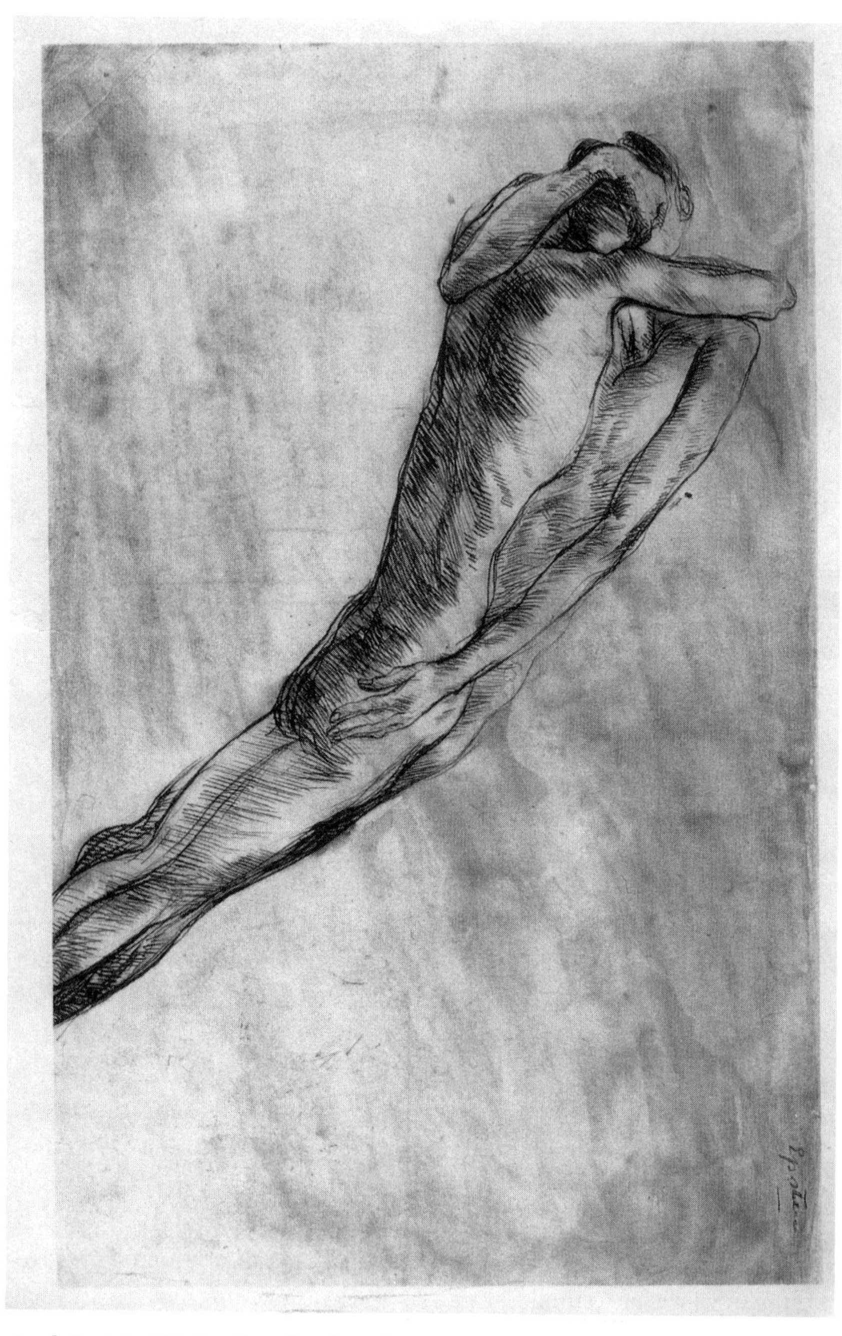

Jacob Epstein, *"We Two Boys Together Clinging" for W. Whitman, Calamus, in* Leaves of Grass, c. 1902. Pen and ink and colored wash.

Beth Lipkin Collection

deed, and by stimulating friendship, the lofty idealism of youth, to create a sensitive consciousness to conditions about it . . . so that youth, when it matures, shall become the strength of the nation to the end that idealism shall govern conduct." The young men in the Promethean and other clubs enacted this call to social improvement and nation strengthening through involvement in various movements, including supporting labor unionization and lobbying for tenement house reform.[51]

The expressions of youth club members suggest that ideals of male "friendship" and "fraternity" were embedded in a utopian vision of a democratic and classless society developed in opposition to the materialism, "selfishness and cynicism" of industrialized urban society.[52] Yet these clubs were constrained by the very class-based society they criticized, in that they were located in social settlements supervised by middle- and upper-class reformers and dependent on philanthropic funding. Within the clubs, liberal capitalist tenets of improvement and social uplift through education were often in tension with the more leveling ideals of democratic brotherhood. This tension is evident within the youth club rhetoric, which speaks of "brotherhood" in the privileged language of Western male intellectuals. Although this ideal may have intersected with patterns of working-class male camaraderie and solidarity in the streets and taverns of New York's tenement house districts, its goal was to transform and "uplift" the men who inhabited this milieu through the privileged realm of literary culture. Moreover, the life trajectories of these young men, many of whom went on to play prominent social roles as businessmen, scholars, and political reformers, suggest that their introduction to "culture" in the settlements served primarily to help them achieve individual social advancement.[53]

The tension between vertical and horizontal forms of male relationships was also evident in the careers of Elliott and Stover. Their movement "down" into the immigrant neighborhoods conformed in many ways to the similar erotic and political male "descents" enacted elsewhere in turn-of-the-century New York. As we have already seen, men who fashioned themselves as social reformers, like Charles Loring Brace and Horatio Alger, coupled their own "descent" with the "uplift" of the young men they encountered in the "slums." Similar stories were reenacted and renarrated in Stover's and Elliott's own time by other prominent New Yorkers, including Charles Parkhurst, Jacob Riis, and Theodore

Roosevelt, who gave sensational accounts of their escapades.[54] During the same period, middle-class men, in search of sexual pleasure and freedom from the constraints of "respectable" culture, frequented the bars and streets of immigrant neighborhoods.[55] Although many sought sex with working-class women, others participated in a burgeoning "fairy culture" based on gender inversion, and still others pursued sexual relations with "rough" working-class men, whose appearance and masculine style they eroticized. Many, like Stover and Elliott, heralded Walt Whitman "as a prophetic spokesman" and identified with his notion of "the manly love of comrades."[56]

The careers of Elliott and Stover point to the area where erotic and reform models of "descent" overlapped and illustrate the tense coexistence of vertical and horizontal models of class relations. The trajectories these reformers enacted and told and the stories that were told about them had a more horizontal structure than those of typical "slummers." After their initial "descent," both remained in immigrant neighborhoods throughout their lives and formed long-lasting relationships with men who lived there. Like other reformers, they recounted their experiences to middle-class audiences through publications, but they also built constituencies within the neighborhoods in which they lived. Their moves to costume themselves as "simple" men, for example, registered not only with middle-class audiences but also with those living in the tenement districts, many of whom interpreted the absence of "dress suit" and "high hat," along with the desire to form close relationships with "even the humblest laborer," as signs of humility and solidarity.[57] Moreover, each developed a politics that, in its advocacy of benefits for working-class people, was interpreted as radical by other reformers. Stover, for example, was criticized not only for his attempts to build playing fields in Central Park but also for the campaign he led to open museums to working people on Sundays. Likewise, Elliott's efforts to help convicted criminals from his Chelsea neighborhood and to assist neighborhood youths resisting the draft in World War I were met with great suspicion by many of his counterparts.[58]

The tense interplay between vertical and horizontal models of class- and age-differentiated eroticized male relationships is perhaps best illustrated by the "Socratic role" performed by Elliott and Stover, which had significant explanatory and legitimating power for both. Like Whitman,

Socrates was a historical figure through which these men located themselves in relation to the young immigrants with whom they worked and lived. The influence of Socrates was not lost on those who surrounded them. Settlement leader Stanton Coit, for example, claimed that "Stover was different—and in the same way—from every other mortal whom I have ever known as was Socrates from all the other Athenians of his day."[59]

Elliott's colleagues and students likewise referred to Socrates as his "revered hero" and spoke of "the kind of Socratic probing [Elliott] liked to practice."[60] Indeed, he performed the role with great enthusiasm. His ethics classes, organized as Socratic dialogues, frequently revolved around accounts of Greek devotion to the beauty of the male body and the role of pedagogy in the development of this beauty. After asking his students to recite the Athenian oath, Elliott narrated stories about "those Greek boys . . . each one with his teacher or pedagogue," who:

> would start out in the morning about day light and they stayed there until sundown. They would go through the streets in a kind of procession until they came to a place set aside for gymnastic exercises and there, from sun-rise until noon, they would exercise and play games in the open air. Think of the tremendous skill and strength they would get—twisting and turning and rolling over in the dirt by the hour. It would really make them strong and skillful. Then they had what they called dancing. They wanted to make their boys wonderfully strong, skillful and beautiful.

In other lessons, Elliott theorized about the kinds of male friendships forged in the Greek gymnasia. "Finer, stronger, and more powerful . . . than the individual friendship between two men," "the social friendship" would bring about a renewed "social feeling" throughout society, transcending interest in the individual. The creation of such friendship, he argued, was the responsibility of the social worker.[61]

The links Elliott made between a democratic form of "social friendship" and an eroticized Socratic pedagogy did not go unnoticed or unchallenged by all of his colleagues or students. Lucy Mitchell, who taught with Elliott at the Fieldston School, remembered complaining to Felix Adler that Elliott's entire pedagogy was based on "the study of the life and conditions [of] that man . . . The Greek . . . the one who took hemlock." She felt that this preoccupation with Socrates "had become a joke among the pupils." Mitchell also raised the specter of the "unspeakable" when discussing Elliott's relationships with his students. When asked to give an anecdote, she responded: "Oh dear me, not anything I'd want to tell. . . . It was more what the children said and what the children thought and that isn't anything to be repeated." Others, recounting their memories of Elliott after his death, expressed unease when asked to talk about his relationship with his charges. One woman, when asked about Mark McCloskey's relationship with Elliott, characterized it as "a very different kind of relationship . . . a very close one" and told her interviewer, "if you and I were simply talking as people I might tell you things that I haven't today but I can't neglect the purpose of your inquiry."[62]

The troubled response to Elliott's interactions with his students reflects the uneasy connection between Socratic pedagogy and pederasty, which inheres in a pedagogical model that eroticizes youthful male bodies within a vision of society built around bonds between men. The role of the Socratic pedagogue—the older man who instills this ideal of male friendship in young men—proved especially troubling because it resonated with contemporary fears about the sexual corruption of youth. Such fears circulated widely in late-Victorian America and became the subject of numerous reform crusades. When the fears dealt with sexual relations between men, they were much more troublesome and more difficult to address. Indeed, the emergence of a Socratic form of pedagogy at British universities earlier in the nineteenth century had caused similar "problems." Troubled by the role of Socrates as a "corrupter of youth" and the simultaneous recovery of "Greek Love," British classicists like Benjamin Jowett were accused of corrupting youth and promoting "boy love." Such connections between pederasty and Socratic pedagogy motivated an uneasy, if hesitant, critique of Elliott as well.[63]

Because Elliott and Stover drew so heavily on male traditions of cross-class homoeroticism and on privileged male access to public space, their careers differed in significant ways from those of their more prominent female counterparts. Most important, settlement women formed their primary relationships not with working-class clients but with one another. But they shared the male settlement reformers' belief that a reimagined sexuality was essential for bridging the chasm between social classes. Indeed, a class-based analysis of sexuality was central to the concept of "human brotherhood" espoused by Jane Addams, the movement's most prominent social thinker. "Tak[ing] a page from the Greeks," Addams argued that the "fundamental sex susceptibility . . . suffused the world with its deepest meaning and beauty."[64] She felt, however, that sexuality had become misdirected in industrial society and manifested itself in "vice and enervation." She located "vice" primarily in the commercialized street life of working-class neighborhoods and "enervation" within the confines of the middle-class family that thwarted young peoples' desire to participate in the cultivation of democratic civic life.[65] Drawing on Plato's dialogue between Socrates and Diotima, Addams argued that the sexual impulse must be freed from both limited family reproduction and mere sensual pleasure. Redirected to "the affairs of imagination" by people of all classes, the sexual impulse would bring renewed life to the city.[66]

These connections between Addams's writing on sexuality and the careers of Elliott and Stover carry three implications for our understanding of the settlement movement and its historical legacy. First, a reformation of American sexuality stood at the center of settlement house ideology. Both male and female leaders of the movement believed that refashioning sexual desire was crucial to the project of overcoming class difference. Although they shared a broad middle-class perception that working-class neighborhoods were highly sexualized spaces, they also saw that characteristic as a source of great possibility for the creation of new forms of social organization. Such a reorganization never came to be, but these men and women established sexual identities and practices that conformed neither to the middle-class norms of their day nor to current binary notions of heterosexuality and homosexuality.

Second, the settlement movement was not organized solely along the lines of gendered identity. It promoted collaboration among men and women who did not subscribe to dominant gender and sexual roles. This collaboration remained fruitful and held out the possibility for a transcendence of strict gender categories well into the twentieth century. Indeed, Elliott and Stover maintained close friendships with Addams and Wald throughout their lives. The friendship between Elliott and Wald grew especially close: Wald even requested that "her dear friend John

Elliott" speak at her funeral and serve as executor of her will.[67] Correspondence between the two aging reformers suggests that an understanding of each other's sexuality comprised a primary bond. In one 1933 letter, for example, Elliott wrote to Wald raving about the controversial film *Maedchen in Uniform*, which depicted lesbian relationships in a German boarding school.[68] During the same year, Wald wrote to Elliott about her "very, very nice" new companion with language of playful gender inversion: "I call her 'Everyman'," she wrote, "and she is very pleasing."[69] These exchanges point to the intriguing possibility that in addition to the gendered networks of the "female dominion," settlement reformers developed networks of sexual subjectivity that crossed gender lines.

Third, the shared connections between male and female settlement reformers offer some insight into their eventual career paths and the potent anti-same sex discourse that would take hold in American political culture in the twentieth century. Feminist historians have shown that as medical models of homosexuality gained greater authority and circulation in the first decades of the century, women involved in politics—especially those who remained unmarried and those who espoused leftist and feminist convictions—were increasingly stigmatized as perverted, pathological, and un-American. The vilification of these women through this rhetoric of sex and gender significantly circumscribed the social and political changes they were able to achieve.[70] The growing discomfort with male settlement reformers' same-sex relations in the same period suggests that some men experienced a similar fate. Indeed, as the next chapter makes clear, male reformers were increasingly configured as threats to sexual and political order.

5

Daddy George and Tom Brown

Sexual Scandal, Political Manhood, and Self-Government Reform

On January 16, 1916 an overflow crowd of more than 3,500 gathered at New York City's Carnegie Hall to attend a protest meeting. The local press characterized the event as "remarkable in the history of New York" because of the unusual social composition of the audience. Attendees included not only the city's leading public figures—among them such notables as Dr. Felix Adler, head of the Society for Ethical Culture, and the settlement reformer Lillian D. Wald—but also hundreds of ex-convicts.[1] The *New York Tribune* reported that those on the platform included "doctors, lawyers, clergymen, bankers, brokers, retired capitalists, and active philanthropists," while in the audience, "pickpockets rubbed elbows with women of another stratum, a-glitter with diamonds, while burglars were sleeve to sleeve with burghers whose possessions at another time might have been of engrossing professional interest to them."[2]

The purpose of this meeting was to express public opposition to the recent grand jury indictment of Thomas Mott Osborne, the charismatic prison reformer and warden of the notorious Sing Sing Penitentiary in nearby Ossining, New York. Journalists linked this unlikely commingling of the respectable and the criminal to the reforms Osborne promulgated throughout his career. In numerous speeches and articles, he defied conventional wisdom by asserting that there was no such thing as a distinct and identifiable "criminal class." He argued instead that criminal acts stemmed from a multitude of causes, including economic inequality, and that all classes of society harbored individuals who had broken the law. Moreover, Osborne heralded the rehabilitative potential of prisons and maintained that distinctions between prison culture and the culture at large must be minimized. To this end, he had instituted at Sing Sing a Mutual Welfare League, an ostensibly "self-governing" body, which allowed inmates a degree of authority in prison affairs and discipline.[3]

Featured speakers at Carnegie Hall heralded Osborne as a courageous and innovative force in reform and linked his work to broader Progressive efforts to achieve good government and social equity. They argued that the Mutual Welfare League had been successful in producing "good citizens," not merely "good prisoners," and that Osborne's reforms were not an isolated experiment or "one-man product" but fit squarely "with the most advanced authoritative educational practice." They stressed that the benefits extended beyond prison walls. Felix Adler, for example, characterized Osborne as a representative of "a great redemptive movement": "For Mr. Osborne is not only redeeming the prisoner," he proclaimed, "he is trying to redeem us."[4]

The grand jury indictment, initiated by the state's Department of Corrections, painted a very different picture of Osborne's reforms. It alleged that the Mutual Welfare League, rather than "redeeming" prisoners, allowed "unworthy and unfit inmates control, direction, and management of the discipline and police" of Sing Sing, thereby undermining the authority of guards and administrators and "affording the inmates opportunities to commit diverse crimes."[5] Osborne's defenders, in speeches at the Carnegie Hall meeting and in numerous editorials, denied such charges and insisted that the indictment represented a "frame-up." One typical editorial suggested that Osborne was being persecuted by "politicians regretful of lost patronage, and purveyors of supplies who are bemoaning the good old days when they could 'do business' with the prison on terms better worth their while."[6]

Osborne partisans sought not only to situate him at the center of Progressive innovation in penology and education but also to present him as a man whose noble character stood in stark contrast to the charges of his critics. Charles W. Eliot, president of Harvard and Osborne's friend, called him "an upright, conscientious, pure, and honorable man whose nature has carried him with ardor into several forms of philanthropic work."[7] An editorialist from the *New York Times* similarly characterized him as a reform hero—an independently wealthy man who nonetheless bravely and selflessly conducted his work in "an environment, which to most men of his breeding and training would be repulsive."[8] Such depictions were often qualified with references to Osborne's image as temperamental, even eccentric, indicating a certain defensiveness on the part of his defenders. Eliot, for example, referring to Osborne's tendency to "strong emotion" and "quick sympathies," opined that "a man of [Osborne's] temperament suffers severely in body and soul from unreasonable criticism." Another supporter asserted that he had "the temperament of the reformer, its noble enthusiasms, its indiscretions and eccentricities, if you will."[9]

These attempts to defend Osborne's "temperament" implicitly made reference to the most incendiary charges leveled against him—which his defenders proved extremely reluctant to address directly. Whereas Osborne's supporters represented his passionate commitment to reform as motivated by pure selflessness, his accusers maintained that it stemmed from the basest of motives: his desire for sexual relations with the prisoners he purported to reform. Indeed, state prosecutors charged not only that Osborne not only had covered up incidents of "sodomy" within Sing Sing but also had engaged in sexual relations with prisoners. His opponents imbued such sexual allegations with a political dimension; they suggested that he installed "known sodomists"—whom they identified as belonging to the group of "long timers" and repeat offenders in the prison population—as leaders of the Mutual Welfare League, thereby disempowering the more "worthy" short-term prisoners, including white-collar criminals and younger, first-time offenders.[10]

Many Osborne supporters in the reform community professed disbelief at the charges of "immorality" leveled against him. Maintaining that his character was "beyond suspicion," a *New York Times* editorialist, for example, held that "the gross and monstrous acts with which he is charged are unbelievable. Nobody believes them."[11] Others pointed to Osborne's status as a widower and father of four sons, as well as to his impressive physique and aggressive "masculine" style, as evidence of the absurdity of such charges. Yet rumors about sexual impropriety had circulated in political and reform circles for quite some time. Osborne, who often disguised himself in a variety of working-class personae, had been arrested more than once while he rode the rails in hobo costume. His political enemies charged that on one of these occasions, he was caught engaging in sex with a young man in a boxcar. Even though most reformers dismissed such allegations as mere rumor, they had grown familiar with the shadow of sexual suspicion cast on Osborne by the time of his indictment.[12]

The reform community had, only three years earlier, dealt with another sexual scandal involving an associate of Osborne's in the "self-government" reform movement: William R. George, founder of the George Junior Republic, a "self-governing" community of "bad boys and girls," most from New York City, in the rural upstate town of Freeville. George, popularly referred to as "Daddy George" by the community's young citizens, was accused in 1913 of fathering the child of a teenage female, hypnotizing both male and female citizens for unknown purposes, and sleeping in the beds of both males and females. Although the State Board of Charities ultimately dismissed these allegations, George's defense that he suffered "memory lapses" and could not recall episodes in which he occupied the beds of his young charges did not help to instill confidence in his leadership. Indeed, Osborne, who served as the President of the Board of the George Junior Republic (and was known as "Uncle Tom" to the young residents), joined with a state-appointed investigating committee in insisting that George disassociate himself from the republic on the grounds that his passionate investment in and personal connections to the community impeded its efficient and "professional" operation.[13]

It is not difficult to understand how the projects of Osborne and George became subjects of sexual scandal. Like male settlement reformers such as Charles Stover and John Lovejoy Elliott, both men insisted that reform could only be achieved through the establishment of close and intimate relationships between the reformer and his immigrant, working-class, and poor constituents. Moreover, like the settlement reformers, Osborne and George directed their projects primarily toward men and boys; the improved democracy they hoped to create was a decidedly masculine one. They also expressed profound ambivalence regarding their own gender and class positions in relation to these men and youths. They believed that working-class and immigrant men owned a more vigorous and visceral masculinity than did middle-class men, who had been weakened by

Victorian domesticity and an estrangement from physical exertion. Like their settlement counterparts, George and Osborne endeavored to fashion their own masculine images to these standards and therefore sought out and emulated "rough" working-class men and youths. Osborne, as has been noted, went so far as to actually impersonate such men.

Yet, despite such similarities, male settlement reformers were never implicated in the same kind of sexual scandal, even though the possibility of their erotic interest in their constituents became fodder for gossip. The self-government reformers were more susceptible to scandal because of their much closer relationship to the state. Unlike the settlement reformers, who built privately funded organizations, Osborne and George occupied positions of power under the control of increasingly professionalized state institutions. As warden of Sing Sing, Osborne was an employee of the New York State Department of Corrections. George, who accepted guardianship of minors often referred by state orphanages and the juvenile justice system, was subject to the oversight of the State Board of Charities. Moreover, both focused on individuals explicitly defined as state dependents: prisoners and minors.

The fact that these reformers aimed to change the nature of these individuals' relation to the state by promoting greater levels of autonomy—or self-government—within penal and quasi-penal institutions made their projects vulnerable to charges of permitting excessive "license" among people whose claims to independence remained open to question. This vulnerability was only compounded by the fact that Osborne and George concentrated on those whom many considered beyond the reach of reform. Whereas the settlement reformers most often cultivated the brightest and most engaged young men in the neighborhood, Osborne and George loudly asserted that they were interested only in the "roughest," "toughest," and "baddest" young men.[14] Their interest in those defined as criminals—or potential criminals—appealed to the perfectionist philosophies of some Progressives, who often trumpeted the near-miraculous conversions produced by self-government reform. But this interest also raised doubts among more critical commentators, who maintained that hard-line punishment was the only tenable means of dealing with crime. Critics of both men drew on the familiar figure of the misguided sentimental reformer, accusing them of "coddling" offenders who deserved to be punished.

The self-government reformers' interest in "badness" raised other, more damaging, questions related to motivation. As discussed in chapter 1, critics in the late nineteenth century began to deride reformers as sexually suspicious; indeed, they went so far as to conflate Oscar Wilde's desire for sex with men with his reform principles. Moreover, as Mary Blanchard has shown, Americans' experience and critique of Wilde had focused, in part, on his interest in and appeal to working-class youths—especially his affinity for "bad boys."[15] Like Wilde, prison reformers were especially suspect, due at least in part to their sympathy for a population considered to lack sexual morals. A hard-line penologist who investigated Osborne in 1915 broadly criticized "the promiscuous activity of the so-called professional reformers, who, by some strange mental or moral perversion, seem always to be arrayed on the side of the evil-doer and against the law abiding citizen."[16]

The charges against both George and Osborne were eventually dismissed and neither, of course, left concrete evidence that they engaged in sexual relations with their constituents. Like so many reformers who began their careers in the late nineteenth century, both men maintained that crossing class and ethnic lines to produce social change would not only benefit those "reformed" but also "redeem"—to use Felix Adler's term—themselves as well. Like Jane Addams, they believed in the "subjective" power of reform to invigorate and instill a sense of purpose among the privileged classes. But this subjective element presented a paradox inherent in the two predominant meanings of self-government. On one hand, the term connoted political values, including personal liberty, democratic elections, and free-market economics. On the other hand, the term also suggested personal values linked to traditional notions of middle-class respectability: frugality, delayed gratification, and control over sexual impulse.[17] By aligning themselves with and modeling their own personae on poor and working-class men who often rejected such values, George and Osborne appeared to transgress the traditional tenets of individual self-government.

George's and Osborne's cases illustrate the extent to which ideas of "the political" and "the sexual" are mutually constituted—in particular, how the government of one's own gendered and sexualized body was a crucial component of ideals of masculine citizenship in the Progressive Era United States. George, Osborne, and their supporters presented their self-government projects as transforming potentially unruly subjects simultaneously into self-governing individuals *and* citizens of a self-governing republic. In other words, the process of "making" male citizens involved education in the forms of physical and sexual self-regulation associated with ideals of respectable middle-class manliness. Critics of reform projects aimed at ameliorating class inequities remained suspicious that such transformations were possible; they doubted the motivations of middle- and upper-class men who attempted to cross class lines, fearing they strayed so far from respectability that they were incapable of governing their own selves. A close study of George's reform project offers insight into complicated attempts to define citizenship and to produce male citizens at a time of immense demographic change and social upheaval. It also shows how middle-class and elite male reformers of working-class men and youths could become subjects of sexualized critique and scandal.

Self-Government, Sexuality, and Governmentality

At the turn of the twentieth century, prominent Americans invoked the concept of self-government with great frequency. Advocates of women's suffrage claimed denying women the vote violated principles of self-government. Municipal reformers, resistant to political party control of urban affairs, offered local self-government as an alternative to municipal corruption and inefficiency. Critics of Spanish colonial practices argued that colonized populations, in particular Cubans, should be allowed to govern themselves, while some American imperialists alleged that non-European populations were unfit for self-government. Native-born Americans worried that immigrants, particularly Southern and Eastern Europeans and Asians, threatened political and social stability due to their inexperience with or hostility to principles of self-government.[18]

Although definitions and uses of "self-government" varied markedly, they almost always tied the individual citizen to the state; the ability to exercise self-control—most often defined in terms of middle-class respectability, frugality, delayed gratification, and sexual moderation—was a necessary prerequisite for democratic citizenship.[19] A corollary premise held that democratic forms of government thrive only if citizens have learned to control themselves. As a civics periodical proclaimed: "What self-control is to the individual, self-government is to the nation. The nation is best governed which has learned self-government."[20] Thus, the ubiquity of a discourse of self-government might be understood in relation to broader efforts to define the personal and political qualities comprising the "citizen."

However, relations of the individual citizen to government also involve understandings of sexuality. As Foucault has shown, beginning in the eighteenth century, liberal governments concerned themselves with the management of populations, conceived of as living organisms. As governments took responsibility for the reproduction of populations, "sexuality" emerged as a field that linked individual bodies to the collective body; "rational" liberal governments managed its health and reproduction through the exercise of sexual discipline and control on the part of rational liberal subjects.[21]

Thus sexuality might be understood as a constitutive component of multiple and varied arenas of governance that do not, on the surface at least, appear to involve sexual behavior or sexual identity formation. The struggle over party allegiance and patronage, which provided the political context for George's and Osborne's reform projects, was one such arena. Like many other reformers, George and Osborne believed that an unwavering allegiance to party and political patronage prevented men from becoming self-governing citizens; instead, they were subject to the tyranny of political "bosses." Indeed, the Junior Republic and the Mutual Welfare League attempted to produce a new form of male association comprising self-governing citizens free of party sovereignty. In other words, the success of the self-government reform scheme relied on the production of more disciplined selves, or, as political theorist Barbara Cruikshank asserts: "to be self-governing is to be both citizen and subject, both subject to and the subject of government."[22]

The George Junior Republic aimed to reform the behaviors of sexualized and criminalized urban populations in order to produce disciplined citizens who, ostensibly, would become loyal to the democratic system rather than to machine politicians. That the reformers viewed these goals as inherently connected is evinced by continuous and vexed attempts to deal with both sexual and political discipline. Perhaps ironically, this conflation of sexual and political self-government offered a powerful rhetorical framework for those who attacked their efforts.

DADDY'S BOYS: ADVENTURES IN SELF-GOVERNMENT REFORM

Daddy's boys are corkers
They're not the kind that's slow
They're born and bred New Yorkers
I would have you know.
You may talk about your laddies,
Your little Fauntleroys,
They're all back-numbers when compared with Daddy's boys.[23]

In the last years of the nineteenth century, word of "a novel social experiment" reached the American reading public. Daily newspapers and popular periodicals announced the founding of "The Smallest Republic in the World," the George Junior Republic in Freeville, New York, populated by "street gamins from New York City," in densely illustrated accounts of the unique spectacle of "lilliputian citizens" electing government officials, conducting business with tin currency, and, most colorfully, guarding one another in prison cells and on the work gang. Religious publications extolled the "civilizing and Christianizing" power of the republic and beseeched readers to make financial contributions. Prominent intellectuals, notably John R. Commons in the *Journal of Sociology*, assessed the contributions of this "experiment in charity, penology, and pedagogy." These accounts took special notice of the charismatic leadership of William R. George, popularly known as "Daddy George," the organization's adult founder.[24]

This wave of press attention followed George's public announcement in 1897, two years after the community's inception, that "general badness was a qualification for admittance to the Republic, at least so far as it concerned the boy." The idea caught on "like wildfire," according to George—"the very nature of the work calculated to draw it into the limelight"—and resulted in the enrollment of scores of new citizens via New York City's juvenile penal system and the vast network of voluntary philanthropies.[25] Indeed, the entire project evolved from George's growing interest in the "baddest of the bad boys" from the city's tenement districts. Like other middle-class reformers, George found in the boys of the street the means not only to redeem American democracy but also to redefine his own role within a rapidly changing and uncertain world. For George, establishing a "self-governing" community was an opportunity for remaking his own self.[26]

George's entry into the world of juvenile reform mirrors in crucial ways the experiences of a whole coterie of men from the respectable classes who were drawn to "boy work" at the end of the nineteenth century.[27] He was born to a comfortable agricultural family in West Dryden, New York—a village outside of Ithaca—in 1866. He found it difficult to establish friendships with neighborhood boys, who perceived him as nervous and pampered. The diaries he kept in his youth document his growing immersion in an expanding literature targeted to the boy market. George was particularly devoted to adventure stories and remarked that "the Horatio Alger books, telling of poor street gamins, who, after much hardship, finally became useful citizens, gave me special thrills."[28] As Michael Moon has pointed out, works in this genre romanticized cross-class relationships between working-class youths and middle-class men.[29]

George's favorite work of fiction, however, was a different kind of adventure novel: Daniel Defoe's *Robinson Crusoe*, which George rated second only to the Bible as an influence on his life and career.[30] Although published in 1719, *Robinson Crusoe* remained enormously popular throughout the eighteenth and nineteenth centuries in Great Britain and the United States and influenced the writing of juvenile fiction in both countries. Scholars have shown that *Robinson Crusoe* and other books like it inspired committed support for imperialism among generations of Anglo-American boys and men. As Jeffrey Richards has argued, such tales of overseas adventures "energies[ed] and validat[ed] the myth of empire as a vehicle for excitement, adventure and wish-fulfillment through action."[31]

The importance of *Robinson Crusoe* to George suggests that the influence of adventure stories extended beyond the imperial project to an immediate psychological level. Like George, the young Crusoe is an aimless loner who bridled at the expectations imposed on him by his family and sought to escape the constraints of family and society. Crusoe manages to transform himself and make a new world through his adventures at sea and on his seemingly deserted island. This process of self-creation, illustrated so compellingly in the novel, seemed to open enormous possibilities for George and other American men. The journalist Floyd Dell, for example, asserted that an entire generation of American boys "lived in imagination Crusoe's life, and our cramped egotism found free scope in the creation of a world after our own fancy. . . . We learned to believe that we were self-sufficient and all-conquering. We learned that the individual is by right the master of his environment."[32]

Defoe's work also inspired reform-minded men because it presented a portrait of perfected social organization, primarily through Crusoe's relationship with Friday, the young "native" whom he "rescues" and tutors in the ways of industry and Christianity. George claimed that this example taught him about the importance of social connectedness—that values such as patriotism and civic duty held no meaning for the isolated individual.[33] Crusoe's relationship with Friday permits him to extend the virtues he has developed while alone on the island—thrift, ingenuity, and hard labor—into the social realm. George similarly committed himself to teaching such virtues to the "toughs" he encountered in New York City, a process that simultaneously ended his feelings of isolation and uselessness and contributed to the social good. Other American reformers applied this lesson to domestic social problems. The labor activist Henry E. Jackson, for example, in his 1922 book *Robinson Crusoe: Social Engineer,* maintained that "the discovery of Robinson Crusoe solves the labor problem and opens the path to industrial peace." Jackson held up what he believed to be Crusoe's fair and sympathetic treatment of Friday as a model for American employers.[34]

Friday functions as an object of desire and conversion; the taming of his "native" masculinity facilitates Crusoe's social redemption.[35] Literary critics have noted that, in the adventure genre, the protagonist often forges his closest relationship with a racialized male servant like Friday. Scholar Martin Green argues that *Robinson Crusoe* and other adventure tales "told stories about men acquiring power by relating to other men, in loyalty or feud, while women are either absent or play small roles."[36] This homosocial dynamic certainly operates in Defoe's novel. As Ian Watt has argued, when Crusoe grows dissatisfied with his isolation, he "praye[s] for the company of a male slave" rather than for female companionship; moreover, Crusoe and Friday establish a social idyll without the participation of women.[37]

Like Crusoe, George sought out less "civilized" men to provide him with a sense of adventure, companionship, and social purpose. Yet

George's identification with Crusoe suggests some revealing tensions in his reform project, given that he claimed allegiance to the principle of democratic self-government. Crusoe's relationship with Friday, his "willing slave," is, after all, anything but democratic.[38] However, George insisted that he was drawn to reform not only to diminish the rigidity of class distinctions but also to educate young toughs to eschew what he believed was a slavish devotion to the criminal gang and the political machine.[39] Despite such claims, George clearly built a reform praxis that granted him a significant level of control and authority. He struggled to resolve these competing democratic and authoritarian impulses throughout his career.

Upon moving to New York City in 1881, George began to search for his own Friday in the city's poor and immigrant neighborhoods. Following in the footsteps of Alger and countless other "reform slummers," he ventured from his family's uptown townhouse to the Bowery and the Lower East Side on frequent "rambles." Bored with the manufacturing business his family had established for him and complaining of depression and nervous symptoms brought on by desk work, George devoted more of his time to "walking about the slum districts and forming the acquaintanceships of small boys occupied in making bonfires in the streets or vacant lots, playing baseball, 'shooting craps' . . . doing any or all of the many pranks in which the human young male is wont to indulge." Although his letters and diaries stress the pleasure he took in such rambles, his subsequent autobiographical writings describe them as "study of the social conditions of the great city"—a depiction likely inspired by his critics' characterization of him as sentimental and unscientific.[40]

By the early 1890s, George turned his attention to the "toughest" youths—those who belonged to gangs. Influenced by the writings of Jacob Riis, George believed that the much maligned gang actually developed as a "natural" consequence of the need for fellowship among boys and youths. He subscribed to the theory that the problem lay not in the gang's organization but in its criminal activities and its allegiance to the political machine. Likewise, he believed that the gang leader possessed the essential qualities to become a greater leader of men. As Lyman Beecher Stowe, who co-wrote the book *Citizens Made and Remade* with George, put it: "A strong will and the qualities of leadership in a boy are sure to result in his being either a very good or a very bad man. The great criminal leader has the same qualities as the great industrial or political leader. The difference between the two is not in their qualities, but in the use they make of them."[41] This belief led George on a quest to transform the gang into an agent of social good.

George's autobiographical writings describe his attempts to infiltrate two gangs in New York City: the Duffyville Gang in Harlem and the Graveyard Gang on the Lower East Side. In tales embellished in retellings over time, he asserted that he battled the toughest youths in both gangs, one at a time, until he earned their respect and was accepted as a peer and, ultimately, as their new leader. George rented abandoned lofts and established organized boxing clubs for gang members in which he participated. By relating these hyperbolic tales of physical combat and conquest in the slums, he established a persona as an authority on youth reform with the appropriate vigor to deal with gang members on their own terms.[42] Thus, these tales functioned as authorizing narratives, as did similar stories told by contemporaneous reformers, including Theodore Roosevelt and male settlement leaders.

Armed with these stories and with his professed knowledge of the workings of New York's society of street boys, George endeavored to redirect the gangs' alleged criminality. Like Riis, he asserted that militarism offered the best model for instilling obedience and organization, and he began to instruct youths in military drill exercise. George, who had always longed to live "the life of a soldier," had recently "found an outlet for [his] military enthusiasm" as a member of the National Guard.[43] In 1890 he began to take groups of youths upstate during the summer, organizing the boys in military units. He distributed uniforms to all "fresh air soldiers," the majority of whom had been rejected by the Fresh Air Fund because they "were too untidy and too troublesome" to be placed as boarders in rural homes. In the mid-1890s, George arranged a military parade for the returning youths, which closely resembled Waring's street cleaner parades. New York City newspapers heralded the arrival of the "George Industrial Brigade" and marveled at the transformation of "a ragged, unkempt, uncontrolled and uncontrollable little band of scalawags" into a tightly organized company of soldiers, complete with wooden guns and drum corps.[44]

Yet George viewed military training as a means to an end rather than an end in itself. As an advocate of the municipal reform cause that flourished in New York City in the 1890s, he maintained that newly disciplined gangs should be placed in the service of good government and attempted to break their allegiance to Tammany Hall politicians. Indeed, many gangs had affiliated themselves with individual ward politicians; the Duffyville Gang, for example, named itself after city alderman Michael Duffy. To effect this conversion, George offered the services of "his gang" (constituted from members of the Duffyville and Graveyard gangs) to monitor the 1894 election in which reform candidate William Strong was elected mayor. On election day, George's group was sworn in as "Parkhurst cops"—named after the Reverend Charles Parkhurst, whose revelation of police corruption had galvanized the reform community. The boys served as poll watchers and "spotters" who were assigned to follow suspicious voters throughout the day to ensure that they did not vote more than once. After the election, George reorganized this group as the Law and Order Gang, and received authorization to arrest offenders from Theodore Roosevelt, who served as police commissioner under Strong. The Law and Order Gang set about arresting youths involved in policy and craps "rackets." Offenders were brought back to the Eleventh Street loft that served as George's headquarters, where they were reportedly forced to box with gang members, renounce their errant ways, and then dedicate themselves to fighting for "law and order."[45]

The seeming conversion of unruly criminal gangs into disciplined agents of order and honest government received favorable notice in the local press. Flush with this adulation, George concocted a scheme to establish Law and Order gangs throughout the city; each was to serve as an adjunct police force, battling both criminals and electoral corruption.[46] George soon abandoned this plan, later claiming he disbanded the gang when he realized that the youths merely feared his strength and status and had not undergone a "true" conversion to the principles of honest government. He feared that he had replaced the hated "boss" and gang members would readily transfer their loyalty to another leader regardless of the principle espoused. As a result, he focused on the "fresh air" camp, vowing to transform it into a vehicle for inculcating the values of independence and self-government.[47]

George's narrative of the evolution of the George Junior Republic from camp to self-governing community recounts the gradual adoption of self-government principles brought on by a series of "failures." In the camp's first year, George became frustrated by his inability to control the youths' behavior and to convert them to his social and religious values. He was especially dismayed by the campers' enthusiasm for obtaining as much food and clothing as possible, which he feared reinforced tendencies toward "pauperism." He dealt with the perceived transgressions through displays of mastery in the form of daily "whipping bees" behind the woodshed, which involved as many as thirty-four victims per day. But the campers responded to each lash with "catcalls, hoots, and jeers." George claimed that he grew so troubled by the youths' enjoyment of the spectacle of punishment and by his own role "as Judge, Jury, and Grand Executioner" that he experienced an epiphany: the boys should discipline themselves.[48]

George's narrative of the problematic role of punishment in the republic's founding bears a striking resemblance to Michel Foucault's genealogical account of the transition from sovereign to governmental modes of discipline, whereby sovereign power (George's absolute rule) is replaced by liberal juridical systems.[49] Indeed, for George, the "whipping bee" realization prompted a shift in juridical authority to the youths themselves and led to the eventual adoption of the self-government structures that characterized the George Junior Republic: a judicial system, an executive branch, and representative bodies combining features of state and national government, and finally a capitalist economy utilizing Junior Republic currency.[50]

That this transformation grew out of problems concerning crime and punishment is significant. Although George and his supporters played down the community's status as a penal institution, as much as 40 percent of the population was committed by the courts or by poor law officers.[51] Moreover, all citizens under the age of 21 were legally wards of the republic and were not free to leave the grounds without a special pass granted by Daddy George or another administrator. Indeed, citizen "bounty hunters" were often sent after those who tried to "escape" (the term used by citizens) or "run away" (the term used by the adult administration).[52] Thus George, in control until 1913, retained ultimate power over the ostensibly self-governing community despite his professed worries about his own authoritarianism. The republic economy was circumscribed in similar fashion, given that George legally owned all republic property.[53]

The republic's judicial and penal systems immediately became its most heralded and its most problematic features. The popular press offered numerous accounts of punishment as well as visual images of imprisoned and shackled youths and of youths breaking stone in prison garb. Some articles featured long first-person narratives, presented in dialect, of citizens' trials and prison sentences. Similar stories also dominated the pages of *The Junior Republic Citizen*, a publication distributed to supporters and contributors and reportedly edited by the citizens themselves. The records of the early years of the republic reveal a remarkable level of judicial and penal activity, with almost every citizen serving numerous sentences "in jail" or "on the gang" for a wide array of infractions including smoking, swearing, indecency, "self abuse," sodomy, theft, libel, and vagrancy.[54]

At first this level of incarceration was treated by outside observers as picturesque and, more significantly, was held by George and his supporters as proof that the republic was not a dubious "utopian" or "sentimental" project but was instead firmly rooted in the "realities of life in a republic." John R. Commons, for example, warned against "maudlin sympathy from outsiders" who did not comprehend the republic's system of justice.[55] Moreover, such intense publicity served to accentuate a symbolic drama of redemption, in which corrupt and immigrant youths suffered and then emerged from their ordeal as productive and "reformed" American citizens, however much rates of recidivism may have cast doubt on the results.

The centrality of punishment to the George Junior Republic grew problematic after 1900, due in large part to changes within the citizen population. Pleased with his sudden fame and the outpouring of public support for the project, George, in collaboration with Thomas Mott Osborne, the new president of the board of trustees, expanded his vision of the Junior Republic; he believed it would become the model for educating and socializing youths of all classes in the American empire: "One hundred years from now there will be a National Junior Republic to which all Junior Republics will belong. . . . There will be a Republic in the Philippine Islands, Puerto Rico, Cuba, and in all Republic countries. . . . There will be no reform schools and no Homes with a capital 'H.' . . . This will become a system of education for nearly every boy or girl."[56] Indeed, advocates of the self-government cause acted on this plan by establishing new

"Steel Cages in the Jail," from William R. George's 1909 book, *The Junior Republic: Its History and Ideals.*

Junior Republics (seven in total) throughout the country. Even George's imperial plans began to be realized: W. Cameron Forbes, Governor-General of the Philippine Islands and a member of the George Junior Republic board, established a "self-governing penal colony" based on the republic model in 1904.[57]

In accordance with this grand vision, George and his board of trustees began to recruit citizens from middle- and upper-class families in an attempt to "make the Republic a democracy" comprised "of all classes of society. Riches or poverty, so-called goodness or badness."[58] Although relatively few middle-class youths entered the community, their presence was enough to bring on a chorus of criticism directed at the republic's system of punishment. As early as 1897, several middle-class boys from Rochester arrived for a two-week stay and were quickly thrown into the republic's cramped and dirty jail. When news of their travails reached Rochester, leading citizens investigated the republic and related accounts of the horrors of its prison life to the local newspapers. Such publicity dissuaded other middle-class families from sending their children to the Junior Republic and instigated a series of condemnatory reports by juvenile charity organizations throughout the state.[59] The dream of establishing juvenile self-government institutions encompassing all classes would never be realized in George's project, and only partly achieved in the national student government it inspired.[60]

The issue of sexuality and "relations between the sexes" was also of grave concern to observers of the movement. From the moment of its inception, organized charity representatives registered alarm over the "free mixing of the sexes" within the republic. Female citizens were a minority, never comprising more than one third of the population.[61] Most press reporting on the republic reflected this asymmetry by focusing almost exclusively on boy citizens in articles with titles like "The Boy Republic" and "Daddy's Boys," which minimized the presence of female residents. Indeed, a good number of the board of trustees believed that citizenship should be limited to boys for a variety of reasons, ranging from opposition to women's suffrage to the need to avoid charges of immorality between male and female citizens.[62]

Through all the debates surrounding interaction between the sexes, George steadfastly insisted that girls remain as citizens. However, he seemed little invested in the quality of their experience. He expressed ambivalence about their right to vote and left supervision of matters concerning girls in the hands of his wife, known as "Mommy George." In general, female citizens held little status or power within the republic; they were underrepresented in the government, and no girl was elected president during George's tenure. Girl citizens' work opportunities were limited as well; the most common occupations included housemaid, waitress, cook, and laundress.[63]

George's insistence on the presence of girls in the republic reflected the problematic parameters of a social vision and reform project that privileged and romanticized male camaraderie. Like the authors of masculine adventure he so admired, George was more interested in women as they affected men and male relations than as independent, autonomous agents. This functional view (as well as his misogynist interpretation of female sexuality) was strikingly illustrated in a lecture on vice he delivered to New York City youths in the 1890s, described by one observer as follows:

> His favorite appeal was to have beside him on the platform a beautiful girl with golden curls, dressed in white, and call her the City of New York; he then disfigured her with placards, tin cans, dirt marks across her face and throwing ragged clothes about her, and calling all the disfigurements the vices of the City, asking his audience whom they preferred—the girl as she was or as she now appeared.[64]

The treatment of woman as a symbol whose utility to men, rather than her own actions, imbued the polity with either favorable or unfavorable qualities also characterized George's vision of female citizens in the republic. He always described them as marginal, comparing them to a "fine bottle of wine at a banquet" and asserting: "A Republic without girls seems like some fine specimen . . . of human kind who is crippled by the loss of a leg or an arm or some other valuable member of the human organism."[65]

George also described the central function of women in the republic in sexual terms: their presence, he declared, kept men from acting on "unnatural" desires. He was so concerned with the problematic aspects of homosociality that he frequently spoke of the "unnatural" danger that he attributed to sex segregation:

> the moment you introduce unnatural conditions, you introduce unnatural thoughts into the mind, some of which have heretofore given no thought upon the subject at all, and the result is that an unnatural social atmosphere produces unnatural reasoning, and vicious suggestions find root in some lives in which there has never been more than a passing thought about the immoral.

Asserting a correlation between sex segregation and homosexual behavior, George further argued that "[exclusively male] Republics can never expect to reach such high standards of mental, physical, and moral perfection as those which have girls as citizens, any more than a town composed solely of cowboys and miners or a military camp of soldiers can be an ideal community."[66]

The functional presence of girls and young women as second-class citizens did not, in and of itself, prevent the blurring of lines between the male homosocial camaraderie George believed constituted self-government and the corrupting influence of "unnatural" homoeroticism. He expressed opposition to segregation based on race or gender, although he never demonstrated a commitment to racial or gender equality; only a handful of citizens during his tenure came from non-European backgrounds. However, he remained ideologically committed to strict exclusion of the "moral pervert" who threatened to corrupt "normal" individuals and disrupt productive social relations and therefore had "no place" in a republic.[67]

Concerns about sexual propriety in the republic came to a head in 1913, with the previously described investigation by the State Board of Charities. Although cleared of the immediate charges, George was cited for "inappropriate" behavior, and the board ordered the republic to enforce policies that would segregate male and female citizens and institute forms of organization modeled on the family home. Following the board's report, Thomas Mott Osborne, who had grown increasingly critical of George's leadership, resigned as chairman of the board of trustees and George was stripped of direct responsibility for operation of the republic.[68]

TOM BROWN'S PRISON DAYS

Thomas Mott Osborne, William George's chief collaborator, in no way shared the professed aversion to the kinds of "segregated" communities that George believed stood in opposition to the ideal republic. For Osborne, the homosocially organized community represented an ideal and a desired destination that he actively sought throughout his life. Ultimately, he devoted his career to the reform of one such community—the prison. He came to believe that this and other segregated male communities provided the perfect environment for fostering democratic self-government principles.

Throughout his career, Osborne showed little inclination to address the concerns of women in any of his reform projects and writings. Indeed, when the fight for women's suffrage gained strength in the years following World War I, he expressed opposition to the movement and endorsed the position espoused by the Man Suffrage Association Opposed to Political Suffrage of Women (MSA). This organization, chaired by New York City municipal and tariff reformer Everett P. Wheeler, opposed women's suffrage based on an expanded version of the traditional ideology of separate spheres. Rather than disparage women's abilities or political usefulness, the MSA readily admitted that women had played a central role in carrying out a number of Progressive Era reforms. However, it attributed the success of Progressive women to their status as outsiders to the system of electoral politics; it was precisely because they did not have an "interest" in the corrupt workings of the political system that they functioned as reliable and "objective" advocates for the social good. MSA publications claimed that elected officials trusted and followed the advice of female reformers because they were not implicated in the contest for favors and patronage and asserted that women would be best served by staying in this position of political "purity."[69]

Osborne's opposition to women's suffrage appears surprising in light of his background. He counted among his immediate family some of the most renowned women's rights activists in the country's history. His maternal great aunt was Lucretia Mott, the famous abolitionist and co-organizer of the Seneca Falls Convention for the Emancipation of Women in 1848. His maternal grandmother, Martha Coffin Wright, chaired the Seneca Falls Convention. His mother, Eliza Wright Osborne, an agitator for women's political and economic rights, joined Elizabeth Cady Stanton and other suffrage activists in attempting to vote every election day despite the fact that women were barred from the polls. Moreover, Osborne's childhood home in Auburn, New York served as a prominent meeting place for women's rights activists; frequent visitors included Mott, Stanton, and Susan B. Anthony.[70]

By all accounts, Osborne grew up quite happily in a household dominated by activist women and remained close to his mother, three sisters, and female relatives throughout his life. Although no firsthand documentation explaining his eventual stand against women's suffrage exists, an account of his childhood written by his friend and biographer Rudolph W. Chamberlain offers insight into Osborne's commitment to an ideology of separate spheres. Chamberlain suggests that Osborne had significant difficulty negotiating between the homosocially segregated worlds of women and men. He remained unduly attached to the world of girls and women until he left for boarding school in adolescence, at which point he began to look for companionship almost exclusively among men. According to Chamberlain, the only significant relationship Osborne formed with a woman as an adult was with his wife, Agnes Devens Osborne.

In his fascinating 1935 biography, *There Is No Truce: A Life of Thomas Mott Osborne,* Chamberlain associated Osborne's eventual interest in social reform with "the streak of femininity in his own nature." Interestingly, while Chamberlain steadfastly rejected all charges of "unnatural" sexuality leveled against his subject, he nevertheless utilized a model typically linked to male homosexuality in constructing a psychological portrait of Osborne's childhood; Osborne had a remote and stern father and a domineering mother, and was drawn to play activities and interests typically associated with girls.[71] In a chapter entitled "Apron Strings," Chamberlain argued that due to excessive control by his mother, "young Tom came more and more to indulge his own tastes, which were feminine to begin with." These included sewing, knitting, crotcheting, and playing with dolls, all of which reportedly embarrassed his sisters.[72] Chamberlain also intimated that the young Osborne's feminine appearance and exuberant love of finery "embarrassed" other males, asserting that "the masculine code enjoins a high scorn for such things."[73]

As a young man, Osborne began to consciously move away from the female domain of his childhood. Like his friend (and later nemesis) Theodore Roosevelt, he did not fully develop a "masculine" persona until his college years at Harvard. In contrast to his effeminate youthful image, observers of the adult Osborne often noted his large, muscular physique as well as his confident and assertive self-presentation. Osborne's earliest identification with the world of the boy came as a teenager when he discovered the same body of juvenile literature that had so enraptured William George. At Adams Academy and Harvard, where Osborne matriculated in 1880, an overriding ethos of muscular Christianity had taken hold of the university culture; Osborne sought out male camaraderie almost exclusively, participating in organized sports and in fraternal organizations.[74] According to Chamberlain, he finally learned "to play as boys play" and established friendships that "meant more to Tom Osborne than they do to most men." These male friendships "gripped him completely" and "satisfied an unrealized hunger in his soul." At the same time, Chamberlain maintained that he was "apt to feel bewildered or repelled by the attention of female admirers."[75]

Despite this seeming antipathy, at the end of his college career Osborne married Agnes Devens, a young woman from an elite Boston family. In 1886, the couple moved to his hometown of Auburn, where Osborne worked, unhappily, as an executive at his family's successful agricultural machinery business, D. M. Osborne and Company. Osborne's married life lasted only ten years. His wife died in 1896 while giving birth to the youngest of four sons. After that, Osborne turned his attention away from the domestic sphere; he claimed to have no desire to remarry, arguing that such a move would be tantamount to "bigamy." Friends noted a marked change in his temperament and demeanor. Chamberlain asserted that while married, Osborne was "blissfully content in surroundings of domesticity," but in his latter years he "carried with him an atmosphere of the arena and strode among men, wary, belligerent, as if suspecting a foul blow."[76]

As a widower, Osborne devoted himself to two passions: masquerade and reform politics. His love for costume and theatrics had emerged when he was quite young; Chamberlain linked his "delight in impersonation" to his "feminine" fondness for playing imaginary games with dolls and puppets and his love of fancy clothing. Indeed, Osborne continued his involvement in theater throughout his life, appearing in Hasty Pudding productions at Harvard and organizing amateur theatricals in Auburn.[77] Yet, in middle age, he engaged in a very different sort of performing. He disguised himself as a variety of working-class and poor men and sought male companionship in saloons and the streets. Osborne took to "riding the rails" disguised as a "tramp" or "hobo," to use the parlance of the day, and would disappear from his home for days at a time, often traveling to New York City. His diaries reveal that he developed a range of masculine personae, including those he named "Dude, Doctor, Old Gent, Mexican, Italian, and Colored Gent." Osborne's diaries, in which he used the Greek symbol psi to refer to masquerading activities, also indicate that he formed friendships with other tramps over the years.[78] Osborne continued these escapades throughout his life, much to the consternation of his family and friends, who worried about this "unconventional" and "abnormal" behavior.[79]

In spite of such criticism, Osborne invested his penchant for masquerading with a degree of legitimacy by linking his activities to his interest in reform politics. He reversed a long-standing affiliation with the Republican Party after "bolting" to support the election of Cleveland in 1884 (much to the horror and dismay of his mother) and successfully ran as a Democrat for mayor of Auburn in 1896.[80] In that office, Osborne recast his masquerades as investigations into vice in the city and as fact-finding missions to determine the level of public support for his administration. When he was appointed as New York State Public Service Commissioner after serving two terms as mayor, he "tramped" throughout the state on the railroads to investigate safety on the rails, eventually issuing a report, which resulted in stricter regulations.[81]

Other prominent figures of the era, including the Reverend Charles Parkhurst, Theodore Roosevelt, and the muckraker Josiah Flynt, also went undercover to investigate and publicize charges of official corruption and moral turpitude.[82] At a time when reform had not yet professionalized, such publicized investigations could lend a veneer of credibility to reformers eager to present themselves as authorities on a particular social problem. Yet reform masquerades clearly served other, less "objective" functions. Such performances might also be understood to fulfill the emotional/psychological impulses for reform—the "subjective" desires and motivations so lucidly described by Jane Addams. In a sense, impersonation represented a more extreme version of other Progressive strategies to cross class lines, including settlement reformers' relocating to tenement neighborhoods and dressing in the style of the working class. These measures were meant not only to better address the perceived needs of reform constituents but also to enable elite reformers to break free of bourgeois restraints.[83]

Although Osborne established his reform reputation in large part through his spectacular acts of impersonation, his interest in masquerading transcended the reform context. He "tramped" in working-class costume both before and after his career in reform politics, even though such excursions had damaged his reputation and alienated members of his family. Chamberlain characterized this interest in impersonation as a kind of uncontrollable compulsion, maintaining that "Osborne could no more resist the excitements of masquerading than a toper can resist the stimulant."[84] Yet alongside this negative assessment, Chamberlain linked his "fundamental urge" to assume other identities and thereby "unshackle the bolts of identity" to his great success as a reformer: "He put on a convict's livery to see with the convict's eye."[85] According to Chamberlain, Osborne's "capacity for putting himself in another's place" explained "his deep sympathy with his fellow man."[86]

Thomas Mott Osborne (left) and Reverend Samuel Eliot, Hasty Pudding Club show, Harvard (undated). Photo by J. Notman, Boston.

Courtesy The Osborne Family Collection, The George Arents Research Library, Syracuse University, Syracuse, New York

That Osborne attempted to "unshackle the bolts of identity" by masquerading among two specific populations—hoboes and convicts—is interesting for two key reasons. First, it underscores his long-standing desire to establish camaraderie with men whose background differed markedly from his own. Osborne explained his affinity for such rough groups of men in terms of his admiration for their steadfast loyalty to one another and to the masculine code of honor they shared. As the historian George Chauncey argues, these communities were at the core of a thriving bachelor subculture, characterized by "a rejection of domesticity and of bourgeois acquisitivism" and "based on a shared code of manliness and an ethic of male solidarity."[87]

Second, both of these populations offered alternatives to respectable forms of marriage and sexuality through prominent male affectionate and erotic relationships. By the turn of the twentieth century, both the expanding hobo world, comprised primarily of male migrant laborers, and the culture of the prison had become firmly established as social spaces characterized by a high incidence of sexual relationships between men. So close was this association that in 1904 Josiah Flynt contributed an appendix on "Homosexuality Among Tramps" to the second edition of Havlock Ellis's influential text *Sexual Inversion*.[88] Historian Regina Kunzel has shown that same-sex relations, whether configured as "perversion" or in the sexological categories of "inversion" or "homosexuality," permeated discourse about prisons in this period.[89] Moreover, male relations in both of these sites were largely organized in a gendered system that, according to George Chauncey, also characterized urban culture in this period. Relationships often involved a "wolf" or "jocker"—typically an older male who, according to Chauncey, often "combined homosexual interest with a marked masculinity"—and a "punk," a younger and sometimes effeminate partner. While some wolf-punk relationships did not involve sexual relations, many did.[90]

Osborne formed such a "wolf-punk" relationship in the early period of his masquerading. Shortly after the death of his wife, he met a young man who took the alias Louis Schaedeline, whom he "had found in a reform school," and brought him to live in his Auburn mansion. Schaedeline, according to Chamberlain, "was a perfect physical specimen . . . solidly yet gracefully built, with dark skin and strong aquiline features."[91] Schaedeline frequently rode the rails with Osborne; it was he, also dressed in tramp regalia, who was found with Osborne when he was arrested in Syracuse. While no extant documents reveal the exact nature of the relationship between the two men, contemporary observers described them as inseparable. The use of the alias Schaedeline—which may well have functioned as an aural pun on the French term *chatelaine*, meaning "mistress of the manor"—suggests that the relationship may have been romantic. Indeed, legal documents relating to the investigation of Osborne use the latter spelling.[92]

Whether sexual or not, Osborne's relationship with Schaedeline was the first of many similar connections. Throughout his life, Osborne befriended and provided assistance to a number of young men from working-class and poor backgrounds, many of whom became members of his household. This assistance took a number of forms. To some, he offered employment at D. M. Osborne and Company or positions at businesses run by friends. Like the settlement reformers John Lovejoy Elliott and Charles Stover, he aided youths with intellectual ability and aspirations by helping them gain admittance to college and paying their tuition. Osborne looked with special favor on young men with artistic talent, providing patronage and encouragement, as well as capitalizing on his many cultural connections in New York City. Among those he helped early in their careers were the vaudeville and silent film star Raymond Hitchcock (an Auburn native); the violinist and conductor Peter Kurtz, whom Osborne first encountered working in an Auburn shoe shop; and the tenor Charles Hubbard, who eventually established a successful opera career in Paris.[93]

Like George, Osborne worried that his interventions, rather than producing independent and industrious young men in the classic Horatio Alger mode, contributed to "pauperism." Upset that many of the young men whom he helped appeared only to be interested in getting more money from him, he declared, "I have been driven to the belief that help in money is nine times out of ten a mistake."[94] When Osborne visited the Junior Republic in 1896, he became an instant convert, declaring that George had discovered the means to divest philanthropy of its tendency to promote dependence. Osborne maintained that the Junior Republic represented a "perfectly natural evolution from a benevolent tyranny, which, seeking to do its highest duty to the human beings under its charge, had unexpectedly blossomed into a self-governing community."[95] To his friend Spencer Trask, Osborne wrote that it would be impossible to overestimate the importance of the potential of the republic model: "Jail reform, prison reform, school reform, and the literal perfection of Democracy lies in it."[96] He began to make large financial contributions to the Junior Republic and eventually served as chair of the institution's board of trustees.

Despite such professed admiration for the self-government tenets of the Junior Republic, Osborne, like George, found it difficult to reconcile his own desire to influence and befriend young citizens with his commitment to promote independence. Indeed, the two men criticized each other for exercising excessive influence on the republic's boys. Osborne, who had become a frequent visitor to the community, liked to "pal around" with the young men, establishing a coterie of favorites, taking youths on fund-raising trips and vacations, and bringing some to work for his company and live with him in Auburn. Like George, Osborne reportedly favored boys with the worst reputations; one young citizen claimed, "It's funny but if a fellow's in jail or is awful tough, he's just Uncle Tom's kind."[97] George began to resent Osborne's influence, arguing that he undermined his own authority by indulging and providing refuge for discontented youths. Moreover, George expressed concern that Osborne favored the wrong kind of "bad" boy; on at least one occasion, he complained that one of Osborne's favorites—a young man whom Osborne eventually sent to Harvard University—not only had become disrespectful to George but also acted as if he were the "young lover" of an older youth.[98] For his part, Osborne came to argue that, despite his earlier claims to the contrary, the republic remained too much of a "benevolent tyranny." He advocated that George be removed on the grounds that his personal investment in the institution and his excessive control over the young citizens contradicted the ideal of self-government.[99]

Although Osborne officially disassociated himself from the Junior Republic in 1912 after a series of long and bitter conflicts with George, he remained committed to the principles of self-government as espoused and practiced at that institution. When he became active in the prison reform movement in 1910, his ultimate goal was to adapt the Junior Republic model for adult convicts. Osborne emerged as a leading force in prison reform in 1913 when, as chair of a newly formed state prison commission, he voluntarily committed himself as an inmate in the notorious Auburn Penitentiary. Drawing on his long tradition of masquerading,

Osborne assumed the identity of "Tom Brown" and insisted that he be treated exactly as any other inmate. He disseminated an account of his experiences in newspapers and periodicals throughout the country, simultaneously "exposing" deplorable conditions at Auburn and promoting a new self-governing convict organization, the Mutual Welfare League, he formed with inmates at the prison.[100]

Osborne's alias was not selected randomly. During his first year in preparatory school, he discovered a book that carried a significance for him similar to that *Robinson Crusoe* held for William George. Thomas Hughes's *Tom Brown's Schooldays*, published in 1857, is a romanticized tale of the relations between boys in an English public school. Hughes's novel, hugely influential in popularizing the ideals of "muscular Christianity" throughout Great Britain and the United States, addressed issues beyond the public school. According to one critic, Hughes intended to present a model of broader democratic class relations given "that the British constitution would have to come to terms with the inevitable advance of popular democracy and with the extension of the franchise to working men."[101] Other scholars have argued that the novel explores the utility of male romantic and erotic friendships to instill manly virtues and a sense of social "duty" in young men.[102] If *Robinson Crusoe* functioned as a fictional inspiration for William George's own dramatic narratives of desire and domination in New York City's tenement neighborhoods, *Tom Brown's Schooldays* offered a model for Osborne's developing sense of masculine virtue and purpose within a homosocial environment.

Like the fictional Tom Brown, Osborne delighted in the sense of adventure and manly camaraderie he experienced while serving his "sentence," declaring, "not since my college days had I enjoyed such a delightful sense of natural, free, unrestrained comradeship."[103] Osborne also used the persona of Tom Brown to invest himself with an authenticity and authority that other prison reformers lacked. He contended that as Tom Brown, he "lost [his] own identity so completely" that old friends failed to recognize him "among the toughest bunch of fellows in the prison."[104] And he argued that the ease with which he transformed himself into a convict and developed friendship and sympathy with other inmates revealed that the lines drawn between the criminal and the respectable were not as firm as many believed, which led him to conclude "that there is no such thing as a criminal type."[105] He appealed to reform constituents to view convicted criminals as not so different from themselves, asserting that "in the world outside we revere simple goodness; we honor truthfulness and sincerity; we love loyalty and the glorious capacity to live and, if necessary, to die for a friend. All these virtues in their intensest form we find inside the prison."[106] In insisting that convicted criminals did not represent a separate class, Osborne drew on a Progressive theory of social bonds that stressed that all members of society shared common goals and interests and posited environmental factors as the predominant cause of social ills. At the same time, he refuted the countervailing trend, dominant in the burgeoning field of eugenic criminology, to strictly categorize individuals and to define so-called "deviants" as somehow genetically, racially, congenitally different from the respectable population.[107]

Prisons failed, Osborne proposed, because they treated inmates as a distinct and separate class and therefore functioned as "artificial" or "unnatural" environments that bore little resemblance to the outside world. Just as Osborne attempted to break down distinctions between the criminal and the respectable, he proclaimed that the prison environment should resemble society as closely as possible. Foremost, prisoners should learn to govern themselves if they were to become useful members of society after their release. To this end, Osborne developed the scheme for the Mutual Welfare League.[108]

Osborne likely planned the league prior to his voluntary incarceration, but he nevertheless asserted that he concocted the scheme in collaboration with his prison work partner, Jack Murphy. Its principles were described as follows:

> First—The law must decree not punishment, but temporary exile from society until the offender has proven by his conduct that he is fit to return.
>
> Second—Society must brand no man as a criminal, but aim solely to reform the mental conditions under which a criminal act has been committed.
>
> Third—The prison must be an institution where every inmate must have the largest practicable amount of individual freedom, because "it is liberty alone that fits men for liberty."[109]

Orlando Rouland (1871–1939), who also painted portraits of Progressive Era figures Theodore Roosevelt and Chauncey DePew, depicted Osborne in character as Tom Brown, prisoner in New York's Auburn Penitentiary.

From Rudolph W. Chamberlain, There Is No Truce: A Life of Thomas Mott Osborne (1935)

Membership in the league was open to every inmate. Upon joining, members elected officers and a panel of judges called the Board of Review, which ruled on all violations except in cases of assault, refusal to work, strike, and attempted escape. By all accounts, Osborne's idea met with the immediate favor of most of Auburn's inmates, who welcomed the opportunity for more autonomy within the prison. For his part, Osborne, who was elected president of the league although his voluntary "sentence" had ended, immersed himself within prison society.[110] When Osborne was appointed warden of Sing Sing Penitentiary in 1915, he instituted the Mutual Welfare League scheme there as well.

Although Osborne depicted the league as a unique and radical solution for "the prison problem" emerging spontaneously from his interactions with inmates, the plan shared many features with the work of other Progressive Era penologists. According to historian David Rothman, Progressives redefined American penology by insisting that inmates be treated as individuals rather than as a separate class, promoting some level of autonomy and sociability among prisoners, and refiguring the penitentiary not as "an antidote to the external environment, but a faithful replication of it"—all hallmarks of Osborne's concept. Indeed, Rothman describes the league as "the design that best exemplified Progressive ambitions."[111]

Yet Osborne's approach differed markedly from that of other prison reformers in ways that reflected his sympathetic and romantic view of the male convict population. While other prominent reformers limited convict governing bodies to the "best" or most "respectable" men—usually first-time offenders and white-collar criminals with political connections on the "outside"—Osborne maintained that it was the "long timers" (sometimes referred to as "roughnecks" in prison parlance) who, due to the strength of their communal bonds and fierce loyalty to one another, offered the greatest potential for self-government.[112] Osborne asserted that inmates frequently considered the "worst lot" by prison officials actually represented the greatest potential for democracy. Claiming that "the dangerous and desperate criminal is often only the hero gone wrong," he stated that "the very qualities which made . . . the most dangerous of criminals—his skill, ingenuity, boldness, bravery, intellectual power, and loyalty" also represented "assets of the highest value of society."[113] The goal of the prison must not be to undermine these qualities but to turn them away from criminality and toward self-government.

Likewise, Osborne maintained that other prison reformers failed in their approach to discipline by relying on trusted favorites (or "snitches") to report on the wrongdoing of others, which, he contended, worked against an ethos of "honor among thieves" and created distrust, dissension, and violence among inmates.[114] According to Osborne, this method represented not reform but an extension of the corrupt workings of the larger political system in that it promoted self-interest and greed:

> As the criminal looks at society he sees what he calls "graft" everywhere: corruption in the police; corruption in politics; corruption in the district attorney's office, and all too frequently upon the bench. He finds corruption inside the prison, as he found it outside. He often finds the prison run by a combination between corrupt convicts within and corrupt contractors without. He believes that corrupt politics has located the building, built it, sells it supplies and appoints its warden. He sometimes feels himself a helpless unit in a gigantic scheme of corruption, alongside of which his own crime seems like a mere petty piece of boy's play.[115]

Osborne's assertion that modern penology merely replicated the workings of corrupt politics in society at large reveals an important contradiction in his reform ethos. Although he presented himself as a practical reformer who sought to make prisons more closely resemble normal society, he ultimately promoted a more radical and utopian vision: that, through organizations like the Mutual Welfare League, prisons could promote a purer and more effective model of democratic politics than that found outside prison walls.

Osborne's ideal vision posited the prison as a site for the development of democratic principles precisely because it stood apart from society. In this sense, Osborne resembled earlier prison reformers who sought to fashion utopian environments capable of reforming wayward citizens, although he rejected the principle of social isolation promoted by his forbearers. Osborne and his supporters described prisons as "laboratories for democracy" because they removed men from the corrupting influences of society and provided a means of social leveling in that they potentially erased privilege and class distinction. Prison reformers and wardens who privileged "short timers" and white-collar criminals and utilized favored stool pigeons to instill discipline and erode prisoner solidarity wasted this democratic potential by re-creating class divisions and conflicts within prison walls.

In essence, then, Osborne maintained that the prison provided the ideal conditions for democracy. Frank Tannenbaum, a protégé who later established his own reputation as a leading voice in American penology in the 1930s, elucidated this vision in a biography of Osborne. Arguing that the prison environment represented "a real leaven for community government and community responsibility," Tannenbaum outlined the conditions that imbued it with such potential. First, he argued, "physical proximity" and a lack of privacy ("Men eat, sleep, work, play, laugh, and weep, and attend to the needs of nature, all in each other's presence") made "the pressure for socialized action . . . almost inescapable." Second, the absence of economic competition ("Here men do not compete for worldly goods") and poverty produced "a certain sociability and a certain ease" and resulted in communal feeling. Third, inmates were drawn together by the presence of "a common enemy"—namely prison guards and administrators—which, according to Tannenbaum, produced soldierly comradeship.[116] While both Tannenbaum and Osborne implied that a corrupt prison administration represented a suitable common enemy, they insisted that, under a benevolent reform administration, inmates might transfer their animosity to other forms of social corruption.

An implicit element of this depiction of prison was its homosocial organization. The communal solidarity among inmates heralded by both Osborne and Tannenbaum was exclusively masculine, notable for the absence of both the "family claim" and competition for the affections of women. Yet this did not mean that sexual and romantic relations remained absent. As Kunzel has shown, Osborne and others writing on prisons at the time often addressed this "problem."[117] Although he sometimes offered seemingly contradictory explanations for homosexuality, he most often emphasized environmental rather than congenital factors, just as he did when discussing criminality. Calling sodomy "the vice which naturally results from constant confinement," he asserted that "under the best of possible prison circumstances there is bound to be immorality. Wherever there is a community consisting only of men, as in

The Old System—and

The New

Before and after images, Auburn Penitentiary, New York. The image captioned "The New" (bottom) depicts members of the Mutual Welfare League. Photos from undated Mutual Welfare League Association pamphlet.

Courtesy The Osborne Family Collection, The George Arents Research Library, Syracuse University, Syracuse, New York prison, (or in the navy, for that matter), certain unnatural immoral acts are bound to arise, because of the essentially unnatural social conditions. It is inevitable."[118] Although he employed pejorative moral rhetoric, Osborne's assertion that "unnatural acts" were not only inevitable but (seemingly paradoxically) "natural" in prison suggested an inherent and essential connection between sex-segregated communities and same-sex relations. However, Osborne imbued such communities with extraordinary potential for democratic brotherhood, thereby creating a potentially problematic, if unacknowledged, link between his romantic identification with the inmate population and the propensity of that population to engage in "immoral acts."

Osborne's political opponents were quick to make that connection explicit, as evinced by the charges of sexual impropriety brought against him in 1915. Those who brought the indictment against Osborne depicted him as fostering both sexual perversion and a perversion of the social order of the prison, which they saw as inextricably connected. They charged that his interest in the long-term prisoners—or "roughnecks"—stemmed not from a commitment to democratic equality but from his perverse sexual desire. Likewise, they alleged that rather than establishing a system of democratic self-government, Osborne imposed a corrupt and coercive regime in which he and his associates offered favors—ranging from liquor and food to the promise of abbreviated sentences and employment upon release—in exchange for sexual relations and punished those who would not comply. In making these charges, critics implicated Osborne in the dominant reform critique of sex in men's prisons: that sexual relations were inseparable from a broader system of forced indebtedness and obligation.[119] Moreover, they imbued the debate over prison self-government with both political and sexual meanings, charging that roughnecks were incapable of self-government not only because they were ignorant and ill-bred "career" criminals (thereby recapitulating the mugwump critique of universal suffrage) but also because they were "known sodomites" whose inability to govern their own sexual impulses made them unfit to govern in the political sense.[120]

In order to fully understand the lawsuit, it is important to consider the fraught political context in which Osborne served as warden of Sing Sing. From the beginning, Osborne enjoyed little support from the state prison bureaucracy. He was offered the post by Democratic Governor Glynn during his last month in office. Glynn's successor, Republican Charles Whitman, viewed Osborne as a potential political opponent (he was frequently floated as a gubernatorial prospect) and as an estimable competitor for press attention. As a vocal anti-Tammany Democrat, Osborne could count on little support from the leaders of his own party, who, like many other political leaders in the nineteenth-century United States, looked to prisons as an especially lucrative source of patronage.[121] Moreover, Superintendent of Prisons John B. Riley espoused a strict disciplinarian approach to penology and viewed Osborne as an ineffective and sentimental "coddler."[122]

Osborne also faced significant opposition from within Sing Sing itself. His predecessor, a political appointee who had worked as a plumber in New York City before becoming warden, had established the Golden Rule Brotherhood, an inmate governing body superficially modeled after the Mutual Welfare League but comprised of only short timers. The leaders included two men with significant political power: Manhattan banker William J. Cummins, convicted of business fraud, and William Willett, an ex-congressman from Queens convicted of using bribery to secure a judgeship.[123] Osborne, who viewed the Golden Rule Brotherhood as a "ghostly parody" of the league, quickly moved to replace it with an organization modeled after the one he had initiated at Auburn, in which "citizenship was to be determined by the fact that one was a prisoner and not by the fact that one was a good prisoner in the eyes of the authorities."[124] This move infuriated the leaders of the brotherhood, who argued that they had earned the right to govern.[125]

According to Osborne and other observers, the establishment of the league at Sing Sing deepened the division between two "sharply distinguished classes of prisoners": the short timers (also referred to as the "highbrows" and "silk stockings") and the long timers (or roughnecks). Frank Tannenbaum described situation as follows:

> The roughnecks were the gangsters, the thieves, the robbers, the stick-up men, the rough lot, thrown up mainly by city slums, who had lived by a rough and ready code, with little education and social contacts, their hand against every man's with no loyalties except to their little gang. The silk stockings were the bankers, the lawyers, the

> well-to-do, the men of education and family who had found their way into prison. They were clean, intelligent, but with no loyalties within the prison and concerned with no one's welfare but their own. Between them and the roughnecks there was open hostility for the control of the prison. . . . The previous warden . . . had so stacked the cards as to keep the roughnecks out of power.[126]

Many of the short timers complained that Osborne treated them unfairly by curtailing their privileges, subjecting them to solitary confinement, and transferring them to other prisons only to replace them with Osborne's cronies from Auburn. It was this group of inmates, joined by guards and administrators who held that the league threatened their ability to discipline, who launched the complaints that resulted in Osborne's indictment.[127]

The seven-count indictment, delivered on December 28, 1915—one year after Osborne became warden—reflected this class struggle within the prison.[128] In addition to several charges involving "neglect of duty," it accused him of allowing to "certain unworthy and unfit inmates . . . the control, direction, and management of the discipline and police of said prison, thereby causing confusion and rendering the efforts . . . to maintain discipline ineffectual." However, the two most sensational charges—and those that received the bulk of the press attention—alleged sexual impropriety. The sixth count charged that Osborne, "unlawfully and willfully did commit various unlawful and unnatural acts with inmates. . . . Paul Vogel, James Connelly, Max Kleinberg, Henry De Lara, Sidney Welch and various other inmates . . . thereby rendering himself incapable of commanding the respect, esteem and confidence of the inmates . . . and rendering himself incapable of maintaining discipline and proper control over inmates of said prison." The seventh count alleged that Osborne committed perjury by failing to report to prison officials that he had firsthand knowledge of a case in which one prisoner, James Harvey, admitted to having sexual relations with twenty-seven prisoners in one day.[129]

Osborne and his supporters protested that the sexual charges were manufactured in order to so embarrass and discredit him as to force his resignation, for political reasons. A *New York Times* editorial, for example, claimed the suit was instigated by "politicians regretful of lost patronage and purveyors of supplies who are bemoaning the good old days when they could 'do business' with the prison on terms better worth their while."[130] The Westchester District Attorney's office certainly conducted the case in a manner that capitalized on its potential to cause scandal; it leaked information about the "immorality" charges before issuing the indictment and decided to prosecute the perjury case prior to the other counts.[131] Yet the nature of the investigation launched by District Attorney Frederick E. Weeks and Assistant District Attorney William J. Fallon—as well as the responses it elicited from inmates and guards—indicate that the charges represented more than a "frame-up"; they clearly viewed Osborne's alleged interest and participation in same-sex relations as central to his reform project. The testimony gathered for the indictment shows that the district attorney's office pursued three central lines of inquiry intended to make the case that Osborne's "perversion" motivated his interest in reform and corrupted his administration of the prison.

First, Weeks and Fallon attempted to show that Osborne had a long history of engaging in "immoral conduct," from his previous reform efforts through his tenure at Sing Sing. They asked numerous witnesses about his penchant for masquerade, focusing especially on his "tramping" exploits with Schaedeline during his tenure as a public service commissioner; they even called the officer who had arrested the men as a witness.[132] Another witness, William Trefry, testified that the inmates had heard that Osborne "was a degenerate" and had "heard stories of him at Auburn . . . and when he was connected with the George Junior Republic." Trefry also asserted that the men had heard that while working with the Mutual Welfare League at Auburn, Osborne had kept an inmate named Duffy—whom he later had transferred to Sing Sing—as his "punk."[133] From numerous other witnesses, Weeks and Fallon elicited testimony that Osborne surrounded himself with a coterie of "degenerates," many of whom were Auburn inmates who came to Sing Sing with him. Several members of this group—including inmates bearing the colorful nicknames "O.K. Bill," "Dick Richards," and "Jack the Dropper—lived and worked in the warden's house.[134] Whereas Osborne had heralded his attachments to these men as evidence of his camaraderie with and support from the prison population, Weeks and Fallon implied that what tied them together was a shared proclivity for "perversion."

Weeks and Fallon pursued a second line of inquiry meant to show that Osborne's history of same-sex relations and his affiliation with men

known to be "degenerates" subverted order in the prison and promoted corruption—a stark contrast to the image of democratic brotherhood Osborne promoted. The district attorneys elicited testimony from sympathetic witnesses that Osborne's real motivation in instituting the Mutual Welfare League was to replace the "best men" who had led the Golden Rule Brotherhood with "the most notorious propositions in the place." The ex-congressman William Willett, for example, claimed that "the striking thing about them all [cases of sodomy] has been that in almost every case the men that have been involved were either members of the executive committee, members of the board of delegates, assistant sergeants at arms or gallery men [of the league]."[135] Such testimony, of course, drew on broader debates about the fitness of various populations for self-government, yet it posited a propensity to engage in "sodomy" as a prominent addition to the list of disqualifying factors. This point was made explicit in the following question Weeks asked of a witness: "Then it was a fact, was it, that men who were illiterate, men known to be sodomists took the place of the learned, thinking men in prison?"[136]

The grand jury investigation also painted Osborne—famous for his virulent anti-Tammany diatribes—as the "boss" of a corrupt political machine at Sing Sing in which illicit sex replaced cash bribes as the currency of the realm. Several witnesses friendly to the investigation portrayed him as a charismatic leader who ruled with absolute authority (one prisoner claimed the men treated him like an "absolute God") and used the league not as a vehicle to promote self-government but to exercise coercive control over the inmate population. One inmate asserted that Osborne ran the jail like "a political machine, as an organized effort to crush that decent element and get his own men in" and used O.K. Bill, who was reputed to be especially vicious, as a henchman.[137] Several witnesses testified that O.K. Bill and others among Osborne's circle of favorites used threats and violence to coerce younger inmates into "cocksucking" and "buggery."[138]

Weeks and Fallon elicited testimony from a number of inmates that Osborne used Mutual Welfare League officers to procure sex for him. The grand jury transcripts include a number of graphically detailed accounts of such encounters, all of which involved elements of coercion or offers of favorable treatment; Paul Vogel testified that Osborne surreptitiously sabotaged his engagement to a young woman in New York City when he broke off sexual relations; Sidney Welsh charged that Osborne threatened to "draft" him to the feared Clinton Penitentiary if he refused to engage in "foohking matches"; and Max Kleinberg, a tailor, claimed that he was allowed to alter suits on "the outside" for profit in exchange for engaging in sex.[139] In all of these narratives, Osborne functioned as a "wolf," who performed the active role sexually and favored younger, slighter men. Willett and other critics of Auburn maintained that this atmosphere of coercion created conditions for "demoralization" in which young prisoners became corrupted. These charges that so closely resembled the reform critique of machine politics were meant to subvert Osborne's idealistic reformist claims.

A third thematic strand evident in the investigation drew on the popular stereotype of the male reformer as effeminate, impractical, and sentimental. Although Osborne had taken great pains to present himself as manly and practical and often explicitly distanced himself from the ineffectual "sentimentalists" whom he claimed had made a mockery of prison reform in the past, his critics routinely accused him of "pampering and mollycoddling of prisoners."[140] The grand jury investigation contributed to such a characterization by linking the charges of sexual impropriety to an inversion of gendered norms within the prison. This line of inquiry focused on a well-publicized reform Osborne had initiated: "Tom Brown's Knitting Class," a popular program in which inmates would gather nightly to knit "scarves and other garments" for Polish war victims. Osborne's supporters joyfully publicized the image of "hardened convicted murderers" caught up in "the knitting fever" as evidence of an underlying compassion in men considered "vicious" and of the transformation that Osborne's reforms had brought to Sing Sing; Osborne's associate Donald Lowrie claimed that one inmate remarked, "If I'd learned this sooner, I might never have taken to cracking safes."[141]

Critical witnesses interviewed for the investigation presented a different picture. According to Whitmel Smith, a Brooklyn lawyer sent to Sing Sing for grand larceny, "this knitting class was really an opportunity at night for the degenerates to ply their trade." Smith estimated that about two hundred inmates attended the class, which was supervised by Izzy Bloom, an inmate he characterized as "one of the warden's boys." Smith suggested that the real appeal of the knitting class for inmates was the opportunity to participate in unregulated sexual activity: "It was a well-known fact that almost every known degenerate in the place was a member . . . and they had an opportunity to ply their trade as much as they chose because . . . there was a room with four toilets in there . . . and these men could go in there and stay as long as they liked."[142] Weeks and Fallon gathered additional testimony that presented Osborne and his circle as feminized: that he was engaged in knitting himself when he made advances toward inmates; that he kept a Tom Brown doll on his bed; that he broke down in tears while performing fellatio.[143] Other testimony suggested that the prevalence of same-sex relations under Osborne's administration had feminized younger prisoners; several inmates even alleged that, after having sex with Osborne, the young inmate James Connolly "started to act like a woman."[144]

The terminology used in the course of Osborne's investigation evinced multiple and often conflicting understandings of same-sex sexuality. The indictment itself drew on the legal framework for prosecuting sodomy that had emerged from the Christian approbation of same-sex acts as "unnatural" and "sodomitical." In interviewing prisoners, attorneys most frequently asked about incidences of "sodomy." The prisoners often responded using that term as well, but more frequently described Osborne in slang referring to the kinds of acts performed; he was most often referred to as a "cocksucker," and the terms "punk" and "jocker" appeared in several interviews. Charles W. Farr, the prison physician, drew on sexological constructions of homosexuality as biological; he referred to prisoners associated with the case as "congenital sodomists" whom he deemed "diseased and incurable."[145]

The language of "degeneracy" was most often used by politicians critical of Osborne, the district attorneys prosecuting the case, and educated and politically connected prisoners they interviewed. According to historian Peter Boag, the terms "degenerate" and "degeneracy" also dominated commentary on a same-sex scandal involving middle-class men in Portland, Oregon three years earlier.[146] As in Portland, this terminology reflected the prominence of degeneration theory in late nineteenth- and early twentieth-century American culture. The theory identified a decline in Western societies due to a process of "overcivilization," two signs of which were a general feminization of the middle and upper classes and an increase in "abnormal" sexual practices, including same-sex acts. When applied to Osborne—an elite, Harvard-educated man with an interest in theatrical and other cultural pursuits—charges of degeneracy found considerable public resonance. Yet some proponents of the theory—including the influential Italian criminologist Cesare Lombroso—viewed lower-class "criminal types" as degenerate and inclined to sexual abnormality as well. It was this model that Osborne found most objectionable; he referred to the work of Lombroso, as well as the criminological work of Havelock Ellis, as "nonsense" and "preposterous." Yet for those influenced by degeneration theory, the collaboration of an elite degenerate like Osborne with imprisoned criminal degenerates represented a grave danger to sexual and social order.

Conclusion

As was the case with George, the charges against Osborne ultimately failed. The judge dismissed the perjury count and the district attorney's office eventually decided not to prosecute on the remainder of the indictment. As illustrated at the start of this chapter, the reform community rallied around Osborne, portraying the prosecution as a "persecution" by corrupt politicians motivated by greed and self-interest. Indeed, Osborne's defenders could point to considerable successes under his administration: not only had the number of reported disturbances at Sing Sing and Auburn decreased, but Osborne also enjoyed the support and allegiance of the majority of the inmate population at both institutions. He was eventually reinstated as warden of Sing Sing, although he resigned after several months of continued conflict with the prison bureaucracy. Franklin D. Roosevelt, a prominent supporter then serving as Vice Admiral of the Navy, appointed him as warden of the naval prison at Portsmouth, New Hampshire, where Osborne once again was dogged by rumors of sexual impropriety.[147] The taint of sexual scandal effectively ended his political aspirations; he never again ran for public office.[148]

The reform projects Osborne and George instituted suffered after the two scandals. The self-government principles at the core of both the Mutual Welfare League and the George Junior Republic were quickly whittled away after the two charismatic leaders left their posts. By the 1920s, republic citizens retained only limited, largely symbolic power, and the seven established republics soon resembled other hierarchically organized juvenile institutions. With Osborne's resignation, the Mutual Welfare Leagues at Auburn and Sing Sing were essentially defanged; inmates rapidly lost the relative autonomy and privileges they had gained during the reformers' tenure.[149]

The decline of these projects stemmed from multiple factors, not least among them the general retreat from democratic and reformist principles beginning in World War I and lasting through the 1920s. The relatively brief tenure of the self-government movement spearheaded by Osborne and George might also be attributed to inherent tensions within. The reform careers of both men were motivated, at least in part, by the related desires for masculine adventure and for camaraderie with rough immigrant and working-class men. As with many male reformers in the Progressive Era, such desires emerged from a deeply felt sense that these populations of men owned a more vigorous masculinity largely missing in the middle and upper classes, as well as from a belief that the establishment of "fellow feeling" across class lines offered a solution to significant class conflicts and pervasive political corruption. Moreover, both Osborne and George expressed frustration with more mainstream institutional reform movements they deemed insufficient in both promoting cross-class alliances and combating the corrupt political machines that commanded the allegiance of so many working-class men.

The solution they proposed involved winning over "the baddest of the bad" and reorienting their "gang loyalty" toward the principles of good government and economic self-sufficiency, thereby capturing a large and powerful constituency from the machines and converting criminality to respectable and socially "useful" behavior. This vision was inherently problematic: the reformers endeavored to bring the principles of democratic self-government and citizenship to populations that, because they fell under the power of the state, had very little control over their own condition and little capacity to act as independent citizens. Osborne and George resolved this apparent contradiction only by denying the extent to which they held power over these populations, thereby misinterpreting a system of "benevolent tyranny"—to use Osborne's own words—as democratic brotherhood. At the same time, the virulent reaction to these projects suggests that they did hold some potential to shift relations of power, and their projects challenged some of the more hierarchical assumptions about citizenship and self-determination in Progressive Era culture.[150]

The self-government movement also reveals the complex workings of and interrelationships among categories of gender, sexuality, and governance in Progressive Era reform. The sexual scandals in which George and Osborne became embroiled both reflected and shaped broader conflicts over power relations. In the case of the George Junior Republic, the charges that George was "unduly intimate" with young citizens spoke to larger concerns about the gendered meanings of "public" and "private" and the relationship of the family to the state. While many reformers believed that the state served as an appropriate model for an institution comprised of males, even individuals sympathetic to the cause of women's suffrage insisted that the family offered the best possible solution for girls. One critical report, for example, posited that "[a] government . . . be it a republic or other form, is necessarily based upon an aggregation of homes. The total absence of this element in the [Junior Republic] is immediately apparent to the careful observer." This and other published critiques alleged that the dearth of family structures left girls sexually vulnerable and boys without a "civilizing" influence.[151] In this sense, the Junior Republic story demonstrates that, as Foucault suggests, while the family no longer served as a model of government within liberal regimes, it remained a privileged instrument for the government of populations. For critics, the absence of family structure, the basis for a self-governing republic, led to a lack of sexual discipline and made the youths unfit for citizenship.[152]

The question of girls' participation in the George Junior Republic also revealed the vexed relationship among male homosociality, homosexuality, and political governance. Sex segregation in the organization proved problematic for George, who believed that it promoted "unnatural vice," thereby blurring the line between the homosocial camaraderie that animated his ideal of a self-governing republic and homosexual "perversion," which in his view, signified unfitness for self-governance. Osborne faced similar difficulty in negotiating the boundary between the homosocial and the homoerotic; his ideal self-governing democracy was decidedly homosocial, but he also suggested that homosexual relations were "natural" in sex-segregated spaces. His enthusiasm for male camaraderie and intimacy across class lines, with his refusal to condemn homosexual acts in absolute terms, left him vulnerable to charges of "perversion" and "degeneration."

Even more significant is the effectiveness with which charges of lack of sexual self-governance, characterized as a degenerate proclivity to engage in sex with men, became associated with threats to social and political order. This is clearly suggested by the testimony of Sing Sing prisoner Whitmel H. Smith, a politically connected Brooklyn lawyer convicted of grand larceny, who claimed that the interaction of elite degenerate Osborne with lower-class criminal degenerates in prison "degenerated [prison] government into a guerilla government that nobody in the world could control because these men couldn't control themselves."[153]

6

The Problem of the Impracticables

Sentimentality, Idealism, and Homosexuality

During the course of his prison reform career, Thomas Mott Osborne dramatized the history and contemporary debates surrounding the "prison problem" in an unpublished play entitled "The Dawn: A Criminal Morality." In this work, male characters embody abstract ideals such as Honor, Wisdom, and Humanity. At the start of the play, Ignorance and Cruelty, who have long ruled over the prison system, are banished by advocates of the "new penology," represented by Good Intent. Yet Good Intent proves unsuccessful in his attempt to reform the prison. He not only fails to recognize its rehabilitative potential—he believes "Once a crook, always a crook"—but also maintains discipline through the use of "trusties-stool-pigeons, rats, and spies," rewarding inmates who cooperate "with many privileges—endless graft." Thus Good Intent corrodes the spirit of fraternity among the men, the quality from which true reform, rehabilitation, and, ultimately, democracy will be achieved.[1]

Good Intent does not rule over American prison reform alone; he works alongside "silly, maudlin gush" represented in the play by the character Sentimentality. Although a quality typically identified as feminine, Sentimentality is characterized not as a woman, but as an effeminate homosexual man. He first appears in act II "dressed as a Greek, with roses crowning his head" and is engaged in planting pansies—a flower commonly understood to signify male homosexuality—along the base of the prison walls.[2] In the play, Sentimentality represents the worst qualities of the reformer. He is vain and self-aggrandizing; he stages his acts of benevolence for "the keen reporters of the daily press." Although he is more willing to interact with inmates than Good Intent, his motives are corrupt and sexually suspicious. He describes the inmates as "poor, dear things; many of them young and so good-looking" and takes sadistic pleasure in their punishment:

> For my part, I like to have these dangerous animals feeding out of my hand; to put my foot upon their necks—knowing all the time they could rise and destroy me—but they won't. We've bribed them not to. Oh, the feeling is too delicious: These delightful, dangerous, wicked men!

Sentimentality is also portrayed as ineffectual and overcivilized; he believes that planting "rare and lovely" flowers will improve the plight of the "poor unfortunate men" and he holds "a pink tea in the mess-hall once a week" at which he leads discussions on "Bernard Shaw" or "Freud" or "some such latest fad."

In the third act of the play, two newly introduced characters, Wisdom and his "strong ally . . . Common Sense," challenge the rule of Good Intent and Sentimentality. Osborne depicted these two sets of characters in stark opposition. Whereas Good Intent and Sentimentality apply abstract theory and maudlin emotion to the prison problem, Wisdom and Common Sense refuse "to twist the facts to justify a theory; but patiently to learn the facts; and thus let Truth emerge in just conclusions." While the former treat inmates as a separate class and promote a corrupt system of patronage, the latter forge "true brotherhood" and "equality" by allowing inmates to participate freely in their own government. The drama ends with the triumphant "dawn" of a new era in penology, led by Wisdom and Common Sense in cooperation with Humanity and the State.[3]

Osborne's juxtaposition of practical wisdom drawn from experience with theoretical reform motivated by feminine emotion—as well as his scornful treatment of sentimentalism—reflected broader currents in late nineteenth- and early twentieth-century thought and politics. Social thinkers and critics attacked unrestrained idealism and sentimentalism as detached from, and potentially harmful to, the vital, practical, and masculine spirit of modern America. At the same time, the modern "science" of sexology identified the stereotypical male homosexual as effeminate, impractical, sentimental, and a potential threat to normal, "red-blooded" manhood. The overlapping of these discourses produced an inextricable link between sentimentalism—and even idealism—and homosexuality. The powerful connection between the sentimentalist or "impracticable idealist"—to use Theodore Roosevelt's term—and the homosexual was a useful rhetorical weapon in the fiercely waged battles over the future of reform politics; leveling charges of sentimentalism or idealism against rival reformers and their visions enabled men with political ambition—including Roosevelt—to narrow the ideological terrain of Progressive Era reform.

The Sentimental and the Practical

The broad reaction against sentimentalism and idealism emerged from a variety of sources. In literature, a new generation of realist and naturalist writers condemned sentimental and genteel fiction as dissipated, imitative, and artificially feminine. According to literary scholar Leland Krauth, in the new age of realism, "stoicism not sympathy, competition not compassion, survival not self-sacrifice . . . were increasingly the prescribed norms for manly behavior, and in literature the imagined real was more apparent than the imagined ideal."[4] Endorsing the gendered critique of sentiment, Mark Twain declared that "Sentiment is for girls. . . . I have not the slightest sympathy for what the world calls Sentiment—not the slightest."[5] Many of these writers, Twain among them, promoted realism as the literary mode of the future, differentiating themselves from past writers whose idealism and sentimentalism, they argued, failed to reflect the practical and active qualities of American life.[6]

Idealism and sentimentalism in the realm of politics also came under attack during this period, most aggressively by conservative proponents of social Darwinism. Yale sociologist William Graham Sumner harshly criticized social reformers for their "absurd attempt to make the world over." He believed that reformers attempted to impose sentimental solutions on the natural and competitive workings of the human struggle for survival.

To interfere in this inevitable and cosmically determined process, then, was "the greatest folly of which a man can be capable." "The great stream of time and earthly things will absorb the efforts at change and take them into itself as new but trivial components."[7]

Sumner maintained that social reformers failed to apply scientific method to the study of society, and thereby confused motives (ideals) with consequences ("facts in the world of experience"). "To act from notions, pious hopes, benevolence or ideals, is sentimentalism," because such "notions" emerge from the human intellect and emotion, rather than from external "truth and reality." Thus, Sumner characterized all forms of idealism as impractical products of the imagination:

> Every ideal is a phantasm; it is formed by giving up one's hold on reality and taking a flight into the realm of fiction. When an ideal has been formed in the imagination the attempt is made to spring and reach it as a mode of realizing it. The whole process seems to me open to question; it is unreal and unscientific; . . . it is not a legitimate mental exercise. . . . The fashion of forming ideals corrupts the mind and injures character.[8]

Because Sumner viewed laissez-faire capitalism as a natural and rational product of human evolution, he argued that any attempt to promote "socialistic and semi-socialistic" forms of government was irrational, sentimental, and doomed to failure.

Turn-of-the-century pragmatic philosophers also offered a critique of idealism, albeit much more complex and nuanced—and far less pessimistic. Pragmatists rejected the material determinism of conservative social Darwinists, emphasizing instead the power of the human will to shape and change social "reality." While critical of formal idealism, they argued that abstract ideals still held crucial value insofar as they yielded practical consequences. According to William James:

> Now pragmatism, devoted though she be to facts, has no such materialistic bias as ordinary empiricism labors under. Moreover, she has no objection whatever to the realizing of abstractions, so long as you get about among particulars with their aid and they actually carry you somewhere.[9]

This instrumental view of idealism, of course, appealed to many social reformers. Indeed, prominent Progressives like Jane Addams, who called for a reform praxis based on direct engagement with constituent populations and careful study of material conditions, influenced—and in turn were influenced by—American pragmatists.[10]

If pragmatists and pragmatist reformers eschewed a formal idealism divorced from experience, they also warned against a similarly detached emotional interpretation of the world—or sentimentalism. Pragmatist educational reformer John Dewey, for example, maintained that "sentimentalism is the necessary result of the attempt to divorce feeling from action" and argued that there was "no greater evil" facing the reform movement.[11] Philosopher George Santayana also criticized sentimentalism in American life. Although his series of essays on the "genteel tradition" primarily chided American scholars and writers for their wan and "unworldly" idealism, he also remarked on emotional deficiencies, which he characterized using gendered terminology. He described the American intellect as "shy and feminine" and compared the minds of leading American writers Poe, Hawthorne, and Emerson to "an old music-box, full of tender echoes and quaint fancies." He contrasted these men to "the normal practical masculine American," whose character was an "all aggressive enterprise."[12]

Thomas Mott Osborne also characterized the sentimental idealist in gendered terms. Yet Santayana embodied the "genteel tradition" in a benign and unthreatening form; he employed the metaphor of the "sedate" and "spectacled Grandmother"; Osborne's characterization of Sentimentality as a ridiculous and corrupt effeminate male carried a harsher, more bitter critique. This difference can be explained by the very different positions and purposes of the two men. The philosopher Santayana viewed the American political—and even intellectual—scene from a distance; indeed, soon after delivering his first lecture on the "genteel tradition," he left the country altogether.[13] Moreover, his critique pertained as much to the breathless materialism of the practical (masculine) American mind as it did to the tradition of "shy, feminine" intellect. The reformer Osborne, in contrast, found himself directly implicated in debates over the gendered/sexualized meanings of the "ideal," the "sentimental," and the "practical": he faced charges of sentimentality and unrestrained idealism in his prison reform project and was suspected of acting on "corrupt" sexual motives.

Considered in the context of Osborne's embattled reform career, his theatrical representation of Sentimentality might be viewed as an attempt to defend himself against these ideological and sexual charges. Throughout his career, Osborne struggled to present his conception of prison reform as grounded in practical knowledge acquired from his interaction with inmates and prison administrators. Likewise, he (and his supporters) often stressed that the reforms he proposed were not "utopian" but a realizable program based on traditional American political and economic principles. He constructed his self-presentation as vigorous and masculine; his popularity with the "rough" prison population attested to the success of this effort. Osborne's carefully constructed persona stood in opposition to the effete and effeminate figure he identified as Sentimentality.

Osborne's characterization might also be understood in relation to the ideal of sympathy, a quality closely associated with sentimentalism. As recent scholarship on the history and literature of the early republic has shown, sympathy—primarily expressed in the form of male friendship—functioned as a means of pulling disparate groups of men together within the new nation. In other words, the concept allowed men to imagine themselves as confederated citizens and thereby produce a shared national identity. Such an ideal of sympathy, which permeated American literature and political rhetoric, often found expression in romantic friendships among men. In recent years, scholars have shown that such friendships, established among both the generation of "founding fathers" and the abolitionists, worked to establish national cohesion as well as a spirit of cooperative political endeavor.[14]

By the dawn of the Progressive Era, however, that ideal had become less influential. As Caleb Crain has argued, while in the early republic "sympathy had the force of a biological fact," the rise of Darwinism, which emphasized competition rather than cooperation, undermined its explanatory power.[15] To conservative social Darwinists, sympathy seemed an impediment to the proper functioning of American political and economic order. Those who advocated a more egalitarian politics, however, were more reluctant to abandon the notion as a political force and cultural ideal. Progressive reformers sought to redefine sympathy as a pragmatic virtue that combined the two strands of Progressive ideology historian Daniel P. Rodgers has labeled "social bonds" and "social efficiency."[16] John Dewey, who defined sympathy as the sole psychological mechanism "which can be relied upon to work the identification of others' ends with one's own interests," nevertheless worried that such identification might too easily produce unproductive sentimentalism.[17] To avoid this danger, he insisted that sympathy must be tempered by a reflective impartiality:

> To put ourselves in the place of others, to see things from the standpoint of their purposes and values, to humble, contrariwise, our own pretensions and claims till they reach the level they would assume in the eye of an impartial sympathetic observer, is the surest way to attain objectivity of moral knowledge.[18]

Dewey called this alternative to sentimentalism "intelligent sympathy," which he defined as "the marriage of emotion with intelligence."[19]

The ideal of sympathy also provoked concern with regard to changing notions about sexuality. Nineteenth-century American literature offered countless examples of sympathetic relationships among men that ranged across a wide spectrum of male homosocial desire, including the romantic and the erotic. Indeed, two of the most famous American men of letters infused the sympathetic ideal with homoerotic sentiment: Ralph Waldo Emerson, especially in his construction of transcendental friendship; and Walt Whitman, who celebrated manly "adhesiveness."[20] While the expressions of same-sex desire produced by both of these writers—especially Whitman—received some criticism during their own lifetimes, it became more pointed and explicit at the end of the century. The "invention" of the homosexual and the heterosexual and the concomitant rise of antigay discourse had the effect of stigmatizing all such expressions of corporeal desire among men.[21]

Osborne's figure of Sentimentality, then, was not only a symbol of the unmanly and impractical reformer but also a marker of the limits of male homosociality; the effete sentimentalist stood apart from the sympathetic fraternal relations Osborne sought to establish in his prison reform career. In light of his possible sexual interest in men—and of the allegations leveled against him—it is important to note that such a characterization did not necessarily connote an indictment of homoerotic desire or relations. Even those who held a largely positive view of homosexual relations marginalized the effeminate man. Edward Carpenter, the poet of "homogenic" love, for example, identified two types of homosexual men: the "normal type" and the "distinctly effeminate type." The "normal type"—who was "not distinguishable in exterior structure" from heterosexual men—possessed an enormous capacity for sympathetic relations. The "effeminate type," whom he described as "sentimental, lackadaisical, mincing in gait and manners," proved too vain and emotionally undeveloped to act in cooperation with other men: "His affection . . . is often feminine in character, clinging, dependent and jealous, as of one desiring to be loved almost more than to love."[22]

Theodore Roosevelt's "Impracticable Idealist"

The effeminate figure of Sentimentality resembled the characterization of mugwump civil service reformers as members of an "intermediate" sex. Still, Osborne's invocation of this figure illuminates a substantial shift. Previously such charges had been made by politicians who sought to present political reformers and their causes as outside the manly traditions of party. However, during the Progressive Era, self-identified reformers used similar derogatory rhetoric not only to distinguish themselves from the preceding generation of mugwumps but also to attack their contemporaries. For example, William Randolph Hearst, who pursued elective office as an independent Democrat throughout the first two decades of the twentieth century (mostly without success) and espoused such popular reform causes as municipal ownership of utilities, leveled charges of effeminacy against his opponents in the reform community. He used these charges to appeal to the working-class voters he hoped to attract, implying that the alleged effeminacy of his opponents rendered them ill-suited for participation in the manly world of cross-class politics.[23]

The most influential Progressive reformer to employ such gendered rhetoric against other reformers was Theodore Roosevelt. By the turn of the twentieth century, Roosevelt had become the most influential political figure of his generation. When he emerged as the hero of the Rough Riders at the end of the Spanish–American War, he addressed the state of American manhood in a series of popular and influential lectures and essays on the "strenuous life." Primarily targeting the well-off and educated, he called for such men, whom he believed had become soft, effeminate, and "overcivilized," to lead lives of manly vigor and action. Roosevelt's conception of strenuousness involved a host of binary categories. As Gail Bederman has shown, the central tenet of this brand of manhood involved combining elements of "primitive" masculinity with the qualities of industriousness and self-control associated with the established ideal of genteel manhood.[24] Yet Roosevelt also described strenuous manhood as situated between other qualities and values he identified as "extreme": the strenuous man should be intellectual but never "bookish" or snobbish about his knowledge; he should participate in rough sports but not to the point of obsession; he must fight to defend honor or family but should never bully or act cruelly; he must be "morally straight" but by no means "priggish"; he should avoid both "callousness" and sentimentalism.[25]

Politics also played a central role in Roosevelt's doctrine of strenuousness. Like George William Curtis a generation earlier, Roosevelt urged elite and educated young men to participate in electoral politics. In a 1907 lecture to Harvard undergraduates—one of many such addresses he gave at American universities—he asserted that to "neglect . . . political duties . . . shows either a weakness or worse than a weakness in a man's character." He warned the young men not to become "too fastidious, too sensitive to take part in the rough hurly-burly of the actual work of the world," contending that physical, moral, and mental strength—indeed, the quality of one's manhood—depended on such participation. Declaring that colleges should never "turn out mollycoddles instead of vigorous men," he cautioned that "the weakling and the coward are out of place in a strong and free community." Roosevelt further warned: "if you are too timid or too fastidious or too careless to do your part in this work, then you forfeit the right to be considered one of the governing and you become one of the governed."[26]

Roosevelt's exhortation extended beyond merely encouraging participation in electoral politics; it also defined the form of such participation:

> It means to take an intelligent, disinterested and practical part in the everyday duties of the average citizen, of the citizen who is not a faddist or doctrinaire, but who abhors corruption and dislikes

> inefficiency; who wishes to see decent government prevail at home, with genuine equality of opportunity for all men so far as it can be brought about.[27]

Roosevelt situated manly participation in politics between two extremes: the ideal and the practical. The excessively practical man, according to him, pursued politics either for mercenary interest or to achieve party victory as an end in itself; the excessively idealistic man proved unable to compromise and achieve results. Roosevelt advocated pursuing a middle course that should "combine worthy ideals with practical good sense."[28]

Roosevelt's notion that successful engagement in politics required a balance of the practical and the ideal fit squarely within the pragmatist currents of turn-of-the-century American life. Indeed, as scholar Henry May has shown, Roosevelt served as the "greatest spokesman" for the predominant moral philosophy of the period, which May names "practical idealism." May argues that "practical idealism" was rather broadly and loosely defined: "it was possible to be mostly practical or mostly idealistic as long as one maintained some touch with both qualities."[29] More recently, Sarah Watts has offered an intellectual framework for understanding Roosevelt's conception of politics; she argues that Roosevelt saw the world in binary terms and that "blended with Social Darwinist notions of continual flux and the political idea that America served as the vanguard of civilization, the polarity of the opposites seemed to dictate an all-or-nothing choice between two social extremes."[30]

In terms of domestic politics, Roosevelt's binary poles comprised the self-serving and venal politician and the impractical idealist who was at best ineffective and at worst mortally dangerous. While Roosevelt criticized excessively practical men—namely, spoils politicians—in the familiar and conventional terms of good government reformers, he saved his greatest vitriol for those he deemed overly idealistic. His characterization of this type—the impracticable idealist—resembled the figure of the "third-sex" reformer invoked by party politicians; his lack of manly vigor rendered him unable to compete in the rough give-and-take of practical politics.

Like the third-sex reformer, the impracticable idealist shared significant attributes with the predominant stereotype of the homosexual man. Although in his published writings on reformers Roosevelt rarely used the explicit sexual language employed by Senator Ingalls and other party politicians, he did resort to a more coded form of name-calling, occasionally referring to political opponents as "Miss Nancys"—by the end of the century a popular epithet for the effeminate homosexual—and "mollycoddles." Roosevelt is credited with popularizing the term "mollycoddle" in the early twentieth century; it rarely appeared in print before that time. As scholars have shown, the term is derived from "molly," as applied in Britain to effeminate "sodomites" in the eighteenth and early nineteenth centuries. In the first decades of the twentieth century, it came into common usage in ways that reflected animus toward effeminate men and boys. Although it did not always imply same-sex desire, it was often deployed to that end.[31] That Roosevelt connected a deficiency of practicality to homosexuality is also suggested by his critique of ancient Greek culture. Roosevelt chastised a friend who desired "to have lived in Greece in the classic age" by asserting that that would require abandoning "present conventions of morality" as well as "the beautiful love of husband and wife." While he shared his friend's admiration of the intellectual achievements of the Greeks, Roosevelt concluded that they "lacked the self-restraint and political common sense necessary" to survive as a civilization.[32]

Roosevelt's construction of the impracticable idealist also closely resembled sexological models of homosexuality. Medical "experts" at the turn of the century amplified the threat of the degenerated and mentally diseased homosexual. Roosevelt used similar Darwinist and psychological terms to identify the impracticable idealist as a potential danger to the proper functioning of male political relations. In this sense, his characterization of the excessively idealistic and effeminate reformer differed from previous incarnations. The sexual stigma attached to the mugwump identified him as detestable but impotent, more ridiculous than threatening—his greatest flaw was his inability to produce political progeny. This reflected a dominant critique of sodomy—and eventually homosexuality—on the grounds that it deviated from "normal" heterosexual reproduction. By the turn of the century, however, "scientific" models of homosexuality tended to emphasize the "invert" as a corrupting social influence. Roosevelt imbued the impracticable idealist with a similar potential to corrupt.[33]

Roosevelt developed his critique most fully in a 1900 essay, "Latitude and Longitude Among Reformers," in which he defined such men as "vain prattlers" committed to a "mere visionary adherence to a nebulous . . . ideal."

Employing familiar gendered tropes, he portrayed the practical reformer as "strong," "decent," "sound," and "manly," while the unyielding idealist was "weak," "timid," and "vain." Moreover, the impracticable reformer was "slightly disordered mentally," a man with a "twist in [his] mental make-up." What had been a tendency toward unrestrained idealism became a fixed bodily condition; the impracticable was a "man constitutionally incapable of working for practical results." Roosevelt warned that "These little knots of extremists are found everywhere" and that, although the reforms they espoused might seem to differ, "in mental and moral habit they are fundamentally alike." He invoked a fear of contagion—"these little knots of men . . . affect for evil a certain number of decent men"—and warned that those "men who strive for honesty, and for the cleansing of what is corrupt in the dark places of our politics, should emphatically disassociate themselves from the men whose antics throw discredit upon the reforms they profess to advocate."[34]

Roosevelt's rhetoric, which reconfigured effeminate reformers as innately mentally defective, organized into "knots," and a potential danger to "sane and healthy men" mirrors the literature on sexual deviance in American cities produced by medical professionals and antivice reformers in the last two decades in the twentieth century. One of the leading experts of the period, criminal anthropologist Dr. G. Frank Lydston, warned in 1889 that "there is in every community of any size a colony of sexual perverts" who were "usually known to each other" and were "likely to congregate together" and, at times, "operate in accordance with some definite and concerted plan."[35] Likewise, experts on sexual vice claimed that inversion resulted from an inborn biological defect, but also offered evidence that seemingly "normal" men could be drawn into sexual contact with groups of perverts.[36] These reports coincided with the increased policing of homosexuality in American cities, evinced by a marked increase in sodomy prosecutions beginning in the 1880s and 1890s. Roosevelt served as New York City Police Commissioner during this period (1895 and 1897) and spearheaded a concerted effort to rid the city of sexual vice.

The invention of the impracticable idealist allowed Roosevelt to pathologize his critics and the policies they espoused and to assign them underhanded and secretive motives. He contended, for example, that although these groups of impracticable men claimed "that they are striving for righteousness . . . in reality, [they] do their feeble best for unrighteousness."[37] Such a combination of secrecy and organization carried sinister implications for a public consumed with worry about the strength of radical political ideologies among the immigrant working classes in American cities. Although Roosevelt maintained that the "wholesome common sense of the American people" minimized the strength of radical politics, he compared the impracticable idealists in the United States to corresponding "little knots of impracticables" who had produced political unrest in France.

Moreover, using the figure of the impracticable reformer, Roosevelt portrayed as subversive individuals from across the political spectrum. He contended that although impracticable idealists "may be socialists of twenty different types, from the followers of Tolstoi down and up, or they may ostensibly champion some cause in itself excellent, such as temperance or municipal reform," they were bound together by "moral and mental habit."[38] The reference here to "Tolstoi down and up" expands a critique that Roosevelt had leveled at anarchists for years. As historian Terence Kissack shows, Roosevelt proposed that the United States "exclude absolutely not only all persons who are known to be believers in anarchistic principles of members of anarchistic societies, but also all persons who are of low moral tendency or unsavory reputation."[39]

Insight into Roosevelt's conflation of political and sexual aberrance and danger can be gained through a consideration of literature generated by American criminal anthropologists, who classified a range of individuals defined as exhibiting antisocial behaviors as a discrete criminal type. G. Frank Lydston, the expert who reported on "colonies of perverts," offers a case in point. Lydston identified anarchists, for example, as just one variety of "true criminal . . . whose instincts are largely antisocial." Like Roosevelt, he cited unrestrained idealism as the root cause of the antisocial actions: "the true anarchist is . . . a mistaken, misguided philosopher, an idealist whose conceptions of what ought to be are not in harmony with what is . . . He forgets that social perfection is not possible in the presence of . . . human imperfection."[40] Lydston expanded his analysis beyond the political anarchist, arguing that "every criminal may be justly termed an anarchist in action, whatever his theories of social conditions may be; if, indeed, he has any theories."[41] He linked sexual perversion to unfettered idealism as well, attributing same-sex relations in boarding schools, for example, to an excessive investment in the romantic ideal. Although Lydston did not cite idealism as the cause of all instances of "sexual perversion and inversion," he maintained that the danger of such cases—and of all forms of criminality—resulted from the privileging of one's own desires over the common weal.[42]

This criminological conflation of sexual and political crimes, defined as such because they represented threats to social order, provides a context for understanding the transformation of the familiar figure of the effete and effeminate reformer—mollycoddle in Roosevelt's palance—into an elusive and sinister threat to the American political system. This figure combined the qualities of elitism, genteel effeminacy, and idealism associated with the third-sex reformer, the pathological degeneracy of the sexual pervert, and the subversive threat of the political radical. By defining the "impracticable idealist" in this way, Roosevelt presented his own brand of politics as both manly and centrist, as mediating between the corrupt venality of the party boss and the dogmatic righteousness of the reformer.

Roosevelt's contempt for such idealists grew, in part, from a bitter falling out with a group of reformers, many of whom he once considered his friends and colleagues. One significant factor contributing to this division was the debate over U.S. imperialism. To be sure, Roosevelt joined other advocates of imperial policy and military "preparedness" in attacking anti-imperialists as soft, cowardly, and effeminate.[43] Yet the conflict extended to domestic politics as well. After his election to political office in the 1880s, Roosevelt began to critique previous allies in the municipal reform movement for what he believed to be their excessive allegiance to a position of political "purity." This rift became even more acrimonious in 1898, when a delegation of New York City reformers, including John Jay Chapman and Richard Welling, requested that Roosevelt run for Governor of New York on an independent slate that included Osborne for Lieutenant Governor and Colonel George E. Waring for State Engineer.[44]

Believing that Roosevelt had consented, the delegation grew irate when they learned that he had agreed with the reviled boss Thomas Platt to accept only the nomination of the Republican Party. The betrayed independents railed against Roosevelt as lacking manly honor and a puppet of Platt. Chapman, for example, concluded that "Roosevelt . . . can never again furnish such a terrible illustration of the power of the boss as he did when he refused to allow his fellow-citizens to vote for him except on the Platt ticket."[45] Chapman and others believed that their most promising advocate had succumbed to his desire for self-aggrandizement and viewed Roosevelt's capitulation to Republican politicians as a horrible blow to the good government movement. Stung by such criticism, Roosevelt, who easily won the governorship, lashed out vehemently and introduced the figure of the impracticable idealist in his essays and addresses.

The division between Roosevelt and his former colleagues involved more than just disagreement over electoral strategy; it encompassed substantial differences in political ideology. By the last years of the nineteenth century, a significant number of the men who began their reform careers with Roosevelt in the good government movement became frustrated and disillusioned with the slow progress and shortcomings of reform on a number of levels. Recognizing the resiliency of political machines as well as the willingness of men like Roosevelt to compromise with spoils politicians, many believed that the fight against corruption in electoral politics was all but lost. A good many also grew frustrated with their inability to attract working-class and immigrant voters to the movement and a seeming lack of significant improvement in the living and working conditions of the urban poor. This led them to doubt the efficacy of meliorative reform measures. Moreover, alarmed by the state violence directed at striking workers, some began to question whether a political system aligned with—or even controlled by—commercial forces was capable of providing a substantial measure of social equity.

In response to these concerns, many of these men came to embrace political ideologies explicitly critical of industrial capitalism and the American political system—namely a variety of forms of socialism and anarchism. A number of these individuals joined together to found the Social Reform Club in New York City in 1894.[46] Although the club's constitution called for a nonsectarian emphasis on practical and immediate reforms leading to "the improvement of the condition of wage earners," more radical members soon gained the strongest voice in the organization.[47] Its first president was Ernest Howard Crosby, a staunch antimilitarist and Christian anarchist widely recognized as a leading American authority on the work of Leo Tolstoy. Other leaders included Edmond Kelly, the former president of the City Club, who became increasingly radicalized throughout the 1890s and eventually joined the Socialist Party;[48] and James Graham Phelps Stokes, a wealthy member of the New York elite who married a former garment worker from a Jewish immigrant family (Rose Pastor Stokes) and who also became an active member of the Socialist Party.

Many Social Reform Club members had at one time associated with Roosevelt. Crosby had succeeded Roosevelt as a Republican assemblyman in the New York State Legislature in the late 1880s and, like his predecessor, championed such good government causes as electoral and excise reform.[49] Kelly had played a leading role in the municipal reform movement of the 1880s and 1890s as a member of the City Reform Club and as the founder of the City Club and its affiliated Good Government clubs. Stokes too had been a prominent supporter of independent reform causes in New York City during this period. Yet, like the more conservative reformers who had asked Roosevelt to run for governor as an independent in 1898, this group of men experienced a dramatic and acrimonious split with their prominent former colleague. When Roosevelt addressed the club on his police reform work in 1897, he was roundly criticized by socialist Moses Oppenheimer for violating the civil liberties of those he arrested and for his self-aggrandizing "Haroun al Raschid midnight rambles."[50] Roosevelt took great offense at this attack: he insisted that he had been "set up" by club's leaders and persuaded Jacob Riis to resign his membership. Thereafter, Roosevelt loudly and publicly attacked the club as a haven for impracticable radicals.[51]

The purpose of relating these disagreements between Roosevelt and New York City reformers is not to reduce a broader debate over political ideology to a narrative of internecine personal conflict. Similar battles over political ideology and reform practice were waged throughout the nation at the turn of the century. However, these particular struggles shed significant light on the history of reform politics in the Progressive Era. Theodore Roosevelt emerged as the most prominent and powerful advocate of a brand of meliorative and regulatory reform politics designed to correct some of the gross inequalities and examples of political and economic corruption without challenging the basic legitimacy and efficacy of American political and economic systems.[52] As New York governor and then United States president, he played a crucial role in situating this brand of reform at the center of Progressive Era politics. Roosevelt also served as a primary architect and popularizer of a new ideal of political manhood based on qualities of competitiveness and militarism. As such, he contributed powerfully to a discourse that marginalized both principled critics of party corruption and advocates of leftist political ideology as effeminate and potentially subversive.

Resisting the Rooseveltian Model: John Jay Chapman, Ernest Howard Crosby, and the Problem of Homosexuality

Roosevelt's influence in shaping ideals of political manhood is attested to by the vociferous reaction to his preachments on "the strenuous life." Virtually every reformer at odds with Roosevelt felt compelled to situate himself vis-à-vis Roosevelt's influential doctrine. Such responses encompassed considerable variety. For example, the self-government reformers Thomas Mott Osborne and Richard Welling, whose political philosophy differed little from Roosevelt's, accepted the basic tenets of his ideal of strenuousness but criticized him for not being strenuous enough. Osborne believed that Roosevelt's willingness to compromise with the state political machine gave the lie to his "big stick" philosophy; he maintained that Roosevelt's "unforgivable sin" was that he "hit softly."[53] Welling, who published several accounts of his college friendship with Roosevelt, was less openly critical. Instead, he used Roosevelt as a yardstick with which to measure his own strenuousness; he compared his title as "strongest man at Harvard" to Roosevelt's "kindergarten stage of physical development."[54] Moreover, both Osborne and Welling—who believed that they too were exemplars of a rough and practical mode of reform—resented Roosevelt's seemingly exclusive claim to strenuous manhood.[55]

Others presented more substantive critiques of Rooseveltian strenuousness and offered alternative models of political manhood. Edmond Kelly, for example, challenged the social evolutionism at the core of Roosevelt's thinking on politics and gender. Although he initially espoused a Spencerian defense of laissez-faire capitalism, his interaction with working-class people in the Good Government and Social Reform clubs caused him to rethink this position. In a series of published works, including *Evolution and Effort* (1895) and *Government or Human Evolution* (1900, 1901), Kelly steadfastly rejected all forms of determinism as explanations for human behavior. He maintained that while man had successfully struggled to gain his position "at the head of the animal kingdom," the future progress of society necessitated that he "overcome the very qualities of the ape and the tiger."[56] A man's strength was no longer based on his competitive participation in the struggle for survival in the natural world, but rather on the effort he exerted to transcend this struggle through cooperative action:

> It is the faculty by effort of making the ethical inclination greater than the natural one which has been termed freedom of the will. Now those persons who have this faculty and who exercise it are universally recognised as strong men; those who have not this faculty and who fail to exercise it are universally recognised as weak men. The strong men are those who are capable of advancing humanity; the weak men are those who retard it.[57]

Kelly's belief that "the principle of the survival of the fittest is no longer applicable to the development of man" also led him to conclude that women, as well as men, could occupy such a position of strength. He maintained that the inferior status of women came from the privileging of physical strength in the "natural world"; human ethical development required the willful abandonment of such distinctions.[58]

Two of Roosevelt's former reform colleagues, Ernest Howard Crosby and John Jay Chapman, developed even more fully elaborated alternatives to the ideal of strenuous manhood. These two men followed very different paths after their participation in the municipal reform movement. After completing his tenure in the New York legislature in 1889, Crosby served for two years as an international judge in Egypt. Alarmed by great disparities of wealth as well as by the cruelties committed under English imperial rule, he returned to New York a staunch and vocal anti-imperialist and a committed disciple of Tolstoy's philosophy of egalitarian brotherhood. Although he shared much of the philosophy of the anarchist movement, Crosby never identified with a single dogma. As a passionate advocate of particular causes—including anti-imperialism and antimilitarism, the rights of labor, the direct election of U.S. citizens, antiracism, and open immigration—he worked with others regardless of ideological affiliation.[59] Chapman, in contrast, ceased active involvement in the reform movement after the disastrous falling out with Roosevelt. He grew distrustful of organized movements thereafter, but continued to agitate for reform in his journal of political commentary, *The Political Nursery* (1897–1901), as well as in books and essays. Chapman took up many of the same causes as Crosby, although in the 1920s his writing displayed a pronounced anti-Catholic and anti-Semitic bent.

Despite these significant differences, Crosby and Chapman had a great deal in common. Like Kelly, both rejected philosophical determinism and rejected the idea that natural selection played a significant role in human political and social life. Both also stood as proud individualistic idealists; they believed that one must fight firmly for what he believed to be right, however unpopular the cause, and must never compromise with a corrupt or evil system for the sake of practical results. Their idealism was shaped by similar influences: namely the Greek political philosophers, Emersonian transcendentalism, and especially William Lloyd Garrison's doctrine of nonresistance. Both men also attempted to redeem the reputation of idealistic reform—historical and contemporary—from the stigma of effeminacy, thereby resisting the Rooseveltian model of the impracticable idealist. Yet their attempts to present idealism as noble and manly betrayed considerable insecurity; to varying degrees, both reformers associated the idealists they so admired with effeminacy and homosexuality and struggled to make sense of such associations within their own reform visions.

Chapman and Crosby leveled explicit criticism against Roosevelt's brand of practical reform politics and his ideology of strenuous manhood. Although Chapman had been an early admirer, he later concluded that Roosevelt had become thoroughly corrupted by his desire for power and fame. Chapman viewed such desire as a sign of weakness. He maintained that, by betraying his idealistic convictions, Roosevelt had lost his core identity, precisely what had made him a strong man—if indeed such a man had ever existed. Chapman expressed this in the pages of the *Political Nursery*:

> Perhaps some old friend of his, by rummaging with a strong arm in him, could find the original Theodore Roosevelt, or put together the broken pieces that had once gave the thought and made the world believe that there was such a man. But the chances are that you might, with as much hope, grope in a tree for the sapling.[60]

Chapman believed that Roosevelt's failure to act on principle made him a mere political pawn easily manipulated by others. Referring to Roosevelt as "muddle-headed," he asserted that "the only way with such a man is to be right behind him with a club."[61] Roosevelt's political malleability meant that, rather than wielding his own "big stick," he was subject to the dictates of others who possessed the essential strength of conviction.

Chapman's analysis of a failure of idealism extended beyond this example; he believed that far too many American men sacrificed individuality and principle in the practical pursuit of political or economic gain. Yet he felt Roosevelt to be more blameworthy because he presented "expediency and compromise" as virtues to be emulated and admired; to Chapman this represented sophistry, a quality he treated with typical contempt in one of his essays on Greek philosophy:

> And who and what, then, were the Sophists? The meaning of the word has not changed during the last two thousand years. They were exactly the same people they are today, namely, persons who are skeptical of abstractions of any kind, who think that expediency is the criterion of truth in political matters and of success in private life. They are the opportunists; . . . in a democratic age they become demagogues; in a dialectical age they will, by their own views, be driven into some sort of pragmatism.[62]

Chapman believed firmly—and, it seems, incorrectly—that history would reveal the sophistry lurking behind Roosevelt's bluster. He wrote that Roosevelt's fame would "fade out with the generation of small boys living at the time of his death. . . . He's a monster of political sagacity—force and personal charm—all of which will evanesce with the epoch."[63]

When Roosevelt died in 1919, Chapman commented that his "testy condemnation of the idealist as an enemy to society" had continued long after such attacks served a viable political purpose. To Chapman, who confessed pleasure at finding on Roosevelt "the marks of my claws," this seemingly obsessive concern with the idealist betrayed an insecurity as to his own righteousness: "In this world . . . the Prophet is always the enemy of the King."[64] More than a decade earlier, Crosby made a similar observation about Roosevelt. Writing in *The Whim*, a small journal of political and literary commentary that he edited, Crosby remarked that "there is only one thing of which our strenuous President is afraid and that is the Weakling," a figure to which Roosevelt seemed unduly attached: "it is almost impossible for Mr. Roosevelt to make a speech or draw up a public document without the Weakling creeping into it."[65]

Crosby offered two possible explanations for this preoccupation with "the Weakling"—a variant of the mollycoddle and impracticable idealist. First, he suggested that Roosevelt employed this figure as a phantom rhetorical foe; the imagined opposition worked to legitimate Roosevelt's beliefs and policies. Referring to Roosevelt's tendency to vaguely define "the Weakling" as one who "shrinks from his national responsibilities," Crosby claimed that, with the exception of war profiteers and monopolists, he knew of no such "shrinkers." He concluded, therefore, that Roosevelt simply dismissed as weaklings those who disagreed with him about what constituted an individual's "national responsibilities."[66] Second, Crosby ascribed a psychological meaning to "the Weakling," suggesting that Roosevelt was "haunted" by something that lurked within his own nature. He pointed to deeper sexual insecurities contributing to Roosevelt's preoccupation, charging that "It is a sort of obsession, such as the wise men of the Middle Ages classified under the heads of incubi and succubi."[67]

Like Chapman, Crosby also criticized the doctrine of strenuousness as promoting "superficial" action at the expense of intellect; he claimed that Roosevelt showed "all the external attributes of strength, except the central and indispensable one of profound and strenuous thought." Crosby argued that the country already possessed far too much of Roosevelt's brand of strenuous living, resulting in rampant commercialization and self-seeking. Using the example of the "Stock Exchange," he maintained that the "upshot of Mr. Roosevelt's preaching" was to convince young men "to make money faster"—something he likened to "recommending rapacity to the wolves." Moreover, Crosby associated rampant "strenuosity" with modern nervous conditions, classified at the time under the diagnosis of neurasthenia. Unlike many prominent medical experts, who viewed neurasthenia as the product of overcivilization and prescribed strenuous action as a remedy, Crosby inverted the diagnosis, asserting that strenuous living, especially in pursuit of wealth, "filled the land with nervous prostration, lunatics, and wrecks of various kinds."[68] In short, he argued that strenuousness, in that it privileged action over thought—and the material over the ideal—produced weakness rather than strength.[69]

Chapman and Crosby also offered alternative models of political manhood built on a philosophy of nonresistant idealism. It is important to note that these alternative models did not necessarily subvert important central assumptions about gender; both men portrayed manliness as strong and assertive and disdained effeminacy as soft and weak. Neither posed a significant challenge to gender inequalities. While both offered nominal support for women's rights and suffrage, neither paid significant attention to the problems facing women, nor did they question commonly accepted distinctions between the sexes. Rather, Crosby and Chapman struggled to reclaim idealism as a manly quality. In doing so, they, like their foe Roosevelt, employed a masculinist rhetoric that positioned women on the margins of American political life.

In the two volumes on political philosophy he published at the turn of the century—*Causes and Consequences* (1898) and *Practical Agitation* (1900)—John Jay Chapman challenged the kind of "practical reform" that men like Roosevelt advocated. Chapman invented the term "practical agitation" in order to call into question the tenets of that reform philosophy. Whereas practical reform was profoundly oriented toward the achievement of goals, Chapman's theory of practical agitation held that means and end—and cause and consequence—are one and the same. He viewed the practical agitator as a force of influence who, by acting unselfishly in communion with others, would eventually bring about social change. "In an enterprise whose sole aim is to raise the moral standard," he argued, "idealism always pays." Likewise, he believed that a setback in a fight for principle represented "pure gain" because it "records the exact state of the cause" and educated other members of society.[70]

Chapman also presented his views on the politics of idealism in a decidedly masculinist light; practical agitation belonged not to the mollycoddle but to the fully red-blooded American man. He described the give-and-take over moral ideals in politics as a "struggle . . . between two men across a table, my force against your force."[71] He expanded on the notion that practical agitation involved constant struggle by enveloping the doctrine in the language of militarism:

> Every man is born under the yoke, and grows up beneath the oppression of his age. He can only get a vision of the unselfish forces in the world by appealing to them, and every appeal is a call to arms. If he

> fights he must fight, not one man, but a conspiracy. He is always at war with a civilization.[72]

Chapman further argued that the abuse heaped on idealists by practical politicians and reformers required special strength and fortitude to endure. He likened the practical agitator to "Atlas, lifting the entire universe,"[73] and asserted that he must be prepared to live a "rough, hard-hitting life . . . full of rebuffs, knotty points, and recriminations. A life of agitation does not always make men bitter but it is apt to make them rough."[74]

Chapman's philosophy of practical agitation might be viewed as an attempt to legitimize and masculinize the politics of moral suasion—the hallmark strategy of the abolitionist movement. Although many women actively resisted being relegated to the sphere of private morality and strove to achieve more direct political power through suffrage and social reform activism, the ideology of separate spheres and the gender-essentialist understanding of women's power as rooted in their maternal and marital influence on boys and men still held considerable sway in the years after the Civil War.[75] As has been discussed, women's association with the exercise of influence outside electoral politics had contributed to the characterization of reform, in general, as feminine. To reclaim the politics of moral suasion as appropriately manly, Chapman called on the memory of the abolitionist William Lloyd Garrison. Believing that Garrison had been neglected or treated dismissively by his generation, Chapman presented a portrait of a fierce and noble visionary: a "hot coal of fire" who "plunges through the icy atmosphere like a burning meteorite from another planet."[76] In his 1913 biography of Garrison, Chapman depicted him as a bold "man of action" who defied the timidity of his time:

> The age was conciliatory: Garrison is aggressive. . . . Conciliation was the sin of that age. Now this anti-type, this personified enemy of his age,—Garrison,—must in his nature be self-reliant, self-assertive, self-sufficient. He relates himself to no precedent. He strikes out from his inner thought. He is even swords-drawn with his own thought of yesterday.[77]

Chapman attempted to banish the image of a shrill and impractical moralist, instead presenting him as a manly hero of practical agitation: "a man who saw in ideas the levers and weapons with which he might act upon the world."[78]

Ernest Crosby also found inspiration in Garrison's philosophy of nonresistance. Like Chapman, Crosby penned a celebratory biography—*Garrison the Non-Resistant* (1905)—in which he emphasized Garrison's aggressive manliness.[79] In this volume, he explicitly distanced Garrison from the stigmatized image of the effeminate idealist; asserting that hr was free from "the common defects of reformers" and that "there was nothing abnormal about him," Crosby emphasized Garrison's strong constitution and aptitude for sports.[80] Moreover, he argued that Garrison, who "expressed the obligation of non-resistance in its strongest form," offered ample proof that "the non-resistant is no weakling." Indeed, the potential nonresistant must follow in Garrison's manly footsteps: "Let us beware, however, of imitations and travesties of non-resistance," he warned. "It is no colorless, negative quality, and should have no taint of timidity, no suspicion of effeminacy." Crosby also warned readers to pay no heed to those who criticized them as impracticable for acting on moral principles; he claimed that "the fact that they are impracticable is the very source of their strength, for the attempt to apply them tends to transform the world."[81]

Crosby offered his ideal of manly nonresistance not only in opposition to the image of the impracticable reformer but also as an alternative to the model of military manliness he believed permeated American life, especially with regard to the new quest for empire. He asserted that despite such enthusiasm, "The strenuous man is not the soldier on horseback with saber drawn, but rather the man with folded arms who sees a new truth and utters it regardless of consequences." Moreover, Crosby contended, the nonresistant man possessed superior courage and fortitude because "no one can injure a man who refuses to be hurt; you may kill him but you cannot touch the man in him."[82]

In contrast to the brave nonresistant, Crosby characterized the militarist as weak and cowardly. The project of imperialism displayed special cowardice, he argued, because it involved "unmanly . . . unequal contests" against opponents who did not possess the "advantages of modern artillery."[83] Crosby also criticized what he called "the military idea of manliness" for promoting effeminate qualities, including a fondness for pomp and material finery as well as a tendency toward petty quarrels:

> Why is it that military people are constantly plotting and counter-plotting . . . ? And it is noticeable that such backbitings are usually considered, either rightly or wrongly, as feminine idiosyncrasies while the military profession claims to be of all professions, the most manly. Is it possible that the soldier is effeminate? . . . It seems to me that the position of the military man is a false one . . . his feeling of superiority above his fellows makes him abnormally self-conscious, and hence supersensitive and overtouchy.[84]

Crosby extended this critique to encompass sexuality, arguing that the military life not only inverted gender roles but also promoted "unnatural vices" because it removed "active young men . . . far from the restraining influences of home and . . . of woman's society."[85] Other critics of militarism made similar charges, including anarchist Emma Goldman, who asserted that "the growth of the standing army inevitably adds to the spread of sex perversion; the barracks are the incubators."[86]

That Crosby condemned homosexual acts and defined them as "peculiarities" associated with the military institutions he so despised is somewhat surprising, given that many of the thinkers he admired expressed a vision of social brotherhood in homoerotic terms. These included Walt Whitman and Edward Carpenter as well as J. William Lloyd, an American anarchist and poet who wrote of "the manly love of comrades."[87] Crosby, who published a vast number of poems collected in the volumes *Plain Talk in Psalm and Parable* (1899) and *Swords and Plowshares* (1902), emulated the work of these men in his own verse;[88] some of his poems celebrated manly camaraderie and male physical beauty. "Love's Patriot," for example, embodied a utopian vision of democracy in the figure of "a beautiful lad, with a far-off look in his eye," who engaged in the following exchange with the poet:

> "Then you do as you like in your Land of Love,
> Where every man is free?"
> "Nay, we do as we love," replied the lad,
> And his smile fell full on me.[89]

Crosby also shared the belief that sexuality transcended a mere procreative function: "Sexual love is the origin not only of the human race, but of all our altruism, all our idealism, all our art, all our religion," he declared. "Falling in love, in its larger implication, is the one thing in life worth doing."[90]

Yet, Crosby found it difficult to integrate what he called "these troublesome questions of sex"—and especially same-sex relations—into his vision of a democracy founded on transcendental love.[91] His treatment of Edward Carpenter, whom he considered "the living man who writes the noblest English," illustrates this ambivalence.[92] In his brief biographical study, *Edward Carpenter: Poet and Prophet* (1901), Crosby praised Carpenter for his commitment to the concept of "universal unity" and for renouncing the privileges of wealth and status—for "falling in love with the classes that do the hard work of the world" and joining them in a life of labor. Crosby also endorsed Carpenter's claim that sexual love played a central role in the forging of social unity and praised his "courage and frankness" in addressing same-sex relations:

> Carpenter's idea of sex as the basis of universal unity naturally involves the question of the relationship to each other of members of the same sex, as well as of those of the opposite sexes. . . . Such sentiments are not often spoken of publicly in these days, but it is irrational to condemn them offhand as inverted and abnormal. All variations from the commonplace are abnormal, the good as well as the bad. Genius and philanthropy are abnormal, and the race would come to a standstill if it did not have such abnormal variations among which to choose its pathway.

Crosby further defended Carpenter's celebration of homogenic love, arguing that if "all affection has its basis in sexual instincts," then all forms of love that did not lead to procreation—including the "love of the father for the son" or the love "of sisters for each other"—must also be considered "inverted."[93]

Crosby also expressed reservations about same-sex relations. While he felt Carpenter's ideas worthy because they encouraged a "general, all-embracing love," he was reluctant to endorse the free sexual expression of such love; in effect, he marked a division between the homosocial and the homosexual. He encompassed his critique of homosexuality in the context of the more general "problem of sex": although he criticized the "present system of intersexual relations," which, he argued, encouraged "the binding together for life of ill assorted pairs," he also believed that marriage promoted social stability and contentment—qualities he felt could not be offered by same-sex relations. He did "not believe that much is to be expected from close friendships of a romantic nature between persons of the same sex," asserting that such relationships "involve all the jealousies and selfishness and normal courtship and have none of the physiological and domestic sanctions."[94] Crosby also expressed such reservations in personal terms: after reading Carpenter's pamphlet on "Homogenic Love," he wrote to a friend: "In the future I shall be more lenient to Carpenter's homogeneous friends, but I am thankful I am not built that way."[95]

John Jay Chapman proved far less amenable to positive interpretations of homosexuality. In the numerous essays he published on politics and literature in the early twentieth century, he attempted to disassociate the tradition of idealism from any suggestion of homosexuality and effeminacy. His treatment of Walt Whitman and Ralph Waldo Emerson provides two important cases in point. While Chapman expressed admiration for Whitman's proud eccentricity and bodily vigor, he asserted that Whitman had been erroneously understood, especially by the English, as an authentic representative of the American man, who was very unlike Whitman in his conformist and practical nature. Moreover, Chapman charged that Whitman displayed a lack of intellectual rigor and dismissed his brand of idealism as consisting of mere "rattletrap theories."[96] He singled out the homoeroticism in Whitman's work as particularly "false" and unrepresentative:

> As to his talk about comrades and Manhattanese car-drivers, and brass-founders displaying their brawny arms round each other's brawny necks, all this gush and sentiment in Whitman's poetry is false to life. It has a lyrical value, as representing Whitman's personal feelings, but no one else in the country was ever found who felt or acted like this.[97]

Chapman concluded that while Whitman was "a delightful appearance and a strange creature," he "solve[d] none of the problems of life and [threw] no light on American civilization."[98]

Chapman's critique of Emerson displayed a great deal more ambivalence. Emerson stood alongside Garrison as a major influence on Chapman's intellectual development and political thought. Indeed, at one point, Chapman went so far as to describe Emerson as "the cure and antidote of all the ills of this country."[99] In his influential essay, "Emerson, Sixty Years After" (1898), he heaped on further praise, asserting that Emerson's individualist and idealist attack on the "moral cowardice" of his day should inspire reformers and intellectuals in the present. Yet, as would Santayana more than a decade later, Chapman criticized Emerson for living too much in the world of ideas; he asserted that Emerson suffered from a deficiency of the "lower registers of sensation" that separated him from the world around him.[100]

Chapman charged that this "natural asceticism" caused Emerson to offer misguided and potentially "harmful" advice about sex and love. He directed especially sharp criticism against Emerson's seeming subjugation of heterosexual relations to the broader social ideal of transcendental love:

> This perpetual splitting up of love into two species, one of which is condemned, but admitted to be useful—is it not degrading? There is in Emerson's theory of the relation between the sexes neither good sense, nor manly feeling, nor sound psychology. It is founded on none of these things. It is a pure piece of dogmatism.[101]

Chapman suggested that a crucial problem with Emerson's privileging of universal love was that it failed to distinguish between the sexes: "If an inhabitant of another planet should visit the earth," he asserted, "he would learn from the Italian opera that there were two sexes; and this, after all, is probably the fact with which the education of such a stranger ought to begin."[102] Thus, Chapman found Emerson's doctrine on these issues dangerous and "unmanly"; it even threatened to blur the distinction between the homosocial and homoerotic.

In an unpublished 1919 essay, Chapman leveled a similar critique against Plato and his "revolting provisions" on matters of love and sex. According to Chapman, Plato, much like Emerson, was "a man devoid of sexual instinct, and of all those cognate human feelings which make the home, educate the next generation, and sanctify life." As he had in his analysis of Emerson, Chapman conflated charges of asceticism and homoeroticism, only much more overtly. For example, he complained bitterly that Plato's dangerous teachings on "the relations of the sexes" had been exploited by men like Benjamin Jowett, "the homosexual British classicist," who, because he refused to criticize Plato's sexual morals, allowed "the young Oxford student [to] jog off happily with his license in his pocket."[103]

Chapman attacked Plato's thinking on two levels. First, he insisted that Plato's sexual doctrines—including his proposal of a community of wives—were misguided "practical suggestions" linked to his interest in "brotherly love." Thus, he asserted, Plato's writings on sexual relations must be dismissed as a form of sophistry and should be separated from the worthy idealism proffered elsewhere in his works.[104] Second, Chapman asserted that Plato's Socrates must be differentiated from the historical Socrates. He depicted the latter as "full of common sense, whimsical, humble," a man who met "all comers like a sort of local prizefighter" and who felt comfortable consorting "with link-boys, mechanics, bathmen, and harlots." This Socrates—a "pugnacious" man of the people, Chapman argued—did not share Plato's "unnatural" sexual views; rather, Plato projected them onto his version of Socrates in the *Republic*.[105]

In the last years of his life, Chapman offered an even bolder critique of Plato's sexuality in his volume *Lucian, Plato, and Greek Morals*, in which he directly referred to Plato as an "abnormal pederast" and praised Lucian, who had publicly denounced Plato's interest in young men, for striking a "manly . . . blow against pederasty."[106] Chapman confessed to friends that he had been delighted to discover that Lucian "felt the same way" that he did; he had been troubled by the subject for a long time, and he asserted that "pederasty" (which he defined as synonymous with homosexuality) was the "false note" he had identified in Greek philosophy.[107] In Lucian, Chapman finally found a Greek philosopher whose idealism was free of the "troubling" element of homosexuality.

The attempts by Chapman and Crosby to offer alternatives to the Rooseveltian doctrines of strenuous manhood and practical reform reveal the circumscribed boundaries of the discourse of political manhood in the Progressive Era. Both men shared much the same philosophy as their more powerful foe; they equated manhood with strength, honor, and assertiveness and condemned negative qualities—defined as timidity, cowardice, and snobbery—as effeminate. Moreover, both bespoke an admiration for the values of militarism, despite protestations to the contrary. Indeed, Crosby's peers noted that despite his staunch opposition to all forms of militarism, the allusions and images of warfare permeated his essays and speeches.[108] This was not, of course, anomolous. Leading figures, among them Santayana and both William and Henry James, identified the character of the age as practical, forceful, active—all characteristics they associated with masculinity. The nervous attempts by Crosby and especially Chapman to disentangle the traditions of homoeroticism and idealism reveal that such a model of masculinity implied heterosexuality as well.

Crosby's and Chapman's opposition to Roosevelt ultimately reinforced his narrowing of political culture. The emphasis that all these reformers placed on strenuous and practical qualities worked to solidify the association of politics with masculinity and thereby challenged claims to political power made by Progressive women.[109] Moreover, their attempts to excise homosexuality from ideals of political manhood contributed to a deepening current of antihomosexual sentiment in American public life.

Epilogue

Red Bloods and Mollycoddles in the Twentieth Century and Beyond

In the 1907 essay on "Red-Bloods and Mollycoddles" invoked at the beginning of this book, Goldsworthy Lowes Dickinson offered a critique of the model of red-blooded Rooseveltian manhood. He extended it by speculating about the meaning of the American affinity for "Red-blooded" qualities for the future of this ascendant national power. He voiced skepticism that "a Mollycoddle will ever be produced strong enough to breathe the American air and live" and asserted that this "crucial question" was synonymous with "the question [of] whether America will ever be civilized." Although he recognized that these categories were "the ideal extremes between which the Actual vibrates," he cautioned that the simultaneous embrace of the "Red-blood" and contempt for the "Mollycoddle" would lead to corruption and dysfunction, given that the qualities of both were essential for the production of an ethical and democratic national culture.[1]

Dickinson elaborated on these potential dangers in other essays in the same volume, warning that a current emphasis on assertive and acquisitive individualistic masculinity might produce deep and sustained divisions between rich and poor and an animus toward socialism, manifested in a lack of concern for the plight of poor and working-class people. Bereft of the idealistic and democratic commitments he associated with the mollycoddle, America would, he feared, "fossilize in the form of her present Plutocracy."[2]

Recent historical scholarship on masculinity in American culture suggests that Dickinson's observations were in many ways prescient. Literature on the early twentieth century demonstrates the extent to which an ideal of white masculinity coalesced around valorization of aggressive strenuousness and anxious distrust of qualities believed to be "soft" and feminine. Kristin Hoganson and Sarah Watts have shown that an investment in strenuous manhood profoundly influenced U.S. military intervention abroad and shaped the racist and often brutal military and colonial policies pursued in the late nineteenth and early twentieth centuries. Marlin Ross and Martin Summers have demonstrated that a model of strenuous masculinity shaped African American conceptions of respectable manhood at the same time that a dominant discourse of racialized masculinity positioned black men as inferior and lacking self-control. John F. Kasson has demonstrated the extent to which the virile model of masculinity permeated popular culture and shaped white men's conceptions of themselves and their position in the world, constructed as one of superiority.[3] Gail Bederman has shown that the remaking of white manhood through the discourse of civilization at the turn of the twentieth century reinforced male dominance and white racial superiority. Bederman's work is especially compelling in demonstrating the extent to which this discourse legitimated, and even popularized, acts of violence against African American men and women.[4]

Recently, historians have demonstrated that the model that emerged at the turn of the twentieth century shaped dominant discourses of American national power and proved especially influential in the political culture and foreign policy of the Cold War era.[5] Robert D. Dean's compelling examination of Cold War foreign policy explicates the direct and powerful impact of Roosevelt and other elite men of his generation on the political worldview and conceptions of masculinity of the Cold War–era foreign policy elite, whom he terms the "imperial brotherhood." Dean shows that a commitment to the virtues of the strenuous life, "grounded in prescriptive lessons learned in a series of exclusive male-only institutions—boarding schools, Ivy League fraternities and secret societies, elite military service, metropolitan men's clubs," permeated elite male culture.[6] Boarding schools, for example, "inculcated a masculine code of strength, loyalty, stoic service, and engagement in struggle" and shaped policies intended to assert American global dominance.[7] The "imperial brotherhood" included such men as Dean Acheson, James Forrestal, and George Kennan. As members of Truman's postwar administration, they developed the policy of Cold War containment, both tough and practical, as befit their conception of strenuous manhood.

Despite this masculinist stance, Cold War foreign policy elites found themselves under attack as unmanly. Conservative politicians, drawing on the associations of elite education and refinement with mollycoddle-ish effeminacy, characterized members of the "imperial brotherhood" as too soft and weak—and too identified with European culture—to effectively serve American interests on the global stage. These attacks were generated, in part, by the association of these men with the social policies of the New Deal, criticized as socialist. K. A. Cuordileone, in an exceptionally insightful study of Cold War political culture, argues that elite liberals responded by simultaneously distancing the liberal tradition from communist ideology and reinfusing it with an ethos of nationalist masculine toughness. Cuordileone offers an extended analysis of elite liberal historian Arthur Schlesinger Jr.'s influential 1949 book, *The Vital Center*, arguing that the formulation of "the vital center" and the broader political consensus in the 1950s positioned all forms of political "extremism"—from fascism on the right to communism on the left—as both un-American and "deficient in manliness."[8]

As Dean, Cuordileone, and others have shown, prominent American men interpreted the domestic and international crises of the Cold War era through the lenses of gender and sexuality. Fears about the American ability to emerge triumphant found expression in the diagnosis of "The Crisis of American Masculinity," the title of a 1958 *Esquire* article by Schlesinger.[9] In many ways, this "crisis" resembled that of the late nineteenth and early twentieth centuries: it was understood as a product of conformity and loss of individualism within the corporate workplace, estrangement from vigorous activity related to the domestication of boys within the female-dominated home, and the expansion of women's social, cultural, and political power. Cuordileone argues, however, that the mid-twentieth-century "crisis" differed in that it bespoke "nagging doubts that a male body naturally possessed a male identity,"[10] influenced in large part by psychological writing on the malleability of gender identity and manifested in growing concerns about the stability of male identity and a growing self-consciousness among men. Schlesinger maintained, for example, that "today men are more and more conscious of maleness not as a fact but as a problem."[11] Cuordileone shows that these concerns focused largely on homosexuality, associated with effeminacy, weakness, and pathology; the assertion of masculine identity and power required the affirmation of heterosexuality.

Scholarship on the political culture of the Cold War has amply demonstrated the centrality of homosexuality to constructions of nationalist masculinity during this period. Robert Dean and David K. Johnson show that the links between the "red scare" and the "lavender scare" extend beyond the rhetorical. Men accused of homosexuality found themselves vilified as morally weak and pathological traitors. The careers of foreign service officials were ruined, employees of the State Department and other federal offices were fired and sometimes imprisoned, and the red-baiting of Joseph McCarthy and J. Edgar Hoover often associated homosexuality with communist sympathy and treasonous acts. Indeed, communism and homosexuality were deeply imbricated within postwar anticommunist ideology. Schlesinger, for example, asserted that communists could "identify each other (and be identified by their enemies) on casual meetings by the use of certain phrases, the names of certain friends, by certain enthusiasms and certain silences," and likened this to forms of identification and association among homosexual men.[12]

My work suggests that, while worries about the stability of male identity and related concerns about the meaning and effects of homosexuality may have been more pervasive in Cold War culture, this nexus became firmly established in the late nineteenth and early twentieth centuries, at the very same time the "sexual invert" was identified as a particular social, cultural, and political type. In different ways, the reformers discussed in this book understood their own gendered identities as unstable or, in Schlesinger's terms, as a "problem" rather than as a "fact." Stover, Elliott, and Osborne, for example, consciously crafted masculine images in the Whitmanesque mold in order to assert an identity that encompassed both toughness and an eroticized vision of male homosociality. Chapman and Crosby too worked to demonstrate that political idealism could be congruent with masculinity, disavowing historical figures they had once admired or making nervous attempts to disassociate those figures from models of homosexuality. Even Roosevelt's self-construction as exemplar of practical and strenuous American masculinity contained anxieties about his own gendered body, manifested by his obsession with athleticism and muscularity and by the opportunist use of political invective to portray opponents as undesirable mollycoddles who were not quite male. Although anxieties about male subjectivity did not always draw explicitly on medical models of gender and sexual inversion, they always addressed a perceived instability of the binary gender categories. Thus, medical/psychological concerns might best be understood as responding to—as well as generating—models of gender and sexuality that asserted both unstable gender and non-normative sexual desire. The emergence of the term "third sex" in political discourse before it appeared in sexological literature illustrates this point.

Although the term "mollycoddle" did not often appear in Cold War discourse, its popular usage in the first half of the twentieth century elucidates some of the connections between turn-of-the-century and Cold War understandings of gender instability and homosexuality. Despite attempts by Dickinson and others to redefine the term more positively, its use in the United States largely followed the Rooseveltian definition: the mollycoddle was a social problem and a threat to normative American sex and gender categories. In the early twentieth century, for example, child care experts offered advice to parents on how not to raise a mollycoddle son; this literature offered similar prescriptive advice from medical professionals who warned of the dangers of "acquired inversion": for example, boys were to engage in competitive physical activity, be prevented from engaging in activities associated with girls, and be dissuaded from establishing a close identification with their mother.[13]

The mollycoddle was also a ubiquitous figure in popular culture. Film scholar Gaylyn Studlar shows that the actor Douglas Fairbanks Jr. built his early cinematic career embodying a mollycoddle who undergoes a transformation and emerges as a red-blooded American man.[14] In Victor Fleming's 1920 film, *The Mollycoddle*, for example, Fairbanks plays Richard Marshall V, who at first looks a great deal like the young and effete Theodore Roosevelt (he dons a monacle and pocket square and carries a cane). Marshall, who moved to Europe as a child, appears so much the mollycoddle that he is mistaken for a European by a group of American tourists: "That fellow is contrary to the Constitution of the United States," exclaims one American character. Through a series of character-building exploits—including hard physical labor and militarist interaction with American Indians in the West—Marshall becomes masculinized and Americanized. At the end of the film he emerges as a red-blooded man, a worthy descendent of forefathers who fought in the Revolutionary War and "pioneered" the American frontier.[15]

Fairbanks's mollycoddle roles also gave dramatic shape to white male anxieties about homosexuality. In *The Mollycoddle,* for example, the Fairbanks character is first indoctrinated into heterosexuality by forging a relationship with a virtuous and feminine American woman. In an earlier film, *Double Trouble* (1915), Fairbanks plays a character who suffers from a split personality. He has lived as two men defined in polar terms that closely align with Roosevelt's construction of political manhood. He began life as Florian Amidon, an effete and effeminate upper-class northeastern mollycoddle identified as both a Christian reformer and a Sunday school teacher. After he is accidentally hit on the head, he assumes a new personality, that of Eugene Brassfield, a tough working-class type who achieves success as a corrupt, womanizing machine politician. The event that causes the character to recognize and ultimately reconcile these two identities is presented as a moment of homosexual panic. When Fairbanks's character reverts to the Florian persona on vacation, a homosexual hotel porter, presented in negative and stereotypically effeminate terms, perceives him as homosexual and makes a pass at him. The film ends with Florian/Eugene eschewing the homosexual effeminacy of the mollycoddle and the venal and corrupt qualities of the "tough" and embracing a red-blooded and heterosexual persona positioned between these two poles.[16]

The 1906 novel upon which the film *Double Trouble* was based, Herbert Quick's *Double Trouble, or, Every Hero His Own Villain,* is even more explicit in its psychological and political framing of the mollycoddle. The first page contains a neurological diagnosis of Florian, in which he is described as both neurasthenic and sexually inverted based on symptoms that include "fondness for the poetry of Whitman and Browning (see Nordau); . . . pronounced nervous[ness] and emotional irritability during adolescence; aversion to young women in society; stubborn

Douglas Fairbanks Jr. in *The Mollycoddle*, 1920.

Courtesy Kino International

clinging to celibacy."[17] In this version, the central character changes personality multiple times and his political positions transform accordingly, which is a source of much anxiety and confusion for his fiancée, Elizabeth Waldron. Elizabeth warns the ward-heeler Brassfield, "you have confined yourself too closely to the practical and productively utilitarian," and beseeches him to work to lift the city's "civic life to a higher plane." As Florian, however, the protagonist proves so attached to the idealized promotion of governmental and sexual purity that his platform is ridiculed and ultimately ignored by other politicians. Elizabeth too proves critical of excessive purity in men; in a letter to a friend she expresses a desire to take the "Miss Nancy" qualities of men like Florian and the "forceful" qualities associated with Brassfield and "grind [them] to a pulp and mix them, the compromise would be my ideal."[18]

The transformation of these mollycoddle characters corresponds to an Anglo-American literary tradition explicated by Eve Sedgwick, in which heterosexual male identity, always unstable, is defined as that which is not homosexual; the homosexual functions primarily as a negative referent for the assertion of heterosexual male identity and power. It also recalls in important ways the continuum of political manhood defined by Roosevelt, in which the effeminate mollycoddle stands outside of, and defines the limits of, proper male homosociality in American life. Cinematic narratives of mollycoddle transformation also reinforced the prescriptive notion that, through indoctrination and socialization, boys and men might rid their identities of the vestiges of effeminacy and become red-blooded American men.[19]

Narratives of mollycoddle transformation also forecast the negotiation of masculine identity and power within the political culture of the Cold War. Ubiquitous and repetitive narratives, exemplified by Fairbanks's cinematic characters, worked not to secure and stabilize a definition of white manhood but to underscore its shaky foundations. In Schlesinger's terms, such public hand-wringing about the contours of masculine identity produced a "self-consciousness" that he viewed as undermining American national power.[20] Cuordelione shows that Schlesinger and other Cold Warriors attempted to naturalize national male power by laying out a broad swath of terrain—"the vital center"—as both American and manly and by identifying both the homosexual and the communist, often configured as overlapping or indistinguishable, as gendered and political threats. Of course, this formulation owes a great deal to Roosevelt, seen as emblematic of the kind of masculinity necessary for the anticommunist struggle. Indeed, the extent to which Schlesinger borrowed from Roosevelt's model of a masculine American "center" is remarkable. Schlesinger figured communists in a way that closely resembled Roosevelt's depiction of anarchists, despite the gap in ideology between the two, and he used similar phrases and terms to describe political threats to American manhood and American national interests.[21]

Attempts by Schlesinger and other liberal Cold Warriors to identify a stable model of American political manhood proved unsuccessful, as had the efforts of Roosevelt and his supporters. As David Johnson has shown, the persecution and demonization of homosexuals in the name of securing national interests and fighting communism, while immensely damaging to individual lives and reputations, also worked to widen the discursive terrain on which homosexuality was defined and discussed and helped to launch the postwar homophile movement. Drawing on the example of the civil rights movement, homophiles reconfigured homosexuals as a minority population deserving of rights and protections.[22]

The homophile movement, a progenitor of the more recent movement for LGBT rights, complicated but in no way ended the vexed and vituperous negotiation of the political meanings attached to gender and sexuality, as is evinced by recent U.S. political history. In the 1976 presidential election, Ronald Reagan drew on the red-blooded cinematic image of John Wayne to construct himself as a credible presidential candidate committed to a hard-line foreign policy that would reassert American global power. His supporters ridiculed incumbent Jimmy Carter as soft, sentimental, and weak. Patrician George W. Bush, reacting in part to the popular characterization of his father as an elitist "wimp," carefully honed his image as a rough, "straight-shooting" Texan, devoted to the priorities of the "common man," despite his clear affinity for serving the interests of corporate elites.[23] Bush's 2004 reelection campaign worked aggressively to sustain the red-blooded image of a masculine protector who would bring terrorists to justice, "dead or alive," and caricatured the Democratic opponent as an effeminate and suspiciously "French" patrician, domesticated by feminism and profoundly unprepared to carry out the masculine duties of a commander-in-chief. If the Bush campaign proved somewhat circumspect about linking Kerry's effeminacy directly to homosexuality, its interlocutors did not. Journalists and cultural commentators portrayed Kerry and his running mate, John Edwards, as overly and physically affectionate with each other and connected this appearance of "gayness" to their alleged support of feminist causes and LGBT rights.[24]

These examples and countless others in the recent past illustrate that despite massive transformations in the histories of the United States and the world, and despite important challenges to gender and political order waged by feminists, human rights activists, and others, dominant constructions of American national power and political leadership remain organized by a gendered vision that exalts red-blooded masculine power, most often tethered to a male body and produced through the marginalization or repudiation of individuals and qualities defined as feminine or homosexual. Recent attempts by conservative politicians to recuperate the legacy of Theodore Roosevelt—including presidential political advisor Karl Rove's invocation of Roosevelt as the tough and virile model for George W. Bush's domestic "populism" and "aggressive" foreign policy, and Harvard government professor Harvey Mansfield's call for a renaissance of Rooseveltian "manliness" in American life—testify to the tenacity of this red-blooded ethos.[25] At the same time, an association of femininity and homosexuality with the qualities of weakness and un-American political ideologies often works to relegate a whole range of causes—from equitable social provision to diplomatic international engagement—to the suspect domain of the mollycoddle.

Notes

INTRODUCTION

1. Theodore Roosevelt, "The College Man: An Address Delivered at the Harvard Union," 1907. This lecture is transcribed in Donald Wilhelm's *Theodore Roosevelt as an Undergraduate* (Boston: John W. Luce and Company, 1910), 78–90.

2. Roosevelt defined these ideals of strenuous manhood in a number of essays and lectures between 1899 and 1901—among them "The Strenuous Life," "Fellow-Feeling as a Political Factor," "Civic Helpfulness," Character and Success," "Promise and Performance," "The American Boy," "National Duties," and "Christian Citizenship"—published collectively in his *The Strenuous Life: Essays and Addresses* (New York: The Century Co., 1901). A search of indexed periodicals and newspapers turns up relatively few uses of the term "mollycoddle" before 1907; an abundance of such usages, a number of which are addressed in chapter 1, appear after Roosevelt's famous speech.

3. Goldsworthy Lowes Dickinson, "Red-Bloods and 'Mollycoddles,'" in his *Appearances: Notes of Travel, East and West* (New York: Doubleday, 1914), 180–86. See also Dennis Proctor, ed., *The Autobiography of G. Lowes Dickinson and Other Writings* (London: Duckworth, 1973). Proctor's introduction quotes from unpublished autobiographical writings that addressed Dickinson's self-identification as "homosexual" (1–32).

4. Dickinson, *Appearances*, 181–82.

5. Dickinson, *Appearances*, 184. For compelling analyses of the intersection of nationalism and strenuous manhood in Roosevelt's career and the impact of this nationalism broadly, see Sarah Watts, *Rough Rider in the White House: Theodore*

Roosevelt and the Politics of Desire (Chicago: University of Chicago Press, 2003); and Kristin L. Hoganson, *Fighting for American Manhood: How Gender Politics Provoked the Spanish-American and Philippine-American Wars* (New Haven and London: Yale University Press, 1998).

6. Dickinson, *Appearances*, 184.

7. In addition to Watts, *Rough Rider*, and Hoganson, *Fighting for American Manhood*, see Arnaldo Testi, "The Gender of Reform Politics: Theodore Roosevelt and the Culture of Masculinity," *Journal of American History* 81, no. 4 (Mar. 1995): 1525–26; and Gail Bederman, *Manliness and Civilization: A Cultural History of Gender and Race in the United States, 1880–1917* (Chicago and London: University of Chicago Press, 1995), 170–216.

8. See Jennifer Terry, *An American Obsession: Science, Medicine, and Homosexuality in Modern Society* (Chicago: University of Chicago Press, 1999), chaps. 1–2; Jay Hatheway, *The Gilded Age Construction of Modern American Homophobia* (New York: Palgrave MacMillan, 2003); Jonathan Ned Katz, *The Invention of Heterosexuality* (New York: Penguin, 1995), 1–82.

9. On the mugwump movement, see John G. Sproat, *"The Best Men": Liberal Reformers in the Gilded Age* (New York: Oxford University Press, 1968); Matthew Josephson, *The Politicos, 1865–1896* (New York: Harcourt, Brace & World, 1938); Gerald W. MacFarland, *Mugwumps, Morals and Politics, 1884–1920* (Amherst: University of Massachusetts Press, 1975); David M. Tucker, *Public Moralists of the Gilded Age* (Columbia and London: University of Missouri Press, 1998); and Geoffrey Blodgett, "The Mugwump Reputation, 1870 to Present," *Journal of American History* 66, no. 4 (Mar.ch 1980): 867–87. On Gilder, see Herbert F. Smith, *Richard Watson Gilder* (New York: Twayne, 1970); and Arthur John, *The Best Years of the Century: Richard Watson Gilder,* Scribner's *Monthly, and the Century Magazine, 1870–1909* (Urbana: University of Illinois Press, 1981). On Curtis, see Gordon Milne, *George William Curtis and the Genteel Tradition* (Bloomington: Indiana University Press, 1956); and Edward Cary, *George William Curtis* (Boston and New York: Houghton, Mifflin, 1895).

10. Eve Kosofsky Sedgwick developed the theory of homosocial desire in *Between Men: English Literature and Male Homosocial Desire* (New York: Columbia University Press, 1985). See also Richard Dellamora, *Apocalyptic Overtures: Sexual Politics and the Sense of an Ending* (New Brunswick, NJ: Rutgers University Press, 1994); and Linda Dowling, *Hellenism and Homosexuality in Victorian Oxford* (Ithaca, NY: Cornell University Press, 1994).

11. See, for example, Seymour J. Mandelbaum, *Boss Tweed's New York* (New York: John Wiley, 1965); Alexander B. Callow Jr., ed., *The City Boss in America: An Interpretive Reader* (New York: Oxford University Press, 1976); Leo Hershkowitz, *Tweed's New York: Another Look* (New York: Doubleday, 1977). More recent studies of "bossism" have revised this formulation and identified more collaboration of reformers and bosses. See Thomas R. Pegram, "Who's the Boss? Revisiting the History of American Urban Rule," *Journal of Urban History* 28, no. 6 (2002): 821–35.

12. This includes the classic studies by Paul Boyer, *Urban Masses and Moral Order*

in America, 1820–1920 (Cambridge: Harvard University Press, 1978); Nell Irvin Painter, *Standing at Armageddon: The United States, 1877–1919* (New York: Norton, 1987); and McGerr, *A Fierce Discontent: The Rise and Fall of the Progressive Movement in America* (Oxford and New York: Oxford University Press, 2002). In recent years, the class dynamics of Progressive reform have been reinterpreted with more attention to middle-class—though not elite—radicalism and the collaboration of working-class and middle-class individuals. An influential example of this approach is Robert D. Johnston, *The Radical Middle Class: Populist Democracy and the Question of Capitalism in Progressive Era Portland, Oregon* (Princeton: Princeton University Press, 2003).

13. This history is addressed and cited in depth in chapter 1 of this study.

14. On Roosevelt's attempts to present himself as practical and centrist, see Watts, *Rough Rider*, 9–20; and Henry May, *The End of American Innocence: A Study of the First Years of Our Own Time*, 1912–1917 (New York: Knopf, 1959), 9–19.

15. Jane Addams, *The Spirit of Youth in the City Streets* (New York: Macmillan, 1909), 16–17.

16. Ernest H. Crosby, quoted in Leonard D. Abbott, *Ernest Howard Crosby: A Valuation and A Tribute* (Westwood, MA: The Ariel Press, 1907), 20.

17. See Terry, *An American Obsession*, chapters 1 and 2; Katz, *The Invention of Heterosexuality*, 1–56.

18. On women's influence on American political culture in this period see, for example, Paula Baker, "The Domestication of Politics: Women and American Political Society, 1780–1920," *American Historical Review* 89 (1984): 620–47; Robin Muncy, *Creating a Female Dominion in American Reform* (New York: Oxford University Press, 1991); Camilla Stivers, *Bureau Men, Settlement Women: Constructing Public Administration in the Progressive Era* (Lawrence: University of Kansas Press, 2000); and Kathryn Kish Sklar, *Florence Kelley and the Nation's Work: The Rise of Women's Political Culture, 1830–1900* (New Haven: Yale University Press, 1995). Useful historiographical essays on this subject include Elizabeth Israels Perry, "Men Are from the Gilded Age, Women Are from the Progressive Era," *Journal of the Gilded Age and Progressive Era* 1, no. 1 (2002): 25–48; Michael E. McGerr, "Political Style and Women's Power, 1830–1930," *The Journal of American History* (Dec. 1990): 864–85; Lisa D. Bush, "Gender and the Uses of History," *Journal of Urban History* 29, no. 2 (2003): 216–25; and Robin Muncy, "Ambiguous Legacies of Women's Progressivism," *Magazine of History* (May 1999): 15–20.

19. On the scholarly investment in the idea of masculinity in crisis, see Bryce Traister, "Academic Viagra: The Rise of American Masculinity Studies," *American Quarterly* 52, no. 2 (2000): 274–304. Scholarship on the "crisis of masculinity" in this period includes: Clyde Griffen, "Reconstructing Masculinity from the Evangelical Revival to the Waning of Progressivism: A Speculative Synthesis," in Mark C. Carnes and Clyde Griffen, eds., *Meanings for Manhood: Constructions of Masculinity in Victorian America* (Chicago: University of Chicago Press, 1990); J.A. Mangan and James Walvin, eds., *Manliness and Morality: Middle-Class Masculinity in Britain and America, 1800–1940* (New York: St. Martin's Press, 1987); and Anthony Rotundo,

American Manhood: Transformations in Masculinity from the Revolution to the Modern Era (New York: Basic Books, 1993).

20. Socialist and anarchist politics of the period are addressed throughout this study. For a useful overview of these movements, see Painter, *Standing at Armageddon*. On socialism, see Daniel T. Rogers, *Atlantic Crossings: Social Politics in the Progressive Age* (Cambridge, MA: Harvard University Press, 1998); James Weinstein, *The Long Detour: The History and Future of the American Left* (Boulder, CO: Westview Press, 2003), 1–132; and Mary Jo Buhle, *Women and American Socialism, 1870–1920* (Urbana: University of Illinois Press, 1983). On anarchism, see Francis Robert Shor, *Utopianism and Radicalism in Reforming America, 1888–1918* (Westport, CT: Greenwood Press, 1997).

1. Of Mugwumps and Mollycoddles: Patronage and the Political Discourse of the "Third Sex"

1. *Minneapolis Journal*, April 14, 1907. Copy found in Richard Watson Gilder Papers, New York Public Library Rare Books and Manuscripts Collection, Box 32, Scrapbook #13, "1906 (Gilder-Hearst Affair)."

2. Richard Watson Gilder, "William R. Hearst's Long-Cherished Design," *New York Times*, Oct. 18, 1906, 8.

3. Gilder, "William R. Hearst's Long-Cherished Design," 8.

4. "The Question of Manliness," *New York Times*, Oct. 28, 1906, 8.

5. This remark was made by Representative Mark Sullivan, Democrat of Massachusetts, on February 13, 1906. Sullivan also questioned Hearst's masculinity on the grounds that he made "cowardly newspaper attacks" rather than criticizing opponents face to face. Quoted in David Nasaw, *The Chief: The Life of William Randolph Hearst* (New York: Houghton Mifflin, 2000), 187–88.

6. The *New York Times* editorial page backed up Osborne's characterization in an editorial of the same day entitled "A New and Sinister Figure." "Osborne Flays Hearst as Foe of Democracy" and "A New and Sinister Figure," *New York Times*, Oct. 24, 1906, 4. Reformer Jacob A. Riis and poet Edwin Markham defended Gilder and criticized Hearst in similar fashion. Jacob A. Riis, "Letter to the Editor of the *New York World*," reprinted in "Hearst Insults Gilder, Jacob A. Riis Replies," *New York Times*, Oct. 28, 1906, 8. Edwin H. Markham, "Reply to Mr. Gilder," *New York Times*, Oct. 19, 1906, 8.

7. *New York Journal*, Oct. 20, 1906.

8. Already in 1906 Hearst had challenged the masculinity of prominent reformer R. Fulton Cutting, to whom he referred as an "overfed, too delicate, quite worthless poodle," as well as his Republican opponent, Charles Evans Hughes, whom he dismissed as an "animated featherduster." This characterization of Cutting ran in the *New York Journal*, May 19, 1906. The criticism of Hughes was reported in the *Chicago Tribune*, Oct. 31, 1906. Sources were collected in a scrapbook compiled by Gilder. Richard Watson Gilder Papers, New York Public Library Rare Books and Manuscripts Collection, Box 32, Scrapbook #13.

9. On the "fairy" as "intermediate sex" in urban America at the turn of the century, see George Chauncey, *Gay New York: Gender, Urban Culture, and the Making of the Gay Male World, 1890–1940* (New York: Basic Books, 1994), especially 47–64.

10. The term "homosexual" was invented in 1868 by German physician Karl Westphal. However, it did not enter into popular use until the early part of the twentieth century. Jonathan Ned Katz, *The Invention of Heterosexuality* (New York: Penguin, 1995), 10; Jennifer Terry, *An American Obsession: Science, Medicine and Homosexuality in Modern Society* (Chicago: University of Chicago Press, 1999), 36.

11. On the mugwump movement, see John G. Sproat, *"The Best Men": Liberal Reformers in the Gilded Age* (New York: Oxford University Press, 1968); Matthew Josephson, *The Politicos, 1865-1896* (New York: Harcourt, Brace & World, 1938); Gerald W. MacFarland, *Mugwumps, Morals and Politics, 1884–1920* (Amherst: University of Massachusetts Press, 1975); and David M. Tucker, *Public Moralists of the Gilded Age* (Columbia and London: University of Missouri Press, 1998). On Gilder, see Herbert F. Smith, *Richard Watson Gilder* (New York: Twayne, 1970); and Arthur John, *The Best Years of the Century: Richard Watson Gilder,* Scribner's *Monthly, and the* Century *Magazine, 1870–1909* (Urbana: University of Illinois Press, 1981). On Curtis, see Gordon Milne, *George William Curtis and the Genteel Tradition* (Bloomington: Indiana University Press, 1956); and Edward Cary, *George William Curtis* (Boston and New York: Houghton Mifflin, 1895). On mugwumps and the presidential election of 1884, see Mark Wahlgren Summers, *Rum, Romanism, and Rebellion: The Making of a President, 1884* (Durham: University of North Carolina Press, 2000).

12. On the history of sexological models of the "third sex" in medical discourse, see Terry, *An American Obsession*; Vernon A. Rosario, ed., *Science and Homosexualities* (New York and London: Routledge, 1997); Jay Hatheway, *The Gilded Age Construction of Modern American Homophobia* (New York: Palgrave MacMillan, 2003); Vern L. Bullough, "The Development of Sexology in the USA in the Early Twentieth Century," in Roy Porter and Mikulas Teich, eds., *Sexual Knowledge, Sexual Science: The History of Attitudes to Sexuality* (Cambridge: Cambridge University Press, 2004), 303–22; and Nancy Ordover, *American Eugenics: Race, Queer Anatomy, and the Science of Nationalism* (Minneapolis: University of Minnesota Press, 2003).

13. Social and urban social histories of homosexuality include: Chauncey, *Gay New York*; Nan Alamilla Boyd, *Wide Open Town: A History of Queer San Francisco to 1965* (Berkeley: University of California Press, 2003); Lillian Faderman, *Odd Girls and Twilight Lovers: A History of Lesbian Life in Twentieth-Century America* (New York: Columbia University Press, 2001); and Peter Boag, *Same-Sex Affairs: Constructing and Controlling Homosexuality in the Pacific Northwest* (Berkeley: University of California Press, 2003). Literary and cultural studies include Michael Moon, *Disseminating Whitman: Revision and Corporeality in* Leaves of Grass (Cambridge, MA: Harvard University Press, 1991) and *A Small Boy and Others: Imitation and Initiation in American Culture from Henry James to Andy Warhol* (Durham: Duke University Press, 1998); Siobhan B. Somerville, *Queering the Color Line: Race and the Invention of Homosexuality in American Culture* (Durham: Duke University Press, 2000); and

Michael Trask, *Cruising Modernism: Class and Sexuality in American Literature and Social Thought* (Ithaca, NY: Cornell University Press, 2003).

14. Richard Hofstadter, *Anti-Intellectualism in American Life* (New York: Knopf, 1962), 187–91.

15. Geoffrey Blodgett, "The Mugwump Reputation, 1870 to Present," *Journal of American History* 66, no. 4 (Mar. 1980): 867–87. On gender and criticism of the mugwumps, see also David G. Pugh, *Sons of Liberty: The Masculine Mind in Nineteenth-Century America* (Westport, CT: Greenwood Press, 1983), 100–109; and Arnoldo Testi, "The Gender of Reform Politics: Theodore Roosevelt and the Culture of Masculinity," *Journal of American History* 81, no. 4 (Mar. 1995): 1525–1527. On gender and party politics, see Rebecca Edwards, *Angels in the Machinery: Gender in American Party Politics from the Civil War to the Progressive Era* (New York: Oxford University Press, 1997).

16. Blodgett, "The Mugwump Reputation," 882–83.

17. Harlen Makemson, "A 'Dude and Pharisee': Cartoon Attacks on *Harper's Weekly* Editor George William Curtis and the Mugwumps in the Presidential Campaign of 1884," *Journalism History* 29, no. 4 (Winter 2004): 179–89. Makemson quotes "Dudes, Cads and Boys," *New York Daily Tribune*, Apr. 22, 1883.

18. On the history of the "dude," see Richard A. Hill, "You've Come a Long Way, Dude: A History," *American Speech* 69, no. 3 (Autumn 1994): 321–27.

19. On the periodical press and this perceived feminization, see Ann Douglas, *The Feminization of American Culture* (New York: Knopf, 1977), 227–58.

20. George William Curtis, *Orations and Addresses of George William Curtis*, ed. Charles Elliot Norton (New York, 1894), II:386–87.

21. Kristin L. Hoganson, *Fighting for American Manhood: How Gender Politics Provoked the Spanish-American and Philippine-American Wars* (New Haven and London: Yale University Press, 1998).

22. Politician Joseph Foraker described the illiberal Republican contingent at the 1884 Republican convention as effete and effeminate snobs who wore "their hair parted in the middle, banged in front, wore an eyeglass, rolled their r's and pronounced the word either with the *i* sound instead of the *e*." Joseph B. Foraker, *Notes of a Busy Life* (Cincinnati, 1917), I:167–68.

23. Blaine's cousin Gail Hamilton (Mary Abigail Dodge) introduced the term "political hermaphrodite." See Blodgett, "The Mugwump Reputation," 883–84. According to Sproat, Theodore Roosevelt also used the term in reference to the mugwumps. See Sproat, *"The Best Men"*, 133. See also *New York Sun*, Apr. 20, 1897.

24. Charles Francis Adams, "Individuality in Politics: A Lecture" delivered at Steinway Hall, New York, April 21, 1880. Pamphlet published by Independent Republican Association (New York, 1880), 4–5. Richard Rogers Bowker Papers, New York Public Library Rare Books and Manuscripts Collection.

25. George William Curtis, "Machine Politics and the Remedy," lecture delivered May 20, 1880. Pamphlet published by the Independent Republican Association (New York, 1880), 3. Richard Rogers Bowker Papers, New York Public Library Rare Books and Manuscripts Collection.

26. On the critique of partisanship in the Gilded Age, see, for example, John M. Dobson, *Politics in the Gilded Age: A New Perspective on Reform* (New York: Praeger, 1972); and Mark Wahlgren Summers, *Party Games: Getting, Keeping, and Using Power in Gilded Age Politics* (Chapel Hill: University of North Carolina Press, 2004).

27. Adams to Charles Milnes Gaskell, May 24, 1875, in Harold D. Cater, ed., *Henry Adams and His Friends: A Collection of His Unpublished Letters* (Boston: Houghton Mifflin, 1947), 67.

28. R. R. Bowker quoted in Michael E. McGerr, *The Decline of Popular Politics: The American North, 1865–1928* (New York and Oxford: Oxford University Press, 1986), 56.

29. Adams, "Individuality in Politics: A Lecture," 14; Curtis, "Machine Politics and the Remedy," 4.

30. Sproat argues that the "myopic mugwumps . . . overestimated their strength and importance" and questions their claim to have swung the 1884 presidential election to Cleveland. Sproat, *"The Best Men"*, 127, 139–41. Geoffrey Blodgett contends that Massachussetts mugwumps' "influence at the ballot box was hardly as telling as they would have had it. . . . Their flirtation with the Democratic party, dictated by their bolt in 1884, did contribute to a striking Democratic revival in the state around 1890, but resulted in no permanent change in the structure of state politics." Blodgett, "The Mind of the Boston Mugwumpery," *Mississippi Valley Historical Review* 48 (Mar. 1962): 614. John M. Dobson concludes: "The problem the Mugwumps faced—how best to alter existing system—troubles reformers today as well. The Mugwumps chose to abandon their party positions and try to influence the course of political events from outside the regular organizations. In the long run, this tactic proved unsuccessful. Those Independents who stayed with the Republican party were the ones who ultimately helped determine what changes would occur." Dobson, *Politics in the Gilded Age*, 188.

31. Sproat, *"The Best Men"*, 127. Among those refusing to bolt were Henry Cabot Lodge and Theodore Roosevelt. See Dobson, *Politics in the Gilded Age*, 112–17.

32. Blaine quoted in Sproat, *"The Best Men"*, 141; Conkling's remarks come from an interview with the *New York Herald*, Nov. 9, 1877.

33. Two excellent and thorough overviews of the civil service reform movement are Ari Hoogenboom, *Outlawing the Spoils: A History of the Civil Service Reform Movement, 1865–1883* (Urbana: University of Illinois Press, 1961); and Paul P. Van Riper, *History of the United States Civil Service* (Evanston, IL: Row, Peterson, 1958). See also Brian J. Cook, *Bureaucracy and Self-Government: Reconsidering the Role of Public Administration in American Politics* (Baltimore: Johns Hopkins University Press, 1996), 65–97.

34. Letter of June 30, 1876, from Curtis to Hayes. Quoted in Milne, *George William Curtis and the Genteel Tradition*, 152.

35. Hayes quoted in David M. Jordan, *Roscoe Conkling of New York: Voice in the Senate* (Ithaca, NY and London: Cornell University Press, 1971), 267. Hayes wrote Curtis that the two issues on his platform he cared most about "were the Civil Service, and the South." Hayes to Curtis, July 10, 1876, quoted in Hoogenboom, *Outlawing the Spoils*, 143.

36. According to Ari Hoogenboom, most state legislators were opposed to civil service reform but passed legislation in response to public pressure. Over the next several years, party politicians enacted laws that "took the starch out" of these civil service measures. Hoogenboom, *Outlawing the Spoils*, 256–58.

37. Curtis, "Machine Politics and the Remedy," 10–11.

38. Some mugwumps proved more likely than others to invoke such prejudices. While Curtis avoided ethnic stereotypes, others, including *The Nation* editor E. K. Godkin, resorted to anti-Irish rhetoric. In an editorial criticizing New York political organization Tammany Hall, Godkin referred to Irish men as "bummers, rowdies, drunkards, gamblers, pugilists, bilks, shysters, and deadbeats." E. L. Godkin, "Tammany Apologists," *The Nation* (Jan. 26, 1893):60.

39. On charges of elitism in civil service examinations, see Robert Maranto and David Schulz, *A Short History of the U.S. Civil Service* (Lanham, MD: University Press of America, 1991), 41–44. George Washington Plunkitt railed against civil service examinations as testing for arcane and impractical knowledge: "questions about Egyptian mummies and how many years it will take for a bird to wear out a mass of iron as big as the earth by steppin' on its once in a century." George Washington Plunkitt, "The Curse of Civil Service Reform," *Plunkitt of Tammany Hall: A Series of Very Plain Talks on Very Practical Politics*, ed. William Riordan (New York: E. P. Dutton, 1963). In a similar facetious vein, an 1884 New York editorial referred to the "examination of men in Greek and Latin to see if they can lay brick or paint fences." *New York Tribune*, Oct. 2, 1884, 6.

40. Ingalls made this statement in a fascinating "photographic interview" for the *New York World*, Apr. 13, 1890, 19–22. He also stated: "Patronage will allure the ambitious, force will coerce the timid, demagogism will gull the credulous, fraud will rule the weak, money will buy the mercenary." His words were widely reported and criticized in the liberal press. *The Nation*, for example, excoriated Ingalls for these comments twice in 1890 (June 19), 480; and Nov. 13, 418). Ingalls defended his remarks as "legitimate political warfare" on the floor of the Senate. *Congressional Record—Senate*, 51st Cong., 2nd sess. (Jan. 14, 1891), 1278.

41. George William Curtis, "The Duty of the American Scholar to Politics and the Times: an oration delivered before the Literary Societies of Wesleyan University, Middletown, Conn., August 5, 1856," in Norton, ed., *Orations and Addresses of George William Curtis*, 13, 32.

42. George William Curtis, "The Public Duty of Educated Men: an oration delivered at the commencement of Union College, June 27, 1877," in Norton, ed., *Orations and Addresses of George William Curtis*, 269–70.

43. George William Curtis, "The Relation Between Morals and Politics, Illustrated by the Civil-Service System: an address delivered before the Unitarian conference at Saratoga, N.Y., September 20, 1878," in Norton, ed., *Orations and Addresses of George William Curtis*, 130.

44. See E. Anthony Rotundo, *American Manhood: Transformations in Masculinity from the Revolution to the Modern Era* (New York: Basic Books, 1993), 271. On abolitionist notions of manhood, see Donald Yacovone, "Abolitionists and the 'Language of

Fraternal Love,'" in Mark C. Carnes and Clyde Griffin, eds., *Meanings for Manhood: Constructions of Masculinity in Victorian America* (Chicago: University of Chicago Press, 1990), 85–95. For a more comprehensive examination of nineteenth-century models of manliness, see Gail Bederman, "'Civilization,' the Decline of Middle-Class Manliness, and Ida B. Wells's Antilynching Campaign (1892–1894)," *Radical History Review* 52 (Winter 1992): 5–32. On middle-class gender roles in antebellum America, see Mary P. Ryan, *Cradle of the Middle Class: The Family in Oneida County, New York, 1790–1865* (Cambridge and New York: Cambridge University Press, 1981).

45. Of course, women played leading roles in antislavery politics and men who supported abolitionism were attacked as feminine. See Michael D. Pierson, *Free Hearts and Free Homes: Gender and American Antislavery Politics* (Chapel Hill: University of North Carolina Press, 2003); and Bruce Dorsey, *Reforming Men and Women: Gender in the Antebellum City* (Ithaca, NY: Cornell University Press, 2002).

46. James Russell Lowell quoted in McGerr, *The Decline of Popular Politics*, 56.

47. Richard Rogers Bowker, *Christian Union*, Apr. 26, 1876.

48. Curtis expressed this view as follows: "Armed with the arbitrary power of patronage, party overbears the free expression of the popular will and entrenches it in illicit power. It makes the whole Civil Service a drilled and disciplined army whose living depends upon carrying elections at any cost for the party which controls it." George William Curtis, "Party and Patronage: an address prepared for the eleventh annual meeting of the National Civil Service Reform League in Baltimore, April 28, 1891," in Norton, ed., *Orations and Addresses of George William Curtis*, 489.

49. Twain made this statement in 1884 in an effort to convince independent-minded Republicans not to vote for Blaine for president. Quoted in Sproat, *"The Best Men"*, 128.

50. Curtis, "Machine Politics and the Remedy," 9.

51. Committee of the National Civil Service Reform League, "To the Voters of the United States" (October 31, 1882). Pamphlet Collection of the New York Public Library.

52. Elliott J. Gorn, *The Manly Art: Bare Knuckle Prize Fighting in America* (Ithaca, NY: Cornell University Press, 1990), 252. On nineteenth-century working-class masculinity, see also Roy Rosenzweig, *Eight Hours for What They Will* (Cambridge: Cambridge University Press, 1983), 56–64; and David Montgomery, *The Fall of the House of Labor* (Cambridge: Cambridge University Press, 1987), 86–93. For an exhaustive account of "sporting life" in New York City, see Timothy Gilfoyle, *City of Eros*, especially chapter 5. For an in-depth discussion of the prominence of the saloon in male working-class life in the late nineteenth century, see Perry R. Duis, *The Saloon: Public Drinking in Chicago and Boston, 1880–1920* (Urbana and Chicago: University of Illinois Press, 1983).

53. Michael McGerr, "Political Style and Women's Power, 1830–1930," *The Journal of American History* (Dec. 1990):866. On manliness and the political culture of the "party period," see also McGerr, *The Decline of Popular Politics*; Paula Baker, "The Domestication of Politics: Women and American Political Society, 1780–1920," *American Historical Review* 89:620–47; and Jean H. Baker, *Affairs of Party: The*

Political Culture of Northern Democrats in the Mid-Nineteenth Century (Ithaca, NY: Cornell University Press, 1983).

54. Tammany leader Richard Croker claimed that patronage produced citizens: "And so . . . we need to bribe them [poor New Yorkers] with spoils. Call it so if you like. Spoils vary in different countries. Here they take the shape of offices . . . I admit it is not the best way. But it is for practical purposes the only way. Think what New York is and what the people of New York are. One half, more than one half, are of foreign birth. We have thousands upon thousands of men who are alien born, who have no ties connecting them with the city or the state. They do not speak our language, they do not know our laws, they are the raw material with which we have to build up the state." Quoted in W. T. Stead, "Mr. Richard Croker and Greater New York," *Review of Reviews* (October 1897):345.

Likewise, George Washington Plunkitt argued that an end to patronage meant an end to patriotism for urban men: "I have good reason for sayin' that most of the Anarchists in this city today are men who ran up against civil service examinations. Isn't it enough to make a man sour on his country when he wants to serve it and won't be allowed unless he answers a lot of fool questions about the number of cubic inches of water in the Atlantic and the quality of sand in the Sahara desert? There was once a bright young man in my district who tackled one of these examinations. The next I heard of him he had settled won in Herr Most's saloon smokin' and drinkin' beer and talkin' socialism all day. Before that time he had never drank anything but whisky. I knew what was comin' when a young Irishman drops whisky and takes to beer and long pipes in a German saloon. That young man is today one of the wildest Anarchists in town. And just to think! He might be a patriot but for that cussed civil service." George Washington Plunkitt, "The Curse of Civil Service Reform," in Riordan, ed., *Plunkitt of Tammany Hall.*

55. Terry, *An American Obsession*, 35. German sexologist Karl Heinrich Ulrichs first wrote on sexual inversion in 1864. German medical professionals Karl Westphal and Richard von Krafft-Ebing developed Ulrichs's formulation. On sexual inversion and medical discourse in Europe and the United States, in addition to Terry, see Hatheway, *The Gilded Age Construction*, 101–56; Lisa Duggan, *Sapphic Slashers: Sex, Violence, and American Modernity* (Durham and London: Duke University Press, 2000), 156–79; George Chauncey Jr., "From Inversion to Homosexuality: Medicine and the Changing Conceptualization of Female Deviance," *Salmagundi* 58–59 (1982–83):114–46; and Vernon Rosario, ed., *Science and Homosexualities* (New York: Routledge, 1997).

56. Terry, *An American Obsession*, 78. See also Hatheway, *The Gilded Age Construction*, 1–10; Bullough, "The Development of Sexology in the USA in the Early Twentieth Century," 303–22; and Margaret Gibson, "The Masculine Degenerate: American Doctors' Portrayals of the Lesbian Intellect, 1880–1949," *Journal of Women's History* 9, no. 4 (Winter 1998).

57. E. C. Spitzka, "A Historical Case of Sexual Perversion, Medical Record (August 20, 1881)," excerpted in Jonathan Ned Katz, *Gay/Lesbian Almanac* (New York: Harper & Row, 1983), 179–80. Like every other scholar who works on same-sex sexu-

ality in the United States, I am enormously indebted to Katz for his scholarship and for the work he has done to produce an archive for this area of study.

58. Hatheway, *The Gilded Age Construction*, 113.

59. On "sodomitical" or "molly" cultures in the Anglo-American world, see Rictor Norton, *Mother Clap's Molly House: The Gay Subculture in England 1700–1830* (London: GMP Publishers, 1992); Thomas A. Foster, *Sex and the Eighteenth-Century Man: Massachusetts and the History of Sexuality in America* (Boston: Beacon Press, 2006); Clare A. Lyons, *Sex Among the Rabble: An Intimate History of Gender and Power in the Age of Revolution* (Chapel Hill: University of North Carolina Press, 2006); and Jonathan Ned Katz, *Love Stories: Sex Between Men Before Homosexuality* (Chicago: University of Chicago Press, 2001), 45–90.

60. Patricia U. Bonomi, *The Lord Cornbury Scandal: The Politics of Reputation in British America* (Chapel Hill: University of North Carolina Press, 1998).

61. Letter from Samuel Galloway to Abraham Lincoln, Saturday, August 22, 1863. Abraham Lincoln Papers at the Library of Congress. Transcribed and annotated by the Lincoln Studies Center, Knox College, Galesburg, Illinois.

62. Gail Hamilton's May 29, 1880, *New York Tribune* essay was reproduced in its entirety in the *New York Times*, Oct. 24, 1884, 4. Blaine used the term in a November 4, 1884 campaign speech in reference to Senator Hoar. *New York Times*, Nov. 4, 1884, 2. The term "hermaphrodite" was used in political contexts in the 1870s. A "German-American" letter writer to the *New York Times* referred to Horace Greeley as the "Hermaphrodite Candidate," July 30, 1872, 5. A *New York Times* editorial referred to the *New York Tribune* as an example of "the neutral, hermaphrodite, or 'independent' press." "Grumbling as a Fine Art," Oct. 8, 1874, 4. The *New York Times* used the term "political hermaphrodite" in reference to Hoar's Massachusetts contingent on Oct. 24, 1884; Nov. 5, 1884, 2; and Dec. 26, 1884, 2.

63. *Congressional Record*, 49th Cong., 1st sess., March 1886, 2786. Quoted in Hofstadter, *Anti-Intellectualism in American Life*, 188. The speech is also quoted in Burton J. Williams, *Senator John James Ingalls: Kansas' Iridescent Republican* (Lawrence: University of Kansas Press, 1972), 107–109.

64. "Only One Vote to Spare," *New York Times*, Mar. 27, 1886, 4; "The Republican Spirit," *Harper's Weekly* 30, no. 1529 (Apr. 10, 1886): 226.

65. Hofstadter, *Anti-Intellectualism in American Life*, 188–91.

66. Ingersoll quoted in Francis Curtis, *The Republican Party: A History of Its Fifty Years' Existence and a Record of Its Measures and Leaders, 1854–1904* (New York: G. P. Putnam's Sons, 1904), 476. Hay quoted in Blodgett, "The Mugwump Reputation, 1870 to Present," 883.

67. Thomas Collier Platt, *Autobiography of Thomas Collier Platt* (New York: B.W. Dodge & Company, 1910), 220–21.

68. Riordan, ed., *Plunkitt of Tammany Hall*, 11.

69. On social Darwinism in the United States, see, for example, Robert C. Bannister, *Social Darwinism: Science and Myth in Anglo-American Social Thought* (Philadelphia: Temple University Press, 1979); Carl N. Degler, *In Search of Human Nature:*

The Decline and Revival of Darwinism in American Social Thought (New York: Oxford University Press, 1992); Mike Hawkins, *Social Darwinism in European and American Thought, 1860–1945: Nature as Model and Nature as Threat* (New York: Cambridge University Press, 1997); and Richard Hofstadter, *Social Darwinism in American Thought* (Philadelphia: University of Pennsylvania Press, 1944).

70. Quoted in "Arrested Development," *New York Tribune,* Oct. 1, 1884.

71. Mugwump reformers also used Darwinian rhetoric to argue *for* civil service reform. Dorman B. Eaton, for example, argued that the merit system would promote competition for positions, which would, in turn, lead to national success. He wrote: "Wherever there is life and growth, there is competition, in which the development and the survival of the fittest are the conditions of superiority and progress." Dorman B. Eaton, "A New Phase of the Reform Movement," *North American Review* 132 (June 1881): 555; quoted in Gerald W. McFarland, "Partisan of Nonpartisanship: Dorman B. Eaton and the Genteel Reform Tradition," *Journal of American History* 55 (Mar. 1969): 806–22.

72. Terry, *An American Obsession*, 46.

73. In addition to Terry, *An American Obsession*, chaps. 1–2, see Hubert Kennedy, *Ulrichs: The Life and Works of Karl Heinrich Ulrichs, Pioneer of the Modern Gay Movement* (Boston: Alyson Publications, 1988); and Harry Oosterhuis, "Richard von Krafft-Ebing's 'Step-Children of Nature': Psychiatry and the Making of Homosexual Identity," in Vernon A. Rosario, ed., *Science and Homosexualities* (New York and London: Routledge, 1997), 67–88.

74. It is possible that the theory of inversion achieved greater circulation through the writing of George M. Beard, an American neurologist who first "discovered" the illness of neurasthenia, a phenomenon that received considerable attention in the popular press. In 1884, Beard cited Spitzka's article on Lord Cornbury and Ulrichs's theory of inversion as part of a broader discussion of "sexual perversion," which he described as symptomatic of the neurasthenic condition. George M. Beard, *Sexual Neurasthenia* (New York: E. B. Treat, 1884), 99–107. On Beard and neurasthenia, see F. G. Gosling, *Before Freud: Neurasthenia and the American Medical Community, 1870–1910* (Urbana: University of Illinois Press, 1987); and Gail Bederman, *Manliness and Civilization: A Cultural History of Gender and Race in the United States, 1880–1917* (Chicago: University of Chicago Press, 1995), 77–120.

75. Recent works on the history of manhood in the United States have commented on the political rhetoric of Ingalls and Roscoe Conkling but have not linked this rhetoric to the work of sexologists. See, for example, Rotundo, *American Manhood*, 271–74; Hoganson, *Fighting for American Manhood*, 23–24, 34–37; and Testi, "The Gender of Reform Politics: Theodore Roosevelt and the Culture of Masculinity," 1525–1526.

76. This strand of degeneration theory intersected with American conceptions of the disease of neurasthenia, which, as Gail Bederman has shown, was understood to endanger "middle- and upper-class businessmen and professionals whose highly evolved bodies had been physically weakened by advances in civilization." Bederman, *Manliness and Civilization*, 87.

77. The *Frank Leslie's* cartoon (figure 1.1) likens mugwumps to the biological

"freaks" on display in the dime museum. Ingalls's speech, quoted above, also suggests constitutional abnormality, as does the *Minneapolis Journal* essay on the "mollycoddle controversy." On degeneration, see Hatheway, *The Gilded Age Construction*, 86–89; Terry, *An American Obsession*, 45–50; Boag, *Same-Sex Affairs*, 128–137, and Somerville, *Queering the Color Line*, 29–33.

78. On effeminacy and male same-sex desire, see Katz, *Love Stories*, 50–54. On the use of female names and pronouns to denote same-sex desire, see Mary Warner Blanchard, *Oscar Wilde's America: Counterculture in the Gilded Age* (New Haven: Yale University Press, 1998), 12. The term "man-milliner" was most often associated with George William Curtis, who was pilloried as such in a speech by New York Senator Roscoe Conkling in 1877. Richard Hofstadter has suggested that the term had come to connote homosexuality later in the century, citing as an example the fact that Conkling's nephew, who published the speech in an 1889 biography, replaced it with asterisks. Hofstadter, *Anti-Intellectualism in American Life*, 189.

Colin A. Scott suggested that these connections had become part of the general formulation of inversion by 1896: "'The Fairies of New York" shared characteristics with European "societies of inverts . . . Coffee-clatches, where the members dress themselves with aprons, etc., and knit, gossip, and crochet; balls, where men adopt the ladies' evening dress." Colin A. Scott, "Sex and Art," *The American Journal of Psychology* 7, no. 2 (Jan. 1896): 216.

79. On the history of the production and reception of sexology in the United States at the turn of the twentieth century, see Terry, *An American Obsession*, 74–119; and Bullough, "The Development of Sexology in the USA in the Early Twentieth Century," 303–22. On sexuality and urban bohemians, see Christine Stansell, *American Moderns: Bohemian New York and the Creation of a New Century* (New York: Owl Books, 2001). On urban subcultures, see Chauncey, *Gay New York*; and Boyd, *Wide Open Town*. On the Alice Mitchell trial, see Duggan, *Sapphic Slashers*.

80. References to the "inverted mugwump" include: "Mr. Daton and the Civil Service," *New York Times*, June 7, 1893, 4; untitled editorial, *New York Times*, Apr. 1, 1894, 4; and Everett P. Wheeler, "The First Year of the Cleveland Administration," *New York Times*, Apr. 16, 1894, 5. On historians' assessment of Cornbury, see Bonomi, *The Lord Cornbury Scandal*.

81. *New York Sun*, April 8, 1895. Thanks to Greg Robinson for informing me of this source and for his analysis of New York press coverage of the Wilde trials in his unpublished essay, "'Speaking the 'Unspeakable': New York City Newspaper Coverage of the Oscar Wilde Trials in 1895." For an expanded discussion of Wilde's reception in the United States, see Blanchard, *Oscar Wilde's America*; and Boag, *Same-Sex Affair*, 125–56.

82. Carroll Smith-Rosenberg, "The New Woman as Androgyne," in *Disorderly Conduct: Visions of Gender in Victorian America* (New York and Oxford: Oxford University Press, 1985), 245–96.

83. Quoted in Williams, *Senator John James Ingalls*, 155.

84. "Osborne Flays Hearst as Foe of Democracy," *New York Times*, Oct. 24, 1906, 4.

85. Richard Rogers Bowker, "An Open Letter to Mr. Curtis," *New York Evening Post*, Sept. 2, 1879.

86. Sproat, *"The Best Men"*, 133–38.

87. Theodore Roosevelt, *An Autobiography* (New York: The Outlook Company, 1913), 147. Roosevelt recounts his break with the mugwumps on 85–88.

2. THE TAMMANY WITHIN: GOOD GOVERNMENT REFORM AND POLITICAL MANHOOD

1. W. T. Stead, "Mr. Richard Croker and Greater New York," *The Review of Reviews* (Oct. 1897):354–55.

2. Matthew P. Breen, *Thirty Years of New York Politics* (New York, 1899), 778–83.

3. On Godkin and the mugwump movement, see Gerald W. McFarlane, *Mugwumps, Morals and Politics, 1884–1920* (Amherst: University of Massachusetts Press, 1975); William M. Armstrong, *E. L. Godkin: A Biography* (Albany: State University of New York Press, 1978); and Thomas Bender, *New York Intellect* (New York: Knopf, 1987), 185–91.

4. Some mugwumps proved more likely than others to invoke such prejudices. While George William Curtis avoided ethnic stereotypes of Tammany men, others, including Godkin, resorted to anti-Irish rhetoric. Indeed, Godkin, who considered Tammany men "bummers, rowdies, drunkards, gamblers, pugilists, bilks, shysters, and dead-beats," contended that although "a swarm of 'Mikes' may succeed a swarm of 'Barneys' and 'Jerrys'," the nature and goals of the organization would never change. E. L. Godkin, "Tammany Apologists," *The Nation* (Jan. 26, 1893):60.

5. On the histories of the City Reform Club, the City Club, and other good government organizations in New York City in the 1880s and 1890s, see David C. Hammack, *Power and Society: Greater New York at the Turn of the Century* (New York: Columbia University Press, 1987), 140–41, 205–326; John Louis Recchiutti, *Civic Engagement: Social Science and Progressive-Era Reform in New York City* (Philadelphia: University of Pennsylvania Press, 2007); Richard L. McCormick, *From Realignment to Reform: Political Change in New York State, 1893–1910* (Ithaca, NY: Cornell University Press, 1981), 117–37; Edwin G. Burrows and Mike Wallace, *Gotham: A History of New York City to 1898* (New York and Oxford: Oxford University Press, 1999), 1185–1208; David I. Aronson, "The City Club of New York: 1892–1912," Ph.D. diss., New York University, 1975; Gregory Weinstein, *The Ardent Eighties and After* (New York: The International Press, 1947); Richard W.G. Welling, *As the Twig Is Bent* (New York: G. P. Putnam's Sons, 1942), 40–90.

6. See Alexander B. Callow Jr., *The Tweed Ring* (New York: Oxford University Press, 1965).

7. John Jay Chapman, *Causes and Consequences* (New York: Charles Scribner's Sons, 1898), 30–31.

8. Historian David C. Hammack defines "swallowtails" as the "politically active group of . . . merchants, bankers, and lawyers who directed the city's economy." Hammack shows that elite "swallowtails"—so named because of the frock coats they

favored—openly dominated New York City mayoral politics from Tweed's demise in 1870 until 1903. Hammack, *Power and Society*, 110–11.

9. On the Henry George campaign and the mayoral election of 1886, see Edwin G. Burrows and Mike Wallace, *Gotham: A History of New York City of 1898* (New York: Oxford University Press, 1999), 1097–1110; and Charles A. Barker, *Henry George* (New York: Oxford University Press, 1955).

10. See Hammack, *Power and Society*, 215–17. See also McCormick, *From Realignment to Reform*; and Harold F. Gosnell, *Boss Platt and His New York Machine: A Study of the Political Leadership of Thomas C. Platt, Theodore Roosevelt, and Others* (Chicago: University of Chicago Press, 1924).

11. Hammack, *Power and Society*, 215–17; McCormick, *From Realignment to Reform*, 69–103.

12. George Gunton, "The Peril of Popular Government," *Lecture Bulletin of the Institute of Social Economics* 4, no. 5 (1901): 104–105.

13. See, for example, Carl Schurz, "The Blindness of Party Spirit," *Harper's Weekly* (Oct. 30, 1897): 1071.

14. Lincoln Steffens, *The Autobiography of Lincoln Steffens, Volume I* (New York: Harcourt, Brace & World, 1931), 233–38.

15. Lincoln Steffens, *The Shame of the Cities* (New York: S. S. McClure, 1902).

16. John Brooks Leavitt, "Criminal Degradation of New York Citizenship," *The Forum* 17 (Aug. 1894): 659–65.

17. Kelly, who was the first Roman Catholic leader of Tammany, also served in the U.S. House of Representatives. On Kelly, see Oliver E. Allen, *The Tiger: The Rise and Fall of Tammany Hall* (Reading, MA: Addison-Wesley, 1993), 144–69; Gustavus Myers, *The History of Tammany Hall* (New York: Boni & Liverwright, 1901), 259–66.

18. William L. Riordan, ed., *Plunkitt of Tammany Hall: A Series of Very Plain Talks on Very Practical Politics* (1905; reprint, New York: E. P. Dutton, 1963), 3.

19. *Mazet Investigation*, 5 vols. (Albany: State of New York, Official Publication, 1900), I:352. Quoted in Lothrop Stoddard, *Master of Manhattan: The Life of Richard Croker* (New York: Longmans, Green, 1931), 120.

20. Richard Croker, "Tammany Hall and the Democracy," *North American Review* 154 (Feb. 1892): 225–30. Similarly, Plunkitt contended that "Politics is as much a regular business as the grocery or the dry-goods or the drug business. You've got to be trained up to it or you're sure to fail." Riordan, ed., *Plunkitt of Tammany Hall*, 19.

21. Similarly, Hugh J. Grant successfully ran for the mayor's office as a "reformer" and representative of the "New Tammany" in the 1888 election. Croker's successor, Charles Francis Murphy, a man whose tastes and habits bespoke a solid bourgeois respectability, also cast himself as a "reformer."

22. John D. Townsend, *Wine and Spirits Gazette*, May 4, 1894, excerpted in Townsend, *New York in Bondage* (New York: privately published to subscribers, 1901), 157.

23. Richard W.G. Welling, "Reform in Municipal Government: Two Addresses Delivered by Invitation before the Massachusetts Reform Club, Saturday, February 17, 1894" (Boston: Press of Geo. H. Ellis, 1894), 23–24.

24. Edward M. Shepard, "Political Inauguration of the Greater New York," *Atlantic Monthly* (Jan. 1898): 108, 111. On Shepard, see Jack Gable, "Edward M. Shepard, Militant Reformer," Ph.D. diss., New York University, 1967.

25. Citizens' Union, "To Voters of Open Mind: New York, Oct. 31, 1901," Citizens' Union campaign handbill. Citizens' Union Records [hereafter CUR], Columbia University Rare Books and Manuscripts Library, box W4, file 2.

26. Ibid.

27. The latter poster also includes the following poem: "Now let us all speak easy— / Sh! do not mention Tam— / If I hide behind a Shepard / They will take me for a lamb. / So purrs the hungry Tiger / That preys on rich and poor / You must vote the fusion ticket / if you'd drive him / from your door." Cartoon by W. A. Rogers originally published in *Harper's Weekly*, CUR, Scrapbook W25: "Citizens' Union Campaign Literature, 1901."

28. *New York Tribune*, Sept. 8, 1897, quoted in Stoddard, *Master of Manhattan*, 177.

29. One 1901 Citizens' Union pamphlet included a poem entitled "The Lament of the English Emigrant, or the Theme of an Absentee Landlord—Squire Croker of Wantage, England" which read, in part: "He is the Squire of Wantage town / Quite English, you know," from his heel to his crown; / His heel is quite English when once it is placed / On the neck of the Irish, that he has disgraced." CUR, Scrapbook W25: "Citizens' Union Campaign Literature, 1901."

30. Stead, "Mr. Richard Croker and Greater New York," 345.

31. Riordan, ed., *Plunkitt of Tammany Hall*, 14.

32. Some contemporary observers have suggested that Croker's nomination of Shepard represented an even more Machiavellian ploy to undermine reform forces, especially the Citizens' Union. The *Brooklyn Standard Union*, for example, maintained that Croker realized that Tammany stood little chance of defeating Low and therefore nominated Shepard to divide the reform effort: "Croker would have to be born over again," the paper asserted in an October 2, 1901, editorial, "before he consented to such a programme unless it was his design to utilize inevitable defeat to weaken and perhaps destroy a political organization that has aspired to rival Tammany." Shepard accepted the nomination for diverse reasons, including his belief that he could reform Tammany from within and his fierce opposition to the growth of imperialism on the national level. (He believed a reformed Democratic Party offered the only vehicle through which the battle against imperial policy could be waged.) For a thorough analysis of Shepard's mayoral candidacy, see Jack Gabel, "Edward Morse Shepard: Militant Reformer," Ph.D. diss., New York University, 1967, 320–75.

33. The Committee of Fifteen and Edwin R.A. Seligman, eds., *The Social Evil: With Special Reference to Conditions Existing in the City of New York* (G. P. Putnam's Sons, 1902), 155–59. On antivice reform in this period, including reform accusations of Tammany and police involvement in promoting prostitution, see Timothy J. Gilfoyle, *City of Eros: New York City, Prostitution, and the Commercialization of Sex, 1790–1920* (New York: Norton, 1992), 251–315; and David J. Pivar, *Purity Crusade: Sexual Morality and Social Control, 1868–1900* (Westport, CT: Greenwood Press, 1973), 131–254.

34. "To the Citizens of the Lower East Side [first edition 25 June 1901]." CUR, Scrapbook W25: "Citizens' Union Campaign Literature, 1901."

35. This citation comes from the continued campaign against the cadet system by the Citizens' Union on behalf of Seth Low after his bid for reelection as mayor in 1903 failed. Undated pamphlet, "The Woman's Municipal League Bulletin," CUR, File: "Citizens Union—Campaign—Literature (1903–1906)."

36. Riordan, ed., *Plunkitt of Tammany Hall*, 37.

37. Riordan, ed., *Plunkitt of Tammany Hall*, 25–26.

38. Stead, "Mr. Richard Croker and Greater New York," 253–54. For a similar claim by a Republican politician of the same period, see Louis J. Lang, ed., *The Autobiography of Thomas Collier Platt* (New York: B. W. Dodge, 1910).

39. In the past, good government reformers had recognized that Tammany's organizational acuity had contributed to its electoral success. In fact, the Citizens' Union itself, as well as the affiliated City Club and good government clubs, were formed with the intention of bringing Tammany-like cohesion to the reform cause. Yet, without patronage positions, these organizations had little success in winning over working-class constituencies.

40. Henry Childs Merwyn, "Tammany Points the Way," *Atlantic Monthly* 74 (Nov. 1894):680–89.

41. Theodore Roosevelt, "Machine Politics in New York City," *The Century* (Nov. 1886), reprinted in Roosevelt, *American Ideals and Other Essays, Social and Political* (New York and London: G. P. Putnam's Sons, 1906), 175–221.

42. Henry Childs Merwyn, "Tammany Hall," *Atlantic Monthly* (Feb. 1894):240–46.

43. Kelly quoted in Merwyn, "Tammany Points the Way," 686. Historian Daniel Czitrom offers an insightful case study of mobility within Tammany Hall in "Underworlds and Underdogs: Big Tim Sullivan and Metropolitan Politics in New York, 1889–1912," *The Journal of American History* (Sep. 1991):536–58.

44. Robert H. Wiebe, *The Search for Order, 1877–1920* (New York: Hill and Wang, 1967).

45. Oswald Garrison Villard, "Tammany Tactics," *Boston Transcript* (Nov. 5, 1893).

46. Ibid.; Roosevelt, "The Manly Virtues in Practical Politics," *The Forum* (July 1894).

47. Theodore Roosevelt, "Machine Politics in New York City," *The Century* (Nov. 1886); reprinted in Roosevelt, *American Ideals and Other Essays, Social and Political* (New York: G. P. Putnam's Sons, 1906), 187–88.

48. "Dude's Reform Club," *New York World*, Apr. 15, 1883.

49. Quoted in Gail Bederman, *Manliness and Civilization: A Cultural History of Gender and Race in the United States, 1880–1917* (Chicago and London: University of Chicago Press, 1995), 170–71; and Edmund Morris, *The Rise of Theodore Roosevelt* (New York: Coward, McCann & Geoghegan, 1979), 162.

50. Jane Addams, "The Subjective Necessity for Social Settlements," 1910, reprinted in *Jane Addams: A Centennial Reader* (New York: Macmillan, 1960), 10. This essay was first presented as a lecture at a meeting of the Ethical Culture Society in 1892.

51. Bederman, *Manliness and Civilization*, 170–71.

52. Theodore Roosevelt, "The College Graduate and Public Life," *Atlantic Monthly* (Aug. 1890).

53. See, for example, Kristin L. Hoganson, *Fighting for American Manhood: How Gender Politics Provoked the Spanish-American and Philippine-American Wars* (New Haven and London: Yale University Press, 1998), 170–216; Donna Harraway, "Teddy Bear Patriarchy: Taxidermy in the Garden of Eden, New York City, 1908–1936," in Amy Kaplan and Donald E. Pease, eds., *Cultures of United States Imperialism* (Durham: Duke University Press, 1993), 237–91; Morris, *The Rise of Theodore Roosevelt*, 543–661; and Sarah Watts, *Rough Rider in the White House: Theodore Roosevelt and the Politics of Desire* (Chicago: University of Chicago Press, 2003), 123–25.

54. M. A. DeWolfe Howe, *John Jay Chapman and His Letters* (Boston: Houghton Mifflin, 1937), 10–47.

55. Chapman wrote to Timmins, "Oh Minna, suppose such a defect like that in yourself—that made you imperfect in giving yourself to the man you loved—and opened yourself to—and he sympathized over it with someone else." This term appears in a letter from John Jay Chapman to Minna Timmins, November 2, 1887. John Jay Chapman Papers [hereafter JJC], Houghton Library, Harvard University, file 4512–4513.

56. Letter from John Jay Chapman to Minna Timmins, November 11, 1887. JCC, file 4522–4523.

57. Richard B. Hovey, *John Jay Chapman: An American Mind* (New York: Columbia University Press, 1959), 50–51. Elsewhere in this study Hovey, who employs a Freudian frame of analysis, attributes to Chapman "an overplus of unconscious fear of homosexual elements in his own makeup" (335).

58. Letter from John Jay Chapman to Minna Timmins, November 2, 1887. JJC, file 4512–4513.

59. In another expression of this concern, Chapman wrote, "What makes me angry is that this cost me my life—and one only has one life— . . . I want to die, not figuratively but literally—because the system of life—which makes life worthwhile—the reproductive system got destroyed and burnt up and pulled out of me." Letter to Minna Timmons dated November 29, 1887, JJC, file 4530–4531.

60. Ibid.

61. Quoted in Hovey, *John Jay Chapman*, 51.

62. Quoted in Hovey, *John Jay Chapman*, 59, 63; Howe, *John Jay Chapman and His Letters*, 66.

63. Richard Welling, "The Arrested Development of Johnny Doe," unpublished autobiographical essay. Welling Papers, NYPL, box 28, folder 2.

64. Richard Welling, *As the Twig Is Bent* (New York: G.P. Putnam's Sons, 1942), 241.

65. Welling, "The Arrested Development of Johnny Doe."

66. John Jay Chapman, *Practical Agitation* (New York: Charles Scribner's Sons, 1900), 75.

67. Ibid., 137.

68. Roosevelt wrote: "The terms machine and machine politician are now undoubtedly used ordinarily in a reproachful sense. . . . On the contrary, the machine is often a powerful instrument for good; and a machine politician really desirous of doing honest work on behalf of the community is fifty times as useful an ally as is the average philanthropic outsider. "Machine Politics in New York City," *The Century*, 1886; reprinted in Roosevelt, *American Ideals and Other Essays*, 176.

69. On muscular Christianity, see, for example, Clifford Putney, *Muscular Christianity: Manhood and Sports in Protestant America, 1880–1920* (Cambridge, MA and London: Harvard University Press, 2001); Gail Bederman, "'The Women Have Had Charge of the Church Work Long Enough': The Men and Religion Forward Movement of 1911–1912 and the Masculinization of Middle-Class Protestantism," *American Quarterly* 41 (Sept. 1989): 432–65; and E. Anthony Rotundo, *American Manhood: Transformations in Masculinity from the Revolution to the Modern Era* (New York: Basic Books, 1993), 224.

70. William James, "The Moral Equivalent of War," *The Popular Science Monthly* (Oct. 1910).

71. Josiah Strong, *The Twentieth Century City* (New York, 1898), 109.

72. Roosevelt, "The Manly Virtues and Practical Politics," 78–79.

73. Letter from Theodore Roosevelt to Samuel J. Colgate, October 8, 1882, in *The Letters of Theodore Roosevelt*, ed. Will Irwin (New York: Scribners, 1946), 1:57.

74. *Theodore Roosevelt, An Autobiography* (New York: Charles Scribner's Sons, 1913), 56.

75. City Reform Club minutes, October 13, 14, and 16, 1882. *City Reform Club Minute Books*, Vol. 1, New York Public Library.

76. *Tammany Times*, December 4, 1895, 10.

77. On the gendering of the political sphere, see, for example, Richard Hofstadter, *Anti-Intellectualism in American Life* (New York: Knopf, 1962), 187–91; Lori D. Ginzberg, *Women and the Work of Benevolence: Morality, Politics, and Class in the Nineteenth-Century United States* (New Haven: Yale University Press, 1990); Mary P. Ryan, *Women in Public: Between Banners and Ballots, 1825–1880* (Baltimore: Johns Hopkins University Press, 1990); Paula Baker, "The Domestication of American Politics: Women and American Political Society, 1780–1920," *American Historical Review* 89 (1984): 620–47. On "purity politics" associated with vice, see Pivar, *Purity Crusade*.

78. City Reform Club minutes, December 22, 1882. *City Reform Club Minute Books*, Vol. 1, NYPL.

79. Welling, *As the Twig Is Bent*, 43. See also *City Reform Club Minute Books*, Vol.1, 1882–1890, NYPL; Robert Muccigrosso, "Richard W.G. Welling: A Reformer's Life," Ph.D. diss., Columbia University, 1966, 39–44; John Jay Chapman, *Retrospections*, unpublished mss., JJC.

80. Letter from Richard Welling to M.A. DeWolfe Howe, quoted in Howe, *John Jay Chapman and His Letters*, 67–68.

81. Ibid., 68–69.

82. During this period, club members also participated in the effort to bar G. W.

Plunkitt's plan to build a speedway in Central Park. Welling, *As the Twig Is Bent*, 42–48; Muccigrosso, *Richard W.G. Welling*, 40–58.

83. Aronson, "The City Club of New York: 1892–1912," 45–72.

84. City Club Papers of Incorporation, quoted in Aronson, "The City Club of New York: 1892–1912," 61.

85. Criticism of the idealism of Chapman and other Goo Goos was especially intense in 1895 when the good government clubs refused to back fusion candidates and ran their own candidates for office. These quotes are from a representative editorial of that time, "Keep the Goo Goos Straight!," *New York Sun*, Oct. 5, 1895.

86. "Roosevelt to Preble Tucker," *New York Times*, Oct. 23, 1895.

87. Hammack, *Power and Society*, 110–11.

88. For an excellent examination of Murphy's career, see Nancy Joan Weiss, *Charles Francis Murphy, 1858–1924: Respectability and Responsibility in Tammany Politics* (Northampton, MA: Smith College, 1968).

3. WHITE ARMY IN THE WHITE CITY: CIVIC MILITARISM, URBAN SPACE, AND THE URBAN POPULACE

1. Edward Bellamy, *Looking Backward 2000–1887* (1887; reprint, New York: New American Library, 1960), 212–13.

2. Jacob A. Riis, *A Ten Years' War: An Account of the Battle with the Slum in New York* (1900; reprint, Freeport, NY: Books for Libraries Press, 1969), 168.

3. Although Lears maintains that middle- and upper-class men embraced militarism in part to bolster themselves against the perceived "threat of anarchists, immigrants, strikers, tramps, and criminals," he interprets "the martial ideal" principally as a backward-looking psychic response to a "weightless modernity" as well as to the perceived feminization of American life and culture. Indeed, Lears argues that the "return to militancy" of the 1890s was largely rhetorical and had very little real impact on domestic politics in the United States, save for the emergence of a largely ineffective advocacy for draconian criminal punishment and the limited institution of military drilling in education. T.J. Jackson Lears, *No Place of Grace: Antimodernism and the Transformation of American Culture, 1880–1920* (Chicago: University of Chicago Press, 1981), 98–139. Analyses of the importance of militarism at the turn of the twentieth century can also be found in recent works on the history of manhood in America. These include E. Anthony Rotundo, *American Manhood: Transformations in Masculinity from the Revolution to the Modern Era* (New York: Basic Books, 1993), 232–39; Michael Kimmel, *Manhood in America: A Cultural History* (New York: The Free Press, 1995), 181–86; and Gail Bederman, *Manliness and Civilization: A Cultural History of Gender and Race in the United States, 1880–1917* (Chicago: University of Chicago Press, 1995), 170–216.

4. Kristin L. Hoganson, *Fighting for American Manhood: How Gender Politics Provoked the Spanish-American and Philippine-American Wars* (New Haven: Yale University Press, 1998). See also: Michael C.C. Adams, *The Great Adventure: Male Desire and the Coming of World War I* (Bloomington: Indiana University Press,

1990); Mary W. Blanchard, "The Soldier and the Aesthete: Homosexuality and Popular Culture in Gilded Age America," *Journal of American Studies* 30 (Apr. 1996): 25–46; Martin Green, *Dreams of Adventure, Deeds of Empire* (New York: Basic Books, 1979); and John Pettegrew, "'The Soldier's Faith': Turn-of-the-Century Memory of the Civil War and the Emergence of Modern American Nationalism," *Journal of Contemporary History* 31, no. 1 (Jan. 1996): 49–73.

5. On Coxey's Army, see, for example, Lucy G. Barber, *Marching on Washington: The Forging of an American Political Tradition* (Berkeley: University of California Press, 2002); Dimitri Palmateer, "Charity and the 'Tramp': Itinerancy, Unemployment, and Municipal Government from Coxey to the Unemployed League," *Oregon Historical Quarterly* 107, no. 2 (Summer 2006); Carlos A. Schwantes, *Coxey's Army: An American Odyssey* (Moscow: University of Idaho Press, 1994); and Nell Irvin Painter, *Standing at Armageddon, 1877–1919* (New York and London: Norton, 1987), 117–21. Washington Gladden, *Social Facts and Forces* (1897; reprint, Port Washington, NY: Kennikat Press, 1971), 189–90, quoted in Paul Boyer, *Urban Masses and Moral Order in America* (Cambridge, MA and London: Harvard University Press, 1978), 174.

6. Edward Bellamy, *Looking Backward 2000–1887* (1887; reprint, New York: New American Library, 1960), 212–13.

7. On Bellamy's influence, see Daphne Patai, ed., *Looking Backward, 1988–1888: Essays on Edward Bellamy* (Amherst: University of Massachusetts Press, 1988); Arthur Lipow, *Authoritarian Socialism in America: Edward Bellamy and the Nationalist Movement*, (Berkeley: University of California Press, 1982); John L. Thomas, *Alternative America: Henry George, Edward Bellamy, Henry Demarest Lloyd, and the Adversary Tradition* (Cambridge, MA: Belknap Press of Harvard University Press, 1983); Toby Widdicombe and Herman S. Preiser, eds., *Revisiting the Legacy of Edward Bellamy, American Author and Social Reformer* (Lewiston, ME: Edwin Mellen Press, 2002).

8. William James, "The Moral Equivalent of War," reprinted in John J. McDermott, ed., *The Writings of William James: A Comprehensive Edition* (Chicago: University of Chicago Press, 1967), 660–71. James also notes that H. G. Wells espoused a similar concept of civic militarism in his 1908 work "First and Last Things." Like Bellamy, James believed that a militarist ethos could coordinate and organize labor in the service of the state. To this end, James suggested that young men be conscripted to perform a broad array of domestic work: "to coal and iron mines, to freight trains . . . to road-building and tunnel-making, to foundries and stoke-holes, and to the frames of skyscrapers."

9. Ibid.

10. On masculinity at the turn of the twentieth century, see Bederman, *Manliness and Civilization*; Rotundo, *American Manhood*, 222–83; Kimmel, *Manhood in America*, 81–190; Hoganson, *Fighting for American Manhood*, 15–42; and Clifford Putney, *Muscular Christianity: Manhood and Sports in Protestant America, 1880–1920* (Cambridge, MA and London: Harvard University Press, 2001), 1–44. On James and manhood, see Kim Townsend, *Manhood at Harvard: William James and Others*

(New York: Norton, 1996); and Robert D. Richardson, *William James: In the Maelstrom of American Modernism: A Biography* (Boston: Houghton Mifflin, 2006).

11. On masculinity, militarism, and the New Deal, see Michael Willrich, "Home Slackers: Men, the State, and Welfare in Modern America," *Journal of American History* 87, no. 2 (Sept. 2000), 460–89; Bryant Simon, "New Men in Body and Soul: The Civilian Conservation Corps and the Transformation of Male Bodies and the Body Politic," in Virginia Scharff, ed., *Seeing Nature Through Gender* (Lawrence: University Press of Kansas, 2003); and Neil M. Maher, "A New Deal Body Politic: Landscape, Labor, and the Civilian Conservation Corps," *Environmental History* 7, no. 3 (July 2002): 435–61.

12. Jacob A. Riis, Scrapbook, 1895. Jacob A. Riis Collection, Reel 6, Library of Congress, Manuscript Division.

13. Jacob A. Riis, *The Battle with the Slum* (New York: Macmillan, 1902).

14. See Jacob A. Riis, "Letting in the Light," *The Atlantic Monthly* 84, no. 505 (Nov. 1899): 495–505. On Riis and the demolition of Mulberry Bend, see Max Page, *The Creative Destruction of Manhattan, 1900–1940* (Chicago: University of Chicago Press, 1999), 73–91; and Tyler Anbinder, *Five Points: The Nineteenth-Century New York City Neighborhood That Invented Tap Dance, Stole Elections, and Became the World's Most Notorious Slum* (New York: The Free Press, 2001), 346–61.

15. "Mulberry Bend Park Opened," *New York Times*, June 16, 1897, 7.

16. See, for example, Jacob A. Riis, *How the Other Half Lives: Studies Among the Tenements of New York* (1890; reprint: New York: Bedford Books, 1996), 96–105.

17. Lincoln Steffens, *The Autobiography of Lincoln Steffens* (New York: Harcourt Brace, 1931). On Riis's career as journalist and photographer, see Maren Stange, *Symbols of Ideal Life: Social Documentary Photography in America, 1890–1950* (Cambridge: Cambridge University Press, 1989), 1–46; Keith Gandal, *The Virtues of the Vicious: Jacob Riis, Stephen Crane, and the Spectacle of the Slum* (New York: Oxford University Press, 1997); Edith Patterson Meyer, *Not Charity But Justice: The Story of Jacob A. Riis* (New York: Vanguard Press, 1974), 26–107; Lewis Fried, *Makers of the City: Jacob Riis, Lewis Mumford, James T. Farrell, and Paul Goodman* (Amherst: University of Massachusetts Press), 10–63.

18. Riis, *How the Other Half Lives*, 17.

19. For Riis's account of his career as photographer, see his autobiography, *The Making of an American* (New York: Macmillan, 1902), 265–73. For a lengthier account of Riis as photographer, see Alexander Alland, *Jacob A. Riis: Photographer and Citizen* (New York: Aperture, 1973). More critical interpretations of Riis's photographic work can be found in Stange, *Symbols of Ideal Life*, 1–46.

20. See, for example, "The Lesson Taught Us by the Gang," *Pratt Institute Monthly* 6, no. 2 (Nov. 1897); and *The Battle with the Slum.*

21. In his introduction to *How the Other Half Lives*, Riis wrote, "The Five Points had been cleared, as far as the immediate neighborhood was concerned, but the Mulberry Street Bend was fast outdoing it in foulness not a stone's throw away" (14).

22. Riis, *How the Other Half Lives*, 49.

23. Riis, *How the Other Half Lives*, 52.

24. "Lady Henry in the Slums: A Midnight Visit to the Places of Vice and Poverty," *New York Evening Sun*, November 28, 1891. Jacob A. Riis Collection, Library of Congress, Manuscript Division, Reel 6, Scrapbook page 132.

25. Jacob A. Riis, "The Other Half and How They Live; Story in Pictures, Address by J. A. Riis, Washington Convention of Christians at Work," *The Temple-Builder* 2, no. 5 (Jan. 1895).

26. Jacob A. Riis, "The Clearing of Mulberry Bend," *Review of Reviews* (1896):172–78.

27. Riis, *The Making of an American*, 264.

28. For a history of the representation of tramps in the nineteenth century, see Todd DePastino, *Citizen Hobo: How a Century of Homelessness Shaped America* (Chicago: University of Chicago Press, 2003), 3–94; and Tim Cresswell, *The Tramp in America* (London: Reaktion Books, 2001), 171–218.

29. Riis, *How the Other Half Lives*, 67. Scholar Keith Gandal also notes Riis's interest in the tough and argues that the Riis combined a conventional moralistic interpretation of this figure with concepts drawn from contemporary psychology. Gandal, *The Virtues of the Vicious*, 91–95.

30. Maren Stange, a historian of photography, argues that these two photographs may actually have been taken by an associate, Richard Hoe Lawrence. Riis, however, presented them as if they were his own. See Stange, "Jacob Riis and Urban Visual Culture: The Lantern Slide Exhibition as Entertainment and Ideology," *Journal of Urban History* (May 1989):274–303. For an expanded version of this argument, see Stange, *Symbols of Ideal Life*, 1–46.

31. Historians have noted that as much as 80 percent of the Italian immigrant population in New York between 1880 and 1900 was male. See Samuel Bailey, "The Adjustment of Italian Immigrants in Buenos Aires and New York, 1870–1914," *American Historical Review* 88:280–305. Writing of the Italian population in Harlem, Robert Orsi argues that Italian immigrants during this period "lived in a largely male world." See Orsi, *The Madonna of 115th Street* (New Haven: Yale University Press, 1985), 21. See also Donna Gabaccia, "Inventing 'Little Italy,'" *Journal of the Gilded Age and Progressive Era* 6, no. 1 (Jan. 2007): 7–41.

32. Stange, "Jacob Riis and Urban Visual Culture," 281–83.

33. Riis, "The Other Half and How They Live," 411.

34. Jacob A. Riis, "Goodbye to the Bend," *The Evening Sun*, May 25, 1895. Significantly, one of the article's subheadings is, "Its History of Bloodshed."

35. Other contemporary writers frequently referred to Italian noncooperation with law enforcement authorities, citing this situation as an example of lawlessness and passion and frequently ignoring the lack of protection extended to immigrants by police officers and within the justice system. The Italian immigrant press, in contrast, sometimes reported on unfair police and judicial treatment of Italian immigrants. For an overview of press reporting on these issues see George E. Pozzetta, *The Italians of New York City, 1890–1914*, Ph.D. diss., University of North Carolina, Chapel Hill, 1971, 181–230.

36. William Noyes to Gino Speranza, May 31, 1906, Gino Speranza Papers, 1906 Correspondence File (New York: The New York Public Library); quoted in Pozzetta, *The Italians of New York City*, 166. Pozzetta writes about Italian immigrant resistance to organized charity, 65–167.

37. "Perils of Photographers," *Photographic Times*, Feb. 3, 1888, 59. Quoted in Stange, *Symbols of Ideal Life*, 23.

38. Pozzetta, *The Italians of New York City*, 28–29. Pozzetta writes of the continued usefulness of *omerta* within immigrant communities in the United States on page 192.

39. Gino Speranza, "The Industrial & Civic Relations of the Italian in Congested Districts," undated draft of article. Gino Speranza Papers, Box 35, The New York Public Library, Rare Books and Manuscripts Division.

40. Gino Speranza, "The Influence of Italy on American Citizenship," undated draft of lecture, Gino Speranza Papers, Box 35, The New York Public Library, Rare Books and Manuscripts Division.

41. Pozzetta, *The Italians of New York City*, 318–21. About the picture for itinerant men at the national level, historian Eric H. Monkkonen asserts that, at the turn of the century, "the percentages of foreign-born among the samples of homeless men are substantial—between 22 and 55 percent. Immigrants were known to pursue certain kinds of migrant work. Scandinavians preferred lumber work, Poles construction or lumber work, Finns mining, and Italians railroad section work." Monkkonen, *Walking to Work: Tramps in America, 1790–1935* (Lincoln: University of Nebraska Press, 1984), 216.

42. Riis, "The Other Half and How They Live," 412. Riis offered a different, somewhat less hostile version of this story in *How the Other Half Lives*. For example, the published version does not include the last line, "As he sits there, he is worth a quarter, and that is all he is worth" (111–12).

43. See, for example, Virginia Yans-McLaughlin, *Family and Community: Italian Immigrants in Buffalo* (Ithaca, NY: Cornell University Press, 1977), 83–108; Pozzetta, *The Italians of New York City*, 305–64; Thomas Kessner, *The Golden Door: Italian and Jewish Immigrant Mobility in New York City 1880–1915* (New York: Oxford University Press, 1977), 51–59.

44. Kessner, *The Golden Door*, 51–59; Bailey, "The Adjustment of Italian Immigrants," 284–85.

45. Gino Speranza, "Characteristics of the Italian Soldier," undated draft of article. Speranza Papers, Box 45, The New York Public Library, Rare Books and Manuscripts Division.

46. Gino Speranza, "The Bright Side of the Life of Our Immigrants," undated draft of article. Speranza Papers, Box 35, The New York Public Library, Rare Books and Manuscripts Division.

47. Riis, "The Other Half and How They Live," 412.

48. Riis, *The Battle with the Slum*, 48.

49. Todd DiPastino, writing about Riis's image and other representations of tramps at the turn of the twentieth century, shows that they frequently combined humor that

presented tramps as inadequate with a sense of threat of transient men. DiPastino, *Citizen Hobo*, 47–58.

50. On anti-Italian sentiment, see Appleton Morgan, "What Shall We Do with the 'Dago'?," *The Popular Science Monthly* 38 (Dec. 1890): 172–79; Dale T. Knobel, *America for the Americans: The Nativist Movement in the U.S.* (New York: Twain, 1996); Salvatore Mondello, *The Italian Immigrant in Urban America, 1880–1920, as Reported in the Contemporary Periodical Press* (New York: Arno Press, 1994), 112–77; Thomas A. Guglielmo, "'No Color Barrier': Italians, Race, and Power in the United States," in Jennifer Guglielmo and Salvatore Salerno, eds., *Are Italians White? How Race Is Made in America* (New York: Routledge, 2003), 29–43.

51. Jacob A. Riis, *Theodore Roosevelt the Citizen* (New York: Outlook, 1903), 131–32. For Roosevelt's version of this encounter see Roosevelt, *An Autobiography* (New York: The Outlook Company, 1913), 169.

52. Roosevelt, *An Autobiography*, 169. On Roosevelt's experience on the New York City Police Commission, see H. Paul Jeffers, *Commissioner Roosevelt: The Story of Theodore Roosevelt and the New York City Police, 1895–1897* (New York: Wiley, 1994); Edmund Morris, *The Rise of Theodore Roosevelt* (New York: Coward, McCann & Geoghan, 1979), 481–515; Jay Stuart Berman, *Police Administration and Progressive Reform: Theodore Roosevelt as Police Commissioner of New York* (New York: Greenwood Press, 1987).

53. Theodore Roosevelt, "The Strenuous Life," in *The Strenuous Life: Essays and Addresses* (New York: The Century Co., 1900), 1–21. It is likely that Roosevelt's theories about manhood and ethnicity were influenced by his experiences with Riis on the Lower East Side. In his autobiography, Roosevelt credits Riis with introducing him to the conditions of immigrant life.

54. Thomas G. Dyer, *Theodore Roosevelt and the Idea of Race* (Baton Rouge: Louisiana State University Press, 1980), 123–42. On Roosevelt's idea of race, see also Sarah Watts, *Rough Rider in the White House: Theodore Roosevelt and the Politics of Desire* (Chicago: University of Chicago Press, 2003), 24–25; and Gail Bederman, *Manliness and Civilization: A Cultural History of Gender and Race in the United States, 1880–1917* (Chicago: University of Chicago Press, 1995), 170–216.

55. Charles Pearson, *National Life and Character* (New York, 1894).

56. Dyer, *Theodore Roosevelt and the Idea of Race*, 143–67. This excellent study traces Roosevelt's evolving thinking on theories of race through private letters, public speeches, and published essays, the source of the Roosevelt quotes presented here.

57. Quoted in Justin Kaplan, *Lincoln Steffens* (New York: Simon and Schuster, 1974), 76.

58. Ibid., 78.

59. Riis, *The Making of an American*, 268. Riis describes taking pictures in immigrant neighborhoods as invasion.

60. Stange, *Symbols of Ideal Life*, 23. Stange quotes an 1888 account of such a confrontation with Italian immigrants.

61. Morgan, "What Shall We Do with the 'Dago'?"

62. Historian Richard Hofstadter argues that Roosevelt, in recasting reform in this fashion, helped to invigorate American reform efforts and paved the way for their success in the Progressive Era. Hofstadter, *Anti-Intellectualism in American Life* (New York: Knopf, 1962), 191–96.

63. Charles W. Gardner, *The Doctor and the Devil, or Midnight Adventures of Dr. Parkhurst* (New York: The Vanguard Press, 1894). An account of Parkhurst's visit to Mulberry Bend can be found on pages 41–45. See also Edward Robb Ellis, *The Epic of New York* (New York: Old Town Books, 1966), 423–34.

64. Many published accounts of Roosevelt's nighttime excursions exist. See, for example, Nathan Miller, *Theodore Roosevelt: A Life* (New York: William Morrow, 1992), 228–41.

65. Jacob Riis, "The Lesson Taught Us By the Gang," 40.

66. Jacob Riis, "On Whom Shall We Shut the Door?," in *The Battle with the Slum*, 225.

67. Jacob Riis, "The Making of Thieves in New York," *Century* (Nov. 1894).

68. Jacob Riis, "The Genesis of the Gang," in *The Battle with the Slum*, 246–55.

69. Jacob Riis, "The Genesis of the Gang," in *The Battle with the Slum*, 246.

70. For further information on the recapitulation theory of play see Dominick Cavallo, *Muscles and Morals: Organized Playgrounds and Urban Reform, 1880–1920* (Philadelphia: University of Pennsylvania Press, 1981); and Benjamin G. Rader, "The Recapitulation Theory of Play: Motor Behaviour, Moral Reflexes and Manly Attitudes in Urban America, 1880–1920," in J. A. Mangan and James Walvin, eds., *Manliness and Morality: Middle-Class Masculinity in Britain and America, 1800–1940* (New York: St. Martin's Press, 1987), 123–34.

71. Community Services Society Collection, Box 297, Photograph #1891, Columbia University, Rare Books and Manuscripts Library, New York. On Hall's influence and the emergence of a militarist ethos in work with boys, see David. I. MacLeod, *Building Character in the American Boy: The Boy Scouts, YMCA, and Their Forerunners* (Madison: University of Wisconsin Press, 1983); and Putney, *Muscular Christianity*, 105–16. Waring supported military drilling for boys as well. He published a fiery defense of the practice in response to complaints made by the Woman's Christian Temperance Union. It concludes: "March on boys! May a bloodless victory be yours and may you destroy all the enemies of your cause by making them your friends." Waring, "Military Drill for Boys' Clubs," *The Charities Review* 4, no. 5 (Mar. 1893).

72. Riis apparently delivered this lecture between 1899 and 1901. A number of reviews can be found in Riis's clippings scrapbook in the Jacob A. Riis Collection, Library of Congress (Reel 6). Quotations come from the following : *Milford, Massachusetts Gazette* (Jan. 4, 1901); "Riis's Fight on Slums," *Indianapolis News* (Feb. 19, 1900); "Jacob A. Riis Speaks to Large Audience," *Hartford Connecticut Times* (Jan. 24, 1900); and "Move for Slum Parks," *Chicago Tower Herald Report* (Nov. 11, 1899).

73. Cavallo, *Muscles and Morals*, 55–60; Rader, "The Recapitulation Theory of Play," 129–30.

74. Rotundo, *American Manhood*, 255–62.

75. Steffens, *Autobiography*, 262–63. For an account of Roosevelt's "boyishness," see also Rotundo, *American Manhood*, 258–59.

76. Gandal suggests that "slum ethnographers" like Riis and Stephen Crane saw their work as a quest for masculine adventure. Gandal, *The Virtues of the Vicious*, 10–21.

77. Rotundo, *American Manhood*, 261.

78. The frontispiece of *A Ten Years' War* is a portrait of Waring, and the book includes a lengthy analysis of Waring's contributions to the Mulberry Bend campaign and other reform efforts. Riis, *A Ten Years' War*, 171–76.

79. Riis, "Letting in the Light," 271.

80. Riis, *The Battle with the Slum*, 416. On Waring's career, see Martin V. Melosi, *Garbage in the Cities: Refuse, Reform, and the Environment, 1880–1980* (College Station: Texas A & M University Press, 1981), 51–78; Richard Skolnik, "George Edwin Waring, Jr.: A Model for Reformers," *New York Historical Society Bulletin* 52 (Oct. 1968): 354–75; Daniel Eli Burnstein, "Clean Streets and the Pursuit of Progress: Urban Reform in New York City in the Progressive Era," Ph.D. diss. Rutgers University, 1992, 85.

81. William Potts, "George Edwin Waring, Jr.," *The Charities Review* 8 (Nov. 1898): 461–68.

82. Everett P. Wheeler, *Callanan's Monthly* 4, no. 7 (June 1901): 1. Publisher Henry Holt called Waring "the most talked of and best talked of man in New York" in the late 1890s. Henry Holt, *Garrulities of an Octogenarian Editor* (Boston: Houghton Mifflin Company, 1923), 157. Thomas Wentworth Higginson also offers effusive praise for Waring in his memoirs. Higginson, *Part of a Man's Life* (Boston: Houghton Mifflin, 1905), 304.

83. Potts, "George Edwin Waring, Jr.," 462.

84. *New York Times*, Dec. 24, 1901.

85. Richard Skolnik, "George Edwin Waring, Jr.: A Model for Reformers," *New York Historical Society Bulletin* 52 (Oct. 1968): 354–75.

86. George E. Waring Jr., *Whip and Spur*, 67–68. Quoted in Melosi, *Garbage in the Cities*, 65.

87. George E. Waring Jr., "Education at West Point," *The Outlook* 59:825–37.

88. Ibid., 827.

89. Many reformers—including Waring and Bellamy—held German militarism in particular esteem, citing Bismarck's achievement of national unity and imperial greatness through the creation of a modern, rationalized military force. Reform-oriented publications also praised Bismarck as a manly hero worth emulating. In 1895, for example, *Harper's Weekly* held that he epitomized such admirable qualities as "the power of daring initiative, sturdy, defiant self-assertion, promptness in resolving and in acting." It is important to note that admiration for Bismarck was not confined to those who favored an imperial role for the United States: even anti-imperialists championed his success in bringing militarized order to Germany's internal bureaucracy and instilling national civic pride in the German population. The white army represented an attempt to bring Bismarckian-style order to the American city—to bring unity to an American population that many believed was as fractured as the former German states.

"Bismarck's Birthday," *Harper's Weekly* (Mar. 30, 1895):290. Other positives assessments of Bismarck include "Bismarck's Eightieth Birthday," *Leslie's Weekly* (Apr. 11, 1895); and George W. Hinman, "Bismarck in the Wilhelm Strasse," "Bismarck in the Reichstag," and "Bismarck at Home," *Leslie's Weekly* (Apr. 1895).

90. Quoted in Lipow, *Authoritarian Socialism in America*. Analyses of Bellamy's influence on American politics also include: John L. Thomas, *Alternative America: Henry George, Edward Bellamy, Henry Demarest Lloyd and the Adversary Tradition* (Cambridge, MA: Harvard University Press, 1983); and Daphne Patai, ed., *Looking Backward, 1988–1888: Essays on Edward Bellamy* (Amherst: University of Massachusetts Press, 1988).

91. George Francis Knerr, "The Mayoral Administration of William L. Strong, New York City, 1895 to 1897," Ph.D. diss., New York University Department of History, 1957, 64–71.

92. Ibid., 71.

93. Col. George E. Waring Jr., "The Necessity for Excluding Politics from Municipal Business," *Proceedings of the Third National Conference for Good City Government and of the Second Annual Meeting of the National Municipal League* (Philadelphia: National Municipal League, 1896), 273.

94. George E. Waring Jr., "Government by Party," *The North American Review* 163, no. 480 (Nov. 1896): 587; George E. Waring Jr., "The Cleaning of a Great City," *McClure's Magazine* 9 (Sept. 1897): 916.

95. Quoted in Lipow, *Authoritarian Socialism in America*, 27.

96. Lipow, *Authoritarian Socialism in America*, 25–27.

97. *Monthly Bulletin Issued by The City Club of New York* 3 (Jan. 1896).

98. *New York Tribune*, Mar. 1, 1895, 4.

99. Colonel George E. Waring Jr., "The Labor Question in the Department of Street Cleaning," *Municipal Affairs* 2 (1898): 226–34. Waring's account was reprinted widely in reform publications and excerpted in newspaper editorials.

100. "Reform in Street Cleaning," *New York Times Sunday Magazine Supplement*, Oct. 11, 1896, 2–3.

101. Adler quoted in Daniel Eli Burnstein, "Clean Streets and the Pursuit of Progress: Urban Reform in New York City in the Progressive Era," Ph.D. diss., Rutgers University, 1992, 85. Charles A. Meade, "City Cleansing in New York: Some Advances and Retreats," *Municipal Affairs* 4 (1900): 721–41.

102. Mayoral Papers of William Strong, Municipal Archives of the City of New York, boxes 49 and 50.

103. Waring's military background and bearing were emphasized in newspapers and periodicals. See, for example, Potts, "George Edwin Waring, Jr.," 465–67; "Clean Streets," *Citizens' Union Pamphlet* no. 2 (New York: July, 1897), 4–7; "Clean Streets at Last," *New York Times*, July 28, 1895, 28; "The Military Element in Colonel Waring's Career," *Century Illustrated Monthly Magazine* 59 (Feb. 1900): 544–47. Waring also heralded his own military accomplishments and militarist approaches to public service in several articles he published while and immediately after serving as com-

missioner. See, for example, "The Cleaning of a Great City," and *Street-Cleaning* (New York: Doubleday & McClure, 1898).

104. On Waring and pragmatic environmentalism, see Martin V. Melosi, "Pragmatic Environmentalist: Sanitary Engineer George E. Waring, Jr.," *Essays in Public Works History* 4 (Apr. 1977). On Riis's environmentalism, see Gandal, *The Virtues of the Vicious*, 8, 32–33, 93–95, 97, 137.

105. M. Christine Boyer, *Dreaming the Rational City: The Myth of American City Planning* (Cambridge, MA: MIT Press, 1983). See also Robert Rydell, *All the World's a Fair: Visions of Empire at American International Expositions, 1876–1916* (Chicago: University of Chicago Press, 1984). On urban transparency and the movement of the military, see Michel Foucault, "Questions on Geography," in Colin Gordon, ed., *Power/Knowledge: Selected Interviews and Other Writings*, 1972–1977 (New York: Pantheon, 1980).

106. "Clean Streets at Last," *New York Times*, July 28, 1895, 28. Two years later the *New York Times* sounded a similar theme: "Nothing connected with the parade was more noteworthy than the size, character and spirit of the crowds along the route, and particularly in what are known as the tenement-house districts. . . . At no point was there the slightest disorder or a sign of anything but enjoyment, sympathy, and pride. Irish, German, Italian, and negro quarters were traversed, and everywhere the temper of the people was the same." "The Street Cleaners Parade," *New York Times*, May 28, 1897, 6.

107. "White Wings Flutter Finely: Waring's Army Delighted Official and Citizens," *New York Recorder*, May 27, 1896. The parades received much coverage in the New York and national press. See, for example, "The Street Cleaners' Parade," *New York Times*, May 28, 1897; "Waring's White Army," *New York Tribune*, May 26, 1896, 13; "Street Cleaners Parade" *New York Times*, May 27, 1896, 1.

108. William Potts, "The White Brigade," *New York Times*, May 27, 1897, 6. Other poems include: anonymous, "The March of the White Brigade," *New York Times*, May 27, 1897, 6; and E.C.L., "To the White Brigade," *New York Times*, May 20, 1897, 6. Others also saw in the parades a magical transformation of workers and populace. One observer reportedly stated, "Waring . . . saw his enemies broken under the wheels of the newly painted ash carts," "First Parade of the Department of Street Cleaning," *New York Herald* (May 26, 1896). Albert Shaw wrote of Waring's tenure as commissioner: "The transforming effect [of Waring's leadership] upon the appearance, comfort, and health of the city was almost magical. His concrete setting-forth of the superior value of non-political business-like administration was more effective as a practical object lesson, than all the speeches and arguments that the reformers could have launched in fifty years." Shaw, *Col. George E. Waring, Jr.: The Greatest Apostle of Cleanliness* (New York, 1899), 14–15.

109. Waring asked that "all citizens . . . aid the department in securing a strict obedience" to the orders that men wear their uniforms at all times when on duty and "whenever appearing in the streets during working hours, whether on duty or not." Officers on the force were also "forbidden to enter liquor saloons, or other places

where liquor is sold, while on duty or in uniform." "Ordered to Wear Their Uniforms," *New York Times*, Jan. 22, 1895, 9.

110. Potts, "George Edwin Waring, Jr." Edward Carey wrote similarly that Waring had transformed "the street-cleaning force, mainly from the old apparently hopeless material, into a body of self-respecting, ambitious, and efficient public servants," in "Tammany Past and Present," *The Forum* (Oct. 1898):204–205. In an article generally favorable to Tammany Hall, Carey cites that organization's opposition to Waring as one of its greatest failures.

111. As historian Donna Gabaccia notes, many "positivist" Americans subscribed not to a social Darwinist conception of "racial competition and domination by the fittest races" but to "Lamarckian notions of racial improvement by means of characteristics acquired through education, social intercourse, and biological amalgamation." Gabaccia, "Race, Nation, Hyphen: Italian-Americans and American Multiculturalism in Comparative Perspective," in Guglielmo, ed, *Are Italians White?*, 51.

112. Quote from "Parade of Col. Waring's Men," *New York Evening Post*, May 28, 1897, 7.

113. "Has a Colored Foreman," *New York Times*, Apr. 4, 1895, 9. This article corrects one from a different (unnamed) New York daily newspaper that had erroneously reported that the department counted four black supervisors. Employment statistics for this period do not exist, and I was not able to establish the total number of workers in the department under Waring. In 1897, the *New York Times* estimated the force at 2,500 men. "The Street Cleaners' Parade," *New York Times*, May 28, 1897, 6. In 1900 the department counted 2,193 workers. "Table 1: Relative Strength of the Top Three Uniformed Departments in NYC, 1900–1950," in Steven H. Corey, "Only Irish Need Apply?: Political Patronage and Sanitation as a Career: 1900–1954," unpublished Ph.D. seminar paper, New York University. I am indebted to Steve Corey for his generosity in sharing this information with me and for his tutorials on the history of sanitation in New York City.

It is possible that the number of African American street cleaners increased somewhat during Waring's tenure. The Department Application Clerk, Cringle, reported in August 1895 that there had been an increase in applications from this group, although the *New York Times* reporter who interviewed him was not able to obtain an accurate count of African American employees. Cringle reported that "colored men sought situations as drivers because they are naturally fond of horses." Another department official told the reporter that "colored men were attracted to the white uniform." "Colored Men as Sweepers," *New York Times*, Aug. 24, 1895, 13.

114. Historian Ira Katznelson shows that Tammany leaders offered street cleaning positions to African Americans between 1897 and 1913 and that these jobs represented 70 percent of the total number of patronage jobs given to African Americans by Tammany during those years. Ira Katznelson, *Black Men, White Cities: Race, Politics, and Migration in the United States, 1900–1930, and Britain, 1948–1968* (London: Oxford University Press, 1973).

115. Thomas Guglielmo, *White on Arrival: Italians, Race, Color and Power in*

Chicago, 1890–1945 (Oxford and New York: Oxford University Press, 2003), 3–13. See also Thomas A. Guglielmo, "'No Color Barrier': Italians, Race, and Power in the United States," in Jennifer Guglielmo, ed., *Are Italians White?*, 29–43; Gabaccia, "Race, Nation, Hyphen"; and Robert Orsi, "The Religious Boundaries of an In Between People: Street Feste and the Problem of the Dark-Skinned Other in Italian Harlem, 1920–1990," *American Quarterly* 44 (Sept. 1992).

116. "The Reform Club," *Tammany Times*, Apr. 6, 1895. Parody was presented as a play with racial and ethnic caricatures. Characters included "Dago Sentinel," "Negro Corporal," and "Herr Damcent."

117. Quoted in "Col. Waring's Labor Brigade," *New York Evening Post*, May 27, 1896, 1.

118. Hiland Flower to George E. Waring, quoted in *New York Times*, Aug. 6, 1895.

119. "Coats Must Be Buttoned, Belts Buckled," *New York Times*, Aug. 23, 1895, 11. In this letter, Waring also spoke of his own military experience in the South, where he performed "arduous" labor in full uniform.

120. "The Waring Battalion," *Tammany Times*, Apr. 20, 1895, 11.

121. Marcus True, "Waring's Mendacity," *Tammany Times* 9, no. 18 (Sept. 12, 1897): 8–10. The article also accused Waring of appointing a "French Maid of All Work" as his personal assistant and of discharging Democratic employees of the department.

Attacks on Waring's Civil War record were preceded by his alleged dismissal of Grand Army of the Republic veterans as "pension bummers." See "The Attack on Waring," *New York Times*, Oct. 22, 1897, 3; "Col Waring in Trouble," *New York Daily Tribune*, Apr. 21, 1895; "Attack on Col. Waring," *New York Times*, Apr. 21, 1895, 9; "Col. Waring Under Fire," *New York Times*, Apr. 23, 1895, 2.

122. The Central Labor Federation letter also accused Waring of adopting the southern Italian "padrone" labor system in an attempt to avoid paying "for the services of American citizens." The claim that Waring was an "idle lackey of the idle class" responded to Waring's earlier characterization of the CLF as "an organization in the interest of idleness." Central Labor Federation letter to Waring, excerpted in "Colonel Waring of Street Cleaning Fame," *Tammany Times* 4, no. 19 (Mar. 16, 1895): 11. On other Tammany and Central Labor Federation claims that Waring enriched himself through his public work, see "The Tiger Snarls at Waring," *New York Tribune*, Oct. 21, 1897, 3; "A Demand on Col. Waring," *New York Times*, Mar. 8, 1895, 2.

123. Asa Bird Gardiner delivered this famous quote in an October 17, 1897 speech, in which he conceded that the only accomplishment Strong's administration could count was "clean streets," but also accused the administration of stealing "about a million a year" in order to accomplish this and furthermore asserted that the main reason streets were cleaner was that the number of horses had declined significantly. "Tammany Hall's Chief Orator Says 'To Hell with Reform,'" *Chicago Daily Tribune*, Oct. 18, 1897, 6.

124. Michael E. McGerr, "Political Style and Women's Power, 1830–1930," *The Journal of American History* (Dec. 1990):864–85. See also McGerr, *The Decline of Popular Politics: The American North, 1865–1928* (New York: Oxford University Press, 1986). On women's influence on American political culture, see, for example, Paula Baker, "The

Domestication of American Politics: Women and American Political Society, 1780–1920," *American Historical Review* 89 (1984): 620–47; and Robin Muncy, *Creating a Female Dominion in American Reform* (New York: Oxford University Press, 1991).

4. SOCRATES IN THE SLUMS: "SOCIAL BROTHERHOOD" AND SETTLEMENT HOUSE REFORM

1. This argument is treated extensively in Robin Muncy, *Creating a Female Dominion in American Reform, 1890–1935* (New York: Oxford University Press, 1991). Among others, prominent women who worked in settlements include Florence Kelley, Eleanor Roosevelt, and Frances Perkins. On the settlement movement in general, see Minna Carson, *Settlement Folk: Social Thought and the American Settlement Movement, 1885–1930* (Chicago: University of Chicago Press, 1990); Allen Davis, *Spearheads for Reform: The Social Settlements and the Progressive Movement, 1890–1914* (New York: Oxford University Press, 1967); and Michael B. Katz, *Under the Shadow of the Poorhouse: A History of Social Welfare in America* (New York: Basic Books, 1986), 158–63. On Hull House see Muncy, *Creating a Female Dominion,* and Katherine Kish Sklar, "Hull House in the 1890s: A Community of Women Reformers," *Signs* 10, no. 4 (Summer 1985): 658–77. On Florence Kelley, see Katherine Kish Sklar, *Florence Kelley and the Nation's Work: The Rise of Women's Political Culture, 1830–1900* (New Haven: Yale University Press, 1995). On Eleanor Roosevelt at New York's College Settlement, see Blanche Wiesen Cook, *Eleanor Roosevelt, Vol. 1, 1884–1933* (New York: Viking, 1992), 135–38.

2. See, for example, Davis, *Spearheads for Reform,* and Sklar, "Hull House in the 1890s."

3. Much scholarship on "romantic friendships" among nineteenth-century women has dealt with settlement women, especially Jane Addams and Lillian Wald. Blanche Wiesen Cook, in "Female Support Networks and Political Activism: Lillian Wald, Crystal Eastman, Emma Goldman," *Chrysalis* 3 (1977): 43–61, argued that Wald and Addams, along with many other political women of the period, could be categorized as lesbians in that they formed their primary attachments to other women. This argument was expanded by Adrienne Rich in her much debated 1980 essay, "Compulsory Heterosexuality and Lesbian Existence," *Signs* 5 (Summer 1980): 631–60. A number of feminist scholars argued that labeling these women "lesbian" was ahistorical but at the same time expressed concerns about the implications of disassociating romantic friendships from lesbian history. On this issue, see Carroll Smith-Rosenberg, *Disorderly Conduct: Visions of Gender in Victorian America* (New York: Oxford University Press, 1985); Esther Newton, "The Mythic Mannish Lesbian: Radclyffe Hall and the New Woman," *Signs* 9 (Summer 1984): 557–75; and Martha Vicinus, "'They Wonder to Which Sex I Belong': The Historical Roots of Modern Lesbian Identity," in Henry Abelove et al., eds., *The Lesbian and Gay Studies Reader* (New York: Routledge, 1993).

4. In many works produced since the 1990s, same-sex relationships among settlement women have been treated in cursory and unsatisfactory fashion. Robyn Muncy asserts that Jane Addams's companion Mary Rozet Smith played the role of "a Victo-

rian wife" (*Creating a Female Dominion* 16). Minna Carson writes briefly on Lillian Wald's "crushes" on female residents at Henry Street (*Settlement Folk* 93). Linda Gordon in her influential *Pitied But Not Entitled: Single Mothers and the History of Welfare* (Cambridge, MA: Harvard University Press, 1994) asserts that settlement women and other female reformers involved with other women shared a "nuns' sensibility" and dismisses their sexual activity as irrelevant (79). Jean Bethke Elshtain asserts: "Celibate lives need not be lonely lives or distorted lives but could be full of love, friendship, and joy—and so they were, for Jane Addams, for Emily Balch, for Ellen Gates Starr, for Addams's companion, Mary Rozet Smith, and for many other college-educated women of their day" (*Jane Addams and the Dream of American Democracy* [New York: Basic Books, 2002]). Victoria Bissell Brown refuses the label "lesbian" for Addams in the absence of evidence of sexual contact. Of Addams's relationship with Smith, Brown writes, "what survives is a record of tenderness and affection, the sort of mutual admiration and devotion that typifies any strong marriage" (*The Education of Jane Addams* [Philadelphia: University of Pennsylvania Press, 2004], 257).

A notable exception to this trend is the work of Leila J. Rupp on the international women's movement. Rupp, whose work addresses, among others, Addams and other American women involved in settlement work, writes, "Given the variety of bonds, we might wonder whether internationally organized women managed to cross the boundaries of sexuality more easily than those of class, religion, and nationality. Certainly the conflicts over sexuality within the movement tended to pit 'respectable' against unconventional behavior rather than same-sex against heterosexual relationships" ("Sexuality and Politics in the Early Twentieth Century: The Case of the International Women's Movement," *Feminist Studies* 23, no. 3 [Autumn 1997]: 595). See also Rupp, *Worlds of Women: The Making of an International Women's Movement* (Princeton: Princeton University Press, 1997). For a fascinating discussion of alternative modes of domesticity and same-sex relationships in settlement houses, see Shannon Jackson, *Lines of Activity: Performance, Historiography, Hull-House Domesticity* (Ann Arbor: University of Michigan Press, 2000), 164–86.

5. On settlement ideology, see Carson, *Settlement Folk*; and Christopher Lasch, ed., *The Social Thought of Jane Addams* (New York: Irvington Publishers, 1982). On Elliott's career, see Tay Hohoff, *A Ministry to Man: The Life of John Lovejoy Elliott* (New York: Harper & Brothers, 1959); and Howard B. Radest, *Toward Common Ground: The Story of the Ethical Societies in the United States* (New York: Frederick Ungar, 1969), 109–21. On Stover see J. K. Paulding, *Charles B. Stover: His Life and Personality* (New York: The International Press, 1938); and Jeffrey Scheuer, "Legacy of Light: University Settlement's First Century" (New York: University Settlement, 1985). On Addams's life, see Jane Addams, *Twenty Years at Hull House* (New York: Macmillan, 1910); and Allen Davis, *American Heroine: The Life and Legend of Jane Addams* (New York: Oxford University Press, 1973). On Wald, see Lillian Wald, *The House on Henry Stree*t (New York: H. Holt, 1915); and Beatrice Siegel, *Lillian Wald of Henry Street* (New York: Macmillan, 1983).

6. Addams made her critique of the "family claim" in two essays, "The Subjective

Necessity for Social Settlements" (1892) and "The College Woman and the Family Claim" (1898), both reprinted in Ellen Condliffe Lagemann, ed., *Jane Addams on Education* (New York: Teachers College Press, 1985). The first essay was originally delivered at a meeting of the Ethical Culture Society, to which both Elliott and Stover belonged. For more on Jane Addams's thought, see Daniel Levine, *Jane Addams and the Liberal Tradition* (Madison: State Historical Society of Wisconsin, 1971); and Lasch, ed., *The Social Thought of Jane Addams.*

7. John Lovejoy Elliott's parents were Isaac and Elizabeth Lovejoy Elliott. His maternal grandfather was antislavery congressman Owen Lovejoy. For further biographical information on Elliott, see Hohoff, *A Ministry to Man;* and Radest, *Toward Common Ground*, 109–21.

8. For biographical information on Stover see Paulding, *Charles B. Stover;* and Scheuer, "Legacy of Light.".

9. Radest, *Toward Common Ground*, 110.

10. Quoted in Paulding, *Charles B. Stover*, 15–16.

11. Paulding, *Charles B. Stover*, 18.

12. Letters to Henry J. Rode, quoted in Paulding, *Charles B. Stover*, 35–38.

13. Paulding, *Charles B. Stover*, 112–13.

14. Paulding, *Charles B. Stover*, 112.

15. Mary K. Simkhovitch, "Recollections and Reflections," in Paulding, *Charles B. Stover*, 136–38.

16. Lillian D. Wald, "Recollections and Reflections," in Paulding, *Charles B. Stover*, 131–35.

17. See, for example: Linda Dowling, *Hellenism and Homosexuality in Victorian Oxford* (Ithaca, NY: Cornell University Press, 1993), 104–54; and Byrne R.S. Fone, *A Road to Stonewall: Male Homosexuality and Homophobia in English and American Literature, 1750–1969* (New York: Twaine Publishers, 1986), 129–56.

18. Edward Carpenter, "Homogenic Love" (1894), in Brian Reade, ed., *Sexual Heretics: Male Homosexuality in English Literature from 1850 to 1900: An Anthology* (New York: Coward-McCann, 1970), 324–47. See also Elaine Showalter, *Sexual Anarchy: Gender and Culture at the Fin de Siècle* (New York: Penguin, 1990), 47.

19. John Lovejoy Elliott to family, January 29, 1893, copy at Ethical Culture Society Archives (ECSA), chronological card file, 1893.

20. Quoted in Hohoff, *Ministry to Man*, 57.

21. Michael Moon, "'The Gentle Boy from the Dangerous Classes': Pederasty, Domesticity, and Capitalism in Horatio Alger," *Representations* 19 (Summer 1987): 87–110.

22. "The Child's Champion" was published in the mass-circulation periodical *The New World.* See Michael Moon, "Disseminating Whitman," in Ronald R. Butters et al., *Displacing Homophobia: Gay Male Perspectives in Literature and Culture* (Durham, NC: Duke University Press, 1989), 235–54.

23. Betsey Erkkila, *Whitman the Political Poet* (New York: Oxford University Press, 1989), 183.

24. Quoted in ibid., 180.

25. For information on Alger's reform activities and his relationships with working-class youths, see Carol Nackenoff, *The Fictional Republic: Horatio Alger and American Political Discourse* (New York: Oxford University Press, 1994).

26. Moon, "The Gentle Boy of the Dangerous Classes," 91.

27. Fone, *A Road to Stonewall*, 57–74.

28. For example, historian Terence Kissack shows that "Whitman's poetry and the homoerotic interpretations of Whitman's work . . . influenced a number of anarchist sex radicals" (109), including John William Lloyd, an American anarchist and publisher of *The Free Comrade,* who modeled himself after Edward Carpenter. Kissack, "Anarchism and the Politics of Homosexuality," Ph.D. diss., City University of New York, 2004, 107–50. On Whitman's influence on the politics of sexuality, see also Nicholas C. Edsall, *Toward Stonewall: Homosexuality and Society in the Modern Western World* (Charlottesville: University of Virginia Press, 2003) and Jonathan Ned Katz, *Love Stories: Sex Between Men Before Homosexuality* (Chicago: University of Chicago Press, 2001).

29. See, for example: Fone, *A Road to Stonewall*, 75–84; Dowling, *Hellenism and Homosexuality in Victorian Oxford*, 130; David S. Reynolds, *Walt Whitman's America: A Cultural Biography* (New York: Knopf, 1995), 578–79; Katz, *Love Stories*, 235–45, 257–87, 321–29.

30. Carpenter, "Homogenic Love."

31. Seth Koven, "From Rough Lads to Hooligans: Boy Life, National Culture and Social Reform," in Andrew Parker et al., eds., *Nationalisms and Sexualities* (New York: Routledge, 1992), 365–91. Koven argues elsewhere that Toynbee reformers disagreed among themselves about the extent to which these relationships should be pursued; Ashbee's connection to working-class boys caused the greatest concern. Koven argues that these relationships tread too close to the boundary separating an ethos of "male friendship-love from homosexuality" (*Slumming: Sexual and Social Politics in Victorian London* [Princeton and Oxford: Princeton University Press, 2004]).

32. See, for example, Heymann Fliegel, "Memorial Address," in Paulding, *Charles B. Stover*, 179–82.

33. One of Stover's colleagues, for example, reported that Stover would take a young man as his roommate at the camp and would take the young man on nature walks. The Papers of the University Settlement Society of New York City (USSNYC), microfilmed by The State Historical Society of Wisconsin, A. J. Kennedy Notes, "SEI-1894, History and Comment," Reel 15.

34. Historians and literary scholars have argued that nineteenth-century writers, influenced by Greek history, often rooted tales of male same-sex love in natural, Arcadian settings. According to Fone, "Arcadia, the pastoral haven of Greek literature, became understood as a code for a homosexual sanctuary" (*A Road to Stonewall* 281). See also Barbara Fasler, "Theories of Homosexuality as Sources of Bloomsbury's Androgyny," *Signs* 5, no. 2 (Winter 1979): 237–51.

35. Gregory F. Gilmartin, *Shaping the City: New York and the Municipal Art Society* (New York: Clarkson Potter, 1995), 241–51.

36. ECSA, Algernon Black Papers, Box: John Lovejoy Elliott.

37. Quoted in "From One Small Room," pamphlet (Hudson Guild, 1945), ECSA, John Lovejoy Elliott Papers, Box: Elliott, pre-1933. For other accounts of the Hurly Burlies and the founding of the Hudson Guild, see Hohoff, *A Ministry to Man*, 41–42, 51–55; Radest, *Toward Common Ground*, 114–20.

38. ECSA, Algernon D. Black Papers, Draft manuscript of "Biography of John Lovejoy Elliott," 43. See also ECSA, "From One Small Room."

39. Reports of the closeness of McCloskey and Elliott abound in Hudson Guild documents, and the relationship is attested to in the early 1960s interviews by Frieda Moss with, among others, Jerome Nathanson, Algernon Black, and Helen Reichenbach, ECSA, Box: Oral History Project. A small amount of correspondence exists at the ECSA in a folder titled "McCloskey, Mark" in the John Lovejoy Elliott Papers. See, for example, letter of February 9, 1942 from McCloskey to Elliott and letter of January 9, 1942 from McCloskey to Elliott.

40. Interview with Bresci Thompson, November 20, 1995.

41. On "Elliott's boys," see, for example, Horace L. Freiss, "John Lovejoy Elliott: A Living Legacy of Ethical Humanism," ECSA, Algernon Black Papers, Box: John Lovejoy Elliott, 1; and "Interview of Helen Reichenbach by Frieda Moss," undated, p. 18, ECSA, Box: Oral History Project. On Elliott's appearance see Hohoff, *A Ministry to Man*, 5; "Interview of Jerome Nathanson by Frieda Moss," 1964, p. 24, ECSA, Box: Oral History Project. Carpenter and Symonds also adopted a rough masculine Whitmanesque style. See, for example, Barbara Fassler, "Theories of Homosexuality as Sources of Bloomsbury's Androgyny," *Signs* 5, no. 2 (Winter 1979): 237–51.

42. Algernon D. Black, draft manuscript, "Biography of John Lovejoy Elliott," 82–83, ECSA. Elliott and Stover's masculine style resembled that of the "slum priests" of London's Oxford House settlement movement more than that of the Toynbee Hall reformers. Seth Koven argues that observers responded to the gendered performances of these men in ways similar to those of Stover and Elliott, described in this essay. Koven writes: "Almost exaggeratedly masculine in their powerful physical presence, these slum priests nonetheless struck many observers as sexually ambiguous" (*Slumming* 257).

43. Stories of Damon and Pythias and David and Jonathan as illustrations of loving male friendships circulated in American culture throughout the nineteenth century, preceding Carpenter and Symonds. The stories became more explicitly imbued with physical and sexual meanings over the course of the century. See, for example, E. Anthony Rotundo, "Romantic Friendship: Male Intimacy and Middle-Class Youth in the Northern United States, 1899–1900," *Journal of Social History* 23, no. 1 (Autumn 1989): 8–10); Michael Lynch, "Here Is Adhesiveness: From Friendship to Homosexuality," *Victorian Studies* 29, no. 1 (Autumn 1985): 67–96; Peter Gay, *The Tender Passion*, vol. 2 of *The Bourgeois Experience: Victoria and Freud* (New York: Oxford University Press, 1986), 238.

44. "Ethics Lesson Plan, Class V, Elliott, 1906," ECSA, Box: Ethics Classes, J. L. Elliott.

45. The story of David and Jonathan appears several times in Elliott's lesson plans.

This quote comes from a plan dated January 5, 1906, ECSA, Box: Ethics Classes, J. L. Elliott.

46. Elliott told the Damon and Pythias story in the following lesson plans: "Class V, Ethics, Lesson, January 5, 1906," "Lesson 18, Ethics, February 23, 1906," "Beta A, Lesson, December 8th, 1905."

47. In addition to Whitman, the boys read Ruskin, Carlyle, and Emerson. Other members of the circle who later achieved renown included Henry Moskowitz and Meyer Bloomfield. See unpublished draft histories of University Settlement clubs, USSNYC, Reel 15, Series 7, Box 1, Clubs. For Epstein's account of his experiences on the Lower East Side, see Jacob Epstein, *Epstein: An Autobiography* (New York: Dutton, 1955), 1–11.

48. Shaw showed the drawings to Robert Ross, Oscar Wilde's literary executor, who awarded Epstein the much sought-after commission to create Wilde's tomb. According to art historian Elizabeth Barker, the *Calamus* drawings were studies for a sculpture. Elizabeth Barker, "New Light on Epstein's Early Career," *The Burlington Magazine* 130, no. 1029 (Dec. 1988): 903–909. Scholar Frank Felsenstein writes that "[Epstein] fell under the spell of Whitman at about the age of sixteen, when he attended classes run by James Kirk Paulding." Felsenstein, relying on notes made by Epstein's widow after his death, incorrectly identifies the "Community Guild" as the location of Paulding's reading group (SEI Club). "Epstein as Book Illustrator," in Evelyn Silber et al., *Jacob Epstein: Sculpture and Drawings* (London: W. S. Maney and Son, 1989), 197–98. Epstein Scholar Silber speculates that Epstein showed the *Calamus* drawings (which represented a significant stylistic and thematic departure from the illustrations he produced for Hutchins Hapgood's 1902 *The Spirit of the Ghetto*) because "he may have thought that Ross . . . would be sympathetic to the sinewy grace of these drawings whose homosexual overtones would make them controversial elsewhere" (*The Sculpture of Epstein* [Oxford: Phaidon Press, 1986], 14).

49. Bernard Hirshberg, "A Tale of Two Souls," *The Emersonian* (Mar. 1911):8–9, USSNY, "Clubs-E," Reel 16.

50. David Colin, "Arise, O Bard," *The Emersonian* (Mar. 1911), USSNY, "Clubs-E," Reel 16.

51. "Preamble of the Promethean Constitution," USSNYC, Reel 15, Series 7, Box 1, "Clubs."

52. Ibid.

53. Many of the boys who were members of the Chadwick Civic Jr. Club and the SEI Club achieved great success. In addition to Epstein, Bloomfield, and Moscowitz, these included the paleontologist Elias Lowe, Albert A. Volk, and Hamilton Holt.

It should be noted that the settlement reformers also taught lessons that reinforced racialized hierarchies. Elliott, for example, infused his teaching on brotherhood with Lamarckian ideas about racial distinctions, characterizing African Americans as members of a "backward race" in need of "uplift." In the same lesson plan, Elliott criticizes British imperialism and the treatment of American Indians, but also insists that it is the duty of Americans to help less developed people and races. He makes the argument that all races have a different place in American society, but also have different capacities. For example, he asserts: "The negroes have their particular gift. They have certain capacity for doing things and we are going to make a tremendous mistake if we are simply going to make them hurt each other and try to change their color." Lesson Plan, January 12, 1906. ECSA, File: Elliott, Ethical Lessons.

Ultimately, Stover and Elliott worked within a framework that configured young people as more impressionable and more susceptible to processes of uplift and Americanization. On uplift and Americanization in Progressive-era urban reform, see, for example: Paul Boyer, *Urban Masses and Moral Order in America, 1820–1920* (Cambridge, MA and London: Harvard University Press, 1978), 220–60; Richard Hofstadter, *The Age of Reform: From Bryan to F.D.R.* (New York: Vintage, 1955), 174–85; Gary Gerstle, *American Crucible: Race and Nation in the Twentieth Century* (Princeton: Princeton University Press, 2001), 14–43.

54. On Parkhurst, see Charles Gardner, *The Doctor and the Devi, or Midnight Adventures of Dr. Parkhurst* (New York: Macmillan, 1890).

55. George Chauncey, *Gay New York: Gender, Urban Culture, and the Making of the Gay Male World* (New York: Basic Books, 1994), 36–67. Historians focusing on the lives of working-class women and on prostitution in the turn-of-the-century city have documented similar erotic economies. See Kathy Peiss, *Cheap Amusements: Working Women and Leisure in Turn-of-the-Century New York* (Philadelphia: Temple University Press, 1986); and Timothy Gilfoyle, *City of Eros: New York City, Prostitution, and the Commercialization of Sex, 1790–1920* (New York: Norton, 1992).

56. Ibid., 104–105.

57. Reminiscence by NYC Parks Department Laborer, Charles B. Stover Papers, USSP, Reel 15. Another Parks Department laborer, Emil T. Delaney, remarked that Stover talked "humbly even with the men of the plainest and most illiterate type." Similar testimonials by Park Department employees were collected by Stanley Bero and are recorded in "Recollections and Appreciations," Paulding, *Stover*, 158–63.

58. Elliott's correspondence with prison inmates from the Hudson Guild neighborhood are extensive. ECSA, Elliott Box, "Prison Correspondence." Elliott was a frequent visitor to Sing Sing, and he often took in recently-released prisoners as "housekeepers"—a subject of great concern to his family and friends. Hohoff, *A Ministry to Man*, 56.

59. Other colleagues who eulogized Stover also referred to Socrates. Remembrances are reprinted in Paulding, *Charles B. Stover*, 129–91. Coit adds that "whoever gained access to [Stover's] mind found within, as Plato says of Socrates, divine and golden images of surpassing beauty" (129).

60. Horace L. Freiss, "John Lovejoy Elliott: A Living Legacy of Ethical Humanism," 6, ECSA, Algernon D. Black Papers, Box: John Lovejoy Elliott, 1.

61. ECSA, Box: Elliott—Ethical Lessons, File: Class V.

62. ECSA, Box: Oral Interviews, "Miss Lucy Mitchell's Oral Interview" by Frieda Moss, January 9, 1964.

63. Dowling, *Hellenism and Homosexuality*, 67–103.

64. Jane Addams, *The Spirit of Youth in the City Streets* (New York: Macmillan, 1909), 16–17.

65. On vice, see ibid., 25–30. On enervation, see "The Subjective Necessity for Social Settlements" (1892) and "The College Woman and the Family Claim" (1898), reprinted in Lagemann, ed., *Jane Addams on Education*.

66. Addams, *The Spirit of Youth*, 16–17.

67. Hohoff, *Minister of Reform*, 67–104.

68. February 4, 1933 letter from J.L.E. to Lillian Wald. ECSA, Box: Hudson Guild—Elliott, File: Wald.

69. November 8, 1933 letter from Lillian Wald to Elliott. ECSA, Box: Hudson Guild—Elliott, File: Wald.

70. See, for example, Nancy F. Cott, *The Grounding of Modern Feminism* (New Haven: Yale University Press, 1987), 175–21; and Smith-Rosenberg, *Disorderly Conduct*, 245–96.

5. DADDY GEORGE AND TOM BROWN: SEXUAL SCANDAL, POLITICAL MANHOOD, AND SELF-GOVERNMENT REFORM

1. Virtually every account of this meeting characterized it as "unique" or "remarkable" because of the social composition of those in the audience. See front-page articles in the following New York newspapers of January 17, 1916: *New York Tribune*, *New York Times*, *New York Sun*, *Brooklyn Daily Eagle*.

2. *New York Tribune*, Jan. 17, 1916, 1.

3. Documents related to Thomas Mott Osborne's career can be found in The Osborne Family Collection, The George Arents Research Library, Syracuse University, Syracuse, New York (hereafter OFC). See also two books on penology written by Osborne: *Within Prison Walls* (New York: D. Appleton, 1914) and *Society and Prisons: Some Suggestions for a New Penology* (1916; reprint, Montclair, NJ: Patterson Smith, 1975). Two biographical studies of Osborne have been published: Rudolph W. Chamberlain, *There Is No Truce: A Life of Thomas Mott Osborne* (New York: Macmillan, 1935); and Frank Tannenbaum, *Osborne of Sing Sing* (Chapel Hill: University of North Carolina Press, 1933).

4. Adler quoted in *New York Tribune* and *New York Sun*, Jan. 17, 1916.

5. The original indictment and all supporting legal documents for the case "New York v. Osborne, 1916" can be found in OFC, Boxes 304–311: "Legal, Suits, New York v. Osborne."

6. "Mr. Osborne's Friends and Enemies," *New York Times*, Aug. 10, 1915.

7. Charles W. Eliot, letter to *New York Times*, quoted in Tannenbaum, *Osborne of Sing Sing*, 240.

8. *New York Times*, July 16, 1916.

9. "Warden Osborne," *New York Times*, Dec. 31, 1915.

10. For narratives of the proceedings brought against Osborne, see Tannenbaum, *Osborne of Sing Sing*, 179–257, and Chamberlain, *There Is No Truce*, 304–64. The

reference to "known sodomists" is from Assistant District Attorney William J. Fallon. For an account of Fallon's involvement in the affair, see the chapter "An Allegation in Lavender" in Gene Fowler, *The Great Mouthpiece: A Life Story of William J. Fallon* (New York: Blue Ribbon Books, 1931), 99–230.

11. "Warden Osborne," *New York Times*, Dec. 31, 1915.

12. William Randolph Hearst, a former college classmate and a bitter political rival of Osborne, reportedly spread stories of Osborne's arrest in New York political circles. See Chamberlain, *There Is No Truce*, 165.

13. For an account of the conflict between Thomas Mott Osborne and William R. George, see Jack M. Holl, *Juvenile Reform in the Progressive Era: William R. George and the Junior Republic Movement* (Ithaca, NY: Cornell University Press, 1971), 129–72; and Frances M. Keefe, "The Development of William Reuben (Daddy) George's Educational Ideas and Practices from 1886 to 1914," Ph.D. diss., Cornell University, 1966, 286–333.

14. On George's interest in "bad boys," see, for example, chapter entitled "A Republic for Bad Boys," in William R. George and Lyman Beecher Stowe, *Citizens Made and Remade: An Interpretation of the Significance and Influence of George Junior Republics* (Boston: Houghton Mifflin, 1912), 65–90; Holl, *Juvenile Reform in the Progressive Era*, 81–82. George wrote that "badness was interesting to [Osborne] as a phenomenon" and quotes one Junior Republic citizen as remarking, "if a fellow's in jail or is awful tough, he's just Uncle Tom's kind" (*The Junior Republic: Its History and Ideals* [New York: D. Appleton, 1909], 206). On American interest in "bad boy" genre of literature in this period, see Kenneth B. Kidd, *Making American Boys: Boyology and the Feral Tale* (Minneapolis: University of Minnesota Press, 2004).

15. Mary Blanchard, *Oscar Wilde's America: Counterculture in the Gilded Age* (New Haven and London: Yale University Press), 14–20. On Wilde's alleged corrupting influence on youth, see also Ed Cohen, *Talk on the Wilde Side* (New York and London: Routledge, 1992); and Terence S. Kissack, "Anarchism and the Politics of Homosexuality," Ph.D. diss., City University of New York, 2004, 90–94.

16. "Memorandum of Rudolph F. Diedling, Prison Commissioner," in "New York v. Osborne, Grand Jury Indictment," 102; OFC, Box 304.

17. On nineteenth-century ideals of self-made manhood, see, for example, E. Anthony Rotundo, *American Manhood: Transformations in Masculinity from the Revolution to the Modern Era* (New York: Basic Books, 1993), 3–25; Judy Hilkey, *Character Is Capital: Success Manuals and Manhood in Gilded Age America* (Chapel Hill: University of North Carolina Press, 1997); and Thomas Edward Augst, *The Clerk's Tale: Young Men and Moral Life in Nineteenth-Century America* (Chicago: University of Chicago Press, 2003).

18. Robert H. Wiebe, *Self-Rule: A Cultural History of American Democracy* (Chicago: University of Chicago Press, 1995); Susan B. Anthony, "Declaration of Rights for Women, 1876," in *History of Woman Suffrage*, ed. Elizabeth C. Stanton et al., 6 vols. (New York, 1887), 3:31–34; Lincoln Steffens, *The Struggle for Self-Government* (New York: McClure, Phillips, and Co., 1906); Josiah Strong, "The Anglo-Saxon and

the World's Future" (1885), reprinted in *Our Country*, ed. Jurgen Herbst (Cambridge, MA: Belknap Press, 1963), 200–18; Amos Steckel, "The Natural Right of Self-Government," *The Arena* 23, no. 5 (1900): 458–63; and Anon., "Dr. White Fears Cuban Annexation," *Harper's Weekly* (Apr. 20, 1907): 561; Matthew Frye Jacobson, *Special Sorrows: The Diasporic Imagination of Irish, Polish and Jewish Immigrants in the United States* (Cambridge, MA: Harvard University Press, 1995).

19. Peter N. Stearns, *Battleground of Desire: The Struggle for Self-Control in Modern America* (New York: New York University Press, 1999).

20. Adolph Roeder, "Civic Aphorisms," *American Magazine of Civics* 7, no. 4 (1895): 422.

21. Michel Foucault, *The History of Sexuality*, trans. R. Hurley, 3 vols. (New York: Vintage, 1976), 1:147.

22. Barbara A. Cruikshank, *The Will to Empower: Democratic Citizens and Other Subjects* (Ithaca, NY: Cornell University Press, 1999), 23.

23. "Daddy's Boys" in Box 12, "GJR Songs," William R. George and George Junior Republic Collection, Department of Manuscripts and University Archives, Cornell University Libraries (hereafter WRGC).

24. James Wilson, "Citizens in Little: The Junior Republic at Freeville, New York," *Strand Magazine* 14, no. 27 (1893): 209–15; Mary Wager Fisher, "'Daddy's Boys': A Novel Social Experiment; A Factory for Good Citizenship," *Rural New-Yorker*, June 24, 1899, 461–62; Harriet Gillespie, "A Miniature Republic," *The Christian Endeavor World*, Feb. 17, 1898, 4; Delavan L. Pierson, "The Little Republic at Freeville," *The Missionary Review of the World* (Nov. and Dec. 1899); Mary Gay Humphreys, "The Smallest Republic in the World," *McClure's Magazine* (July 1897):735–47. These and many other periodical and newspaper articles on the GJR are collected in scrapbooks, WRGC, Box 102.

25. William R. George, "Junior Republic History and Its Basics," *George Junior Republic Bulletin* VI, 1. WRGC, Box 6. See also George and Stowe, *Citizens Made and Remade*, 65–90.

26. Other examples of this type of reform project involving boys include the YMCA and Boy Scouts. "Boy Scouts of America" was founded in 1910, but locally based efforts, many organized by branches of the YMCA and settlement houses, aimed to "build character" in boys and youths. See, for example, David Macleod, *Building Character in the American Boy: The Boy Scouts, YMCA, and Their Forerunners, 1870-1920* (Madison: University of Wisconsin Press, 1983); and Clifford Putney, *Muscular Christianity: Manhood and Sports in Protestant America, 1880–1920* (Cambridge: Harvard University Press, 2001), 99–126. On the Boy Scouts, see Jay Mechling, *On My Honor: Boy Scouts and the Making of American Youth* (Chicago: University of Chicago Press, 2001).

27. Male settlement reformers' interest in "boy work" is addressed in chapter 4. For a fascinating examination of YMCA reformers' interest in urban male youth, see John Donald Gustav-Wrathall, *Take the Young Stranger by the Hand: Same-Sex Relations and the YMCA* (Chicago: University of Chicago Press, 1998). It should be noted that

George struck up a close friendship with YMCA leader Robert McBurney, whom he praised for his "radiant comradeship," while in New York City. Keefe, "The Development of William Reuben (Daddy) George's Educational Ideas," 53. Kenneth B. Kidd offers a useful analysis of the attraction of the subjective attachment to reforming "savage" boys for middle-class and elite reformers and writers in *Making American Boys.*

28. Keefe, "The Development of William Reuben (Daddy) George's Educational Ideas," 40.

29. Michael Moon, "'The Gentle Boy from the Dangerous Classes': Pederasty, Domesticity, and Capitalism in Horatio Alger," *Representations* 19 (Summer 1987): 87–110.

30. George wrote, "the book that made the most deepseated impression upon my mind was *Robinson Crusoe.* In fact I know of no one book, excepting of course, the Bible, that is such a common sense authority on applied sociology. Its simple teachings have played an important part in my life." William R. George, Letter to his daughters, 2, GJRP. Quoted in Keefe, "The Development of William Reuben (Daddy) George's Educational Ideas," 43.

31. Jeffrey Richards, "Introduction," *Imperialism and Juvenile Literature* (Manchester, UK: Manchester University Press, 1989). Studies of the political meanings of *Robinson Crusoe* include Martin Green, *The Robinson Crusoe Story* (University Park: Pennsylvania State University Press, 1990); Manuel Schonhorn, *Defoe's Politics: Parliament, Power, Kingship, and Robinson Crusoe* (Cambridge: Cambridge University Press, 1991); Richard Phillips, *Mapping Men and Empire: A Geography of Adventure* (London and New York: Routledge, 1997), 22–44; Ian Watt, *Myths of Modern Individualism: Faust, Don Quixote, Don Juan, Robinson Crusoe* (Cambridge: Cambridge University Press, 1996); Frank H. Ellis, ed., *Twentieth-Century Interpretations of* Robinson Crusoe*: A Collection of Critical Essays* (Englewood Cliffs, NJ: Prentice-Hall, 1969). For an excellent account of *Robinson Crusoe*'s influence on the making of middle-class masculinity in the mid-nineteenth-century United States, see Shawn Thomson, "Fortress of American Solitude: The Crusoe Topos in Nineteenth-Century America, 1846–1885," Ph.D. diss., University of Kansas, 2006.

32. Floyd Dell, *Intellectual Vagabondage* (New York: George H. Doran, 1926), 27. Quoted in Green, *The Robinson Crusoe*, 24.

33. Keefe, "The Development of William Reuben (Daddy) George's Educational Ideas," 43.

34. Green, *The Robinson Crusoe Story*, 6. Henry E. Jackson, *Robinson Crusoe, Social Engineer: How the Discovery of Robinson Crusoe Solves the Labor Problem and Opens the Path to Industrial Peace* (New York: E. P. Dutton, 1922). It should be noted that this vision of Crusoe as an exemplar of the virtues of self-sufficiency and mastery also appealed to late nineteenth- and early twentieth-century economists, several of whom portrayed him as the archetype of *Homo economicus.* See chapter 7, "Crusoe, Ideology, and Theory," in Watt, *Myths of Modern Individualism*, 172–92.

35. Other narratives of encounters between "civilized" white men and "primitive" or "savage" youths and boys were influential during this period, as documented by Kidd in *Making American Boys.*

36. Watt, *Myths of Modern Individualism*, 169.

37. Green, *The Robinson Crusoe Story*, 23.

38. George, *The Junior Republic*, 3.

39. For example, George maintained that youths who were resident in the republic became "independent in politics." George and Stowe, *Citizens Made and Remade*, 113. One of the Junior Republic's "yells" begins as follows: "Hear ye this! Down with the boss; down with the tram," quoted in William I. Hull, "The George Jr. Republic," *Annals of the American Academy of Political and Social Science* 10 (July 1897): 85.

40. George, *The Junior Republic*, 3. George's diaries and other writings documenting his early life are quoted in Keefe, "The Development of William Reuben (Daddy) George's Educational Ideas," 26–112. George offers a short account of his early life in *The Junior Republic*, 1–18. See also Holl, *Juvenile Reform in the Progressive Era*, 35–86.

41. George and Stowe, *Citizens Made and Remade*, 26. Jacob A. Riis, *The Battle with the Slum* (New York: Macmillan, 1902), 246–55.

42. See, for example, George and Stowe, *Citizens Made and Remade*, 1–20; George, "Notes," quoted in Keefe, "The Development of William Reuben (Daddy) George's Educational Ideas," 65–75.

43. George, *The Junior Republic*, 2–3.

44. "Boys' Camp Broken; The George Industrial Brigade Returns from the Freeville Camp; Parading Up Broadway; Slum Boys from the City Trained as Soldiers," *New York Evening Sun* (Sept. 1896). Undated clipping in scrapbook, WRGC, Box 74.

Clifford Putney shows that the "Boys' Brigade," which originated in Britain and came to the United States in 1890, became replaced by other groups, including the Boy Scouts, which it influenced (*Muscular Christianity* 112). I have uncovered no evidence of any other "boy brigade" being put to direct political purposes.

45. George proposed the Junior Vigilance League in New York City newspapers in January 1895; see clipping, "Junior Vigilance League," in scrapbook, WRGC, Box 74. See also Holl, *Juvenile Reform in the Progressive Era*, 69–75.

46 "Junior Vigilance League"; Holl, *Juvenile Reform in the Progressive Era*, 72–73, 82–83.

47. George, *The Junior Republic*, 1–18; George and Stowe, *Citizens Made and Remade*, 30–32; Holl, *Juvenile Reform in the Progressive Era*, 79–85, 94–101.

48. George, *The Junior Republic*, 37–54.

49. Foucault writes that, in Western Europe and the United States, "by the end of the eighteenth and the beginning of the nineteenth century, the gloomy festival of punishment was dying out," Michel Foucault, *Discipline and Punish: The Birth of the Prison*, trans. Alan Sheridan (1975; reprint, New York: Pantheon, 1978), 8. For a useful explication of a genealogy of the "governmentalization of the state" in the work of Foucault and other scholars of governmentality, see Mitchell Dean, *Governmentality: Power and Rule in Modern Society* (London: Sage Publications, 1999), 102–12. Thomas Mott Osborne viewed the transformation of the republic in similar, if less critical terms, asserting that "the Junior Republic was in its essential features a perfectly natural evolution from a benevolent tyranny, which,

seeking to do its highest duty to the human beings under its charge, had unexpectedly blossomed into a self-governing community." "Introduction," George, *The Junior Republic*, ix.

50. The George Junior Republic Constitution, adopted on March 5, 1898, is published in the first issue of *The Junior Republic Citizen* 1, no. 1 (1898): 9–12, WRGC, Box 17. For George's own account of this transformation, see George, *The Junior Republic*, 19–36. See also Holl, *Juvenile Reform in the Progressive Era*, 96–103 and 176–77.

51. Working with all available records, Catherine Claxton Dong estimates that 83.3 percent of the first 500 residents came from urban areas (through 1906). In 1909, 33.1 percent of the population arrived at the Junior Republic via judicial commitment: 14.3 percent for destitution; 12.8 percent for delinquency; and 6 percent for improper guardianship. Another 7.5 percent arrived via commitment by a poor law officer. Many of those committed by their parents or through other means had previously been arrested and/or institutionalized. Dong, "The Struggle to Define Childhood: Resistance to the Private Sphere from the Junior Republic Movement, 1894–1936," Ph.D. diss., Cornell University, 1995, 23–52.

52. On "runaway" policy, see "Police Log," WRGC, Box 83.

53. Guardianship was granted to Junior Republic Board of Trustees. Dong, "The Struggle to Define Childhood," 31.

54. Press accounts include: Washington Gladden, "The Junior Republic at Freeville," *The Outlook* 54, no. 18 (1896): 778–82; Delavan L. Pierson, "The Little Republic at Freeville, N.Y.," *The Missionary Review of the World* 12, no. 11 (1898): 799–809; Anon., "The George Junior Republic," *The Argosy* 21, no. 4 (1898): 301–305. See also Hull, "The George Junior Republic," 73–86. Firsthand accounts and reprinted police blotters can be found in the first five volumes of the *Junior Republic Citizen* (1898–1902), WRGC, Box 17. Dong reports that arrests averaged "about 5 or 6 per person" per year ("The Struggle to Define Childhood" 237–38).

55. John R. Commons, "The Junior Republic," *The American Journal of Sociology* 3, no. 3 (1898): 437. See also Wilbur H. Crafts, Ph.D., "A Day at the Boys' Republic," *The Christian Endeavor World*, Feb. 17, 1898, 415.

56. "Daddy's Prophecy: Made New Years 1899," WRGC, Box 3.

57. On the national Junior Republic Movement, see Holl, *Juvenile Reform in the Progressive Era*, 173–222; and Keefe, "The Development of William Reuben (Daddy) George's Educational Ideas," 224–58. On Forbes's attempt to institute the GJR system at the Ilwahig Penal Colony in the Philippines, see J. Cameron Forbes, *The Philippine Islands* (New York, 1928); Lyman Beecher Stowe, "A Prison That Makes Men Free," *World's Work* 27 (Apr. 1914): 626–28; and Holl, *Juvenile Reform in the Progressive Era*, 267–72. On Forbes's career, see Peter W. Stanley, "William Cameron Forbes: Proconsul in the Philippines," *The Pacific Historical Review* 35, no. 3 (Aug. 1966): 285–301.

58. George, "Junior Republic History and Its Basics,"3.

59. "Report of the Committee on Placing Out Dependent Children," WRGC, Box 74. See also series of critical assessments of the Junior Republic in the *Rochester Herald*, August 11–14, 1897, clippings in WRGC, Box 74. Dong suggests that the "over-

whelming majority" of citizens from 1897 to 1913 came from the lowest classes. Dong, "The Struggle to Define Childhood," 56.

60. Richard W.G. Welling formed the National Self-Government Committee, which fostered the U.S. student government movement and began the educational program that later became the American Legion's "Boys' State." On the influence of the George Junior Republic on American education, see Holl, *Juvenile Reform in the Progressive Era*, 173–222; and Dong, "The Struggle to Define Childhood," 220–65. On Welling and the National Self-Government Committee, see Richard W.G. Welling, *As the Twig Is Bent* (New York: G. P. Putnam's Sons, 1942); and Robert Muccigrosso, "Richard W.G. Welling: A Reformer's Life," Ph.D. diss., Columbia University, 1966, 95–130.

61. Female citizens were not admitted to the Junior Republic until 1896. Girls' representation ranged from less than 20 percent to 33 percent of the population over time. Dong, "The Struggle to Define Childhood," 19.

62. For example: "Boy Republic," *New York Morning Journal*, July 9, 1895; "Daddy's Boys: A Novel Social Experiment," *Rural New Yorker*, June 24, 1899. On the history of girls' participation in the George Junior Republic, including board member positions, see Keefe, "The Development of William Reuben (Daddy) George's Educational Ideas," 113–86. One critical report on relations between girls and boys was issued by the State Board of Charities of New York on October 15, 1897 and reported in the *New York Sun* on the same date; quoted in Keefe, "The Development of William Reuben (Daddy) George's Educational Ideas," 133–35. Two Belgian criminologists who visited the republic criticized the lack of supervision of interactions between boys and girls. Ugo Conti and Adolphe Prins, "Some European Comments on the American Prison System," *Journal of the American Institute of Criminal Law and Criminology* 2, no. 2 (July 1911): 211–12.

63. On girls' roles in the republic, see George, *The Junior Republic*, 138–54; George and Stowe, *Citizens Made and Remade*, 118–38. Dong reports that few girls received any industrial or clerical training and that even sewing was not treated as an industrial occupation. Dong, "The Struggle to Define Childhood," 173–75. Some girls were elected to the vice president position, which required a great deal of logistical work and lacked the status of the presidency. Judicial and penal institutions were largely segregated and conditions in the girls' jail were less harsh than in the boys'. Dong, "The Struggle to Define Childhood," 224–40.

64. This account comes from George's cousin, Jacob Smith, who visited him in New York City. Jacob Smith, "Memorial Address; William R. George," GJRP. Quoted in Keefe, "The Development of William Reuben (Daddy) George's Educational Ideas," 69. This "functional" treatment of women resembles the "triangulation" of power "between men" in English fiction, as argued by Eve Kosofsky Sedgwick, *Between Men: English Literature and Male Homosocial Desire* (New York: Columbia University Press, 1985).

65. William R. George, "Girls," *Bulletin* XVII, 80, WRGC, Box 6.

66. Ibid., 79. Various drafts of this document with slight variations in wording can be found in WRGC, Box 6. The references to sexuality are more muted in the rendition published as the chapter "Girl Citizens" in *Citizens Made and Remade*, 118–38.

67. George ordered that any new Junior Republic "must exclude all mentally and physically deficient: this includes moral perverts of either sex." George, "Junior Republic History." On the undesirability of girls "with a tendency to moral perversion," see George and Stowe, *Citizens Made and Remade*, 135–38.

68. The findings of the investigatory committee of the State Board of Charities were reported in New York newspapers. See, for example, "Drives George Out of Junior Republic," *New York Times*, Dec. 18, 1913; and "George Must Go, Inquiry Verdict," *New York Times*, Dec. 19, 1913. See also Keefe, "The Development of William Reuben (Daddy) George's Educational Ideas," 286–333.

69. Everett P. Wheeler, "Man-Suffrage Association Opposed to the Political Suffrage for Women." In addition to Wheeler, the Executive Committee included such prominent figures as John Dos Passos, George W. Seligman, and Talcott Williams. Everett P. Wheeler Papers, New York Public Librarym Rare Books and Manuscripts Archives, Box 8; Folder: "Woman Suffrage, 1914–17." See also Susan E. Marshall, *Splintered Sisterhood: Gender and Class in the Campaign Against Woman Suffrage* (Madison: University of Wisconsin Press, 1997), 58–92.

70. Anna Howard Shaw reported that "the best talk I have heard anywhere was that to which I used to listen in the home of Mrs. Eliza Wright Osborne . . . when Mrs. Stanton, Susan B. Anthony, Emily Howland, Elizabeth Smith Miller, Ida Husted Harper, Miss Mills, and I were gathered there for our occasional weekend visits." Anna Howard Shaw, *The Story of a Pioneer* (New York: Harper & Brothers Publishers, 1915), 240–41. See also Chamberlain, *There Is No Truce*, 31–33. On Lucretia Mott, Eliza Coffin Wright, and the nineteenth-century women's movement, see Judith Wellman, *The Road to Seneca Falls: Elizabeth Cady Stanton and the First Woman Rights Convention* (Urbana: University of Illinois Press, 2004); Margaret H. McFadden, *Golden Cables of Sympathy: The Transatlantic Source of Nineteenth-Century Feminism* (Lexington: University Press of Kentucky, 1999); and Sherry H. Penney and James D. Livingston, *A Very Dangerous Woman: Martha Wright and Women's Rights* (Amherst: University of Massachusetts Press, 2004).

71. Historians have argued that the 1930s marked a period of backlash against homosexuals, marked by increased stigmatization and more aggressive policing. See, for example, Jennifer Terry, *An American Obsession: Science, Medicine, and Homosexuality in Modern Society* (Chicago: University of Chicago Press, 1999), 268–96; and George Chauncey, *Gay New York: Gender, Urban Culture, and the Making of the Gay Male World 1890–1940* (New York: Basic Books, 1994), 301–54.

72. Chamberlain, *There Is No Truce*, 41.

73. Chamberlain, *There Is No Truce*, 40.

74. Scholar Kim Townsend notes that Harvard and students embraced a more virile and physical form of manhood in response to economic changes attendant on industrialization and related upper-class insecurities. At the time that Osborne entered Harvard, the university dedicated itself more earnestly to athletics, opening a gym and hiring an athletic director recommended by Theodore Roosevelt. Kim Townsend, *Manhood at Harvard: William James and Others* (New York: Norton, 1996), esp. 97–

120. Scholar Douglass Shand-Tucci identifies the "Whitmanic archetype of the warrior as a gay polarity" and the athlete as "the warrior's derivative" (*The Crimson Letter: Harvard, Homosexuality, and the Shaping of American Culture* [New York: St. Martins Press, 2003], 52–53).

75. Chamberlain, *There Is No Truce*, 72–78.

76. Chamberlain, *There Is No Truce*, 105.

77. Chamberlain, *There Is No Truce*, 42–43. Historian Lisa Duggan asserts that, in the nineteenth century, "the theater created a space for diverging or dissenting performances of class, gender, and sexual relations, for complexly ambiguous interpretations of actors' speech and acts, and for forms of shared living and economic support outside the white home." Lisa Duggan, *Sapphic Slashers: Sex, Violence, and American Modernity* (Durham and London: Duke University Press, 2000), 148.

78. Chamberlain, *There Is No Truce*, 154–61.

79. Chamberlain, *There Is No Truce*, 138, 159.

80. On Osborne's political career, see Charles F. Rattigan, ed., "Hon Thomas M. Osborne: Cayuga County's Candidate for Governor: A Brief Biographical Sketch and History of his Public Service" (New York: Democratic General Committee of Cayuga County, 1910).

81. Chamberlain, *There Is No Truce*, 154–55. Historian Tobias Higbie has identified a group of individuals, some who traveled in disguise like Osborne, to whom he refers as "tramp ethnographers." According to Higbie, they established authority through the deployment of ethnographic methodologies that demonstrated "knowledge of the living and working conditions of their subjects." He argues that these investigators only reinforced class difference and ultimately "mapped out a working-class world that appeared to be a grotesque inversion of middle-class America" (561). Frank Tobias Higbie, "Crossing Class Boundaries: Tramp Ethnographers and Narratives of Class in Progressive Era America," *Social Science History* 21, no. 4 (Winter 1997): 559–92.

82. Josiah Flynt, who also romanticized tramp culture and spent a great deal of time riding the rails, established a successful career as a chronicler of tramp life. See his *Tramping with Tramps* (New York, 1900); *The World of Graft* (New York, 1901); and *The Little Brother: A Story of Tramp Life* (New York, 1902). See also William R. Hunt, "'Which Way 'Bo?': Literary Impressions of the Hobos' Golden Age, 1880–1930," *Journal of Popular Culture* 4, no. 1 (1970): 22–38.

83. For analyses of race, sexuality, and "slumming" during this period in the United States, see Chad Cottrell Heap, "'Slumming': Sexuality, Race, and Urban Commercial Leisure, 1900–1940," Ph.D. diss., University of Chicago, 2001; and Robert Morris Dowling, "Slumming: Morality and Space in New York City from 'City Mysteries' to the Harlem Renaissance," Ph.D. diss., Columbia University, 2001. On the class dynamics of slumming in Great Britain, see Seth Koven's fascinating study, *Slumming: Sexual and Social Politics in Victorian London* (Princeton: Princeton University Press, 2004).

84. Chamberlain, *There Is No Truce*, 70.

85. Chamberlain, *There Is No Truce*, 71.

86. Chamberlain, *There Is No Truce*, 71.

87. Chauncey, *Gay New York*, 79.

88. Josiah Flynt, "Homosexuality Among Tramps," Appendix A in Havelock Ellis, *Sexual Inversion*, by Havelock Ellis, Vol. 4 of *Studies in the Psychology of Sex*, 2nd ed. (Philadelphia: F. A. Davis, 1904), 219–24. On male same-sex relations among "tramping" men in this period, see Peter Boag, *Same-Sex Affairs: Constructions and Controlling Homosexuality in the Pacific Northwest* (Berkeley: University of California Press, 2003), 15–44. Historian Tobias Higbie asserts that relationships organized along "wolf-punk" lines were "pervasive" within hobo communities. Frank Tobias Higbie, *Indispensable Outcasts: Hobo Workers and Community in the American Midwest, 1880–1930* (Urbana: University of Illinois Press, 2003), 124. See also Todd DePastino, *Citizen Hobo: How a Century of Homelessness Shaped America* (Chicago: University of Chicago Press, 2003), 85–91.

89. Regina Kunzel, *Criminal Intimacy: Sex in Prison and the Uneven History of Modern American Sexuality* (Chicago: University of Chicago Press, 2008), chapters 1 and 2.

90. Chauncey, *Gay New York*, 88–96.

91. According to Chamberlain, his physical beauty was such that Osborne used him as a model for the figures of American Indians on murals at a hotel Osborne owned in Auburn (*There Is No Truce* 154–55).

92. The spelling "Chatelaine" appears in Osborne's "Memorandum in Support to Quash and Dismiss the Two Indictments against the Defendant," People of State of New York v. Thomas Mott Osborne, 96;, OFC, file: "Osborne, Legal, Suits, New York v. Osborne Trial (i), 1916." This alias may also represent a play on the use of "husband" and "wife" to refer to tramping men who developed relationships. See Higbie, *Indispensable Outcasts*, 124. On the use of these terms in gay urban contexts, see Chauncey, *Gay New York*, 86–96.

93. Chamberlain, *There Is No Truce*, 212–21.

94. Chamberlain, *There Is No Truce*, 222.

95. Osborne, "Introduction," in George, *The Junior Republic*, ix–x.

96. Osborne to Spencer Trask, May 29, 1905, OFC. Quoted in Holl, *Juvenile Reform in the Progressive Era*, 29. On Osborne's enthusiasm for the GJR, see also Chamberlain, *There Is No Truce*, 222–34.

97. Quoted in Chamberlain, *There Is No Truce*, 222.

98. Quoted in Chamberlain, *There Is No Truce*, 226.

99. George to Osborne, December 1898, Box 3, Folder 6, WRGC. This young man ultimately took "Osborne" as his middle name, indicating that Osborne may have adopted him formally or informally.

100. Osborne, *Within Prison Walls*.

101. Andrew Sanders, "Introduction," in Thomas Hughes, *Tom Brown's Schooldays* (Oxford: Oxford University Press, 1989), xix. The novel resonated with Osborne's own school days. It focuses on a mentoring relationship between two roommates and treats the rugby field as an arena for male interaction and education. At Adams Acad-

emy, Osborne was tutored in football by his roommate, Harry R. "Fuddy" Woodward. Osborne and Woodward formed a close relationship that extended through their years together at Harvard. Chamberlain, *There Is No Truce*, 49–57. On the influence of Hughes and the ethos of "muscular Christianity" in the United States, see Putney, *Muscular Christianity*, 11–45.

102. See, for example, George J. Worth, "Of Muscles and Manliness: Some Reflections on Thomas Hughes," in *Victorian Literature and Society*, ed. James R. Kincaid and Albert J. Kuhn (Athens: Ohio University Press, 1989); and Paul M. Puccio, "At the Heart of *Tom Brown's Schooldays*: Thomas Arnold and Christian Friendship," *Modern Language Studies* 25, no. 4 (1995): 57–74.

103. Osborne, *Society and Prisons*, 40.

104. Osborne repeated the contention that friends did not recognize him as Tom Brown on several occasions. In his journal, he wrote: "I must have the marks of 'the Criminal' unusually developed, or else criminals must look a good deal like other folks—barring the uniform. If I had the ordinary theories about prisons and prisoners it might seem rather mortifying that, in spite of every effort, not one of these intimate friends can spot me among the toughest bunch of fellows in the prison." See Tannenbaum, *Osborne of Sing Sing*, 247; and Osborne, *Society and Prisons*, 122.

105. Osborne, *Society and Prisons*, 27. Osborne published a detailed narrative of his experiences as Tom Brown in the State Prison at Auburn: *Within Prison Walls*.

106. Osborne, *Society and Prisons*, 29.

107. On major currents in Progressive Era penology, see David J. Rothman, *Conscience and Convenience: The Asylum and Its Alternatives in Progressive America* (Boston: Little, Brown, 1980); Alexander W. Pisciotta, *Benevolent Repression: Social Control and the American Reformatory-Prison Movement* (New York: New York University Press, 1994); and Blake McKelvey, *American Prisons: A History of Good Intentions* (Montclair, NJ: Patterson Smith, 1977), 234–66. Osborne's experiences were also widely reported in newspapers throughout the country. See, for example, *New York Tribune*, *New York Times*, *New York Evening Post*, *New York Sun*, *Boston Transcript*, *Christian Science Monitor*, *Bridgeport Standard*, Sept. 29–Oct. 6, 1913.

108. In a 1904 address to the National Prison Association, Osborne railed against what he saw as the absurdity of confining prisoners to an institution that bore no resemblance to democratic society: "The prison system endeavors to make men industrious by driving them to work; to make them virtuous by removing temptation; to make them respect the law by forcing them to obey the edicts of an autocrat; to make them farsighted by allowing them no chance to exercise foresight; to give them individual initiative by treating them in large groups; in short, to prepare them again for society by placing them in conditions as unlike real society as they could well be made." Quoted in Osborne, *Society and Prisons*, 1953.

109. Osborne, *Within Prison Walls*, 148.

110. Tannenbaum, *Osborne of Sing Sing*, 71–100.

111. Rothman, *Conscience and Convenience*, 118–19.

112. Osborne argued that other prison reformers inverted the correct order of

classification by privileging short timers: "In other words, the classification of prisoners, as a matter of logic, was perfect; the only trouble being that conclusions were drawn from premises which happened to be exactly contrary to facts. It is not true that men are worse according to terms" (*Society and Prisons*, 7).

113. Osborne, *Society and Prisons*, 230.

114. Osborne asserted that the manipulation of "snitches" contributed to corruption: "The system of 'stool-pigeons,' which the dangerous condition of constant nervous unrest brings about. The authorities feel it necessary to know what is going on among their charges; and rightly so. The only way to do this is to employ spies and informers; so the prison community is honey-combed with suspicion . . . the officer's errandboy, boot-black, valet and general factotum. He has access at all times to his master and can whisper in his ear any accusations he pleases against any inmate for whom he gets a dislike. This convict favorite often becomes a peculiarly obnoxious species of tyrant." Osborne, *Society and Prisons*, 149.

115. Osborne, *Society and Prisons*, 230.

116. Tannenbaum, *Osborne of Sing Sing*, 150–56. Tannenbaum (1893–1969), who also went undercover to expose prison corruption at Sing Sing, wrote several influential books on crime and penology, including *Wall Shadows: A Study in American Prisons* (1922) and *Crime and Community* (1938). Beginning in 1935, Tannenbaum served as professor of Latin American history and Director of University Seminars at Columbia University. See Joseph Maier and Richard W. Weatherhead, *Frank Tannenbaum: A Biographical Essay* (New York: Columbia University, 1974).

117. Regina Kunzel, "Situating Sex: Prison Sexual Culture in the Mid-Twentieth-Century United States," *GLQ: A Journal of Lesbian and Gay Studies* 8, no. 13 (2002): 253–70.

118. Osborne, *Society and Prisons*, 140–41.

119. Kunzel, *Criminal Intimacy*, chapter 2.

120. The original indictment and all supporting legal documents for the case "New York v. Osborne, 1916" can be found in OFC, Boxes 304–311: "Legal, Suits, New York v. Osborne."

121. After his stint at Auburn as Tom Brown, Osborne received a note he believed to have been authored by New York City Tammany boss Charles Murphy reading, "Damn Fool! Pity you are not in for twenty years." Chamberlain, *There Is No Truce*, 261. On the importance of prisons to political patronage in the United States, particularly at the state level, see Howard Stephen Davidson, "Moral Education and Social Relations: The Case of Prisoner Self-Government Reform in New York State, 1895–1923," Ph.D. diss., University of Toronto, 1991, 195–232.

122. Riley testified that he had disapproved of Osborne's methods and of the Mutual Welfare League from the start: "I don't think you can turn fifteen hundred men loose and let them manage their own affairs because the worst elements in the prison, as long as the Warden holds out on that line, will come to the front." He also asserted that Osborne had misrepresented himself and his policies to "a large number of very wealthy people whose intentions are good" and claimed that he had recommended to

Governor Whitman that Osborne be dismissed, but Whitman had decided against it because such a move would "make a martyr" of Osborne. Testimony of John B. Riley, November 24, 1915; reprinted in "New York v. Osborne," "Memorandum in Support of Motion to Quash," 55–67, OFC. Osborne was also referred to as a "coddler" by unsympathetic journalists. One wrote: "Coddled by Thomas Mott Osborne, who until he was made warden of Sing Sing, unofficially ran the institution here . . . a majority of the 1,300 male convicts are permitted more liberties than in a boarding-school." Quoted in Chamberlain, *There Is No Truce*, 287.

123. Willett and Cummins cooperated in the prosecution of Osborne. See "Testimony of William Willett and William J. Cummins," "New York v. Osborne," OFC, legal files. Chamberlain asserts that Cummins, especially, enjoyed special privileges under the previous administration, including the liberty to pursue business matters unimpeded. See Chamberlain, *There Is No Truce*, 311–13. On Willett, see also Fowler, *The Great Mouthpiece*, 114–15.

124. Tannenbaum, *Osborne of Sing Sing*, 76.

125. See testimony of Willett and Cummins, "New York v. Osborne," OFC, legal files.

126. Tannenbaum, *Osborne of Sing Sing*, 184.

127. See Tannenbaum, *Osborne of Sing Sing*, 179–218; Fowler, *The Great Mouthpiece*, 109–30; Chamberlain, *There Is No Truce*, 304–42.

128. Contemporaneous sexual scandals also encompassed classed political and social struggles in other parts of the United States. See, for example, Peter Boag's account of a 1912 YMCA same-sex scandal in Portland, Oregon: "Sex and Politics in Progressive Era Portland and Eugene: The 1912 Same-Sex Vice Scandal," *Oregon Historical Quarterly* 100, no. 2 (Summer 1999): 158–81. See also George Chauncey's analysis of the scandal involving the Newport, Rhode Island Naval Training Station and Newport Branch of the YMCA in 1919: "Christian Brotherhood or Sexual Perversion?: Homosexual Identities and the Construction of Sexual Boundaries in the World War I Era," in *Hidden from History: Reclaiming the Gay and Lesbian Past*, ed. Martin Duberman, Martha Vicinus, and George Chauncey Jr. (New York: Penguin, 1989), 294–317.

129. "New York v. Thomas Mott Osborne"; "Indictment for Neglect of Duty, filed December 28, 1915"; OFC, Box 304—"Legal, Suits." The indictment was widely reported in New York newspapers. See, for example, *New York Times* (Dec. 29, 1915); *New York Sun* (Dec. 29, 1915); *New York Daily Tribune* (Dec. 29, 1915). It is interesting that the only paper not to report the immorality charges leveled against Osborne was the *New York Times*.

130. Anon., "Mr. Osborne's Friends and Enemies," *New York Times* (Aug. 10, 1915).

131. William J. Fallon's biographer emphasizes the political motivations for prosecuting the case against Osborne, but argues that Fallon believed Osborne to be guilty of the "allegation in lavender." Fowler quotes Fallon as later remarking about the case: "The mistake I made was being too aggressive at the wrong time. I turned a prosecution into a persecution. And that is always bad." Fowler, *The Great Mouthpiece*, 111–26.

132. The officer questioned was Michael W. Kelly, who arrested Osborne and Chatelaine in Auburn and gave "hearsay" evidence of a similar arrest in Syracuse ("the

Syracuse incident"). Kelly testified that he found Osborne and Chatelaine sleeping together in a boxcar. Testimony excerpted in "New York v. Osborne," "Memorandum in Support of Motion to Quash," 95–97, OFC, Box 311.

133. Testimony of William Trefry, excerpted in "New York v. Osborne," "Memorandum in Support of Motion to Quash," 78–81; OFC, Box 311.

134. See testimony of Thomas J. Alger, William Trefry, William Willett, Samuel Stroock, Henry DeLara, Whitmel H. Smith, and John A. Qualey, inter alia. "New York v. Osborne," "Witness Interviews," OFC, Boxes 307–10.

135. Testimony of William J. Willett (Oct. 19, 1915), 58–59; "New York v. Osborne," OFC, Box 310.

136. Testimony of John A. Qualey (Oct. 19, 1915), 50; "New York v. Osborne," OFC, Box 310.

137. Ibid. See also testimony of Willett, Smith, and Alger; OFC, Boxes 310–311.

138. See testimony of Whitmel Smith (Nov. 18, 1915) on Osborne's valet, Alexander Monet; Thomas J. Alger on "O.K. Bill"; Connolly on "O.K. Bill" and "Jack the Dropper" or "Kid Dropper," 571–73; "New York v. Osborne," OFC, Box 310.

139. See testimony of Paul Vogel, Max Kleinberg, Sidney Welsh, James Connolly, Miller (no first name), Andrew Daly, Henry DeLara, Samuel Stroock, inter alia. "New York v. Osborne," OFC, Boxes 310–311.

140. Quoted in Chamberlain, *There Is No Truce*, 287.

141. Donald Lowrie, "The Tom Brown Knitting Class," MSS copy, OFC, Box 234.

142. Testimony of Whitmel Smith (Nov. 18, 1915), 418. "New York v. Osborne," OFC, Box 310.

143. On the doll, see testimony of Osborne, 1307–10; see also testimony of Sidney Welsh, Paul Vogel, James Connolly, Max Kleinberg, "New York v. Osborne," OFC, Boxes 310–311. Several of the prisoners (Welsh, Connolly, and Kleinberg) reported that they felt coerced by Osborne but also reported receiving sexual pleasure (and achieving orgasm) during sexual engagement with him.

144. See, for example, testimony of Thomas J. Alger, excerpted in "New York v. Osborne," "Memorandum in Support of Motion to Quash," 82–84, OFC, Box 311.

145. Interview of Charles W. Farr, prison physician, excerpted in "Memorandum in Support of Motion to Quash," 44–45.

146. Boag shows that the Oscar Wilde trial was also interpreted through degeneration theory in the Pacific Northwest (*Same-Sex Affairs* 127–47). On degeneration theory and sexology in the United States, see Terry, *An American Obsession*, 45–50; and Hatheway, *The Gilded Age Construction*, especially 122–29.

147. According to Chamberlain, "slanders on his personal character were carried to such a degree of vileness that Osborne threatened the *Army and Navy Register* with a libel suit" (*There Is No Truce* 379). On Osborne at Portsmouth, see also Tannenbaum, *Osborne of Sing Sing*, 278–90.

148. When the reformist spirit reemerged in the 1930s, the late Osborne enjoyed a reputation as a pioneer in prison reform; President Roosevelt wrote the introduction to one of the two favorable biographies published during this period, and Ben Shahn

designed a publicly funded mural for Riker's Island depicting Osborne as a liberator of downtrodden convicts. Franklin D. Roosevelt, "Introduction," in Tannenbaum, *Osborne of Sing Sing*, ix–x. A study for Shahn's mural is reprinted in Deborah Martin Kao, Laura Katzman, and Jenna Webster, eds., *Ben Shahn's New York: The Photography of Modern Times* (New Haven: Yale University Press, 2000).

149. McKelvey, *American Prisons*, 342; Rothman, *Conscience and Convenience*, 145; Davidson, "Moral Education and Social Relations," 312–49.

150. Both Osborne and George were criticized for exceeding the parameters of the central ideologies of penal and juvenile reform. On Osborne, see Norval Morris and David J. Rothman, eds., *Oxford History of the Prison: The Practice of Punishment in Western Society* (Oxford: Oxford University Press, 1997), 176–86. On George, see Holl, *Juvenile Reform in the Progressive Era*, 32–34.

151. New York State Board of Charities, "Report of the Special Committee on the George Junior Republic," in *Annual Report of the State Board of Charities* (1913), 407–510.

152. In his 1978 lecture on governmentality, Foucault argues that the family shifted from the model of governmentality to the instrument of government under liberal regimes. Burchell et al., eds., *The Foucault Effect: Studies in Governmentality* (Chicago: University of Chicago Press, 1991), 100. See also Foucault, *The History of Sexuality*, 1:106.

153. Testimony of Whitmel Smith, excerpted in "Memorandum in Support of Motion to Quash," 50–52. Smith also characterized the knitting class as evidence of degenerated government.

6. THE PROBLEM OF THE IMPRACTICABLES: SENTIMENTALITY, IDEALISM, AND HOMOSEXUALITY

1. Thomas Mott Osborne, *The Dawn: A Criminal Morality*, unpublished manuscript, The Osborne Family Collection, The George Arents Research Library, Syracuse University, Box 251. An earlier draft of the play entitled "Which? A Criminal Morality" is also included in Osborne's papers.

2. By the 1920s, the pansy was commonplace slang for homosexual men in the United States. See, for example, Fred R. Shapiro, "Earlier Citations for Terms Characterizing Homosexuals," *American Speech* 63, no.3 (Autumn 1988): 283–85. Pansy tattoos signified homosexuality in European prisons in the late nineteenth century. See Nicholas Dobelbower, "*Les Chevaliers de la guirlande*: Cellmates in Restoration France, "in Jeffrey Merrick and Michael Sibalis, eds., *Homosexuality in French History and Culture* (New York: Haworth Press, 2001), 145.

3. Osborne, *The Dawn*, unnumbered ms. pages.

4. Leland Krauth, *Proper Mark Twain* (Athens and London: University of Georgia Press, 1999), 137. On sentimentalism and gender in American literature, see also Ann Douglas, *The Feminization of American Culture* (New York: Doubleday, 1977); Shirley Samuels, ed., *The Culture of Sentiment: Race, Gender, and Sentimentality in Nineteenth-Century America* (New York.: Oxford University Press, 1992); Daniel

Wickberg, "What is this History of Sensibilities?: On Cultural History, Old and New," *American Historical Review* 112, no. 2 (June 2007); and Christophe Den Tandt, "Amazons and Androgyne: Overcivilization and the Redefinition of Gender Roles at the Turn of the Century," *American Literary History* 8, no. 4 (Winter 1996):639–64.

5. Krauth, *Proper Mark Twain*, 139.

6. On realism, sentimentalism, and masculinity, see Michael Anton Budd, *The Sculpture Machine: Physical Culture and Body Politics in the Age of Empire* (New York: New York University Press, 1997); Stanley Coben, "The Assault on Victorianism in the Twentieth Century," in Daniel Walker Howe, ed., *Victorian America* (Philadelphia: University of Pennsylvania Press, 1976), 160–81; Richard Dellamora, *Masculine Desire: The Sexual Politics of Victorian Aestheticism* (Chapel Hill: University of North Carolina Press, 1990).

7. William Graham Sumner, "The Absurd Effort to Make the World Over," *Forum* 17 (Mar. 1894): 92–102; reprinted in Albert Galloway Keller and Maurice R. Davie, eds., *Essays of William Graham Sumner* (New Haven: Yale University Press, 1911), 1:91–106. For further information on Sumner's social thought, see Richard Hofstadter, *Social Darwinism in American Thought* (Philadelphia: University of Pennsylvania Press, 1944), 51–66; and Robert C. Bannister, *Social Darwinism: Science and Myth in Anglo-American Social Thought* (Philadelphia: Temple University Press, 1979), 97–113.

8. William Graham Sumner, "The Scientific Attitude of Mind," address to initiates of the Sigma Xi Society, Yale University, Mar. 4, 1905; in Keller and Davie, eds., *Essays of William Graham Sumner*, 1:51.

9. William James, *Pragmatism: A New Name for Some Old Ways of Thinking* (1907); reprinted in John J. McDermott, ed., *The Writings of William James: A Comprehensive Edition* (Chicago and London: University of Chicago Press, 1977), 387.

10. See, for example: Christopher Lasch, ed., *The Social Thought of Jane Addams* (New York: Irvington Publishers, 1982); James Livingston, *Pragmatism and the Political Economy of a Cultural Revolution, 1850–1940* (Chapel Hill: University of North Carolina Press, 1994); and Alan Dawley, *Struggles for Justice: Social Responsibility and the Liberal State* (Cambridge, MA: Harvard University Press, 1991), 98–138. On pragmatism, see James T. Kloppenberg, *Uncertain Victory: Social Democracy and Progressivism in European and American Thought, 1870–1920* (Oxford: Oxford University Press, 1986); James Livingston, *Pragmatism, Feminism, and Democracy: Rethinking the Politics of American History* (New York: Routledge, 2001) and *Pragmatism and the Political Economy of a Cultural Revolution.*

11. John Dewey, *My Pedagogic Creed* (New York: E. L. Kellogg, 1897).

12. George Santayana, "The Genteel Tradition in American Philosophy," *University of California Chronicle* 12, no. 4 (Oct. 1911), reprinted in Douglas L. Wilson, ed., *The Genteel Tradition: Nine Essays by George Santayana* (Lincoln and London: University of Nebraska Press, 1967), 37–64.

13. On Santayana, see John McCormick, *George Santayana: A Biography* (New York: Knopf, 1987); and Henry Samuel Levinson, *Santayana, Pragmatism, and the Spiritual Life* (Chapel Hill and London: University of North Carolina Press, 1992).

14. On the importance of sympathy in the early republic, see: Andrew Burstein, *Sentimental Democracy: The Evolution of America's Romantic Self-Image* (New York: Hill and Wang, 2000); Caleb Crain, *American Sympathy: Men, Friendship, and Literature in the New Nation* (New Haven: Yale University Press, 1999); Elizabeth Barnes, *States of Sympathy: Seduction and Democracy in the American Novel* (New York: Columbia University Press, 1997); Bruce Begnett, *Sentimental Bodies: Sex, Gender and Citizenship in the Early Republic* (Princeton: Princeton University Press, 1998); and Dana Nelson, *National Manhood: Capitalist Citizenship and the Imagined Fraternity of White Men* (Durham and London: Duke University Press, 1998). On romantic friendships among abolitionist men, see Donald Yacovone, "Abolitionists and the 'Language of Fraternal Love,'" in Mark C. Carnes and Clyde Griffin, eds., *Meanings for Manhood: Constructions of Masculinity in Victorian America* (Chicago: University of Chicago Press, 1990), 85–95.

15. Crain, *American Sympathy*, 4.

16. Daniel P. Rodgers, "In Search of Progressivism," *Reviews in American History* (1982):113–27.

17. John Dewey, "Ethics" (1908), in Jo Ann Boydston, ed., *John Dewey: The Middle Works* (Carbondale: Southern Illinois University Press, 1978), 5:128.

18. John Dewey, *Theory of the Moral Life* (New York: Irvington Publishers, 1908), 130.

19. John Dewey, *A Common Faith*, in Boydston, ed., *John Dewey: The Later Works*, 9:53.

20. On the homoerotics and gendered meanings of Emerson's writing on transcendental friendship, see Crain, *American Sympathy*, 148–237; Byrne R.S. Fone, *A Road to Stonewall: Male Homosexuality and Homophobia in English and American Literature, 1750-1969* (New York: Twaine Publishers, 1986), 41–56; David Leverenz, "The Politics of Emerson's Man-Making Words," in Leverenz, *Manhood and the American Renaissance* (Ithaca, NY: Cornell University Press, 1989); and Julie Ellison, "The Gender of Transparency: Masculinity and the Conduct of Life," *American Literary History* 4, no. 4 (Dec. 1992): 584–606. On same-sex sexuality and sentimental friendship, see Jonathan Ned Katz, *Love Stories: Sex Between Men Before Homosexuality* (Chicago: University of Chicago Press, 2001), 331–43.

21. Ibid., 331–43; Fone, *A Road to Stonewall*, 333–44. On the emergence of a binary model of sexuality organized by categories of heterosexuality and homosexuality, see Jonathan Ned Katz, *The Invention of Heterosexuality* (New York: Penguin, 1995).

22. Edward Carpenter, *The Intermediate Sex*, 196–97, quoted in Fone, *A Road to Stonewall*, 154–55. On Carpenter's influence in the United States, see Terence S. Kissack, "Anarchism and the Politics of Homosexuality," Ph.D. diss., City University of New York, 2004; and Katz, *Love Stories*, 321–29. On critical assessments of Emerson, see Sarah Ann Wider, *The Critical Reception of Emerson: Unsettling All Things* (Rochester, NY: Camden House, 2000).

23. David Nasaw, *The Chief: The Life of William Randolph Hearst* (New York: Houghton Mifflin, 2000), 125–85.

24. Gail Bederman, *Manliness and Civilization: A Cultural History of Gender and Race in the United States, 1880–1917* (Chicago: University of Chicago Press, 1995), 1–44. On Roosevelt and strenuous masculinity, see ibid., 170–216, and Sarah Watts, *Rough Rider in the White House: Theodore Roosevelt and the Politics of Desire* (Chicago: University of Chicago Press, 2003), 79–122.

25. Roosevelt defined these ideals of strenuous manhood in a number of essays and lectures between 1899 and 1901—among them "The Strenuous Life," "Fellow-Feeling as a Political Factor," "Civic Helpfulness," Character and Success," "Promise and Performance," "The American Boy," "National Duties," and "Christian Citizenship"—published collectively in his *The Strenuous Life: Essays and Addresses* (New York: Century Co., 1901).

26. Theodore Roosevelt, "The College Man: An Address Delivered at the Harvard Union," 1907. This lecture is transcribed in Donald Wilhelm's *Theodore Roosevelt as an Undergraduate* (Boston: John W. Luce, 1910), 78–90.

27. Ibid., 83.

28. Ibid., 88.

29. Scholar Henry May argues convincingly that Roosevelt's embrace of "practical idealism" represented a broader tendency among the American population. Henry F. May, *The End of American Innocence: A Study of the First Years of Our Own Time, 1912–1917* (New York: Knopf, 1959), 9–19.

30. Watts, *Rough Rider in the White House*, 36.

31. A search of the full text archive of multiple publications, including the *Chicago Tribune* and the *New York Times*, yields only a handful of hits for the term "mollycoddle" prior to Roosevelt's 1907 speech. According to a *New York Times* editorialist, writing in 1916, "The word was not in general use so long ago, and although its origin is far more ancient, it was not a popular or familiar designation until Colonel Roosevelt first employed it, ten or a dozen years ago" (*New York Times*, June 4, 1916, 20). This writer and others commented on Roosevelt's invocation of the term to demean those who disagreed with him. See, for example, "The Only One," *New York Times*, May 7, 1907, 8. A June 24, 1907 front-page *Chicago Tribune* story suggests that "mollycoddle" was immediately associated with both effeminacy and same-sex practices. It tells of a boy from Spartan, Illinois who ran away from home because his brother was a "mollycoddle" who "was wont to perfume his hair and go down to the depot to see the trains come in." "Mollycoddle Gets Blame," *Chicago Tribune*, June 24, 1907, 1. For other examples of Roosevelt's use of gendered and sexual vituperative rhetoric, see Watts, *Rough Rider in the White House*, 118–22.

32. Letter from Roosevelt to Goerge Otto Trevelyan, Oct. 7, 1905, reprinted in Joseph Bishop Bucklin, ed., *Theodore Roosevelt and His Time Shown in His Own Letters* (New York: Charles Scribner's Sons, 1920), 2:154.

33. On negative assessments of sexual inversion and the emergence of the language of homosexuality and heterosexuality, see Jennifer Terry, *An American Obsession: Science, Medicine, and Homosexuality in Modern Society* (Chicago: University of Chicago

Press, 1999), 74–158; and Lillian Faderman, *Odd Girls and Twilight Lovers: A History of Lesbian Life in Twentieth-Century America* (New York: Penguin, 1991), 37–61.

34. Theodore Roosevelt, "Latitude and Longitude Among Reformers," *The Century* (June 1900), reprinted in *The Strenuous Life*, 41–62.

35. G. Frank Lydston, "Sexual Perversion, Satyriasis, and Nymphomania," *Philadelphia Medical and Surgical Reporter* 61, no.11 (Sept. 14, 1889): 281–85. Excerpted in Jonathan Ned Katz, *Gay/Lesbian Almanac* (New York: Harper & Row, 1983), 213–14 and quoted in Terry, *An American Obsession*, 92. On Roosevelt's tenure as police commissioner, including his experiences with "vice," see H. Paul Jeffers, *Commissioner Roosevelt: The Story of Theodore Roosevelt and the New York City Police* (New York: John Wiley, 1994). Other medical experts who reported on urban male homosexuals congregating included George M. Beard and Allan McLane Hamilton. See George Chauncey, *Gay New York: Gender, Urban Culture, and the Making of the Gay Male World, 1890–1940* (New York: Basic Books, 1994), 140; and Terry, *An American Obsession*, 92.

36. See, for example, Chauncey, *Gay New York*, 65–97.

37. Roosevelt, "Latitude and Longitude Among Reformers."

38. Roosevelt, "Latitude and Longitude Among Reformers," 60–62.

39. Roosevelt, "First Annual Address," 1901, quoted in Kissack, "The Politics of Homosexuality," 36.

40. G. Frank Lydston, *The Diseases of Society (The Vice and Crime Problem)* (Philadelphia and London: J. B. Lippincott, 1910), 229. Lydston also identified the post–Civil War South in terms of political anarchy. Asserting sympathy for the "Southern white," he faulted Reconstruction policies for "bestowing upon some millions of ignorant blacks political equality with the whites, an equality which the recipient did not need, much less know how to use intelligently." Lydston, who perpetrated the dominant racist narrative of an epidemic of sexual crimes committed by black men against white women in the South, linked these "crimes" to the "criminal politics" and "political anarchy" of granting rights to blacks (267–71, 393–99).

41. Ibid., 229.

42. Ibid., 229–32; 307–426. Lydston argues that the unbridled romantic idealism of girls led not only to the pursuit of same-sex relations but also to prostitution and promiscuity (410–16).

43. Kristin L. Hoganson, *Fighting for American Manhood: How Gender Politics Provoked the Spanish-American and Philippine-American Wars* (New Haven and London: Yale University Press, 1998), 175–79.

44. See M.A. Dewolfe Howe, *John Jay Chapman and His Letters* (Boston: Houghton Mifflin, 1937), 138–40; and Edmund Morris, *The Rise of Theodore Roosevelt* (New York: Coward, McCann & Geoghegan, 1979), 665–80.

45. John Jay Chapman, *The Political Nursery* (Oct. 17, 1898), 17.

46. On the Social Reform Club, see Gregory Weinstein, *The Ardent Eighties: Reminiscences of an Interesting Decade* (New York: International Press, 1928), 111–14. Information on the Social Reform Club also can be found in the following manuscript

collections: E. W. Ordway Collection, New York Public Library, Rare Books and Manuscript Division; James Graham Phelps Stokes Papers, Columbia University Rare Books and Manuscripts Library.

47. Pamphlet, "Social Reform Club: Annual Report, Constitution, List of Members" (Nov. 1898). Copy in James Graham Phelps Stokes Papers, Columbia University Rare Books and Manuscripts Library, File: Social Reform Club.

48. On Kelly's conversion to socialism, see Mark Pittenger, "The Great Evasion: Religion and Science in the Socialism of Edmond Kelly," *Journal of American Culture* 14, no.1 (Spring 1991): 13–18.

49. Peter J. Frederick, "A Life of Principle: Ernest Howard Crosby and the Frustrations of the Intellectual as Reformer," *New York History* 54 (Oct. 1973): 399.

50. Oppenheimer's attack on Roosevelt's performance as police commissioner received prominent attention in the New York City dailies. See, for example, "Hot Attack on Roosevelt: Moses Oppenheimer Stirred Him Up After His Speech Before the Social Reform Club," *New York Times,* Mar. 17, 1897, 3.

51. For an account of this conflict, see Weinstein, *The Ardent Eighties*, 113–14. Roosevelt wrote an angry letter denouncing the club. See letter from Theodore Roosevelt to E. W. Ordway, March 1897, E. W. Ordway Papers, New York Public Library, Rare Books and Manuscripts Division.

52. Roosevelt claimed that his political stance—which he defined as "the radical movement under conservative direction"—represented the only possible patriotic and practical response to social and economic inequities. Theodore Roosevelt, "The Radical Movement Under Conservative Direction," address before the Chamber of Commerce, New Haven, Conn., Dec. 13, 1910; reprinted in Hermann Hagedorn, ed., *The Works of Theodore Roosevelt, Vol. XVI: American Problems* (New York: Charles Scribner's Sons, 1926), 86–99.

53. Quoted in Rudolph W. Chamberlain, *There Is No Truce: A Life of Thomas Mott Osborne* (New York: Macmillan, 1935), 126–27.

54. Richard W.G. Welling, *As the Twig Is Bent* (New York: G. P. Putnam's Sons, 1942), 23–29; 161. See also Welling, "My Classmate Theodore Roosevelt," *American Legion Monthly* (Jan. 1929):9–12, 67–68; and Welling, "Theodore Roosevelt at Harvard: Some Personal Reminiscences" *The Outlook* (Oct. 27, 1920):366–69.

55. Osborne, for example, wrote in 1911 that "Roosevelt is going around like a roaring lion, and the papers print pages of his performances. He bores me so I don't know what to do; and the worst of it is he's so often right in what he says! He's simply maddening." Quoted in Chamberlain, *There Is No Truce*, 127. Welling's resentment of Roosevelt's disproportionate fame is clearly indicated in the annotations he made in a copy of Donald Wilhelm's *Theodore Roosevelt as an Undergraduate* (bequeathed to the New York Public Library).

56. Edmond Kelly, *Evolution and Effort: And Their Relation to Religion and Politics* (New York: D. Appleton, 1895), 47.

57. Ibid., 50.

58. Kelly maintained that the importance of love—rather than mere "sexual

passion"—served as evidence that humans were no longer bound to natural processes of evolution. See, for example, chapter 4, "Determinism and the Evolution of Love," in *Evolution and Effort*, 39–51. Kelly also espouses sexual equality in his utopian novel *The Demetrian* (1907), which he published under the pseudonym Ellison Harding.

59. Crosby remains absent from much of the literature on Progressive reform and anti-imperialism. In addition to Peter Frederick's essay, "A Life of Principle," see his book: *Knights of the Golden Rule: The Intellectual as Christian Social Reformer in the 1890s* (Lexington: The University Press of Kentucky, 1976), 185–234. See also Perry E. Gianakos, "Ernest Howard Crosby: A Forgotten Tolstoyan Anti-Militarist and Anti-Imperialist," *American Studies* 13 (Spring 1972): 11–29; Rory William Stauber, "Lifting the Banner of Tolstoyan Non-Resistance in America: Ernest Howard Crosby's Lonely Quest, 1894–1907," Ph.D. diss., Drew University, 1994; and Leonard D. Abbott, *Ernest Howard Crosby: A Valuation and a Tribute* (Westwood, MA: Ariel Press, 1907).

60. John Jay Chapman, "The Catastrophe," *The Political Nursery* (Oct. 17, 1898).

61. Letter from John Jay Chapman to Minna Timmons Chapman, quoted in Howe, *John Jay Chapman and His Letters*, 134.

62. John Jay Chapman, "Plato," undated manuscript; folder #46M-398, John Jay Chapman Papers, Houghton Library, Harvard University.

63. Letter from John Jay Chapman to George Dudley Seymour, Oct. 5, 1930. Quoted in Howe, *John Jay Chapman and His Letters*, 444.

64. John Jay Chapman, "Memorandum by J. J. Chapman," reprinted in Howe, *John Jay Chapman and His Letters*, 141–46.

65. Ernest Howard Crosby, *The Whim* 5, no. 2 (Mar. 1903): 34–42.

66. Ibid., 35.

67. Ibid., 34. Jamake Highwater argues that medieval concern with these demons stemmed from fears related to sexual ambiguity and same-sex desire: "Virtually every fiend was given a sexual connotation, most famously the incubi (the sexually aggressive demons) and the succubi (the sexually passive demons). But these demons were not designated as male or female. They were envisioned as deviants who could take on the appearance of either gender, depending on their lust and their victim." He argues that homosexuals and Jews were configured similarly as "unnatural freaks" in nineteenth-century medical and psychological literature. Jamake Highwater, *The Mythology of Transgression: Homosexuality as Metaphor* (New York: Oxford University Press, 1997), 87.

68. Ibid., 37–38, 42. On strenuousness as cure for neurasthenia, see Bederman, *Manliness and Civilization*, 77–120.

69. Interestingly, G. Frank Lydston offered a similar critique of strenuosity and militarism, both of which he saw as leading to social disorder and degeneration, and chastised Roosevelt for both his commitment to the strenuous life and to his militarist foreign policies. Lydston, *Diseases and Society*.

70. John Jay Chapman, *Causes and Consequences* (New York: Charles Scribner's Sons, 1898), 31–32.

71. Ibid., 75.

72. John Jay Chapman, *Practical Agitation* (New York: Charles Scribner's Sons, 1900), 149.

73. Letter, quoted in Howe, *John Jay Chapman and His Letters*, 151 and in David Stocking, "John Jay Chapman and Political Reform," *American Quarterly* 2, no. 1 (Spring 1950): 70.

74. John Jay Chapman, "Paul Fuller," manuscript dated October 30, 1917; folder #6434: "JJC Compositions," John Jay Chapman Papers, Houghton Library, Harvard University.

75. Lori D. Ginzberg argues that in the late nineteenth century many women eschewed "moral suasion" in favor of more activist political models (*Women and the Work of Benevolence: Morality, Politics, and Class in the Nineteenth-Century United States* [New Haven and London: Yale University Press, 1990]). Susan E. Marshall shows that, for a sizeable group of elite women who opposed women's suffrage, "the ideology of separate spheres . . . enhanced their social influence as cultural arbiters, maintaining the exclusivity of elite social networks while simultaneously promoting new standards of domesticity that enhanced class control" (*Splintered Sisterhood: Gender and Class in the Campaign against Woman Suffrage* [Madison and London: University of Wisconsin Press, 1997], 224). In a classic essay, Paula Baker also argues that antisuffrage arguments wielded considerable influence in the late nineteenth century because women's participation in electoral politics was seen as threatening to the doctrine of separate spheres and, citing the Women's Christian Temperance Union as an example, argues that women ultimately gained more political power, and ultimately the right to vote, by "forg[ing] the political sphere into a broadly based political movement" ("The Domestication of Politics: Women and American Political Society, 1780–1920," *American Historical Review* 89, no. 3 [June 1984], 620–47).

76. John Jay Chapman, *William Lloyd Garrison* (Boston: Atlantic Monthly Press, 1913), 34.

77. Ibid., 35.

78. Ibid., 162.

79. Ernest H. Crosby, *Garrison the Non-Resistant* (Chicago: Public Publishing Company, 1905).

80. Ibid., 58–59.

81. Ibid., 71–75.

82. Ernest H. Crosby, *The Whim* 5, no. 3 (April 1903): 73–74. Crosby repeated these assertions using similar language in various writings. See, for example, *Garrison the Non-Resistant*, 72.

83. Ernest H. Crosby, *The Whim* 4, no. 5 (Dec. 1902): 14.

84. Ernest H. Crosby, *The Whim* 7, no. 1 (Feb. 1904): 12–13. Crosby published numerous works lambasting militarism as unmanly, including his parodic novel—influenced by the similar work of Mark Twain—entitled *Captain Jinks, Hero* (New York: Funk & Wagnalls, 1902). See also the following works by Crosby: *The Absurdities of Militarism* (Boston: American Peace Society, 1901); "Militarism at Home," *Arena* 31 (Jan. 1904): 70–74; "Why I am Opposed to Imperialism," *Arena* 28 (July 1902): 10–11;

and "The Military Idea of Manliness," *The Independent* 53 (April 8, 1901): 873–75. In the last essay Crosby characterized "the new manliness" associated with militarism: "it takes shape in my mind in the guise of that human turkey-cock, the drum-major, magnificent with padded chest and towering hat and plumes, whirling his glittering baton in an inextricable maze of bass-drums and puffing cheeks, while the humble civilian world bows prostrate before him." Robyn Muncy argues that Crosby's critique also addressed the new accommodation of corporate hierarchies in the name of strenuous white manhood. Robyn Muncy, "Trustbusting and White Manhood in America, 1898–1914," *American Studies* 38, no. 3 (Fall 1997): 34–35.

85. Ernest H. Crosby, *The Whim* 5, no. 5 (June 1903): 134. This notion that segregated male environments promoted same-sex behavior aligned with concerns expressed by William George and Thomas Mott Osborne. Sexologists and reformers also argued that sex-segregated environments might induce men to partake in same-sex behavior. See Regina Kunzel, "Situating Sex: Prison Sexual Culture in the Mid-Twentieth Century United States," *GLQ* 8, no. 3 (2002): 253.

86. Emma Goldman, *Anarchism and Other Essays* (New York: Mother Earth Publishing, 1911), 144.

87. On J. William Lloyd, see Kissack, "The Politics of Homosexuality."

88. Ernest H. Crosby, *Swords and Plowshares* (New York: Funk & Wagnalls, 1902) and *Plain Talk in Psalm and Parable* (Boston: Small, Maynard, 1899).

89. Ernest H. Crosby, "Love's Patriot," in *Plain Talk in Psalm and Parable*, 50–51.

90. Quoted in Abbott, *Ernest Howard Crosby*, 20.

91. Ernest H. Crosby, *Edward Carpenter: Prophet and Poet* (Philadelphia: The Conservator, 1905), 46.

92. Ernest H. Crosby, *The Whim* 6, no. 1 (Aug. 1903): 37.

93. Crosby, *Edward Carpenter*, 45.

94. Ibid., 46–47.

95. Quoted in Leonard D. Abbott, "Some Reminiscences of Ernest Crosby," *Mother Earth* (Feb. 1907):22–27.

96. John Jay Chapman, "Walt Whitman," in *Emerson and Other Essays* (New York: Scribners, 1898), 123.

97. Ibid., 127.

98. Ibid., 127.

99. Quoted in Howe, *John Jay Chapman and His Letters*, 77.

100. John Jay Chapman, "Emerson, After Sixty Years," reprinted as "Emerson" in *Emerson and Other Essays*, 186.

101. Ibid., 189.

102. Ibid., 190.

103. John Jay Chapman, "Plato," undated manuscript (1919), 37–39, John Jay Chapman Papers, Houghton Library, Harvard University.

104. Ibid., 36.

105. Ibid., 5–7.

106. Chapman wrote: "Thus Lucian's bold stroke at the greatest of Greek writers,

falling as it did no the precise spot where the intellect and the senses meet—the nexus and nerve-centre of sex—seemed to explain my inability to sympathize with the Greek temperament. The Attic mind was abnormal." John Jay Chapman, *Lucian, Plato, and Greek Morals* (Boston: Houghton Mifflin, 1931). Chapman also argued that he was directing this study to the contemporary acceptance of homosexuality and prided himself on being bold enough to tackle the subject directly.

107. Chapman's private letters on the publication of *Lucian, Plato and Greek Morals* are quoted in Howe, *John Jay Chapman and His Letters*, 445–57. In one letter Chapman explained his use of the term "pederasty": "'Homosexual' is to me a more unpleasant word than pederasty. Homosexual is a sneaking, allusive—pseudo-scientific, lurching, smirking, loathly word—while pederasty is simply pederasty. You have heard of pederasty. Every one knows what it means. It conveys no falsetto modesty."

108. Abbott, *Ernest Howard Crosby*, 19.

109. Of course, many reform-minded women resisted the brush of sentimental idealism; indeed, many embraced discourses of the "practical," as is amply demonstrated by the development of the work of women in the burgeoning social sciences. See, for example, Helene Silverberg, ed., *Gender and American Social Science: The Formative Years* (Princeton, NJ: Princeton University Press, 1998). However, many women were still attacked as ideological and dangerous for supporting welfare legislation and other progressive causes, especially after World War I. See, for example, Cott, *The Grounding of Modern Feminism*, 243–67.

EPILOGUE: RED BLOODS AND MOLLYCODDLES IN THE TWENTIETH CENTURY AND BEYOND

1. G. Lowes Dickinson, *Appearances: Notes on Travel, East and West* (Garden City, NY: Doubleday, Page, 1915), 184.

2. Dickinson saw the origins of red-blooded acquisitive commitment in the "pioneer" tradition of the United States. He made the Turnerian argument that in the nineteenth century the American focus on individualism flourished because of the vast availability of space and natural resources but that in the future, as resources diminished and immigration increased, opportunities for social mobility would decrease and exploitative individualism would become less tenable. He equated the greater openness to socialism in Europe as a manifestation of a greater commitment to democratic values and asserted, "it is an error to think of America as democratic; her Democracy is all on the surface." "A Continent of Pioneers," in Dickinson, *Appearances*, 148–49.

3. Kristin L. Hoganson, *Fighting for American Manhood: How Gender Politics Provoked the Spanish-American and Philippine-American Wars* (New Haven and London: Yale University Press, 1998); Sarah Watts, *Rough Rider in the White House: Theodore Roosevelt and the Politics of Desire* (Chicago: University of Chicago Press, 2003), 193–235; Martin Summers, *Manliness and Its Discontents: The Black Middle Class and the Transformation of Masculinity, 1900–1930* (Durham: University of North Carolina Press, 2004); Marlon B. Ross, *Manning the Race: Reforming Black Men in the Jim Crow Era* (New York: New York University Press, 2004), 66–110, 90–

144; John F. Kasson, *Houdini, Tarzan, and the Perfect Man: The White Male Body and the Challenge of Modernity in America* (New York: Hill and Wang, 2001), 19.

4. Bederman's insightful analysis illuminates challenges to this discourse as produced in the antilynching activism of Ida B. Wells and the valorization of violence against "primitive" Africans, especially in the form of lynching, in Edgar Rice Brroughs's popular *Tarzan* fiction, first serialized in 1912. Gail Bederman, *Manliness and Civilization: A Cultural History of Gender and Race in the United States, 1880–1917* (Chicago: University of Chicago Press, 1995), 45–76; 217–40.

5. Gary Gerstle, for example, argues that Theodore Roosevelt's understanding of nationalism, which encompassed his embrace of strenuous masculinity, influenced the two models of twentieth-century American nationalism: "civic nationalism" and "racial nationalism." Gerstle's evaluation of Roosevelt's gender and racial politics is far more sympathetic than my own and that of other authors cited here, notably Bederman and Watts. Gary Gerstle, *American Crucible: Race and Nation in The Twentieth Century* (Princeton: Princeton University Press, 2001). Two exemplary books examine the political meanings attached to masculinity during the Cold War: Robert D. Dean, *Imperial Brotherhood: Gender and the Making of Cold War Foreign Policy* (Amherst: University of Massachusetts Press, 2001); and K. A. Cuordileone, *Manhood and American Political Culture in the Cold War* (New York and London: Routledge, 2005).

6. Dean, *Imperial Brotherhood*, 5.

7. Dean, *Imperial Brotherhood*, 19.

8. Cuordileone, *Manhood and American Political Culture*, 1–2.

9. Arthur M. Schlesinger Jr. "The Crisis of American Masculinity," *Esquire* (Nov. 1958):63–65; reprinted in *The Politics of Hope* (Boston: Houghton Mifflin, 1962), 237–46.

10. Cuordileone, *Manhood and American Political Culture*, 15.

11. Schlesinger, "The Crisis of American Masculinity," 237–38; quoted in Cuordeli-one, *Manhood and American Political Culture*, 15.

12. Schlesinger, *The Vital Center*, quoted in David K. Johnson, *The Lavender Scare: The Cold War Persecution of Gays and Lesbians in the Federal Government* (Chicago: University of Chicago Press, 2004), 33–34.

13. Examples of advice to parents on mollycoddle boys include: Louis Welzmiller, "Why It Is that Some Boys Grow Up to Be Mollycoddles," *New York Times*, Mar. 28, 1909, 9; "No Mollycoddle Children form This Method," *New York Times*, Nov. 21, 1915, SM20; and George R. Lyons, "Cause for the Mollycoddle," *Chicago Daily Tribune*, Apr. 18, 1909, E9. On homosexuality and childrearing, see Jennifer Terry, *An American Obsession: Science, Medicine, and Homosexuality in Modern Society* (Chicago: University of Chicago Press, 1999), 214–19; and Julia Grant, "A 'Real Boy' and Not a Sissy: Gender, Childhood, and Masculinity, 1890–1940," *Journal of Social History* 37, no. 4 (Summer 2004): 829–51.

14. Gaylan Studlar, *This Mad Masquerade: Stardom and Masculinity in the Jazz Age* (New York: Columbia University Press, 1996), 1–121.

15. *The Mollycoddle*, directed by Victor Fleming (1920; Los Angeles: Douglas Fairbanks Pictures, Corp.).

16. *Double Trouble*, directed by Christy Cabanne (1915; Los Angeles: Fine Arts Film Company). Studlar offers an excellent reading of the operation of gender in this film (*This Mad Masquerade* 31–38).

17. Herbert Quick, *Double Trouble, or, Every Hero His Own Villain* (Indianapolis: Bobbs-Merrill, 1906), 1. "Nordau" refers to Max Sinom Nordau's influential book, *Degeneration*, first published in English in 1895, which tied sexual inversion to degeneracy. On Nordau's influence in the United States, see Peter Boag, *Same-Sex Affairs: Constructing and Controlling Homosexuality in the Pacific Northwest* (Berkeley: University of California Press, 2003), 128–29.

18. Quick, *Double Trouble.*

19. Studlar, *This Mad Masquerade*, 54–76; Grant, "A 'Real Boy' and Not a Sissy."

20. Schlesinger interpreted upper-class interest in the working class, such as that exhibited by many of the reformers addressed in this study, as a sign of self-indulgent weakness, "the intellectual's somewhat feminine fascination with the rude and muscular power of the proletariat." Schlesinger, quoted in Cuordelione, *Manhood and American Political Culture*, 25.

21. Schlesinger named the undesirable other to strong American masculinity the Progressive "doughface." This figure shared many of the qualities of the "impracticable idealist." He is a "wailer" who is "notable for the distortion of facts by desire." Schlesinger accuses him of "sentimentality." For an excellent discussion of Schlesinger's construction of the "doughface" and of Roosevelt's influence on Schlesinger, see Cuordileone, *Manhood and American Political Culture*, 17–36.

22. Johnson, *The Lavender Scare*, 101–208.

23. The workings of homophobia and gender stereotyping in American electoral politics in the late twentieth century have been well documented. See, for example, Stephen J. Ducat, *The Wimp Factor: Gender Gaps, Holy Wars, and the Politics of Anxious Masculinity* (Boston: Beacon Press, 2004); Bruce Curtis, "The Wimp Factor," *American Heritage* (Nov. 1989):40–49; David Corn, *The Lies of George W. Bush: Mastering the Politics of Deception* (New York: Three Rivers, 2003); and Catherine V. Scott, "Bound for Glory: The Hostage Crisis as Captivity Narrative in Iran," *International Studies Quarterly* 44, no. 1 (Mar. 2000): 177–88.

24. On gender, homosexuality, and the 2004 U.S. presidential election, see W. C. Harris, "'In My Day It Used to Be Called a Limp Wrist': Flip-Floppers, Nelly Boys, and Homophobic Rhetoric in the 2004 U.S. Presidential Campaign," *The Journal of American Culture* 29, no. 3 (Sept. 2006): 278–95; Frank Rich, "How Kerry Became a Girlie-Man," *New York Times*, Sept. 5, 2004; Laura Blumenfeld, "John Kerry: Hunter, Dreamer, Realist," *Washington Post*, June 1, 2003, A1; and Richard Goldstein, "Who's the Man? The Democrats Scramble to Find a Scream-Proof Alpha," *Village Voice* (Jan. 28–Feb. 3, 2004).

25. Harvey Mansfield, "The Manliness of Theodore Roosevelt," *The New Criterion* 23, no. 7 (Mar. 2005) and *Manliness* (New Haven: Yale University Press, 2006). Karl Rove, "Lessons from a Larger-than-Life President," *Time* (June 25, 2006).

Bibliography

MANUSCRIPTS

Algernon D. Black Papers. Society for Ethical Culture Archives. New York.

Citizens' Union Records. Rare Books and Manuscripts Library, Columbia University, New York.

City Reform Club Minute Books. Rare Books and Manuscripts Collection, New York Public Library, New York.

Community Services Society Collection. Rare Books and Manuscripts Library, Columbia University, New York.

E. W. Ordway Papers. Rare Books and Manuscripts Collection, New York Public Library, New York.

Gino Speranza Papers. Rare Books and Manuscripts Collection, New York Public Library, New York.

Jacob A. Riis Collection. Manuscript Division, Library of Congress, Washington, DC.

James Graham Phelps Stokes Papers. Rare Books and Manuscripts Library, Columbia University, New York.

John Jay Chapman Papers. Houghton Library, Harvard University, Boston.

John Lovejoy Elliott Papers. Society for Ethical Culture Archives, New York.

Mayoral Papers of William Strong. Municipal Archives of the City of New York, New York.

Oral History Project. Society for Ethical Culture Archives, New York.

The Osborne Family Collection. The George Arents Research Library, Syracuse University, Syracuse, New York.

The Papers of the University Settlement Society of New York City. The State Historical Society of Wisconsin, Madison.

Richard Rogers Bowker Papers. Rare Books and Manuscripts Collection, New York Public Library, New York.

Richard Watson Gilder Papers. Rare Books and Manuscripts Collection, New York Public Library, New York.

Richard Welling Papers. Rare Books and Manuscripts Collection, New York Public Library, New York.

William R. George and George Junior Republic Collection. Department of Manuscripts and University Archives, Cornell University Libraries, Ithaca, New York.

PRIMARY SOURCES

Abbott, Leonard D. *Ernest Howard Crosby: A Valuation and a Tribute.* Westwood, MA: Ariel Press, 1907.

——. "Some Reminiscences of Ernest Crosby." *Mother Earth* (Feb. 1907):22–27.

Adams, Charles Francis. "Individuality in Politics: A Lecture." Delivered at Steinway Hall, New York, Apr. 21, 1880. Pamphlet published by Independent Republican Association, New York.

Addams, Jane. *The Spirit of Youth in the City Streets.* New York: Macmillan, 1909.

——. *Twenty Years at Hull House.* New York: Macmillan, 1910.

——. *Jane Addams: A Centennial Reader.* New York: Macmillan, 1960.

"Alas the Mollycoddle!" *Minneapolis Journal,* Apr. 14, 1907.

"Arrested Development." *New York Tribune,* Oct. 1, 1884.

Bellamy, Edward. *Looking Backward 2000–1887.* 1887; reprint, New York: New American Library, 1960.

"Bismarck's Birthday." *Harper's Weekly,* Mar. 30, 1895, 290.

"Bismarck's Eightieth Birthday." *Leslie's Weekly,* Apr. 11, 1895.

Bowker, Richard Rogers. "An Open Letter to Mr. Curtis." *New York Evening Post,* Sept. 2, 1879.

Breen, Matthew P. *Thirty Years of New York Politics.* New York, 1899.

Carey, Edward. *George William Curtis.* Boston and New York: Houghton Mifflin, 1895.

——. "Tammany Past and Present." *The Forum* (Oct. 1898):204–205.

Chamberlain, Rudolph W. *There Is No Truce: A Life of Thomas Mott Osborne.* New York: Macmillan, 1935.

Chapman, John Jay. *The Political Nursery.* New York, 1897–1901.

——. *Causes and Consequences.* New York: Charles Scribner's Sons, 1898.

——. *Emerson and Other Essays.* New York: Charles Scribner's Sons, 1898.

——. *Practical Agitation.* New York: Charles Scribner's Sons, 1900.

——. *William Lloyd Garrison.* Boston: The Atlantic Monthly Press, 1913.

——. *Lucian, Plato, and Greek Morals.* Boston: Houghton Mifflin, 1931.

"Clean Streets at Last." *New York Times,* July 28, 1895, 28.

The Committee of Fifteen, and Edwin R.A. Seligman, ed. *The Social Evil: With Special Reference to Conditions Existing in the City of New York*. New York: G. P. Putnam's Sons, 1902.

Commons, John R. "The Junior Republic." *The American Journal of Sociology* 3, no. 3.

Conkling, Alfred. *The Life and Letters of Roscoe Conkling: Orator, Statesman, Advocate*. New York: Charles L. Webster, 1889.

Croker, Richard. "Tammany Hall and the Democracy." *North American Review* 154 (Feb. 1892): 225–30.

Crosby, Ernest H. *Plain Talk in Psalm and Parable*. Boston: Small, Maynard, 1899.

——. *Swords and Plowshares*. New York: Funk & Wagnalls, 1902.

——. *The Whim*. New York, 1902–1907.

——. *Edward Carpenter: Prophet and Poet*. Philadelphia: The Conservator, 1905.

——. *Garrison the Non-Resistant*. Chicago: Public Publishing Company, 1905.

Curtis, Francis. *The Republican Party: A History of Its Fifty Years' Existence and a Record of Its Measures and Leaders, 1854–1904*. New York: G. P. Putnam's Sons, 1904.

Curtis, George William. "Machine Politics and the Remedy." Lecture delivered May 20, 1880. Pamphlet published by the Independent Republican Association, New York.

——. *Orations and Addresses of George William Curtis*. New York, 1894.

Dell, Floyd. *Intellectual Vagabondage*. New York, 1926.

Dewey, John. *My Pedagogic Creed*. New York: E. L. Kellogg, 1897.

——. *Theory of the Moral Life*. New York: Irvington Publishers, 1908.

"Drives George Out of Junior Republic." *New York Times*, Dec. 18, 1913, 6.

Eaton, Dorman B. "A New Phase of the Reform Movement." *North American Review* 132 (June 1881): 555.

Epstein, Jacob. *Epstein: An Autobiography*. New York: E. P. Dutton, 1955.

Fisher, Mary Wager. "Daddy's Boys: A Novel Social Experiment; A Factory for Good Citizenship." *Rural New-Yorker*, June 24, 1899, 461–62.

Flynt, Josiah. *Tramping with Tramps*. New York, 1900.

——. *The World of Graft*. New York, 1901.

——. *The Little Brother: A Story of Tramp Life*. New York, 1902.

Foraker, Joseph B. *Notes of a Busy Life*. Cincinnati, 1917.

Forbes, J. Cameron. *The Philippine Islands*. New York, 1928.

Fowler, Gene. *The Great Mouthpiece: A Life Story of William J. Fallon*. New York: Blue Ribbon Books, 1931.

Gardner, Charles W. *The Doctor and the Devil, or Midnight Adventures of Dr. Parkhurst*. New York: Macmillan, 1890.

"George Must Go, Inquiry Verdict." *New York Times*, Dec. 19, 1913, 20.

George, William R. *The Junior Republic: Its History and Ideals*. New York: D. Appleton, 1909.

George, William R. and Lyman Beecher Stowe. *Citizens Made and Remade: An Interpretation of the Significance and Influence of George Junior Republics*. Boston: Houghton Mifflin, 1912.

Gilder, Richard Watson. "William R. Hearst's Long-Cherished Design." *New York Times*, Oct. 18, 1906.

Gillespie, Harriet. "A Miniature Republic." *The Christian Endeavor World*, Feb. 17, 1898, 4.

Gladden, Washington. *Social Facts and Forces*. 1897; reprint, Port Washington, NY: Kennikat Press, 1971.

Godkin, E. L. "Tammany Apologists." *The Nation*, Jan. 26, 1893.

Gosnell, Harold F. *Boss Platt and His New York Machine: A Study of the Political Leadership of Thomas C. Platt, Theodore Roosevelt, and Others*. Chicago: University of Chicago Press, 1924.

Gunton, George. "The Peril of Popular Government." *Lecture Bulletin of the Institute of Social Economics* 4, no. 5 (1901): 104–105.

Hagedorn, Hermann, ed. *The Works of Theodore Roosevelt, Vol. XVI: American Problems*. New York: Charles Scribner's Sons, 1926.

Hinman, George W. "Bismarck in the Wilhelm Strasse," "Bismarck in the Reichstag," and "Bismarck at Home." *Leslie's Weekly*, Apr. 1895.

"Hot Attack on Roosevelt: Moses Oppenheimer Stirred Him Up After His Speech Before the Social Reform Club." *New York Times*, Mar. 17, 1897, 3.

Howe, M.A. DeWolfe. *John Jay Chapman and His Letters*. Boston: Houghton Mifflin, 1937.

Hughes, Thomas. *Tom Brown's Schooldays*. Oxford: Oxford University Press, 1989.

Humphreys, Mary Gay. "The Smallest Republic in the World." *McClure's Magazine*, July 1897, 735–47.

Irwin, Will, ed. *The Letters of Theodore Roosevelt*. New York: Scribner's, 1946.

"It Will Be a Struggle in Which There Will Be No Use for Political Hermaphrodites." *New York Sun*, Apr. 20, 1897.

Jackson, Henry E. *Robinson Crusoe Social Engineer: How the Discovery of Robinson Crusoe Solves the Labor Problem and Opens the Path to Industrial Peace*. New York: E. P. Dutton, 1922.

"Jacob A. Riis Speaks to Large Audience." *Hartford Connecticut Times*, Jan. 24, 1900.

Josephson, Matthew. *The Politicos, 1865–1896*. New York: Harcourt, Brace & World, 1938.

Keller, Albert Galloway and Maurice R. Davie, eds. *Essays of William Graham Sumner, Vol. I*. New Haven: Yale University Press, 1911.

Kelly, Edmond. *Evolution and Effort: And Their Relation to Religion and Politics*. New York: D. Appleton, 1895.

Kelly, Edmond (as Ellison Harding). *The Demetrian*. 1907.

"Keep the Goo Goos Straight!" *New York Sun*, Oct. 5, 1895.

Lang, Louis J., ed. *The Autobiography of Thomas Collier Platt*. New York: B. W. Dodge, 1910.

Leavitt, John Brooks. "Criminal Degradation of New York Citizenship." *The Forum* 17 (Aug. 1894): 659–65.

Lydston, G. Frank. *The Diseases of Society (The Vice and Crime Problem)*. Philadelphia and London: J. B. Lippincott, 1910.

"The March of the White Brigade." *New York Times*, May 27, 1897, 6.

McDermott, John J., ed. *The Writings of William James: A Comprehensive Edition*. Chicago: University of Chicago Press, 1967.

Meade, Charles A. "City Cleansing in New York: Some Advances and Retreats." *Municipal Affairs* 4 (1900): 721–41.

Merwyn, Henry Childs. "Tammany Hall." *Atlantic Monthly* (Feb. 1894):240–46.

——. "Tammany Points the Way." *Atlantic Monthly* (Nov. 1894):680–89.

Morgan, Appleton. "What Shall We Do with the 'Dago'?" *The Popular Science Monthly* 38 (Dec. 1890): 172–79.

"Move for Slum Parks." *Chicago Tower Herald Report*, Nov. 11, 1899.

"Mr. Osborne's Friends and Enemies." *New York Times*, Aug. 10, 1915.

"Mulberry Bend Park Opened." *New York Times*, June 16, 1897, 7.

Myers, Gustavus. *The History of Tammany Hall*. New York: Boni & Liverwright, 1901.

National Civil Service Reform League, "To the Voters of the United States." [New York], Oct. 31, 1882.

Norton, Charles Eliot, ed. *Orations and Addresses of George William Curtis*. New York: Harper & Brothers, 1894.

"Only One Vote to Spare," *New York Times*, Mar. 27, 1886.

Osborne, Thomas Mott. "Osborne Flays Hearst as Foe of Democracy." *New York Times*, Oct. 24, 1906, 4.

——. *Within Prison Walls*. New York: D. Appleton, 1914.

——. *Society and Prisons: Some Suggestions for a New Penology*. 1916; reprint, Montclair, N.J.: Patterson Smith, 1975.

"Parade of Col. Waring's Men." *New York Evening Post*, May 28, 1897, 7.

Pearson, Charles. *National Life and Character*. New York, 1894.

Pierson, Delavan L. "The Little Republic at Freeville." *The Missionary Review of the World* (Nov. and Dec. 1899).

Platt, Thomas Collier. *Autobiography of Thomas Collier Platt*. New York: B.W. Dodge, 1910.

Potts, William. "The Professional Reformer." *Tammany Times*, Dec. 4, 1895.

——. "The Republican Spirit." *Harper's Weekly* 1529 (Apr. 10, 1886): 30.

——. "The White Brigade." *New York Times*, May 27, 1897, 6.

——. "George Edwin Waring, Jr." *The Charities Review* 8 (Nov. 1898): 461–68.

——. "The Question of Manliness." *New York Times*, Oct. 28, 1906, 8.

Riis, Jacob A. "Perils of Photographers." *Photographic Times*, Feb. 3, 1888, 59.

——. *How the Other Half Lives: Studies Among the Tenements of New York*. New York: Macmillan, 1890.

——. "The Making of Thieves in New York." *Century* (Nov. 1894).

——. "Goodbye to the Bend." *The Evening Sun*, May 25, 1895.

——. "The Clearing of Mulberry Bend." *Review of Reviews* 12, no. 2 (Aug. 1895):172–78.

——. "The Lesson Taught Us By the Gang." *Pratt Institute Monthly* 6, no. 2 (Nov. 1897): 40.

——. *A Ten Years' War: An Account of the Battle with the Slum in New York.* 1900; reprint, Freeport, NY: Books for Libraries Press, 1969.

——. *The Battle with the Slum.* New York: Macmillan, 1902.

——. *The Making of an American.* New York: Macmillan, 1902.

——. *Theodore Roosevelt: The Citizen.* New York: Outlook, 1903.

Riordan, William L., ed. *Plunkitt of Tammany Hall: A Series of Very Plain Talks on Very Practical Politics.* 1905; reprint, New York: E. P. Dutton, 1963.

Roosevelt, Theodore. "The College Graduate and Public Life." *Atlantic Monthly* (Aug. 1890).

——. "The Manly Virtues in Practical Politics." *The Forum* (July 1894).

——. "Roosevelt to Preble Tucker." *New York Times*, Oct. 23, 1895.

——. *The Strenuous Life: Essays and Addresses.* New York: Century Co., 1900.

——. *American Ideals and Other Essays, Social and Political.* New York and London: G. P. Putnam's Sons, 1906.

——. *An Autobiography.* New York: The Outlook Company, 1913.

Schurz, Carl. "The Blindness of Party Spirit." *Harpers Weekly* (Oct. 30, 1897):1071.

Shaw, Anna Howard. *The Story of a Pioneer.* New York: Harper & Brothers, 1915.

Shepard, Edward M. "Political Inauguration of the Greater New York." *Atlantic Monthly* (Jan. 1898):108, 111.

Stead, W. T. "Mr. Richard Croker and Greater New York." *The Review of Reviews* (Oct. 1897):354–55.

Steffens, Lincoln. *The Shame of the Cities.* New York: S. S. McClure, 1902.

——. *The Autobiography of Lincoln Steffens, Volume I.* New York: Harcourt, Brace & World, 1931.

Stoddard, Lothrop. *Master of Manhattan: The Life of Richard Croker.* New York: Longmans, Green., 1931.

Stowe, Lyman Beecher. "A Prison that Makes Men Free." *World's Work* 27 (Apr. 1914).

Strong, Josiah. *The Twentieth Century City.* New York, 1898.

Tannenbaum, Frank. *Osborne of Sing Sing.* Chapel Hill: University of North Carolina Press, 1933.

Townsend, John D. *New York in Bondage.* New York: privately published to subscribers, 1901.

Villard, Oswald Garrison. "Tammany Tactics." *Boston Transcript*, Nov. 5, 1893.

Wald, Lillian. *The House on Henry Stree*t. New York: H. Holt, 1915.

"Warden Osborne." *New York Times*, Dec. 31, 1915.

Waring, George E. Jr. *Whip and Spur.* New York: J. R. Osgood and Company, 1875.

——. "Education at West Point." *The Outlook* 59 (1898): 825–37.

——. "The Necessity for Excluding Politics from Municipal Business." *Proceedings of the Third National Conference for Good City Government and of the Second Annual Meeting of the National Municipal League.* Philadelphia: National Municipal League, 1896.

——. "Government by Party." *The North American Review* 163, no. 480 (Nov. 1896): 587–95.

——. "The Cleaning of a Great City." *McClure's Magazine* 9 (Sept. 1897): 916.

——. "The Labor Question in the Department of Street Cleaning." *Municipal Affairs* 2 (1898): 226–34.

Weinstein, Gregory. *The Ardent Eighties: Reminiscences of an Interesting Decade.* New York: International Press, 1928.

Welling, Richard W.G. "Reform in Municipal Government: Two Addresses Delivered by Invitation Before the Massachusetts Reform Club, Saturday, February 17, 1894." Boston: Press of Geo. H. Ellis, 1894.

——. "Theodore Roosevelt at Harvard: Some Personal Reminiscences." *The Outlook*, Oct. 27, 1920, 366–69.

——. "My Classmate Theodore Roosevelt." *American Legion Monthly* (Jan. 1929):9–12, 67–68.

——. *As the Twig Is Bent.* New York: G. P. Putnam's Sons, 1942.

Wheeler, Everett P. *Callanan's Monthly* 4, no. 7 (June 1901): 1.

Wilhelm, Donald. *Theodore Roosevelt as an Undergraduate.* Boston: John W. Luce, 1910.

Wilson, Douglas L., ed. *The Genteel Tradition: Nine Essays by George Santayana.* Lincoln and London: University of Nebraska Press, 1967.

Wilson, James. "Citizens in Little: The Junior Republic at Freeville, New York." *Strand Magazine* 14, no. 27 (1897): 209–15.

SECONDARY SOURCES

Abelove, Henry, et al., eds. *The Lesbian and Gay Studies Reader.* New York: Routledge, 1993.

Adams, Michael C.C. *The Great Adventure: Male Desire and the Coming of World War I.* Bloomington: Indiana University Press, 1990.

Alland, Alexander. *Jacob A. Riis: Photographer and Citizen.* New York: Aperture, 1973.

Allen, Oliver E. *The Tiger: The Rise and Fall of Tammany Hall.* Reading. MA: Addison-Wesley, 1993.

Anbinder, Tyler. *Five Points: The Nineteenth-Century New York City Neighborhood That Invented Tap Dance, Stole Elections, and Became the World's Most Notorious Slum.* New York: Free Press, 2001.

Armstrong, William M. *E. L. Godkin: A Biography.* Albany: State University of New York Press, 1978.

Aronson, David I. "The City Club of New York: 1892–1912." Ph.D. diss., New York University, 1975.

Bailey, Samuel. "The Adjustment of Italian Immigrants in Buenos Aires and New York, 1870–1914." *American Historical Review* 88 (1983): 280–305.

Baker, Jean H. *Affairs of Party: The Political Culture of Northern Democrats in the Mid-Nineteenth Century.* Ithaca, NY: Cornell University Press, 1983.

Baker, Paula. "The Domestication of American Politics: Women and American Political Society, 1780–1920." *American Historical Review* 89 (1984): 620–47.

Bannister, Robert C. *Social Darwinism: Science and Myth in Anglo-American Social Thought*. Philadelphia: Temple University Press, 1979.

Barber, Lucy G. *Marching on Washington: The Forging of an American Political Tradition*. Berkeley: University of California Press, 2002.

Barker, Charles A. *Henry George*. New York: Oxford University Press, 1955.

Barker, Elizabeth. "New Light on Epstein's Early Career." *The Burlington Magazine* 130, no. 1029 (Dec. 1988): 903–909.

Barnes, Elizabeth. *States of Sympathy: Seduction and Democracy in the American Novel*. New York: Columbia University Press, 1997.

Bederman, Gail. "'Civilization,' the Decline of Middle-Class Manliness, and Ida B. Wells's Antilynching Campaign (1892–1894)." *Radical History Review* 52 (1992): 5–32.

——. *Manliness and Civilization: A Cultural History of Gender and Race in the United States, 1880–1917*. Chicago: University of Chicago Press, 1995.

Begnett, Bruce. *Sentimental Bodies: Sex, Gender and Citizenship in the Early Republic*. Princeton: Princeton University Press, 1998.

Bender, Thomas. *New York Intellect*. New York: Knopf, 1987.

Bibby, John F. *Politics, Parties, and Elections in America*. Chicago: Nelson-Hall, 1992.

Blanchard, Mary W. "The Soldier and the Aesthete: Homosexuality and Popular Culture in Gilded Age America." *Journal of American Studies* 30 (Apr. 1996): 25–46.

——. *Oscar Wilde's America: Counterculture in the Gilded Age*. New Haven: Yale University Press, 1998.

Blodgett, Geoffrey. "The Mugwump Reputation, 1870 to Present." *Journal of American History* 66, no. 4 (Mar. 1980): 867–87.

Boag, Peter. *Same-Sex Affairs: Constructing and Controlling Homosexuality in the Pacific Northwest*. Berkeley: University of California Press, 2003.

Bonomi, Patricia U. *The Lord Cornbury Scandal: The Politics of Reputation in British America*. Chapel Hill: University of North Carolina Press, 1998.

Boyd, Nan Alamilla. *Wide Open Town: A History of Queer San Francisco to 1965*. Berkeley: University of California Press, 2003.

Boydston, Jo Ann, ed. *John Dewey: The Middle Works*, Vol. 5. Carbondale: Southern Illinois University Press, 1978.

——. *John Dewey: The Later Works*, Vol. 9. Carbondale: Southern Illinois University Press, 1986.

Boyer, M. Christine. *Dreaming the Rational City: The Myth of American City Planning*. Cambridge, MA: MIT Press, 1983.

Brown, Victoria Bissell. *The Education of Jane Addams*. Philadelphia: University of Pennsylvania Press, 2004.

Burnstein, Daniel Eli. "Clean Streets and the Pursuit of Progress: Urban Reform in New York City in the Progressive Era." Ph.D. diss., Rutgers University, 1992.

Burstein, Andrew. *Sentimental Democracy: The Evolution of America's Romantic Self-Image*. New York: Hill and Wang, 2000.

Burrows, Edwin G. and Mike Wallace. *Gotham: A History of New York City to 1898*. New York: Oxford University Press, 1999.

Butters, Ronald R., et al. *Displacing Homophobia: Gay Male Perspectives in Literature and Culture*. Durham, NC: Duke University Press, 1989.

Callow, Alexander B., Jr. *The Tweed Ring*. New York: Oxford University Press, 1965.

Carnes, Mark C. and Clyde Griffin, eds. *Meanings for Manhood: Constructions of Masculinity in Victorian America*. Chicago: University of Chicago Press, 1990.

Carson, Minna. *Settlement Folk: Social Thought and the American Settlement Movement, 1885–1930*. Chicago: University of Chicago Press, 1990.

Cater, Harold D., ed. *Henry Adams and His Friends: A Collection of His Unpublished Letters*. Boston: Houghton Mifflin, 1947.

Cavallo, Dominick. *Muscles and Morals: Organized Playgrounds and Urban Reform, 1880–1920*. Philadelphia: University of Pennsylvania Press, 1981.

Chauncey, George. *Gay New York: Gender, Urban Culture, and the Making of the Gay Male World, 1890–1940*. New York: Basic Books, 1994.

Cocks, Catherine. "Rethinking Sexuality in the Progressive Era." *Journal of Gilded Age and Progressive Era* 5, no. 2 (Apr. 2006): 93–118.

Cohen, Nancy. *The Reconstruction of American Liberalism, 1865–1914*. Chapel Hill and London: University of North Carolina Press, 2002.

Cook, Blanche Wiesen. "Female Support Networks and Political Activism: Lillian Wald, Crystal Eastman, Emma Goldman." *Chrysalis* 3 (Autumn 1977): 43–61.

——. *Eleanor Roosevelt, Vol. 1, 1884–1933*. New York: Viking, 1992.

Crain, Caleb. *American Sympathy: Men, Friendship, and Literature in the New Nation*. New Haven: Yale University Press, 1999.

Cresswell, Tim. *The Tramp in America*. London: Reaktion Books, 2001.

Cruikshank, Barbara A. *The Will to Empower: Democratic Citizens and Other Subjects*. Ithaca, NY: Cornell University Press, 1999.

Curti, Merle. "Jane Addams on Human Nature." *Journal of the History of Ideas* 22, no. 2 (Apr.–June 1961): 240–53.

Czitrom, Daniel. "Underworlds and Underdogs: Big Tim Sullivan and Metropolitan Politics in New York, 1889–1912." *The Journal of American History* (Sept. 1991):536–58.

Davis, Allen. *Spearheads for Reform: The Social Settlements and the Progressive Movement, 1890–1914*. New York: Oxford University Press, 1967.

——. *American Heroine: The Life and Legend of Jane Addams*. New York: Oxford University Press, 1973.

Degler, Carl N. *In Search of Human Nature: The Decline and Revival of Darwinism in American Social Thought*. New York: Oxford University Press, 1992.

DePastino, Todd. *Citizen Hobo: How a Century of Homelessness Shaped America*. Chicago: University of Chicago Press, 2003.

Dong, Catherine Claxton. "The Struggle to Define Childhood: Resistance to the Private Sphere from the Junior Republic Movement, 1894–1936." Ph.D. diss., Cornell University, 1995.

Dorsey, Bruce. *Reforming Men and Women: Gender in the Antebellum City*. Ithaca, NY: Cornell University Press, 2002.

Douglas, Ann. *The Feminization of American Culture*. New York: Doubleday, 1977.

Dowling, Linda. *Hellenism and Homosexuality in Victorian Oxford*. Ithaca, NY and London: Cornell University Press, 1994.

Duggan, Lisa. *Sapphic Slashers: Sex, Violence, and American Modernity*. Durham, NC and London: Duke University Press, 2000.

Duis, Perry R. *The Saloon: Public Drinking in Chicago and Boston, 1880–1920*. Urbana and Chicago: University of Illinois Press, 1983.

Dyer, Thomas G. *Theodore Roosevelt and the Idea of Race*. Baton Rouge: Louisiana State University Press, 1980.

Edsall, Nicholas C. *Toward Stonewall: Homosexuality and Society in the Modern Western World*. Charlottesville: University of Virginia Press, 2003.

Edwards, Rebecca. "Domesticity versus Manhood Rights: Republicans, Democrats, and 'Family Values' Politics, 1856–1896." In Meg Jacobs et al., eds., *The Democratic Experiment: New Directions in American Political History* (Princeton: Princeton University Press, 2003).

——. *New Spirits: Americans in the Gilded Age, 1865–1905*. New York: Oxford University Press, 2006.

Ellis, Edward Robb. *The Epic of New York*. New York: Old Town Books, 1966.

Ellis, Frank H., ed. *Twentieth-Century Interpretations of Robinson Crusoe: A Collection of Critical Essays*. Englewood Cliffs, NJ: Prentice-Hall, 1969.

Ellison, Julie. "The Gender of Transparency: Masculinity and the Conduct of Life." *American Literary History* 4, no. 4 (Dec. 1992): 584–606.

Elshtain, Jean Bethke. *Jane Addams and the Dream of American Democracy*. New York: Basic Books, 2002.

Erkkila, Betsey. *Whitman the Political Poet*. New York: Oxford University Press, 1989.

Fone, Byrne R.S. *A Road to Stonewall: Male Homosexuality and Homophobia in English and American Literature, 1750–1969*. New York: Twaine Publishers, 1986.

Frederick, Peter J. "A Life of Principle: Ernest Howard Crosby and the Frustrations of the Intellectual as Reformer." *New York History* 54 (Oct. 1973): 399.

——. *Knights of the Golden Rule: The Intellectual as Christian Social Reformer in the 1890s*. Lexington: The University Press of Kentucky, 1976.

Gable, Jack. "Edward M. Shepard, Militant Reformer." Ph.D. diss., New York University, 1967.

Gandal, Keith. *The Virtues of the Vicious: Jacob Riis, Stephen Crane, and the Spectacle of the Slum*. New York and Oxford: Oxford University Press, 1997.

Gerstle, Gary. "Theodore Roosevelt and the Divided Character of American Nationalism." *Journal of American History* 86, no. 3 (Dec. 1999): 1280–1307.

——. *American Crucible: Race and Nation in the Twentieth Century*. Princeton: Princeton University Press, 2001.

Gianakos, Perry E. "Ernest Howard Crosby: A Forgotten Tolstoyan Anti-Militarist and Anti-Imperialist." *American Studies* 13 (Spring 1972): 11–29.

Gilfoyle, Timothy. *City of Eros: New York City, Prostitution, and the Commercialization of Sex, 1790–1920.* New York: Norton, 1992.
Gilmartin, Gregory F. *Shaping the City: New York and the Municipal Art Society.* New York: Clarkson Potter, 1995.
Ginzberg, Lori D. *Women and the Work of Benevolence: Morality, Politics, and Class in the Nineteenth-Century United States.* New Haven: Yale University Press, 1990.
Goldberg, Michael Lewis. *An Army of Women: Gender and Politics in Gilded Age Kansas.* Baltimore and London: Johns Hopkins University Press, 1997.
Gordon, Colin, ed. *Power/Knowledge: Selected Interviews and Other Writings, 1972–1977.* New York: Pantheon, 1980.
Gordon, Linda. *Pitied But Not Entitled: Single Mothers and the History of Welfare.* Cambridge, MA: Harvard University Press, 1994.
Gorn, Elliott J. *The Manly Art: Bare Knuckle Prize Fighting in America.* Ithaca, NY: Cornell University Press, 1990.
Green, Martin. *Dreams of Adventure, Deeds of Empire.* New York: Basic Books, 1979.
——. *The Robinson Crusoe Story.* University Park: Pennsylvania State University Press, 1990.
Guglielmo, Jennifer and Salvatore Salerno, eds. *Are Italians White?: How Race Is Made in America.* New York: Routledge, 2003.
Guglielmo, Thomas A. *White on Arrival: Italians, Race, Color and Power in Chicago, 1890–1945.* New York and Oxford: Oxford University Press, 2003.
Gustav-Wrathall, John Donald. *Take the Young Stranger By the Hand: Same-Sex Relations and the YMCA.* Chicago: University of Chicago Press, 1998.
Hammack, David C. *Power and Society: Greater New York at the Turn of the Century.* New York: Columbia University Press, 1987.
Hansen, Bert. "American Physicians' Earliest Writings About Homosexuals, 1880–1900." *The Milbank Quarterly* 67, Supplement 1 (1989): 92–108.
Hatheway, Jay. *The Gilded Age Construction of Modern American Homophobia.* New York: Palgrave Macmillan, 2003.
Hawkins, Mike. *Social Darwinism in European and American Thought, 1860–1945: Nature as Model and Nature as Threat.* New York: Cambridge University Press, 1997.
Higbie, Frank Tobias. "Crossing Class Boundaries: Tramp Ethnographers and Narratives of Class in Progressive Era America." *Social Science History* 21, no. 4 (Winter 1997): 559–92.
——. *Indispensable Outcasts: Hobo Workers and Community in the American Midwest, 1880–1930.* Urbana and Chicago: University of Illinois Press, 2003.
Highwater, Jamake. *The Mythology of Transgression: Homosexuality as Metaphor.* New York: Oxford University Press, 1997, 87.
Hofstadter, Richard. *Social Darwinism in American Thought.* Philadelphia: University of Pennsylvania Press, 1944.
——. *The Age of Reform: From Bryan to F.D.R.* New York: Vintage, 1955.
——. *Anti-Intellectualism in American Life.* New York: Knopf, 1962.
——. *The Idea of a Party System: The Rise of Legitimate Opposition in the United*

States, 1780–1840. Berkelely, Los Angeles, and London: University of California Press, 1969.

Hoganson, Kristin L. *Fighting for American Manhood: How Gender Politics Provoked the Spanish-American and Philippine-American Wars.* New Haven and London: Yale University Press, 1998.

Hohoff, Tay. *A Ministry to Man: The Life of John Lovejoy Elliott.* New York: Harper & Brothers, , 1959.

Holl, Jack M. *Juvenile Reform in the Progressive Era: William R. George and the Junior Republic Movement.* Ithaca, NY: Cornell University Press, 1971.

Hoogenboom, Ari. *Outlawing the Spoils: A History of the Civil Service Reform Movement, 1865–1883.* Urbana: University of Illinois Press, 1961.

Horowitz, Helen Lefkowitz. *Rereading Sex: Battles Over Sexual Knowledge and Suppression in Nineteenth-Century America.* New York: Knopf, 2002.

Hovey, Richard B. *John Jay Chapman: An American Mind.* New York: Columbia University Press, 1959.

James, Scott C. "Patronage Regimes and American Party Development from 'The Age of Jackson' to the Progressive Era." *British Journal of Political Science* 36 (2006): 39–60.

John, Arthur. *The Best Years of the Century: Richard Watson Gilder,* Scribner's *Monthly, and the* Century *Magazine, 1870–1909.* Urbana: University of Illinois Press, 1981.

Jordan, David M. *Roscoe Conkling of New York: Voice in the Senate.* Ithaca, NY and London: Cornell University Press, 1971.

Kao, Deborah Martin, Laura Katzman, and Jenna Webster, eds. *Ben Shahn's New York: The Photography of Modern Times.* New Haven: Yale University Press, 2000.

Kaplan, Amy and Donald E. Pease, eds. *Cultures of United States Imperialism.* Durham, NC: Duke University Press, 1993.

Kaplan, Justin. *Lincoln Steffens.* New York: Simon and Schuster, 1974.

Kasson, John F. *Houdini, Tarzan and the Perfect Man: The White Male Body and the Challenge of Modernity in America.* New York: Hill and Wang, 2001.

Katz, Jonathan Ned. *Love Stories: Sex Between Men Before Homosexuality.* Chicago: University of Chicago Press, 2001.

—. *The Invention of Heterosexuality.* New York: Penguin, 1995.

Katz, Michael B. *Under the Shadow of the Poorhouse: A History of Social Welfare in America.* New York: Basic Books, 1986.

Katznelson, Ira. *Black Men, White Cities: Race, Politics, and Migration in the United States, 1900–1930, and Britain, 1948–1968.* London: Oxford University Press, 1973.

Keefe, Frances M. "The Development of William Reuben (Daddy) George's Educational Ideas and Practices from 1886 to 1914." Ph.D. diss., Cornell University, 1966.

Kennedy, Hubert. *Ulrichs: The Life and Works of Karl Heinrich Ulrichs, Pioneer of the Modern Gay Movement.* Boston: Alyson Publications, 1988.

Kessner, Thomas. *The Golden Door: Italian and Jewish Immigrant Mobility in New York City 1880–1915.* New York: Oxford University Press, 1977.

Keyssar, Alexander. *The Right to Vote: The Contested History of Democracy in the United States*. New York: Basic Books, 2000.

Kidd, Kenneth. *Making American Boys: Boyology and the Feral Tale*. Minneapolis: University of Minnesota Press, 2004.

Kimmel, Michael. *Manhood in America: A Cultural History*. New York: The Free Press, 1995.

Kincaid, James R. and Albert J. Kuhn, eds. *Victorian Literature and Society*. Athens: Ohio University Press, 1989.

Kissack, Terence S. "Anarchism and the Politics of Homosexuality." Ph.D. diss., City University of New York, 2004.

Knerr, George Francis. "The Mayoral Administration of William L. Strong, New York City, 1895 to 1897." Ph.D. diss., New York University, 1957.

Koven, Seth. *Slumming: Sexual and Social Politics in Victorian London*. Princeton and Oxford: Princeton University Press, 2004.

Kornbluth, Mark Lawrence. *Why America Stopped Voting: The Decline of Participatory Democracy and the Emergence of Modern American Politics*. New York: New York University Press, 2000.

Krauth, Leland. *Proper Mark Twain*. Athens and London: University of Georgia Press, 1999.

Kunzel, Regina. "Situating Sex: Prison Sexual Culture in the Mid-Twentieth Century United States." *GLQ* 8, no. 3 (2002): 253–70.

——. *Criminal Intimacy: Sex in Prison and the Uneven History of Modern American Sexuality*. Chicago: University of Chicago Press, 2008.

Kurland, Gerald. *Seth Low: The Reformer in an Urban and Industrial Age*. New York: Twayne Publishers, 1971.

Lagemann, Ellen Condliffe, ed. *Jane Addams on Education*. New York: Teachers College Press, 1985.

Lasch, Christopher, ed. *The Social Thought of Jane Addams*. New York: Irvington Publishers, 1982.

Lears, T.J. Jackson. *No Place of Grace: Antimodernism and the Transformation of American Culture, 1880–1920*. Chicago: University of Chicago Press, 1981.

Leverenz, David. *Manhood and the American Renaissance*. Ithaca, NY: Cornell University Press, 1989.

Levine, Daniel. *Jane Addams and the Liberal Tradition*. Madison: State Historical Society of Wisconsin, 1971.

Levinson, Henry Samuel. *Santayana, Pragmatism, and the Spiritual Life*. Chapel Hill and London: University of North Carolina Press, 1992.

Lipow, Arthur. *Authoritarian Socialism in America: Edward Bellamy and the Nationalist Movement*. Berkeley: University of California Press, 1982.

Livingston, James. *Pragmatism and the Political Economy of Cultural Revolution, 1850–1940*. Chapel Hill: University of North Carolina Press, 1997.

——. *Pragmatism, Feminism, and Democracy: Rethinking the Politics of American History*. New York: Routledge, 2001.

Lott, Eric. *Love and Theft: Blackface Minstrelsy and the American Working Class.* New York and Oxford: Oxford University Press, 1993.

Maier, Joseph and Richard W. Weatherhead. *Frank Tannenbaum: A Biographical Essay.* New York: Columbia University, 1974.

Makemson, Harlen. "A 'Dude and Pharisee': Cartoon Attacks on *Harper's Weekly* Editor George William Curtis and the Mugwumps in the Presidential Campaign of 1884." *Journalism History* 29, no. 4 (2004): 179–89.

Mangan, J. A., and James Walvin, eds. *Manliness and Morality: Middle-Class Masculinity in Britain and America, 1800–1940.* New York: St. Martin's Press, 1987.

Marshall, Susan E. *Splintered Sisterhood: Gender and Class in the Campaign Against Woman Suffrage.* Madison and London: University of Wisconsin Press, 1997.

Matta, Christina. "Ambiguous Bodies and Deviant Sexualities: Hermaphrodites, Homosexuality, and Surgery in the United States, 1850–1904." *Perspectives in Biology and Medicine* 48, no. 1 (2005): 74–83.

May, Henry F. *The End of American Innocence: A Study of the First Years of Our Own Time, 1912–1917.* New York: Knopf, 1959.

McCormick, John. *George Santayana: A Biography.* New York: Knopf, 1987.

McCormick, Richard L. *From Realignment to Reform: Political Change in New York State, 1893–1910.* Ithaca, NY: Cornell University Press, 1981.

McFarland, Gerald W. "Partisan of Nonpartisanship: Dorman B. Eaton and the Genteel Reform Tradition." *Journal of American History* 55 (Mar. 1969): 806–22.

——. *Mugwumps, Morals and Politics, 1884–1920.* Amherst: University of Massachusetts Press, 1975.

McGerr, Michael E. *The Decline of Popular Politics: The American North, 1865–1928.* New York and Oxford: Oxford University Press, 1986.

——. "Political Style and Women's Power, 1830–1930." *The Journal of American History* (Dec. 1990):864–65.

——. *A Fierce Discontent: The Rise and Fall of the Progressive Movement in America, 1870–1920.* New York and Oxford: Oxford University Press, 2003.

McKelvey, Blake. *American Prisons: A History of Good Intentions.* Montclair, NJ: Patterson Smith, 1977.

Mechling, Jay. *On My Honor: Boy Scouts and the Making of American Youth.* Chicago: University of Chicago Press, 2001.

Melosi, Martin V. *Garbage in the Cities: Refuse, Reform, and the Environment, 1880–1980.* College Station: Texas A & M University Press, 1981.

Miller, Nathan. *Theodore Roosevelt: A Life.* New York: William Morrow, 1992.

Milne, Gordon. *George William Curtis and the Genteel Tradition.* Bloomington: Indiana University Press, 1956.

Montgomery, David. *The Fall of the House of Labor.* Cambridge: Cambridge University Press, 1987.

Moon, Michael. "The Gentle Boy from the Dangerous Classes: Pederasty, Domesticity, and Capitalism in Horatio Alger." *Representations* 19 (Summer 1987): 87–110.

Morris, Edmund. *The Rise of Theodore Roosevelt.* New York: Coward, McCann & Geoghegan, 1979.

Muccigrosso, Robert. "Richard W.G. Welling: A Reformer's Life." Ph.D. diss., Columbia University, 1966.

Muncy, Robin. "Trustbusting and White Manhood in America, 1898–1914." *American Studies* 38, no. 3 (Fall 1997): 21–42.

—. *Creating a Female Dominion in American Reform, 1890–1935.* New York: Oxford University Press, 1991.

Nackenoff, Carol. *The Fictional Republic: Horatio Alger and American Political Discourse.* New York: Oxford University Press, 1994.

Nasaw, David. *The Chief: The Life of William Randolph Hearst.* New York: Houghton Mifflin, 2000.

Nelson, Dana. *National Manhood: Capitalist Citizenship and the Imagined Fraternity of White Men.* Durham, NC and London: Duke University Press, 1998.

Newton, Esther. "The Mythic Mannish Lesbian: Radcyffe Hall and the New Woman." *Signs* 9, no. 4 (Summer 1984): 557–75.

Norton, Rictor. *Mother Clap's Molly House.* London: GMP Publishers, 1992.

Orsi, Robert. *The Madonna of 115th Street.* New Haven: Yale University Press, 1985.

—. "The Religious Boundaries of an In-Between People: Street Feste and the Problem of the Dark-Skinned Other in Italian Harlem, 1920–1990." *American Quarterly* 44 (Sept. 1992).

Page, Max. *The Creative Destruction of Manhattan, 1900–1940.* Chicago: University of Chicago Press, 1999.

Painter, Nell Irvin. *Standing at Armageddon: The United States, 1877–1919.* New York and London: Norton, 1987.

Parker, Andrew, et al., eds. *Nationalisms and Sexualities.* New York: Routledge, 1992.

Patai, Daphne, ed. *Looking Backward, 1988–1888: Essays on Edward Bellamy.* Amherst: University of Massachusetts Press, 1988.

Paulding, J. K. *Charles B. Stover: His Life and Personality.* New York: International Press, 1938.

Peiss, Kathy. *Cheap Amusements: Working Women and Leisure in Turn-of-the-Century New York.* Philadelphia: Temple University Press, 1986.

Phillips, Richard. *Mapping Men and Empire: A Geography of Adventure.* London and New York: Routledge, 1997.

Pierson, Michael D. *Free Hearts and Free Homes: Gender and American Antislavery Politics.* Chapel Hill: University of North Carolina Press, 2003.

Pisciotta, Alexander W. *Benevolent Repression: Social Control and the American Reformatory-Prison Movement.* New York: New York University Press, 1994.

Pittenger, Mark. "The Great Evasion: Religion and Science in the Socialism of Edmond Kelly." *Journal of American Culture* 14, no. 1 (Spring 1991): 13–18.

Pivar, David J. *Purity Crusade: Sexual Morality and Social Control, 1868–1900.* Westport, CT: Greenwood Press, 1973.

Porter, Roy and Mikulas Teich, eds. *Sexual Knowledge, Sexual Science: The History of Attitudes to Sexuality*. Cambridge and New York: Cambridge University Press, 1994.

Pozzetta, George E. "The Italians of New York City, 1890–1914." Ph.D. diss., University of North Carolina, Chapel Hill, 1971.

Puccio, Paul M. "At the Heart of *Tom Brown's Schooldays*: Thomas Arnold and Christian Friendship." *Modern Language Studies* 25, no. 4 (Autumn 1995): 57–74.

Putney, Clifford. *Muscular Christianity: Manhood and Sports in Protestant America, 1880–1920*. Cambridge, MA and London: Harvard University Press, 2001.

Radest, Howard B. *Toward Common Ground: The Story of the Ethical Societies in the United States*. New York: Frederick Ungar, 1969.

Reade, Brian, ed. *Sexual Heretics: Male Homosexuality in English Literature from 1850 to 1900:An Anthology*. New York: Coward-McCann, 1970.

Reichley, James. *The Life of the Parties: A History of American Political Parties*. Lanham, MD: Rowman & Littlefield, 2000.

Reynolds, David S. *Walt Whitman's America: A Cultural Biography*. New York: Knopf, 1995.

Rich, Adrienne. "Compulsory Heterosexuality and Lesbian Existence." *Signs* (Summer 1980):631–60.

Richards, Jeffrey. *Imperialism and Juvenile Literature*. Manchester, UK: Manchester University Press, 1989.

Richardson, Robert D. *William James: In the Maelstrom of American Modernism: A Biography*. Boston: Houghton Mifflin, 2006.

Rodgers, Daniel P. "In Search of Progressivism." *Reviews in American History* (1982):113–27.

Roediger, David. *Towards the Abolition of Whiteness*. New York and London: Verso, 1994.

Rome, Adam. "'Political Hermaphrodites': Gender and Environmental Reform in Progressive America." *Environmental History* 11 (July 2006): 440–63.

Rosario, Vernon A., ed. *Science and Homosexualities*. New York and London: Routledge, 1997.

Rosenzweig, Roy. *Eight Hours for What They Will*. Cambridge: Cambridge University Press, 1983.

Rothman, David J. *Conscience and Convenience: The Asylum and Its Alternatives in Progressive America*. Boston: Little, Brown, 1980.

Rotundo, E. Anthony. *American Manhood: Transformations in Masculinity from the Revolution to the Modern Era*. New York: Basic Books, 1993.

Rupp, Leila. *Worlds of Women: The Making of an International Women's Movement*. Princeton: Princeton University Press, 1997.

Ryan, Mary P. *Cradle of the Middle Class: The Family in Oneida County, New York, 1790–1865*. Cambridge: Cambridge University Press, 1981.

——. *Women in Public: Between Banners and Ballots, 1825–1880*. Baltimore: Johns Hopkins University Press, 1990.

Rydell, Robert. *All the World's a Fair: Visions of Empire at American International Expositions, 1876–1916*. Chicago: University of Chicago Press, 1984.

Samuels, Shirley, ed. *The Culture of Sentiment: Race, Gender, and Sentimentality in Nineteenth-Century America*. New York.: Oxford University Press, 1992.

Scheuer, Jeffrey. *Legacy of Light: University Settlement's First Century*. New York: University Settlement, 1985.

Schonhorn, Manuel. *Defoe's Politics: Parliament, Power, Kingship, and* Robinson Crusoe. Cambridge: Cambridge University Press, 1991.

Schwantes, Carlos A. *Coxey's Army: An American Odyssey*. Moscow: University of Idaho Press, 1994.

Sedgwick, Eve Kosofsky. *Between Men: English Literature and Male Homosocial Desire*. New York: Columbia University Press, 1985.

Senelick, Laurence. "Mollies or Men of Mode? Sodomy and the Eighteenth-Century London Stage." *Journal of the History of Sexuality* 1, no. 1 (July 1990): 33–67.

Shand-Tucci, Douglass. *The Crimson Letter: Harvard, Homosexuality, and the Shaping of American Culture*. New York: St. Martins Press, 2003.

Showalter, Elaine. *Sexual Anarchy: Gender and Culture at the Fin de Siècle*. New York: Penguin, 1990.

Siegel, Beatrice. *Lillian Wald of Henry Street*. New York: Macmillan, 1983.

Silber, Evelyn, et al. *Jacob Epstein: Sculpture and Drawings*. London: W. S. Maney and Son, 1989.

Sklar, Katherine Kish. "Hull House in the 1890s: A Community of Women Reformers." *Signs* (Summer 1985):658–77.

——. *Florence Kelley and the Nation's Work: The Rise of Women's Political Culture, 1830–1900*. New Haven: Yale University Press, 1995.

Skolnik, Richard. "George Edwin Waring, Jr.: A Model for Reformers." *New York Historical Society Bulletin* 52 (Oct. 1968): 354–75.

Smith, Herbert F. *Richard Watson Gilder*. New York: Twayne, 1970.

Smith-Rosenberg, Carroll. *Disorderly Conduct: Visions of Gender in Victorian America*. New York and Oxford: Oxford University Press, 1985.

Sproat, John G. *The Best Men: Liberal Reformers in the Gilded Age*. New York: Oxford University Press, 1968.

Stange, Maren. *Symbols of Ideal Life: Social Documentary Photography in America, 1890–1950*. Cambridge, UK: Cambridge University Press, 1989.

——. "Jacob Riis and Urban Visual Culture: The Lantern Slide Exhibition as Entertainment and Ideology." *Journal of Urban History* (May 1989):274–303.

Stansell, Christine. *American Moderns: Bohemian New York and the Creation of a New Century*. New York: Owl Books, 2001.

Stauber, Rory William. "Lifting the Banner of Tolstoyan Non-Resistance in America: Ernest Howard Crosby's Lonely Quest, 1894–1907." Ph.D. diss., Drew University, 1994.

Stearns, Peter N. *Battleground of Desire: The Struggle for Self-Control in Modern America*. New York: New York University Press, 1999.

Stivers, Camilla. *Bureau Men, Settlement Women: Constructing Public Administration in the Progressive Era.* Lawrence: University of Kansas Press, 2000.

Stocking, David. "John Jay Chapman and Political Reform." *American Quarterly* 2, no. 1 (Spring, 1950): 70.

Summers, John H. "What Happened to Sex Scandals? Politics and Peccadilloes, Jefferson to Kennedy." *The Journal of American History* 87, no. 3 (Dec. 2000): 825–54.

Summers, Mark Wahlgren. *Party Games: Getting, Keeping, and Using Power in Gilded Age Politics.* Chapel Hill: University of North Carolina Press, 2004.

Terry, Jennifer. *An American Obsession: Science, Medicine, and Homosexuality in Modern Society.* Chicago: University of Chicago Press, 1999.

Testi, Arnaldo. "The Gender of Reform Politics: Theodore Roosevelt and the Culture of Masculinity." *The Journal of American History* 81, no. 4 (Mar. 1995): 1509–1533.

Thomas, John L. *Alternative America: Henry George, Edward Bellamy, Henry Demarest Lloyd and the Adversary Tradition.* Cambridge, MA: Harvard University Press, 1983.

Trask, Michael. *Cruising Modernism: Class and Sexuality in American Literature and Social Thought.* Ithaca, NY: Cornell University Press, 2003.

Tucker, David M. *Public Moralists of the Gilded Age.* Columbia and London: University of Missouri Press, 1998.

Van Riper, Paul P. *History of the United States Civil Service.* Evanston, IL: Row, Peterson, 1958.

Watt, Ian. *Myths of Modern Individualism: Faust, Don Quixote, Don Juan, Robinson Crusoe.* Cambridge: Cambridge University Press, 1996.

Watts, Sarah. *Rough Rider in the White House: Theodore Roosevelt and the Politics of Desire.* Chicago: University of Chicago Press, 2003.

Weiss, Nancy Joan. *Charles Francis Murphy, 1858–1924: Respectability and Responsibility in Tammany Politics.* Northampton, MA: Smith College, 1968.

Wider, Sarah Ann. *The Critical Reception of Emerson: Unsettling All Things.* Rochester, NY: Camden House, 2000.

Wiebe, Robert H. *The Search for Order, 1877–1920.* New York: Hill and Wang, 1967.

Williams, Burton J. *Senator John James Ingalls: Kansas' Iridescent Republican.* Lawrence: University of Kansas Press, 1972.

Witcover, Jules. *Party of the People: A History of the Democrats.* New York: Random House, 2003.

Yans-McLaughlin, Virginia. *Family and Community: Italian Immigrants in Buffalo.* Ithaca, NY: Cornell University Press, 1977.

Index